TRIAL BY
FRIENDSHIP

THE FOURTH OF JULY.
1776–1918.

John Bull: "Doth not a meeting like this make amends?"
Uncle Sam: "Sure!"

TRIAL BY FRIENDSHIP

Anglo-American Relations
1917-1918

DAVID R. WOODWARD

THE UNIVERSITY PRESS OF KENTUCKY

Publication of this book was assisted by grants
from Marshall University Foundation, Inc.,
and the Marshall University Graduate School.

Frontispiece: From *Punch*, July 3, 1918.

Copyright © 1993 by The University Press of Kentucky

Scholarly publisher for the Commonwealth,
serving Bellarmine College, Berea College, Centre
College of Kentucky, Eastern Kentucky University,
The Filson Club, Georgetown College, Kentucky
Historical Society, Kentucky State University,
Morehead State University, Murray State University,
Northern Kentucky University, Transylvania University,
University of Kentucky, University of Louisville,
and Western Kentucky University.

Editorial and Sales Offices: Lexington, Kentucky 40508-4008

Library of Congress Cataloging-in-Publication Data

Woodward, David R., 1939-
    Trial by friendship : Anglo-American relations, 1917-1918 / David
R. Woodward.
        p.   cm.
    Includes bibliographical references and index.
    ISBN 0-8131-1833-6 (alk. paper)
    1. World War, 1914-1918—Diplomatic history.   2. World War,
1914-1918—United States.   3. World War, 1914-1918—Great Britain.
4. United States—Foreign relations—Great Britain.   5. Great
Britain—Foreign relations—United States.   I. Title.
D619.W74   1993
940.3'22—dc20   92-36875

I O O O O 9 4 9 I O

This book is printed on recycled acid-free paper meeting
the requirements of the American National Standard
for Permanence of Paper for Printed Library Materials. ⊖

Contents

Illustrations and Maps

Illustrations

Maps

Acknowledgments

Every effort has been made to avoid infringing upon the copyright of any individual or institution. I am obliged to the following individuals and institutions for permission to inspect and to quote documents in which they hold the copyright: the Librarian, Manuscripts and Archives, Sterling Memorial Library, Yale University; the Trustees of the Milner Papers, New College, Oxford; the British Library; the Beaverbrook Foundation; the Masters and Fellows of Churchill College, Cambridge; National Library of Scotland; Trustees of the Imperial War Museum; the National Army Museum; the Bodleian Library; House of Lords Record Office; Liddell Hart Centre for Military Archives; National Library of Scotland; Lord Esher; Lord Scarsdale; and Andrew Rawlinson. Unpublished Crown-copyright material in the Public Record Office and in Oriental and India Office Collections of the British Library is reproduced by permission of the Controller of Her Majesty's Stationery Office. I am also indebted to the Special Collections Branch of the U.S. Army Military History Institute for providing me with photographs from its collection.

A National Endowment for the Humanities Travel to Collections Grant and a sabbatical from Marshall University made possible an extensive research trip to the United Kingdom in 1987. Marshall University also provided me with valuable assistance, including a summer research grant and reassigned time for research and writing. Books, articles, and microfilm were secured from all over the United States by the helpful staff of the Morrow Library.

In addition to the many fine scholars who have instructed me with their treatments of various World War I subjects, I am particularly indebted intellectually to fellow academicians who have generously extended a helping hand. Four specialists in the field, Norman A. Graebner, Edward M. Coffman, Bentley Brinkerhoff Gilbert, and John Gooch, read and commented on my first draft. Their astute vetting of my manuscript immeasurably improved its quality. Colleagues at Marshall University, especially Robert D. Sawrey and Leonard J. Deutsch, have greatly enhanced the readability and organization of this work with their stylistic suggestions and penetrating questions. Two anonymous reviewers for the University Press of Kentucky also made a valuable contribution with their critical evaluations of the manuscript. Michael J. McCarthy, one of my graduate students who is destined to have a distinguished future in history, and Patricia Sterling, a magnificent copyeditor, played a significant part in the production of this book. Finally, I want to recognize the encouragement and sharp proofreading eye of my wife and closest friend, Martha Cobb Woodward. Any mistakes of fact or interpretation in this book, however, are of my own making.

To all who assisted me in this labor of love, I give my heartfelt thanks.

Prologue

On June 28, 1914, in the Bosnian capital of Sarajevo, an assassin's bullet precipitated a chain of events with unforeseen and dramatic results for the destinies of the United States and Great Britain. The great war unleashed by this event accelerated an important trend in international affairs: the replacement of Great Britain by the United States as the world's greatest power.

Britain declared war on Germany on August 4. No British soldiers had fought in Western Europe since Waterloo, but Britain committed its small, elite fighting force to the Continental war. At the center of this decision was the fear of what German domination of Europe would mean, not only for the British Isles but for the British Empire as well. A fundamental issue was whether Britain would survive as a great imperial power.

The British Continental commitment was made easier by the widely held belief that the war would be short. Whatever the duration of the conflict, however, Britain's leaders anticipated with few exceptions that their country's primary role would be in finance, as an arsenal for the Allies, and as the world's premier naval power. It seemed unimaginable that direct involvement in the land war would eventually lead to the deployment of the greatest armed force in one theater in the country's history. Nevertheless, by the summer and fall of 1917, British and Dominion forces constituted the mainstay of the land war against the Imperial Germany Army.

America's part in the war was even more surprising. Forced to abandon its neutrality and its tradition of noninvolvement in European affairs, the United States was drawn into a collective military effort against Berlin. When the war ended, General John J. Pershing commanded the largest force in American history. The two English-speaking democracies, fighting on foreign soil, possessed the two best armies and fleets on the globe. At a frightful cost to their economy and manpower, the British had kept the western front intact in 1917, absorbed the initial blows of the 1918 Germany offensives, and played the leading role in the Allied counterattacks that began in August. For its part, the United States, having achieved global economic ascendancy during the war, was on the verge of dominating the battlefields of Western Europe. The battle-initiated yet still fresh American Expeditionary Force in November was destined to become the army of the future if the war continued into 1919.

The Armistice represented a great triumph for democracy and liberal values in international affairs. The United States and Great Britain appeared to have the opportunity to make and enforce a peace based on their shared liberalism and faith in parliamentary government. Yet though they were joined by their common sacrifices and their essential agreement on many war objectives, the tension between the American and British political and military leadership over the development and manner of employment of an American expeditionary force in Western Europe boded ill for any Anglo-American world order.

The impact of America's military role on British war policy and imperial defense strategy has been largely ignored by British historians. As for U.S. employment of armed force in Western Europe, most American historians have followed the lead of Foster Rhea Dulles, who moves immediately from the end of American neutrality to peacemaking in his volume in the New American Nation Series, *America's Rise to World Power, 1898-1954*.[1] Scholars who have written on Anglo-American relations during the period of cobelligerency have examined subjects secondary to the war against the Imperial Germany Army. Anglo-American war aims, Britain's growing financial dependency upon the United States, commercial and maritime rivalry, and the Anglo-American reaction to the emergence of Communism in Russia have been thoroughly scrutinized.[2] Anglo-American relations in the context of military operations, however, have not received the attention they deserve. Only David F. Trask, who has examined President Woodrow Wilson's efforts to harmonize political and military objectives in the European war, as well as Anglo-American naval relations, 1917-18, has analyzed the power and political aspects of America's extra-Continental activity.[3]

It is not my intention to duplicate Trask's account of the maritime front or to parallel his pioneer examination of the American role in the Supreme War Council. Nor is this binational study written from either a British or an American point of view. Rather, it attempts to address Anglo-American relations in the collective military effort without embracing the perspective of either side. Based on extensive research in the recent literature and in American and British archives, this volume investigates the political and military aspects of the origins, nature, and course of Anglo-American cobelligerency. Unpublished sources provide a fresh perspective for the continuing idealist-realist debate in international affairs. Emphasis is given to the war leadership of David Lloyd George and Woodrow Wilson, the two most powerful political figures in the world during the last phase of the war. In broad terms, this book also serves as a historical case study of the inevitable tension between national self-interest and efforts at collective security, even among powers who share so many common cultural and political values.

1

From Rapprochement to the House-Grey Memorandum

The roots of cobelligerency with its underlying tension can be traced to the Anglo-American rapprochement that developed from 1898 to 1914 as America entered the world stage. Throughout much of the nineteenth century, international trends had favored both Britain and the United States over all other powers. The defeat of Napoleon and the 1814-15 peace settlement created a rare equilibrium in Europe, and Britain's supremacy on the high seas served to shelter both countries from any realistic threat of invasion. Both consequently enjoyed the luxury of maintaining limited peacetime land forces. Britain refused to embrace the mass conscript army that all great European powers possessed, relying instead on a small professional force. The United States, which had momentarily been the world's greatest land power at the end of its Civil War in 1865, maintained at the turn of the century an army more suitable to a Portugal or a Norway than to a great world power.

Without a serious rival on the world scene for most of the nineteenth century, Britain continued to add to its vast empire. On the eve of World War I, Britain had an empire 140 times its own size, constituting almost a quarter of the earth's land surface; some 400,000,000 people at home and abroad were the subjects of George V.

The world map with portions of every continent colored in British red, however, belied Britain's real position at the beginning of the new century. It is true that Britain in absolute terms was the world's premier power if measured by its fleet, financial resources, industrial capacity, trade, and colonies.[1] But fundamental trends in the international situation no longer favored Britain. Industrialization in countries such as Germany, the United States, and Japan created powerful commercial competitors. Japan built a world-class navy and embarked on an expansionist policy in Asia; French overseas expansion, especially in Africa, at times threatened British holdings; Russian imperial designs often collided with British interests in such areas as Persia, India, and the Far East. Germany, with its determination to build a battle fleet that would challenge Britain's and its aggressive policies in Europe and abroad, came to represent the greatest threat after 1905. Consequently, Britain was forced to shift its attention increasingly to European affairs, forming the Triple Entente with France and Russia. The nation's naval strength was concentrated in home waters, and a rapid deployment force—the British Expeditionary Force (BEF), capable of a limited role in any European war—was created.

As British policy became increasingly "defensive" in nature, Washington and London drew closer. Of all the emerging powers the United States seemed most benign to British vital interests. Throughout much of the nineteenth century, Washington had divorced military policy from its foreign policies. Safe from any real foreign threat, the United States was able to make a virtue out of military weakness both before and after the costly Civil War. Even after it extended its influence overseas around the turn of the century—acquiring territories and protectorates in the Caribbean; expanding across the Pacific with the acquisition of Hawaii, Wake, Guam, Samoa, and the Philippine Islands; and taking an activist role in China—American policymakers established no real connection between these new foreign commitments and their country's ability to uphold them. Nor did American leaders believe that the nature of their expansionism, despite its paternalistic disregard for the national sentiment of the colonial peoples, could be compared to British or European imperialism.

In one sense American expansion *was* different: America was a satisfied nation with no emotional or strategical need for additional territory. Its colonies were not considered permanent; rather, they were thought of as temporary dependencies to be "civilized" before being given their independence. It is significant that the United States was the one major power that began and finished World War I without any intention of annexing territory.[2]

America's construction of a modern fleet even seemed to work to Britain's advantage. Unable to disperse its own fleet to every latitude of the globe, London began to turn over to the United States the responsibility of protecting the Western Hemisphere. Another advantage of this informal entente was that the United States, with the notable exception of its difficulties with Japan, pursued policies in the decade before the war that did not threaten to entangle Britain in a dispute with another great power. Equally, from the American point of view, the growing friendship between the Atlantic powers appeared to involve no potential military obligations for the United States beyond the Western Hemisphere.

An extremely important factor in the Anglo-American rapprochement was the prevailing British perspective that the United States was an Anglo-Saxon cousin—a cousin, incidentally, who had grown from an infant with a population of three million at independence to a giant of almost a hundred million by 1914. Never mind the legacy of American distrust of Britain and the ethnic diversity of the American population. The United States, A.E. Campbell has written, "was treated as a branch of the British Empire which, owing to a regrettable misunderstanding, had broken away and achieved political independence in the past."[3]

The British frequently assumed too much in their relationship with the United States because of language, economic ties, and a common culture and history. Modest American expansionist tendencies, writes P.A.R. Calvert, were considered "with a certain sense of paternal pride" as "a predictable stage of development of a power stemming from British origins."[4] American innovation and technical success, though feared for their threat to British economic well-being, were similarly accepted as manifestations of the Anglo-Saxon race's genius.[5] Joseph Chamberlain, the pro-American colonial secretary at the turn of the century, included his American "cousins" when he asserted: "I believe in this race, the greatest governing race the world has ever seen; in this Anglo-Saxon race, so proud, tenacious, self-confident and determined, this race which neither climate nor change can degenerate, which will infallibly be the predominant force of future history and universal civilisation."[6]

Avner Offer's thought-provoking study has shown that the United States was a decisive dimension in London's prewar strategic thinking about the rising German threat. "The real assets of British security," he argues, "were the bonds and resources of the English-speaking world overseas: economic, social, political, sentimental, forming a complex but effective system of practical kinship."[7] This emphasis on the superiority and brotherhood of the Anglo-Saxon race, which was echoed by Theodore Roosevelt and many other Americans, especially in urban areas on the east coast, contributed to British misconceptions about the part that the United States was prepared to play in a war with Germany. The historical and cultural bond between the two countries was to a large degree responsible for the generally pro-British tilt of the American public while their country remained officially neutral. But a wide chasm often existed between the military and civilian leaders of both countries; conflicting national goals and perceptions were differences that could not be bridged by considerations of racial kinship. In reality, the improved political relationship between London and Washington prior to 1914 had been largely one-sided: the British granted concessions without receiving anything in return. "In hard diplomatic coin," Bradford Perkins has observed, "the Americans took but they did not give."[8]

On the eve of World War I, British and American world views on the employment of force and the balance-of-power politics in defense of national interests were in sharp contrast.[9] The experiences of the nineteenth century had ill prepared American statesmen to confront the turbulent new century that ended British domination of the seas and destroyed the balance of power in Europe, the two conditions—other than geography—that had most protected American borders from foreign threat in the nineteenth century. The political struggles of Europe were seen as alien to American interests. For Americans, "isolationism had come to reflect not a favorable geographic position and a satisfactory international equilibrium," Norman Graebner has astutely observed, "but a superior morality."[10] As the "world's major satisfied nation," the United States was the leading proponent of peaceful means such as arbitration to resolve conflicts between nations. If the American position were to be accepted, it "would guarantee the country its international advantages without the necessity of war or extensive military preparations."[11] In sum, America on the eve of World War I aspired to have its world influence match its unquestioned economic power without assuming the inevitable international responsibilities that would ensue and without developing the military means necessary to support a global policy. That the success of American foreign objectives in the twentieth century would depend in large part on its willingness and ability to use force may appear obvious to many students of American diplomacy since 1914. But such a view was clearly at odds with the prewar thinking of America's foreign policy elite, which rejected power politics. And why not? Virtual disarmament and isolation from European conflicts had served both the nation's interests and its ideals in the past and apparently would do so in the future.

It was President Woodrow Wilson's fate to confront a world picture very different from that viewed by his predecessors. Not since 1812 had the international situation been so threatening to the United States. Shortly before he took the oath of office on March 3, 1913, he made a much-quoted remark to a friend: "It would be the irony of fate if my administration had to deal chiefly with foreign affairs."[12] Wilson certainly expressed a legitmate concern. his previous scholarly inquiry had given almost no attention to foreign affairs. As the war clouds grew over Europe, Wilson paid them little or no heed. Before the war, as Arthur Link, his most authoritative biographer, has noted, Wilson "spoke and acted as if foreign problems did not exist."[13] Because Wilson paid fleeting attention to the Spanish-American war, even for a time enthusiastically advocating American overseas expansion, this view has been challenged, but it remains correct in its essentials. The voluminous Wilson papers demonstrate that the new president, dur-

Woodrow Wilson and French president Raymond Poincaré in December 1918. Courtesy of Special Collections, U.S. Army Military History Institute.

ing the decade before he entered the White House, had had almost nothing to say or write about foreign affairs.

Wilson's reaction to the outbreak of war mirrored those of his countrymen: this European civil war, though it soon spread to other corners of the world from Mesopotamia to East Africa to the Shantung province in China, was not the business of Americans. As the local conflict in the Balkans between Austria-Hungary and Serbia threatened to involve the other great European powers, the president told reporters on July 27: "The United States has never attempted to interfere in European affairs."[14] Wilson, however, apparently decided not to define an offer of American mediation of the European conflict as interference: he made an ineffectual attempt on August 4, after the war had begun, to employ the good offices of United States as a go-between for peace.

Britain's decision to deploy the British Expeditionary Force on the European continent to prevent a Germany victory over France altered Wilson's views on American neutrality not one iota. He greatly admired British political institutions and, like many other Americans, felt most at home abroad when visiting the British Isles. But though he was privately more sympathetic to the British than to the Germans, he did not share the British view that Germany was the aggressor nation and must be soundly defeated to preserve future peace.[15] To Wilson's way of thinking, America's and humanity's interests would best be served by a draw. He told a journalist in December 1914 that the best chance of "a just and equitable peace, and of the only possible peace that will be lasting, will be happiest if no nation gets the decision by arms; and the danger of an unjust peace, one that will be sure to invite further calamities, will be if some one nation or group of nations succeeds in enforcing its will upon the others."[16]

To prevent the United States from becoming entangled in the European conflict, he cautioned his countrymen to be "impartial in thought as well as in action," to be "a nation that neither sits in judgment upon others nor is disturbed in her own counsels and which keeps herself fit and free to do what is necessary and disinterested and truly serviceable for the peace of the world."[17]

Wilson's approach to the global crisis was shaped first and foremost by what Link has called his Christian idealism. The son, grandson, and nephew of Presbyterian ministers, Wilson was a devout Christian. When in residence at the White House, he never missed a Sunday service at the Central Presbyterian Church. His Christian ethics provided his sense of right and wrong in foreign relations; he believed that nations no less than individuals should be guided by the moral teachings of Christ.[18] Wilson also had a strong faith in democracy, was optimistic about human nature, and believed with a crusader's zeal that the United States had a mission to lead the world away from world empires, armed alliances, and balance-of-power politics to a new world order based on law and universal values. To the world's most satisfied power, of course, these objectives promised to enhance national interests with virtually no sacrifice. In an international system of democracies based on the rule of law, the United States, with its rapidly growing population and an industry that was on the verge of outproducing all the European states added together,[19] would become the dominant power of the twentieth century without the implicit dangers of militarism.

His pursuit of American national self-interest while he also championed the interests of humanity has led to considerable disagreement about Wilson's motives, which indeed were often more complex than they sometimes appeared at the time. Part of the confusion in London about his policies stemmed from his subtle mind, his aloofness, and especially the mixed signals emanating from the men who were expected to inform him on British policy and faithfully represent his views to the British government. In Anglo-American relations, Wilson was primarily advised by Robert Lansing, who had become secretary of state following the resignation of William Jennings Bryan in mid-1915; Walter Hines Page, the American ambassador in London; and Colonel Edward M. House, his alter ego and closest adviser. Unlike the president, these Anglophiles were concerned with the dire strategic consequences to the United States should Germany triumph over Britain. In contrast to most of their countrymen, they recognized that America's security in large part rested on retaining amicable Anglo-American relations and preventing Germany from dominating the European continent. Of the three men, House unquestionably enjoyed the most influence with the president in strategic questions and relations with Great Britain, particularly after the United States entered the war in April 1917. Lansing, a realist in foreign affairs, provided Wilson with legal justifications for the use of force.[20] But his basic incompatibility with the president placed him increasingly on the fringes of vital questions in Anglo-American relations once America entered the war. Page's strong pro-British sentiments eventually cost him Wilson's confidence, to the extent that the president refused even to read his cables from London.

House's intimate relationship with the president and consequent influence in foreign affairs declined after Wilson remarried. Edith Bolling Galt over time replaced the colonel in the president's affections.[21] On geopolitical and strategic questions and relations with the British, however, House retained his dominance, in considerable part because of an extraordinary breakdown in ambassadorial relations between London and Washington.[22] By persuading the president (not without some justification) that Page and the irascible and nervous British ambassador in Washington, Sir Cecil Spring Rice, were incapable of competently representing Wilsonian views, House increasingly made himself the essential link between London and Washington.

The Wilson-House relationship remains one of the most controversial partnerships in American foreign affairs.[23] An honorary Texas colonel, House was small in stature, stylishly dressed, wealthy, and cosmopolitan. As the president's special representative he achieved intimacy with many British leaders through his self-effacing and ingratiating ways. By collecting and swapping information, he helped shape the president's perceptions of the British government. Unfortunately, he often heard only what he wanted to hear. Certainly his diary provides an unreliable record of his conversations with Wilson and foreign statesmen.[24] Many of the entries seem to have been written to justify his own views on international events. An unsuspecting Wilson believed that House had no political ambitions but only wanted to serve as the president's instrument in achieving a new order in international affairs. "All he wants to do is to serve the common cause and to help me and others," Wilson once wrote of his adviser.[25]

This was not true. The president's almost total and essentially remote control of American policy afforded House, with his ready access to the Oval Office, the opportunity to achieve his ulterior objectives. In 1911-12 he had written anonymously a novel in which one Philip Dru, an enlightened dictator of the United States, created a world peace league through cooperation with Great Britain.[26] "Worst of all, in his near mystical identification of Wilson with Philip Dru," John Milton Cooper has astutely noted, "House spun fantasies that loosened his grip on reality. Often he did not realize how badly he misrepresented situations or how desperately he was seeking to embody his dreams through Wilson and others."[27]

No previous American leader had ever had such great global responsibilities thrust upon him as Wilson, and no other president has assumed a decisive international role with such detachment. "The President lives enveloped in mystery and there are strange stories of the difficulty which is encountered by anyone even in the highest position who desires to have access to him," wrote Spring Rice in describing Wilson's aloofness to his government.[28] Wilson the president resembled Wilson the introverted university professor in making difficult decisions in foreign affairs. His favorite retreat in the White House, his second-story private study, certainly had the appearance of a professor's office. His desk was stacked with papers and books; a portable Corona typewriter, with which he personally triple-spaced many important diplomatic notes, rested in the corner. Before reaching a decision, it was his habit to retire to this study to reflect. Slow to make up his mind, he stubbornly clung to decisions made. He did not read widely in newspapers, and his circle of advisers was small. Confident of his judgment, he often relied on his own principles and instincts. His chief source of information for Anglo-American relations was House, who at critical times, although not always intentionally, did not accurately represent either the president's or the British position. The result was that neither Wilson nor the British government had a consistently correct reading of the other's intentions when House served as the conduit of diplomatic exchange.

British leaders, who were not without experience in clothing their country's self-interest in moralistic terms, expected sympathy, if not outright support, from their Atlantic cousins in the war against German expansionism. Prime Minister Herbert H. Asquith pledged his government to the destruction of the "military domination of Prussia" soon after the war began. The British leadership then and later believed that the great sacrifices of Britain and its empire would have been in vain if the German leadership were not taught that military adventurism did not pay. An unrepentant Germany would continue to threaten the European equilibrium and menace Britain's global position. Statements in this vein were made repeatedly in their inner councils of war during any discussions of peace. The destruction of German militarism (easier to condemn than to find a practical means to end, as the outbreak of another world war was to demonstrate) constituted Britain's major objective in Europe, surpassing even the liberation of Belgium. Outside of Europe the British linked world stability with the preservation of the British Empire. They took for granted that their world leadership "conduced to the general welfare and they felt that all Americans should be able to perceive this obvious fact unless blinded by prejudice."[29]

Wilson, however, did not identify British interests with those of the United States. German U-boats increasingly forced him to take a stand against Berlin to protect American lives at sea, but he remained determined to keep the United States out of the war. As the fighting continued into 1916 with no end in sight, Wilson became bolder in his efforts to mediate the conflict as a means of keeping his country from becoming entangled in the European hostilities. Foreign Secretary Sir Edward Grey, representing the dominant school among British statesmen who believed that present and future British national security depended upon an Anglo-American partnership, was prepared to go quite far in appeasing Wilson. But Grey insisted that if peace negotiations were successful, the United States should continue to play a responsible international role through participation in an international organization that would foster disarmament and peace.[30] Grey was realistic in his concern that America might not prove to be a reliable partner on the international stage after the war. There was a real danger that the United States might turn its back on Europe with the restoration of peace. Given Wilson's desire to shape any peace settlement along the lines of his revolutionary world views, however, the immediate danger was that he would prevent the achievement of a peace that satisfied Britain's vital interests.

On February 17, 1916, Grey and House drafted and initialed in

London the controversial House-Grey Memorandum, which seemed to promise American entry into the war on Britain's side if Germany refused to participate in peace discussions or proved unreasonable once brought to the peace table. In his eagerness to end the war through mediation, House, as Wilson's special emissary, was less than forthright with both Grey and his president. He convinced the British foreign secretary that Wilson was prepared to "intervene on the side of the Allies" if Germany proved to be intransigent.[31] On the other hand, House seriously misrepresented London's willingness to accept the American definition of a favorable British peace at the beginning of 1916. House was not entirely to blame in this respect. British efforts to avoid offending Wilson did not lead to straight talk on their part.

The House-Grey Memorandum forced the British leadership to confront directly for the first time the consequences of what America's participation in world politics might mean for the future security of the British Empire. The desired outcome of peace discussions would be American military cooperation, which might shorten the war. Although confident of victory, the British were becoming concerned about the heavy war burden being placed upon them. With significant help from the Empire, Britain was now playing a central role in the land war in Europe to preserve the anti-German coalition. France had suffered horrendous losses in 1914-15. Russia had been thrown back from the borders of East Prussia and driven from Poland. In southeastern Europe and the Near East, following the failure of the Dardanelles and Gallipoli ventures in 1915, the Central powers were dominant.[32]

As 1916 began, the British government's adviser on grand strategy, the Chief of the Imperial General Staff, General Sir William Robertson, exacted a general commitment (though final approval was not forthcoming until early April) from his government to employ the largest force that Britain had ever sent to any theater of operations in a massive offensive on the western front. With fiscal, manpower, and industrial resources already extended, the maintenance of this vast force on the Continent further threatened to undermine the economy. "We have reached a stage in the development of our resources," Robertson warned the civilians, "when those requirements [to maintain the army's manpower] can only be met by putting the same strain upon the social and business life of the community as has long been borne in France."[33] Although further mobilization for total war might make Britain financially dependent on the United States, the British felt that they had no choice but to support their allies to the fullest as paymaster, shipper, arsenal, and now major participant on the western front.

Despite the apparent advantages of gaining America as a cobelligerent, there were many dangers, not the least of which was the threat posed by Wilson's peace program to the unity of the alliance and to future British security. A British peace could not be obtained just by preventing German hegemony on the Continent; the global threat posed by Berlin's overseas possessions, which was of secondary interest to Britain's European allies, also had to be removed.

In his discussions with the British leadership in January and February, House had seemed to offer a territorial settlement that left intact Germany's overseas possessions, strengthened Berlin's position in Eastern Europe, and left unchecked German influence in the Near East. Moreover, Poland was to be freed from Russian domination, perhaps ruled by a German prince, which in effect would mean the "annexation of Russian Poland to Germany—an outcome that would alienate tsarist Russia, whose contributions to the Allied cause were immense. Berlin was also to be given all or part of Anatolia as "compensation for the loss of Alsace-Lorraine."[34] The British were to be compensated by the liberation of Belgium.

What to Colonel House was a balanced peace was clearly a disaster to the British. To be sure, they had initially gone to war in response to Germany's invasion of Belgium, but that country's independence no longer represented a satisfactory end to the war. To achieve a sound peace, German militarists had to be taught a lesson, German expansionism in the East thwarted, and the future security of the British Empire secured through the elimination of Germany's colonies. Given what is now known about the determination of both the civilian and military leadership of Imperial Germany to become a world power,[35] the American conception of a balanced settlement (in the unlikely event that Germany accepted American terms) would have been detrimental to the long-range security of both Britain *and* the United States. On balance, then, the opening of general peace negotiations threatened to result, first, in a serious division of the anti-German coalition over war aims and, second, a peace settlement that would leave an expansionist Germany unhumbled. And there remained the vital question of whether the United States would join the anti-German coalition if peace negotiations collapsed. Wilson's motives for peacemaking were understandably suspect to many British leaders, although not to Grey.[36]

The first official discussions of the House-Grey Memorandum took place in the War Committee on February 22 and March 21 as the British wrestled with the difficult choices required to achieve a favorable British peace.[37] Secretary of State for War Lord Kitchener raised a central question: what if Berlin unexpectedly took a reasonable stance, accepted Wilson's intervention to end the war, and agreed to the *status quo ante bellum*? Reginald McKenna, chancellor of the exchequer, noted that "the Americans considered that the end of the war would be a draw." In that case, Asquith retorted, a draw would be "much the same as a defeat." Moreover, how could the British be certain that Wilson's mediation efforts were not, in Asquith's words, "humbug, and a mere manoeuvre of American politics?"[38] Britain might be walking into a trap. If peace negotiations began and Berlin would not accept the original American formula, would Wilson really destroy his chances for reelection by declaring war on Germany? "[Wilson] might," Edwin S. Montagu, the Anglo-Jewish millionaire and Liberal political leader, wrote Asquith on March 18, "with the best will in the world be confronted by a demand for what might appear to him slight modifications or the failure of the conference."[39] In that event British security would almost certainly be sacrificed for Wilson's political career. First Lord of the Admiralty Arthur Balfour, a champion of Anglo-American ties, spoke for the British inner political leadership with the exception of Grey when he said during the War Committee's second discussion of the House-Grey Memorandum that the proposal was at that time "not worth five minutes thought."[40]

Wilson's qualified promise to become Britain's ally in the event that Germany blocked a negotiated settlement, however, tilted American policy in favor of the British and constituted an unneutral act. But was he gambling for peace without the military resources or will to back his bluff if it were called? The president naturally was concerned with American domestic considerations and attentive to the overwhelming American desire to remain distant from European affairs.[41] He genuinely sought to open general peace negotiations not to involve the United States in war but to protect American neutrality through a negotiated settlement before his hand might be forced by events beyond his control, such as Germany's campaign of undersea assault. On March 24, 1916, a German submarine attacked an unarmed French passenger vessel, the *Sussex*, injuring several American passengers. Wilson responded on April 18 by threatening a diplomatic rupture with Germany unless Berlin restricted its use of submarine warfare. The British, having broken the German code, were privy to what Wilson told the German ambassador in Washington.[42] They dared to hope that German torpedoes might force Wilson to shift his attention from achieving a balanced peace through mediation to seeking a military victory over Germany.

On April 26 Field Marshal Lord Kitchener, attired in full dress uniform, discussed German provocations with the American military attaché, Lieutenant Colonel George O. Squier, who was paying his respects to the secretary of state for war before returning to the United States. Kitchener, no doubt hoping that his words would influence the American administration, spoke enthusiastically about the president's stern note, expressing the belief (which he surely did not actually hold) that American intervention would bring the war to a close before the end of 1916. Kitchener attempted to assure Squier that Britain, unlike its allies, was "in this war solely on principle, and wants absolutely nothing." With the "two English-speaking peoples working together on broad principles," a "lasting peace" might be ensured. Kitchener concluded his conversation with what must have been the first British attempt to forge a special military relationship with the United States and to involve American soldiers in Western Europe in the event of American belligerency. "Tell your Secretary of War, if he will merely send me a wire for any assistance that I can give, it will be given immediately without the necessity of regular diplomatic channels." He also suggested that American troops complete their training in France, enabling them to enter combat "in the shortest possible time."[43]

Wilson almost certainly never read an account of this interview, nor was he apparently shown by the War Department a paper prepared at the beginning of April by American military and naval attachés in London and Paris and two American officers attached to the BEF. These officers suggested that plans immediately be prepared for the mobilization of American shipping to convey an American army to Europe in the event of war.[44] This astonishing though realistic proposal was not considered at this time by the Joint Army and Navy Board; America's military leadership was all too aware that the furthest thought from the president's mind in April 1916 was sending American forces to Europe. He had taken a tougher diplomatic stance with Germany, in all likelihood, to promote his standing as a peace mediator with the Allies. After the Germans gave an evasive response on May 4, the so-called *Sussex* pledge, Wilson pressed the British to avail themselves of the House-Grey Memorandum.

The British War Office, despite the soothing words of Kitchener, remained adamantly opposed to a Wilsonian peace. When Wilson pressed the British government in late May to take up the House-Grey Memorandum, the Army Council, the governing board of the British army that included Kitchener and Robertson among its members, threatened resignation "if the War Committee insisted on an inquiry into the peace question."[45] With the BEF in the final stages of preparation for its great offensive on the Somme, the army leadership remained optimistic about Britain's ability to defeat the German army.

Another vital consideration for the British civilian leadership continued to be America's apparent unwillingness to back its diplomacy with force—or even to understand the need of coordinating national goals with military policy. When House had discussed American mediation with the inner circle of the British government, David Lloyd George had emphasized the connection between a program of naval and military preparedness and the success of American diplomatic efforts.[46] What were the British to think of the scholar-statesman who earlier had been "too proud to fight" after the sinking of the *Lusitania*?

At first glance the president seemed oblivious of the realities of power politics. The president's first vivid memory as a child growing up in Augusta, Georgia, had been the outbreak of the Civil War. As he was playing in front of his home, he heard a man exclaim, "Lincoln is elected, and there'll be war."[47] Although Augusta remained on the fringes of that destructive conflict, Wilson developed a hatred for war. During his earlier career as an academic, warfare had never engaged his scholarly attention, not even in his account of the Civil War. As president, he tended to be bored by military questions and was uncomfortable in the presence of soldiers. On the eve of American belligerency he told a journalist that "he'd rather have done anything else than head a military machine. All his instincts were against it."[48]

Notwithstanding his hatred of war, Wilson was clearly not averse to the employment of force as a last resort for righteous purposes. "If I cannot retain my moral influence over a man except by occasionally knocking him down, if that is the only basis upon which he will respect me, then for the sake of his soul I have got occasionally to knock him down," he explained before the National Press Club on May 15, 1916. "If a man will not listen to you quietly in a seat, sit on his neck and make him listen."[49]

Some historians have had difficulty reconciling Wilson's aversion to war with his readiness to utilize force to support his diplomacy in Mexico and the Caribbean. Before America intervened in the Great War, Wilson had employed American armed forces in Mexico (twice), Haiti, Cuba, and the Dominican Republic. In fact, he involved his country in more military interventions than any other American president before or since. Yet that statement, although true, is misleading without elaboration. Wilson truly hated war and feared that it would foster militarism in the United States. With the exception of his dispatch of the AEF to Western Europe, Wilson's use of force was extremely limited, involving only a handful of casualties, and was more in line with a police action for economic, humanitarian, or liberal political objectives. The president's rigid control of the military's involvement in Mexico at Veracruz in 1914—and during the Punitive Expedition in 1916—provides an excellent illustration of his carefully managed employment of force to support his diplomacy.[50]

Wilson's view of his constitutional position as commander-in-chief reinforced his determination to assert civilian authority over the army and navy establishments; these he deemed instruments of a national policy to be determined solely by civilians. At the same time, rejecting the idea that he had a dual civilian and military role as commander-in-chief, he reacted angrily in 1918 when someone sent him an etching that depicted him in military dress.[51]

A serious consequence of Wilson's rigid separation of military and civilian authority was that he ignored the machinery that had been created for formulating the nation's strategic policy.[52] He had suggested to the British that he might become their ally without preparing for or even examining the consequences of U.S. belligerency. American generals and admirals were kept in the dark about the House-Grey Memorandum, and no contingency plans were made for collective security.

On Elihu Root's recommendation, the War Department General Staff had been created by an act of Congress in 1903. Its head, the chief of the General Staff, who replaced the commanding general of the army, served as strategic adviser to the secretary of war and the president. As the "brain" of the army, the General Staff was expected to develop into an organization capable of mobilizing, organizing, training, transporting, and supplying the army in time of war. Another essential duty of the General Staff was to gather intelligence and to develop plans for the strategic deployment of the nation's armed forces. In 1908-10 the General Staff had been divided into two sections, one housed in the War Department and the other, the War College Division, placed across town with the Army War College at Washington Barracks. The War College Division (renamed in February 1918 the War Plans Division) was given the responsibility for intelligence gathering and war planning.[53]

In August 1915 the president's hand had trembled with rage as he pointed to a lead article in the *Baltimore Sun* with the provocative heading, "May Call 1,000,000 Men." This article purported to give an account of the General Staff's plans for war with Germany, based on sending an army to Europe. The president believed that American neutrality and contingency planning for any cooperative or offensive military effort were incompatible, even when it appeared that war might be forced upon a reluctant America. The chief of the War College Division of the General Staff, Brigadier General M.M. Macomb, issued a heated and honest denial: the U.S. Army had no plans for offensive war with Germany. Rather, the General Staff had developed fragmentary plans for calling up 1,000,000 men only if Germany attacked the Atlantic coast.[54] The war planners from 1914 to 1916 were strictly defensive in their appreciations, with other formal war plans focusing on defending the west coast against a Japanese attack and countering a British attack on New York.[55] The possibility that the United States might have to fight Germany on European soil was not considered.

Aware of the existing political realities, the General Staff had been treading very warily. Before the *Baltimore Sun* affair, Chief of Staff

Hugh L. Scott, prompted by the secretary of war, had ordered all officers at the Army War College not to discuss in any public forum the course of the war in Europe. A further directive at the beginning of 1916 cautioned all civilian employees of the War College not to discuss the war while at work or offer "any views of a partisan nature in connection therewith." [56] Congress delivered a further blow to the General Staff's effectiveness in its National Defense Act of 1916 by restricting that body to a chief of staff, two general officers of the line, ten colonels, ten lieutenant colonels, fifteen majors, and seventeen captains—a total of fifty-five officers. No more than half of these were allowed to serve in or near the District of Columbia. When war did come, only nineteen officers were attached to the General Staff, eleven of them assigned to the War College Division. With the General Staff limited in personnel and mission, the possibility that the United States might engage in collective military action with Britain or any other power went unexamined. The consideration of such vital questions as the transport, equipment, logistics, and theater of operations for any expeditionary force was left until the eve of American belligerency.

As was the case with the army, American isolationist sentiment precluded any possibility that the U.S. Navy's General Board—the naval general staff, authorized by Congress in 1900—might develop plans for American participation in the European war. Nor did the Joint Army and Navy Board, created in 1903, ever become an effective means of coordinating army and navy planning; after 1913 it practically ceased to exist. The unfortunate consequences of the inability of the General Staff, General Board, and Joint Army and Navy Board to carry out their intended role in the development of the nation's strategic plans was never more apparent than during the ill-conceived preparedness campaign in 1916.

Circumstances by 1915-16 had forced the president to link American military power to the credibility of his efforts to protect American neutral rights and to play a more active role in international affairs. As he told opponents of preparedness in May 1916: "A nation which, by the standards of other nations, however mistaken those standards may be, is regarded as helpless, is apt in general counsel to be regarded as negligible." [57] After the sinking of the *Lusitania*, the president embraced an ambitious naval construction program with the goal of making the U.S. Navy second to none. The subsequent Naval Act of 1916, which appropriated money for a battleship-dominated fleet, did not, however, prepare the United States to participate in the current conflict on the Allied side. A great battle fleet might enable the United States to hold its own with the great naval powers following the conclusion of World War I, but it would be ineffectual in containing the German U-boat threat. Hence the U.S. naval building program ultimately constituted a graver future threat to British primacy on the high seas than to German interests.

The effect of the 1916 preparedness movement on the U.S. Army was even more disappointing to the British. Wilson had campaigned hard in January and February for a buildup of the army as well as the navy. Momentarily, he even supported the War Department's proposal for a national reserve force, the Continental Army, over the opposition of important members of his own party. Unable to muster the necessary votes in Congress, despite his attempt to take the issue to the people, Wilson retreated and left the question of strengthening the army to the isolationist Congress.[58]

The issue of army preparedness, however, would not go away, given American military intervention in Mexico in retaliation against Pancho Villa's raid on Columbus, New Mexico, in March 1916. As the Punitive Expedition advanced into the Mexican interior, Congress passed its first comprehensive plan of national security, the National Defense Act, which Wilson signed into law on June 3, 1916. But this bill, reflecting the dominant isolationist sentiment in Congress and the country, did not prepare the army to fight in Europe. Conscription was rejected, and the mainstay of American land warfare became the militia, a primitive fighting force by twentieth-century European standards. Congress also refused to sanction either the plans or the machinery for national mobilization, which would have been rightly interpreted by the public as the first step toward an interventionist military policy.

As constituted, the U.S. Army was clearly incapable of participating in the European war. Its armament was obsolete and its supply of munitions hopelessly inadequate. Its field artillery had enough rounds to sustain a bombardment on the western front for no more than a few minutes. With no poison gas, flame throwers, tanks, mortars, hand and rifle grenades, heavy field howitzers, or modern aircraft, the U.S. Army remained a nineteenth-century force and a very small one at that. In 1916 it ranked seventeenth in the world.

As the presidential campaign of 1916 intensified, Wilson's actions more and more symbolized the noninterventionist sentiment of the country. When Lindley M. Garrison resigned in protest over Wilson's abandonment of the Continental Army idea, Wilson selected a pacifist, Newton D. Baker, to replace him as secretary of war. With Josephus Daniels as secretary of the navy, both branches of service now had pacifistic civilian leadership. Another signal of American intentions occurred during the Democratic convention in St. Louis in 1916. Keynote speaker Martin Glynn, former governor of New York, praised Wilson for keeping the country out of the war. Spontaneously, members of the audience began to chant, "What did we do? What did we do?" Glynn riposted: "We didn't go to war." During the subsequent campaign, "He kept us out of war" became a powerful Democratic slogan. The British rightly feared that the American political situation rendered worthless Wilson's assurance that he would "probably" enter the war if Berlin did not accept a reasonable peace settlement. Congress would never declare war over such an issue. Just as important, the American preparedness campaign was clearly not designed to enable the Americans to cooperate with the British against Germany.

American actions in the military realm during the months immediately following the House-Grey Memorandum thus did nothing to alter Asquith's initial reaction that he did not see where "the coercive power of the United States" lay. David Lloyd George, then minister of munitions, had agreed and said that the Americans would "possess no coercive power this year."[59] It was natural for the British to assume that the American commitment to ending the war, which suggested the possibility of military cooperation with the British, was insincere.

Lloyd George and Asquith were wrong about America's inability to back its diplomacy with power. America would possess "coercive power" in 1916, not its army or navy but its emerging economic ascendancy over Britain. Given the growing dependency of Britain on America for credit and supplies, this form of American diplomatic leverage represented a far greater threat to British interests than it did to the Central Powers.

The long-awaited British offensive on the Somme in July 1916 momentarily pushed British thoughts of peace into the background. The initial phase of the attack was an unmitigated disaster. Although shaken by the massive casualties suffered by the BEF and its Commander-in-Chief Sir Douglas Haig's frank admission that his attacks must "go well into the autumn" and that another prolonged offensive would be required in 1917, the War Committee at the beginning of August nonetheless supported the continuation of the offensive.[60] During August, with the enemy launching costly counterattacks, the BEF inflicted heavy losses on the Germans. Elsewhere, the French fought stubbornly at Verdun; the Russian steamroller advanced against Austria-Hungary; and the Italians applied pressure on the Isonzo.

The simultaneous pressure on the Central Powers on all major fronts caused some British leaders to worry that Berlin, fearing defeat, might use Wilson to arrange an armistice. When this prospect was discussed by the War Committee on August 10, Grey accurately expressed the sentiments of his associates: Britain wanted any proposal for an armistice with the enemy to be based on conditions "that the United States would accept, which at the same time would be impossible for Germany to accept unless owning that she was beaten."[61] This was wishful thinking, and the British knew it. If Germany sought a ceasefire through Washington, it would almost certainly cinch Wilson's reelection. Wilson, now growing wary of working for peace through London, might try to use the growing British economic dependence on America to force Britain to silence its guns. Lloyd George could bluster that "it would be a declaration of war if they [the United States] stopped the supply of cotton,"[62] but that could not change Britain's economic vulnerability, which was increasing by the week.

Continuing British commitment to victory placed Anglo-American relations in serious jeopardy during the summer and fall of 1916. British retaliation against American firms suspected of trading with Germany—the so-called "black list"—and the suppression of the Easter Rebellion in Ireland provoked an angry reaction in the United States. More ominously, Wilson, angry that the British had not taken up his peace plan, now had serious reservations about London's motives. Having "lived with the English statesmen for the past two years and seen the real inside of their minds," he believed that British goals represented the European militarism and imperialism he so despised.[63]

The British began to harden their position as well. Through the interception of German messages between Washington and Berlin, Asquith's government knew that Wilson had told the German ambassador that it was "in the interest of America that neither of the combatants should gain a decisive victory."[64] It was axiomatic to most British leaders that not only the British Empire but Western civilization as well depended upon the defeat of German militarism. In memoranda circulated within the Cabinet, war objectives were frequently articulated that went beyond the peace terms discussed by Grey and House at the beginning of 1916.[65] Despite the growing strain, the British were in no mood to halt the war until the German threat was destroyed. "It is horrible to allow oneself to think even for a moment that the fruits of victory may be spoiled for us by unsatisfactory terms of peace," Montagu asserted. American efforts for peace, he continued to emphasize, were "contemptible and untrustworthy" and did not consider "civilisation, merits, or the future security of peace, but only the immediate political interests of either party." In equally bitter language the Earl of Crawford, president of the Board of Agriculture, charged that "President Wilson, whose recent action shows how deeply he is obsessed by electioneering ambition, will be quite ready to make such an [armistice] offer, even though he anticipates a refusal, provided his party can profit thereby."[66]

What some British leaders were saying in private, Lloyd George, who had succeeded Kitchener as secretary of state for war, said in public as September came to an end. Lloyd George was pro-American and genuinely believed that the best hope for future world peace depended upon the creation of a Pax Anglo-Americana. "If the United States would stand by Great Britain the entire world could not shake the combined mastery we would hold over the seas," he had told House at the beginning of 1916.[67] Beyond the obvious need to humor the president, Lloyd George had been sincere in his desire to create a "special relationship" between the world's two great English-speaking nations; he was to return to this idea again and again. But he viewed a soft peace as disastrous to British national interests and future world stability. With the climax of the American presidential campaign approaching, he feared that Wilson would take preemptive action to force negotiations upon the British at a time when Allied military fortunes were ebbing. The result might be catastrophic for British efforts to gain a stable peace through the smashing of German military despotism.

In a calculated move in early September, Lloyd George allowed the publication of a War Office interview with an American journalist, Roy Howard. The result was sensational. No British leader had ever spoken so bluntly to the president. The hawkish Welshman warned Wilson not to "'butt in' for the purpose of stopping the European war." Such American intervention in itself would constitute an unneutral act. Having "invested thousands of its best lives to purchase future immunity for civilisation," the British Empire was determined to fight the war "to a finish—to a knock-out."[68]

Grey was naturally furious at Lloyd George's extraordinary intervention in the realm of Anglo-American relations. "It has always been my view," he wrote, "that until the Allies were sure of victory the door should be kept open for Wilson's mediation. It is now closed forever as far as we are concerned." Lloyd George was unrepentant. The American politician has no "international conscience," he replied, and "thinks of nothing but the ticket, and he has not given the least thought to the effect of his action upon European affairs."[69]

Lloyd George was not overly concerned about the possibility that Wilson might retaliate by taking advantage of British reliance on American industry, finance, and raw materials. The war had been responsible for America's biggest economic boom in history. Just as British finances were dependent on America, so also was American prosperity becoming increasingly dependent on its trade and financial ties to the Allies. The former chancellor of the exchequer told the War Committee on October 5 that Britain should, if anything, increase its dependence on America because large orders gave the British "a greater political pull in that country." Big corporations in the United States were very powerful, and "we could use them if we handled them properly." With extraordinary prescience, he also predicted that Germany, growing frustrated over British access to American

THE WHITE HOUSE MYSTERY.

Uncle Sam: "Say, John, shall we have a dollar's worth?"
From *Punch*, January 3, 1917.

resources, was becoming desperate.[70] The United States might soon have no choice but to fight to protect itself from German outrages on the high seas. The risk that Lloyd George was prepared to take was that the militarists in Berlin would force Wilson's hand before the president's mediation efforts created a rupture between Washington and London that might be fatal to British hopes for victory.

Turbulent waters lay ahead for Anglo-American relations. "Here we regard the White House rather as Vesuvius is regarded in Naples, that is as a mysterious source of unexpected explosions," Spring Rice reported to London.[71] An angry President Wilson seemed bent on making the British, especially the pugnacious Lloyd George, pay for ignoring his peace efforts.

2

From Mediator
to "Associate Power"

Wilson's mediation efforts made the British government confront for the first time an America suggesting that it was prepared to take a decisive part in world politics. Confident of victory, the British believed during the spring and summer of 1916 that they could rebuff Wilson's potential threat to a favorable British peace without serious consequences. As the military stalemate continued into the fall, however, this was no longer true. America's economic ascendancy over the British grew by the day. In contrast to Lloyd George, many British leaders were not so sanguine over their country's economic and financial dependency on the United States. Forty percent of British war expenditure was being spent on supplies from North America. On October 31 Maurice Hankey, the secretary of the War Committee, warned in a general review of the war that the Achilles heel of the Entente members was their "staying-power, owing to the prodigious strain of the American orders on their financial resources." If this trend continued, "the Allies will, within the next few months, become entirely dependent upon the goodwill of the President of the United States of America for their power to continue the war."[1]

The deteriorating financial situation was only one of many concerns for the British political leadership. Britain's European allies were nearing exhaustion. Uncertain of their continued reliability, the British were themselves confronted with a serious manpower crisis. Hard fighting on the Somme had cost the BEF almost half a million casualties. Yet, in Robertson's words, the Germans continued to fight "with undiminished vigour." Robertson's grim forecast was that Britain "must expect, and at once prepare for, harder and more protracted fighting and a much greater strain on our general resources than any yet experienced before we can wring from the enemy that peace which we have said we mean to have."[2] The Army Council warned that British forces, depleted by a year of hard campaigning, faced a crisis in 1917. Unless extraordinary measures were taken to bring in more men, it would "be impossible after April next to keep the armies up to strength." Drafting men up to fifty-five years was one extreme measure advocated.[3]

German undersea assault also represented an accelerating threat. Walter Runciman, the president of the Board of Trade, issued a dire warning in early November: "My expert advisers believe that I am far too sanguine in advising the War Committee that the complete breakdown in shipping will come in June, 1917; they are convinced that it will come much sooner than June."[4] These estimates were based on the questionable assumption that Germany planned to continue limited as opposed to all-out U-boat warfare.

Under the circumstances it is not surprising that the prospect of a peace mediated by President Wilson began to be viewed seriously in some quarters. Lloyd George's position of fighting the war "to a finish—to a knock-out" was questioned within the British government by the respected Unionist leader and former foreign secretary, Lord Lansdowne. In a memorandum to the Cabinet, dated November 13, he asked the pertinent question: Would the pursuit of Lloyd George's "knock-out blow" against Imperial Germany destroy rather than save civilization?[5] There now seemed the prospect that the United States might offer the British future security. Wilson, in an extraordinary break with American isolationist tradition, told Grey (through House) that he could be sure "the United States would go any length in promoting and lending her full might to a League for Peace" in the event of a compromise settlement.[6]

But did Wilson really speak for his people in promising a global role for the United States? "The President's assurances as to the desire to take part in the permanent settlement are undoubtedly genuine," Spring Rice reported from Washington. "But between this and the performance there is a gulf. This people will have to abandon the Monroe doctrine and the Washingtonian tradition against entangling alliances. They will also have to have an army and a fleet ready on an instant and distant call for foreign service. The people who could not spare one word to Belgium are now to engage to send their armies and navies to the defence of threatened right. This is a big change."[7]

Renewed American pressure on London to end the hostilities seemed likely because Wilson had been reelected in early November and his opposition to American participation in the war had been a key element in his narrow victory. Now, in an effort to stop the war before German undersea assault forced his hand, he chose to push aggressively a new peace initiative, seeking to arrange a peace conference over which he would preside. Angry with the British, he no longer based his peace formula on Anglo-American cooperation but viewed British navalism in the same light as German militarism.[8] If Berlin responded favorably to his peace efforts and the British did not, he considered pressuring the British to the peace table with America's financial leverage. "We can determine to a large extent who is to be financed and who is not to be financed," he had declared in a public speech as November began.[9] By the end of the month, he had moved to put these threatening words into action by encouraging the Federal Reserve Board to adopt a policy that was tantamount to destroying British credit in the United States. On November 27 the Federal Reserve Board cautioned American banks and private citizens against investing in foreign short-term securities. The following day, when the press reported the Federal Reserve Board's warning, the value of Allied bonds dropped precipitously.[10]

On November 28 the British War Committee held a grim council over the Federal Reserve Board's action, which Balfour characterized as "more serious even than the submarine menace." If the United States withheld credit, announced Reginald McKenna, chancellor of the exchequer, Britain could not purchase the wheat and munitions essential to victory. Montagu expressed an even more alarmist view: "At our present rate of living and of expending munitions we should very shortly have to close down, possibly within a month, if the American supplies were shut down." The British at this time did not have any evidence that Wilson had staged this shock to the British war effort, but Grey and others suspected as much because of Wilson's growing estrangement from London. On November 24 he had instructed House to inform Grey that Americans were now as angry with London as they were with Berlin because of the war's growing infringements on American neutrality.[11]

Had it faced almost certain defeat, Asquith's coalition government might have endorsed peace negotiations. The British leadership, however, did not believe that the Allied military position was desperate. Germany held most of Belgium and the richest part of France, dominated central and southeastern Europe, and had Russia on the ropes. For their part, though, the Allies had strengthened their position on the periphery against Turkey, maintained a tight and painful naval blockade, and still held the strategical initiative on the western front, with almost four million French, British, and Belgian soldiers facing two and a half million Germans. On the other hand, the British did not reckon that the balance of forces so favored them that they could be certain of a favorable negotiated peace. Asquith's rejection of a negotiated peace, however, did not save him from the "ginger" faction, which demanded greater sacrifices from the country for victory on the battlefield.[12]

On December 7 Lloyd George, the author of the "knock-out blow," became prime minister and immediately reorganized the government, creating a War Cabinet of himself and four others. This directorate, committed to seeing the war through to victory rather than peace by negotiation, included Andrew Bonar Law, the Canadian-born leader of the Conservatives; Lord Milner, who was popular with the Tory intelligentsia and the leading advocate of New Imperialism; and Lord Curzon, a former proconsul like Milner and a leading Conservative statesman, who was especially interested in the eastern possessions of the British Empire. The common bond linking these three Conservatives was that they opposed a compromise peace, desired more extreme measures to mobilize Britain for total war, and emphasized the security of the British Empire.[13] The fifth member of the War Cabinet, Arthur Henderson, chairman of the Parliamentary Labour party, was known for his strong support of the war against Germany. The new spirit in London boded ill for Wilson's peace plans. No one in the inner circle of the government had spoken more strongly against keeping the future security of the British Empire out of the uncertain hands of President Wilson or was more identified with fighting the war to a finish than Lloyd George.[14] He was now surrounded with men of like mind.

The view that financial exigencies would have forced the British to accept an unsatisfactory peace underestimates both their moral fiber and the hatred of the enemy aroused by the unprecedented sacrifices being made in the land war in Europe. Unlimited warfare led to the expectation of victory. "The cry which united most British politicians was a demand for victory at almost any price" is the conclusion of the most recent study of British politics during the war.[15] That a compromise peace in 1916 was analogous to defeat was just as true for the working class as it was for the political leadership. In January 1917 the Labour Conference at Manchester overwhelmingly passed a resolution supporting a "fight to the finish."[16] The German people during this period, it should be remembered, were suffering severe hardships because of the British blockade. During the terrible "turnip winter" of 1916-17, the average caloric intake of the German people fell to 1,000 calories per day. In time perhaps as many as 750,000 Germans starved to death. Yet their government chose more extreme measures to win the war—not a compromise peace.

With Lloyd George's government adamantly opposed to an unsatisfactory peace, Wilson's use of economic pressure, although clearly capable of damaging the British war effort, would have undermined Anglo-American relations even more. If a frustrated Wilson had persisted in economic blackmail to start general peace negotiations, the unthinkable might have occurred: Anglo-American relations could have been ruptured, with America assuming an openly unfriendly or even belligerent position. This frightful possibility of Wilson's high-risk peace strategy certainly occurred to the leaders of both countries.

On November 15 Wilson told House that "if the Allies wanted war with us we would not shrink from it. . . . He thought they would not dare resort to this," wrote House, "and if they did, they could do this country no serious hurt."[17]

On December 21 Robertson suggested to the new Lloyd George government that it might be necessary to warn the Canadian government secretly "of the possibility of trouble arising with the United States."[18] Robertson's warning was precipitated by Wilson's intensified pressure on the belligerent capitals for a negotiated peace. On December 12 Berlin, in a surprising and misleading move, had expressed a willingness to negotiate an end to the war. On December 18, as a prelude to a general peace conference, Wilson asked all the warring nations to state their war objectives.

Some British radicals applauded Wilson's peace kite. Henry W. Massingham, editor of *The Nation*, wrote Lloyd George that Wilson's peace initiative was "the best news since Bethlehem" and a way for the world to "escape from its impending ruin."[19] Massingham's favorable view sharply contrasted with the indignant reaction of much of the London press and the new British government. In addition to the dangers implicit in a Wilsonian peace, what infuriated the British was that Wilson publicly put them on the same moral level as the Germans, by implication rejecting their contention that the survival of civilized international behavior depended upon an Entente victory. In a speech to the Senate on January 22, 1917, Wilson spoke directly about the peace he wanted. Arguing that "only a peace between equals can last," he committed the United States to a "peace without victory."[20]

Robertson rather than Massingham spoke for most of his countrymen when he wrote Lord Milner on December 18: "We must have no 'peace' yet. We can bring Germany to her knees if only we persist. Peace now means an intolerable existence later. . . . I think we ought to be very firm with the U.S. We have more supporters in the U.S. than Germany has. Wilson is a poor creature. Let us treat him as Germany has hitherto done."[21]

A break between London and Washington was largely averted by two factors. First, key members of Wilson's foreign affairs establishment—most notably House and Lansing, who earlier had tried to dissuade Wilson from an independent, actually more neutral, peace initiative—falsely reassured the British that the president's primary motive in pressing for general peace negotiations was to pave the way for America's entry into war on the side of the Entente.[22] Second and more important, the Germans no less than the British opposed a compromise peace. On January 9, 1917, the German leadership made its fateful decision at a crown council to defy Wilson and launch unlimited submarine warfare at the beginning of February.

This bid for victory was made on the advice of Germany's army and navy leaders, who overestimated the effect of unlimited submarine warfare on Britain and underestimated the ultimate importance of American participation in the war. The German Admiralty had prepared a position paper arguing that the British would be starved out of the war before the next harvest, and Germany's military leadership was supremely confident that the United States could not affect directly the outcome of the land war in Europe. Admiral von Holtzendorff, chief of the Naval General Staff, promised: "I guarantee on my word as a naval officer that no American will set foot on the Continent!" Field Marshal Paul von Hindenburg, the German supreme commander, was equally contemptuous of America's land forces. "We can take care of America," he blustered.[23]

Wilson's mediation plans were destroyed when he learned on January 31 that Germany was resuming unrestricted submarine warfare. No longer could the president realistically play the role of mediator. During the next two months he agonized over America's response to this German challenge, moving from the severance of relations with Berlin, to an attempt at a negotiated peace through war-weary Austria-Hungary, to armed neutrality.

While Wilson deliberated, popular pressure for war mounted with each new German outrage. On March 1 the nation was shocked at the revelation of a provocative telegram sent by the German foreign secretary, Arthur Zimmermann. A banner headline in the *New York Times* announced: "Germany Seeks Alliance against U.S., Asks Japan and Mexico to Join Her." Meanwhile, unrestricted German submarine warfare took its toll of American lives. On March 18 it was announced that fifteen Americans had been killed when the Germans sank three American merchant ships.

As war fever swept the country, there was little understanding by America's political leadership of what war with Germany might ultimately entail. The existing machinery for the harmonization of military policy with national policy continued to be kept in the background. The chief of staff was Major General Hugh L. Scott, a West Pointer, who had first served in the Seventh Cavalry, replacing an officer killed at Little Bighorn. This old soldier, only months away from retirement, and the General Staff he headed have been unfairly made scapegoats for America's unpreparedness for war.[24]

Scott's assistant chief of staff was Major General Tasker H. Bliss, who briefly succeeded Scott before becoming the American military representative on the Supreme War Council. The son of a classics professor, Bliss was America's most erudite general. He knew geology, history, the arts, French, Spanish, Italian, Russian, Latin, and Greek. A bald man with a drooping mustache, he was as economical with his

THE LAST THROW.

Germany resorts to unrestricted submarine warfare.
From *Punch*, February 21, 1917.

words in conference as he was prolific in reports and correspondence. Scott, Bliss, and the skeleton General Staff were arguably out of their element in mobilizing the country for total war, but they were not to blame for inadequate war planning.[25] Restrictions placed on long-range strategic planning by Wilson and Congress had kept the General Staff from preparing for the war that the United States was most likely to fight. "Any reference to what the army would do if we were drawn in," Bliss's biographer Frederick Palmer has written, "was as heretic as for an American soldier to take sides in partisan politics. It practically amounted to insubordination."[26]

As soon as unrestricted German warfare began, however, the General Staff turned its attention to the possibility of raising a large American army. In personal correspondence Scott wrote, "At the present time we are going ahead and doing what we can in a quiet way. The President desires no step taken towards mobilization. I suppose in the hope that Germany will not do any overt act."[27]

If the political leadership decided to extend American power some 3,000 miles to France, the General Staff would truly face an awesome task. Given the magnitude of the effort required, the U.S. Army was less prepared to fight than during the War of 1812 or even the American Revolution.[28] Wilson's refusal to give the military a role in formulating national policy had prevented any interaction between America's civilian and military leadership concerning the possible consequences of America's extra-Continental involvement. The United States had neither the men, the arms, nor a military plan of action to confront a powerful adversary such as Germany. The separation of civil and military responsibilities meant that the 1916 "preparedness" campaign had had almost no connection with the war that the United States was most likely to fight. In part this was due to the general perception that America must prepare to defend its interests against the victor powers rather than to intervene in the European conflict.

Scott had asked Congress for 1,000,000 men in 1916, a request, he wrote, that was received "with great hilarity. I was asked 'What do you want with a million men. The United States will never be at war with anybody. Do you want them to eat? You certainly cannot have any other use for them.'"[29] On the eve of war the army was some 20,000 men under strength, with only 5,791 officers and 121,797 enlisted men. An additional 80,446 National Guardsmen were on federal service. With no fully organized divisions, corps, or armies, the United States in reality did not have a real army. Moreover, "preparedness" was a word that did not describe the naval establishment. America entered the war with nine out of ten warships inadequately manned, two of three not materially fit, and the required antisubmarine ships, mine-layers, and auxiliaries yet to be produced.[30]

Despite these grave deficiencies, the United States had enormous though largely untapped military potential. In addition to burgeoning industry, the country's greatest asset was its vast manpower. Almost 24,000,000 registered for the draft during the war. Washington had more men available to it than France and Great Britain combined; of the European powers, only Russia had a larger population.

On the day after Germany announced the resumption of unrestricted submarine warfare, Scott directed the War College Division to "submit without delay a statement of a plan of action that should be followed by the United States in case hostilities with Germany occur in the near future." The War College Division's response two days later was to recommend the building of an army of 1,500,000 men through conscription; until this army was organized, trained, and equipped, the War College Division "earnestly" advised that no American troops be sent to Europe. It also emphasized that the success of any military venture would depend on achieving "some definite understanding between ourselves and other belligerents engaged in seeking a common end." The American military cooperation would have to be confined initially to naval and economic support, "but ultimately it may include joint military operations in some theatre of war to be determined by agreement with other nations."[31]

Initial considerations of the employment of American forces overseas did not include the placing of American soldiers alongside the Anglo-French forces in the trenches of the western front.[32] Instead, General Staff attention focused on a theater of operations that American arms might dominate. The first proposal for an expeditionary force to Europe actually predated the resumption of unrestricted German submarine warfare. In a series of reports to the War Department in November and December 1916, Captain Edward Davis, the American military attaché in Athens, advocated sending an American expeditionary force of 500,000 men to Macedonia. Given the White House's attitude toward military contingency planning, the War Department, which forwarded Davis's reports to the War College Division on January 17, viewed these reports with understandable trepidation. The chief of the War College Division, Brigadier General Joseph E. Kuhn, warned Davis that both Scott and Secretary of War Baker were "somewhat apprehensive that reports of this character are fraught with possibilities of harm, in the event that their contents become known to others than the authorities of the War Department."[33]

Davis's reports are of particular interest because of his emphasis on the political as well as the strategical implications of American involvement in a Balkan campaign. Davis, like most policymakers in Washington, believed that America's ideals in international affairs might be tainted by involvement with European powers in a coalition war against the Central Powers. On the other hand, if the United States chose noninvolvement, the result might be a peace settlement that would be detrimental to American national interests. Davis was particularly concerned that the Entente might try to purchase direct Japanese involvement in the European conflict at the expense of America's Far Eastern interests. "It is not only possible but it is probable that the future welfare of the United States will be seriously and adversely affected by decisions made without her knowledge in councils where, as matters now stand, she has neither voice nor authority." He also warned against accepting "some humiliation of a repugnant nature." By turning the other cheek, America might place in jeopardy "the future welfare of the nation."

Davis made the erroneous but appealing argument that America could maintain her complete military and political independence by establishing a front against Bulgaria through operations emanating from a Macedonian port. Ignoring the failures of previous attempts to find "a way around" the siege warfare of the western front, including the deployment of an Allied force against Bulgaria operating from Salonika, Greece, Davis was confident that an American expeditionary force in Macedonia "would be employed in striking hardest, and in the softest part, that antagonist who will quit the easiest." If Bulgaria were driven from the war, Davis predicted, Turkey and Austria-Hungary would soon collapse. American soldiers might not even have to shed their blood to remove the Bulgarians from the war. The armed presence of America, with its "fair diplomacy," would probably encourage Bulgaria to begin peace negotiations.[34]

Davis, it is now known, did more than write strategic appreciations for the War Department. Exceeding his authority, he discussed American involvement in the Balkans with the commander of the Allied forces there, General Maurice Sarrail. Sarrail was as enthusiastic as Robertson was cool when he learned of Davis's efforts. When the Chief of the Imperial General Staff informed the British War Cabinet that the American army was totally unprepared for intervention in the Balkans, the civilians decided to offer Washington no encouragement for military ventures in the eastern Mediterranean.[35]

Despite the amateurish, even daft, quality of Davis's strategical ideas, his advocacy of an independent American theater apparently intrigued Scott and Kuhn. According to Davis, the United States might fight in Europe to protect its national interests yet maintain complete independence in both the military and the political realm. On February 2 Kuhn directed the War College Division to refer to Davis's reports in preparing plans for waging war against Germany; on the following day, Scott, believing that the Dutch might abandon their neutrality because of German attacks on their shipping in the

North Sea, requested a study of an attack on the German army by way of Holland.[36]

There is no evidence that Wilson knew of these strategical appreciations of a land war against Germany that in fact had much to say about America's ability to influence the outcome of the war. Possessing a love for the sea—he had once thought of attending Annapolis—Wilson demonstrated a strong interest in naval matters, but his inclination was not to interfere with his secretary of the navy and admirals.[37] On the other hand, he immediately foresaw a role for the U.S. Navy in the war, and he urged the expansion of its personnel and sought to open lines of communication with the British Admiralty for possible Anglo-American naval cooperation to protect American shipping.[38]

As Wilson struggled with the question of war or continued neutrality, the only strategic appreciation he apparently saw was one written by Herbert Hoover, an engineer who had made a fortune in worldwide mining operations and had become a public figure as head of the Commission for the Relief of Belgium. In a memorandum to House, Hoover argued against sending an American force to Europe; the difficulty of organizing and transporting such a force in the near future seemed insurmountable. Moreover, coalition warfare with the Entente powers would create "political" problems. To help the anti-German coalition, Hoover suggested that the Entente be allowed to recruit in America to fill its depleted ranks. Hoover also advocated having a strong home defensive force "in being when peace approaches. As our terms of peace will probably run counter to most of the European proposals, our weight in the accomplishment of our ideals will be greatly in proportion to the strength which we can throw into the scale." House passed this memorandum on to Wilson, who noted that he was favorably impressed with Hoover's suggestions when he forwarded it to Baker on February 16.[39]

Although Wilson personally visited Baker in the War Department in early February and was decisively involved in the question of whether to adopt the draft,[40] he apparently did not think that an American declaration of war would involve the United States in the land war in Europe. On the eve of his ill-fated peace offensive in December 1916, the president had ruminated about the nature of modern warfare and the course of the great European conflagration. Since this is almost the only record of his thoughts on the trench warfare of the western front, his words require careful attention.

Wilson saw no "glory" in the "systematized destruction" of modern warfare. "Never before in the world's history have two great armies been in effect so equally matched; never before have the losses and the slaughter been so great with as little gain in military advantage. . . . The mechanical game of slaughter of today has not the same fascination as the zest of intimate combat of former days; and trench warfare and poisonous gases are elements which detract alike from the excitement and the tolerance of modern conflict. With maneuver almost a thing of the past, any given point can admittedly be carried by the sacrifice of enough men and ammunition.Where is any longer the glory commensurate with the sacrifice of the millions of men required in modern warfare to carry and defend Verdun?"[41]

It is doubtful that Wilson had changed his mind about the futility of the great offensives on the western front. Hence, he almost certainly opposed committing American forces to the attrition warfare that characterized the bloodstained battlefields of France and Belgium. Believing that American support in the form of finance, war supplies, and naval action would decisively tip the military balance in favor of the Allies, he expected the war to end quickly. The cannons would be silenced not through the sacrifice of thousands of young Americans but because of German recognition that their cause was hopeless once America joined the Allies. "Both sides have grown weary of the apparently hopeless task of bringing the conflict to an end by the force of arms; inevitably they are being forced to the realization that it can only be brought about by the attrition of human suffering, in which the victor suffers hardly less than the vanquished. This may require one year, maybe two," he had written in late November 1916.[42] His faith in reason led him to believe that the threat more than the employment of American land power would demoralize Germany and give the peace elements there the upper hand. The U.S. Army's role was largely destined to be psychological.

At this juncture, by giving his General Staff no part in the formulation of national policy, the president obviously did not understand what might be involved in the use of American power to influence events in faraway battlefields. Nevertheless, the prospect of war forced him increasingly to link his interventionist diplomacy to either the employment or the threat of military force. He told members of the Emergency Peace Federation who visited him in the White House on February 28, 1917, that "as head of a nation participating in the war, the President of the United States would have a seat at the Peace Table, but that if he remained the representative of a neutral country he could at best only 'call through a crack in the door.' "[43]

By stages, Wilson had arrived at the unhappy conclusion that a liberal peace settlement could not be obtained through American neutrality. A danger he saw in choosing sides against Germany, however, was that American involvement would encourage extremism in Allied war objectives and make impossible his "peace without victory." On March 19 he held an extraordinary interview in the White

A DEAD FROST.

President Pygmalion Wilson: "The durned thing won't come to life!"
From *Punch*, January 31, 1917.

House with Frank Cobb, editor of the *New York World*.[44] "What else can I do?" he is said to have told the journalist. "Is there anything else I can do?" Germany was forcing his hand, but he worried that American participation would guarantee an Allied victory, making a just peace difficult to achieve: "A declaration of war would mean that Germany would be beaten and so badly beaten that there would be a dictated peace, a victorious peace."[45] These words proved to be prophetic, but one wonders on what military premises Wilson could make such a prediction. Germany was not going to be defeated if America concentrated, as Hoover suggested, on building a powerful home defense force to use as a negotiating ploy on the eve of peace discussions.

The following day the president placed the question of war or continued armed neutrality before his administration. As excited reporters, clamoring for news, packed the corridors, Wilson canvassed his Cabinet members. The national agitation and the warlike temper of the nation was reflected in the small rectangular chamber where the Cabinet met. According to Lansing's account, every man at this meeting except the president, who was noncommittal, spoke in favor of a declaration of war. The secretary of state characterized the two-and-a-half-hour discussion—significantly, the only attempt by Wilson to involve his Cabinet in the appropriate American response before his war speech to Congress—as a meeting that promised to "change the course of history and determine the destinies of the United States and possibly of the world."[46]

True enough. The emergence of the United States as a great power in Europe proved to be a turning point in the destinies of both the United States and Great Britain in the twentieth century. But this meeting continued to reflect considerable confusion on the part of the civilian leadership about the global military role that the United States might play. Many Cabinet members apparently shared the president's view that American belligerency would hasten the end of the war without much greater sacrifice than the continuation of armed neutrality. Certainly, none of those present seemed to believe that American intervention was necessary at this juncture to save the Entente from defeat.[47] Probably only Lansing believed that the future security of the United States depended upon a British victory.[48]

Initially, America's right to trade across the seas, which had been challenged by both London and Berlin, had been viewed as America's primary national interest in the war. Recent German outrages now made American honor and self-respect an important factor in the Cabinet's decision for war. Believing that an Entente victory was assured, America's leaders did not think their country's participation in the war automatically involved military cooperation with the British and French armies, yet Berlin's acts of aggression made the Cabinet members fighting mad and determined to teach Germany's warlords a lesson. Albert S. Burleson, the Texan who headed the Post Office Department, wanted to show the German leadership that they had "woke up a giant." Other Cabinet members talked of doing "every-thing possible" and "employ[ing] all our resources" to "aid in bringing the Kaiser to his knees." With the U.S. Army lacking the men and equipment to take on the German army, however, the American leadership was inclined to think more in terms of assistance to the Allies in the form of money, ships, and supplies.

With no military or naval professionals invited to this crucial meeting, Baker and Daniels were left to speak for the armed services. Daniels, his eyes brimming with tears, saw no alternative to war but offered no specifics about the role that the U.S. Navy might play. Baker spoke more to the point. The secretary of war favored raising a large army and even of sending that force to Europe, *if* the Allies at a later date appeared in danger of losing because of manpower difficulties. On the other hand, perhaps echoing a prior discussion with the president, Baker held out the hope that "the very knowledge of our preparations" would force the Central Powers "to realize that their cause was hopeless."[49]

On March 29, only four days before the president's war message to Congress, the General Staff produced its first strategic appreciations of a war on European soil. These campaign plans, which concentrated on the Balkans and a surprise attack via Holland on the unprotected German flank in Belgium, had been requested on February 2-3 by the chief of staff. One suspects that they were held back until it was clear that Wilson had decided on war with Germany.

In theory, the proposed theaters of operations in Holland and Macedonia, as alternatives to taking part in the trench warfare of the western front, seemed to promise America a considerable measure of independence. Under professional scrutiny, the reality was seen to be quite different. In the Balkans, where a considerable Entente force had been operating against Bulgaria from the Greek port of Salonika since late 1915, it would not be feasible for the Americans to establish an independent front with their own port of supply. It would be practica-ble only to operate from the Allied port of Salonika; just as obviously, the American forces would have to coordinate their plans with— really, subordinate them to—the existing strategy of the Entente forces in the Balkans. Cooperation with Entente general staffs would be just as essential if America attempted operations in Holland. The element of surprise, essential to a successful attack upon the rear of the western German army, would be lost if America attempted to send its forces piecemeal to Holland. A large force of some 1,000,000 men would have to be assembled in England prior to any cross-Channel demarche.

Kuhn emphasized the obvious when he asserted that it was "impossible" for America to launch land operations against the Central Powers "except in cooperation with the Entente powers." To do otherwise "might aid Germany by embarrassing the armies now operating against her."[50]

After seriously considering war with Germany for almost two months, the War College Division, which apparently did not agree with Wilson that the war was nearing an end through mutual exhaustion, came to appreciate more than ever the difficulty of posing a credible military threat to Germany. First, even if Wilson approved and Congress supported the draft that the General Staff deemed essential, it would take many months to organize and equip an expeditionary force of 500,000 to 1,000,000 men. Then the vital question of shipping remained.

The United States lacked a fleet adequate to the enormous task of transporting and supplying such a force. The Civil War was a distant memory, but the American merchant marine had never recovered from the losses inflicted by Confederate raiders. America's total gross tonnage in 1917 seemed impressive until examined: of 8,800,000 gross tons, 6,300,000 were either coastal or confined to rivers or the Great Lakes.[51] With only 10 percent of its foreign commerce carried in American bottoms, the United States was less able than Norway to transport and supply an army overseas.[52] The War College Division estimated that it would take ten months to transport a force of 500,000 to the Balkans, assuming that 50 percent of American's available oceangoing tonnage could be utilized. Shipping 1,000,000 men and their supplies some 3,000 miles across the Atlantic for any invasion through Holland would take longer, at least fourteen months. This depressing arithmetic indicated that it would probably be 1919 before the United States could organize and transport a formidable force to any European front. A "serious mistake" that America must avoid, Kuhn emphasized, was to rush one or two divisions to Europe "that could not exert any important influence on the war" but would denude the army of many officers necessary to the development of a mass American force.[53]

The president apparently made his decision for war after his discussion with his Cabinet. On March 21 he called Congress into a special session to begin on April 2. He then closeted himself in his private White House study to prepare his war message, which the Cabinet would not be allowed to review. Wilson seems to have identified no strategic interest in becoming Britain's war partner other than earning a decisive role in the peace settlement. Britain's war, in his mind, was not America's war. An overwhelming British victory, supported by American power, would actually make a balanced and durable peace more difficult to achieve. Compelled to fight, he was determined that the American war effort—whatever form it might take—would support American national interests (which he interpreted as the "freedom of the seas" and the higher interests of mankind) rather than the unenlightened and selfish interests of London and other European governments. "We desire no conquest, no dominion. We seek no indemnities for ourselves, no material compensation for the sacrifices we shall freely make. We are but one of the champions of the rights of mankind."[54]

The British government resented Wilson's assumed moral superiority, but it welcomed his promises of support. The United States, the president proclaimed, was prepared "to exert all its power and employ all its resources to bring the Government of the German Empire to terms and end the war." Wilson also expressed support for "the utmost practicable cooperation in counsel and action with the governments now at war with Germany."[55]

Despite his promise to the Allies of full American support and cooperation, Wilson continued to maneuver to protect his position as the honest broker between the warring nations. "The United States Government," Spring Rice informed the Foreign Office, "is going into the war, not as an ally of governments or monarchies, but as the standard bearer of democratic ideas and as the eldest child of freedom."[56]

To a remarkable degree, the president followed the advice of the nation's leading newspapers on the eve of war, as interpreted by Joseph Tumulty, his secretary. On March 24 Tumulty gave Wilson a summary of editorial opinion which echoed the president's fears that the United States, with no choice but to fight, would lose its innocence and moral superiority in league with European powers who placed national self-interest over the rights of mankind. Tumulty made three points: "If we are driven into war by the course of Germany, *we must remain masters of our own destiny. If we take up arms against Germany, it should be on an issue exclusively between that Empire and this Republic. And . . . the United States must retain control of that issue from beginning to end."[57]

Wilson—no doubt because this advice mirrored his own views—pursued these goals, with important ramifications for the American military role in the war. Determined to distance himself from Allied war aims, Wilson chose the designation of "associate" rather than "allied" power. He also made it clear that he was fighting against Imperial Germany and not its allies. (Although the United States did declare war on Austria-Hungary on December 7, 1917, it remained at peace with Turkey and Bulgaria.)

A dual and conflicting focus existed in Wilson's approach to military involvement in the European war. In defense of American neutrality he had tentatively employed his country's position as a world power to influence the outcome of the war. His interventionist foreign policy initially involved U.S.-sponsored mediation without any consideration on his part of the deployment of fleets and armies. Germany's unrestricted U-boat warfare, however, led him to conclude that his peacemaking efforts were futile without, at the very least, the clear threat of America's participation in a collective military and naval effort against Germany. Yet he balked at departing radically from the American tradition of noninvolvement in European affairs. Rather than become a full-fledged member of the anti-German alignment (for example, he would not even accept the earlier Entente agreement against separate peace negotiations with the enemy), the president sought to maintain his country's independence, militarily as well as politically, in order to assert American exceptionalism in foreign policy.[58] Although he spoke of a collective military effort, he treated American belligerency almost as a private affair with the German government.

On April 6, 1917, the House of Representatives, as the Senate had done two days earlier, overwhelmingly approved the war resolution. The United States had taken a giant step into the unknown. Wilson talked of holding back none of America's resources in fighting to make the world safe for democracy. But did the president really expect that American arms would play a pivotal role in the war in Europe? It is more likely that he had spoken these words on April 2 to frighten the Germans out of the war. An American threat to employ all its resources, House had told him earlier, was "bound to break their [the Germans'] morale and bring the war to an earlier close."[59] What House and Wilson did not recognize was that Germany's leaders had already made their assessment of America's potential threat to them. In launching unrestricted U-boat warfare, they were treating the armed services of the United States with contempt.

3

The Balfour Mission
and Americans Abroad

The assessment by the British Chief of the Imperial General Staff of America's ability to influence the outcome of the war differed little from that of the German warlords who gambled for victory with the resumption of unrestricted U-boat warfare in February. On February 13, 1917, Robertson wrote a fellow general, Sir A.J. Murray: "I do not think that it will make much difference whether America comes in or not. What we want to do is to beat the German Armies, until we do that we shall not win the war. America will not help us much in that respect."[1]

Robertson's views were based on reports from British representatives in America and the evaluation of his own staff. The British military believed that the United States was incapable of rapidly developing a mass army. After one year, assuming weapons and equipment were available, the British General Staff predicted that "not more than 250,000 men could be put into the field."[2] British pessimism about America's ability to field an army was hardly surprising or demeaning to the American military establishment. Although short of professional and experienced officers, the British New Armies (composed of volunteers) still had available to them more regular staffs and regular regimental officers than the U.S. Army. Turning civilians into soldiers is a slow process in the best of circumstances. Lord Kitchener had taken a minimum of eight months, typically a year or more, to prepare his New Army divisions for the field.

An even greater concern was that the United States might remain aloof from the European war. Colville Barclay, the British chargé d'affaires in Washington, warned that "there appears to be a strong feeling in the States in favour of limited co-operation for purely American purposes." American leaders would probably "dissociate themselves" from Entente war objectives and not contemplate any military involvement.[3]

The immediate help America could give was thought to be primarily in finance, the possible addition of neutral shipping because of

American participation, and a boost to Allied morale. Significantly, Barclay emphasized that belligerency would not really enhance the value of American industry to the Entente cause. America was not a supplier of such modern weapons as tanks, machine guns, and airplanes; it produced primarily munitions, not the weapons that fired them.[4] With Anglo-French production of munitions now sufficient to meet Entente needs, any increased American production in this area would be of no real assistance. Barclay's assessment proved correct. The U.S. Army in fact was largely equipped for modern war in 1917-18 by Anglo-French industry.

British and American evaluations of America's ability to influence the course of the war in 1917 and even 1918 resulted in many similar conclusions. If America began to prepare immediately and to ship piecemeal divisions to Europe, it would still take a year to put a token force of some 250,000 men on the European continent. Such a small and inexperienced force, whatever its impact on Entente morale, would have no direct influence on the monster battle with the German army. On the other hand, if America, as Hoover recommended to Wilson, initially shipped no troops to Europe but rather concentrated on building a powerful army "in being" at home, American help would be at least two years away. A year or more seemed necessary just to transport an army, once formed, to Europe.

Wilson's inflated view of America's ability to hasten the defeat of Germany and his wishful thinking that the conflict was rushing to a conclusion had been reinforced by Lloyd George, who had suggested to him in February 1917 that American participation "would shorten the war, might even end it very quickly."[5] These sentiments in no way represented Lloyd George's real position. He saw little likelihood of ending the war within the near future, but he was still confident of victory, especially if he could extract greater sacrifices from Britain and the Dominions and redirect the British military effort away from the western front.[6] On March 20 he told the representatives of the Dominions, who attended the inaugural meeting of the Imperial War Cabinet, that it was unlikely that Germany could be forced to accept a British peace that year. Nonetheless, the British Empire must make a supreme effort in 1917 because of the decline of its allies. Victory would come in 1918.[7] British belief in ultimate victory was not at this time dependent upon American military contributions.

It has often been argued—most recently by Robert H. Ferrell—that when America came into the war, "the Allies stood in dire peril of failure—of losing the war." Ferrell contends that had Wilson adhered to neutrality, the Entente would soon have been forced "to ask Germany for terms."[8] However true this may seem in hindsight, it was not the view of the British political and military

Members of the British Imperial War Cabinet, 1917. Front row, left to right: Arthur Henderson, Lord Milner, Lord Curzon, Bonar Law, David Lloyd George, Sir Robert Borden, W.F. Massey, and Gen. Smuts. Second row: Sir S.P. Sinha, the Maharajah of Bikanir, Sir James Meston, Austen Chamberlain, Lord Robert Cecil, Walter Long, Sir Joseph Ward, Sir George Perley, Robert Rogers, and J.D. Hazen. Back row: Capt. L.S. Amery, Adm. Jellicoe, Sir Edward Carson, Lord Derby, Maj.-Gen. F.B. Maurice, Lt.-Col. Sir M. Hankey, Henry Lambert, and Maj. Storr. From Sir William Robertson, *Soldiers and Statesmen* (New York, 1926).

leadership on the eve of American belligerency. Firmly rejecting any peace negotiations with Berlin, the British saw their country as the most powerful military member of the anti-German coalition.[9] As Lloyd George declared on March 20, the victory would be "a victory in which the British Empire will lead. It will easily then be the first Power in the world."[10]

This statement followed on the heels of the British conquest of Baghdad in Mesopotamia, a victory of much greater political than strategical value. On the western front the Anglo-French forces, still holding the strategical initiative with their superior numbers, were poised to launch a spring offensive, which the new French commander-in-chief, Robert Nivelle, rashly promised would smash through the German trenches in twenty-four or forty-eight hours. The role of the British in this offensive was to draw off German reserves at Arras; their attack on April 9 against Vimy Ridge was a brilliant success, initially surpassing any achievement by British arms on the Somme in 1916. It is true that the overthrow of the tsarist monarchy in mid-March introduced an element of uncertainty about Russia's future stability. On the other hand, Austria-Hungary seemed increasingly inclined toward peace.

Finances aside, the gravest threats to Britain's survival as a great power when America entered the war were German undersea assault and the emerging manpower crisis. April was the most successful month of the war for German submarines. The Allies lost a staggering 881,027 gross tons, of which the British share alone was over 500,000 gross tons. If successful measures were not found—and soon— against submarine warfare, the war might indeed be lost. At the end of April the Admiralty began the innovative convoy system. Many anxious months lay ahead, but in time the convoys exceeded all expectations.

An answer to Britain's worsening manpower question proved more difficult to find. On March 21 Lord Rhondda, who chaired a committee to examine means to keep the army up to strength, warned "that the strain on the man-power of the country is becoming acute, especially in view of the heavy industrial and financial responsibilities which have to be borne by this country."[11] Britain naturally began casting covetous glances toward what appeared to be America's almost unlimited reserves of men. Solving British manpower difficulties through the utilization of America's vast population became in time a central theme of London's attempts to coordinate war policy with the United States. Lloyd George and others came to believe by the winter of 1917-18 that Britain's survival as a great power depended upon substituting Americans for their own soldiers. In no other way, they thought, could British industry and the British army both be kept of the first rank.

Spring Rice, whose advice on the United States was usually very perceptive, had reported on February 23, 1917, that it was "wholly out of the question" to expect America to send a large expeditionary force to Europe. The "utmost" it would do, he informed Arthur Balfour, who had replaced Grey as the British foreign secretary in Lloyd George's government, "would be to encourage enlistment."[12] If this were really true, an advantage in enlisting Americans into the Entente forces was that Yanks could be introduced to combat within months rather than years. Lord Eustace Percy, a junior member of the Foreign Office who specialized in American affairs, argued in a paper on April 4 that "an American Expeditionary Force of any size can neither be trained, armed nor transported in time to make itself felt. The only sound war policy the United States can pursue is to encourage enlistment in the British and French Armies."[13]

Although Robertson himself urged this policy upon the civilians, he had little confidence that American public opinion would tolerate sending U.S. citizens to serve as cannon fodder for the Entente forces. On April 12 he wrote Charles à Court Repington, the influential military correspondent for *The Times* (London): "The Americans now with the Canadian Corps are showing a desire to fight under the American Flag."[14]

Robertson was especially interested in educating the American military and political leadership about the enormous task of taking on the German army. Hence, the American military attaché in London, Lieutenant Colonel Stephen L'Hommedieu Slocum, was invited to observe the British Expeditionary Force in France (apparently American neutrality had precluded a previous visit). After visiting the British front, April 19-25, Slocum reported to the War Department, "One simply cannot appreciate the magnitude of this struggle until one comes into contact with it. . . . the British have a tremendously effective military machine in France, and one of vast proportion. . . . If the submarines do not cut off the vital food supplies, England will drive hard for some time to come."[15]

The practical-minded Robertson wanted to send a military mission to Washington as soon as possible to advise the Americans on training and equipment.[16] He and other British leaders naturally assumed that Americans would welcome advice and direction from their more war-experienced British cousins. Lord Percy, the American "expert" in the Foreign Office, believed that America understood "little or nothing of the way in which a war is conducted. The first and main point is that for this reason the administration in Washington will be very ready to follow our lead."[17] The inevitability of an Anglo-Saxon alignment against the Hun seemed confirmed by reports from the head of British intelligence in the United States, Sir William Wiseman, who, as the confidante of Colonel House, reported: "It is generally realised (although, of course, never mentioned) that the war has come to a struggle between Germany on the one side and England and America on the other."[18] It was neither the first nor the last time that the British were deceived by pro-British sentiments expressed by Page, Lansing, and especially House. Unfamiliar with America, many British leaders overestimated the willingness of the American military and political elite to subordinate their country's war policy to what the British perceived as the common good.

As the British assessed the tenor of American belligerency, President Wilson was forced to come to grips with a pivotal question: whether to expand the armed services through volunteers or compulsion. On the day before Wilson's March 20 meeting with his Cabinet, Colonel House had spoken against organizing a large conscript army; he favored permitting "volunteers to enlist in the Allied armies."[19] Faced with war, however, Wilson took the most crucial step of the first days of his war administration, the decision that ultimately made possible an American Expeditionary Force of some 2,000,000 men. Abandoning his 1916 position, he sided with Baker and the General Staff in supporting compulsory military service.

At the time, Wilson did not link his support of the draft with sending a large U.S. force to fight on foreign soil. His position was primarily shaped by domestic considerations, especially the attempt by his old political rival, Theodore Roosevelt, to raise a volunteer army corps to fight in Europe.[20] Opposed to limiting the American role in the war, Roosevelt, who had earlier advocated a volunteer force to fight in Mexico, sought a dramatic military debut for the United States. He agitated for the dispatch to the western front of an all-volunteer force—largely commanded by Ivy Leaguers and including a black regiment and a German-American regiment—to assist the Allies in smashing the forces of Kaiser Bill.

The General Staff objected to Roosevelt's volunteer force of adventurers on the grounds that it would lead to a premature commitment of American arms to battle. When asked by Baker to comment on the old Rough Rider's attention-grabbing proposal, Bliss condemned it as both impractical and detrimental to America's long-range military role in the war. In his critical evaluation, which applied equally to the sending of a token regular army division to Europe for political effect, Bliss stressed that any small American force sent into combat would have to be "accompanied by two or three times its strength in order to promptly meet the excessive losses that an insufficiently trained force will incur. We will have to feed in raw troops to take the place of raw

troops." How would the reckless slaughter of young Americans contribute to support for the war in the United States or, for that matter,
among the Allies, Bliss pointedly asked. Still, Bliss did agree with
Baker that critical Allied manpower needs might force America to
commit its soldiers prematurely to the European conflict to save the
anti-German coalition from defeat. In that event, green American
forces should be sent to France, Bliss argued, but only in numbers
(eventually totaling 1,000,000 men) calculated to have a real impact on
the fighting.[21]

Wilson, who may not have seen this paper by Bliss, was motivated
more by political than by military considerations in reaching a decision
on the draft. Roosevelt's plan represented a serious challenge to the
president's war leadership and threatened to politicize the formation
of America's land forces. The pro-British ex-president in charge of an
American force in the coalition war might also threaten Wilson's
efforts to maintain American independence and effect a balanced
peace settlement. Another consideration for the president was his
desire to organize efficiently for war through "selective" service, which
would lessen the damage to industry by keeping skilled workers out of
the army. His support of the draft also effectively sidetracked suggestions, such as the one made by House, that the United States should
serve as a recruiting ground for Allied armies rather than raise a large
force of her own. Wilson clearly did not want to dissipate America's
influence on the peace settlement by encouraging American citizens to
give their lives under foreign flags.

From the very first he was leery of America's being co-opted by the
anti-German coalition. When the French and British bombarded the
War Department with proposals for coordinating the American mili-
tary effort with their own, Wilson held back.[22] He was also cool to the
War Cabinet's proposal to send a British mission headed by Balfour to
Washington. "The plan has its manifest dangers," he wrote House on
April 6. "A great many will look upon the mission as an attempt to in
some degree take charge of us as an assistant to Great Britain."[23]

In the end, Wilson decided that he could not refuse a visit by Allied
missions (the French decided to send one as well, to coincide with the
British mission). On April 13 the British group led by Balfour left
Liverpool. The War Cabinet could have chosen no better diplomat to
represent its interests in the White House. Wilson's intellectual equal,
dignified and tactful, Balfour believed that the continuation of the
Anglo-American partnership after the war was as essential to peace as
the defeat of Germany. He, unlike Lloyd George, attempted then and
later to be as candid and open with the American leadership as possible. The War Office chose a wounded veteran, Lieutenant General
Tom Bridges, to accompany Balfour as head of the military mission.

Arthur J. Balfour,
British Foreign
Secretary.
Courtesy of
Special Collections,
U.S. Army Military
History Institute.

To hasten America's impact on the course of the war, the War Cabinet instructed Balfour to encourage Wilson to explore every means of rapidly expanding his country's shipping tonnage. Hoping to have access to American bayonets as well as ships, Balfour was also instructed to request that a small force of American regulars be sent to France immediately. A battalion would do. An American presence on the continent was certain to lift the war-weary spirits of the Allies. But Robertson had another, more practical motive. As he wrote Haig on April 10, "I am also urging them to send some troops to France at once even if only a brigade. It would be a good thing to get some Americans killed and so get the country to take a real interest in the war."[24] Balfour was further directed by the War Cabinet to request that this token force be followed by a larger force in August or September. The next two requests on the British wish list required the greatest diplomacy. The War Cabinet hoped, first, that Balfour could persuade the American military and political leadership to send partially trained units to complete their training in France; and, second, that the British, Canadian, and French governments would be allowed to recruit individual Americans for service in their armies.[25]

When the British mission arrived at Halifax, Nova Scotia, on April 20, an urgent message from Spring Rice was waiting. The British ambassador warned that Balfour's task might be more difficult than anticipated: Wilson was being accused of becoming a tool of the British. "The reason which no doubt is at the bottom of antagonism of Americans to Great Britain is the fear of being thought to be relapsing into the condition of a colony," he explained. "There would be the very greatest reluctance to taking part in the war under British control or as part of a British campaign."[26]

On Sunday, April 22, a special train carrying the British mission pulled into Washington's Union Station. Awaiting its members on the platform were Secretary of State Lansing and other American dignitaries. As the British delegation, escorted by cavalry, drove away from the station down streets flying British and French flags, "Washington cheered, clapped, honked, tooted and in other noisy ways showed its approval."[27]

On Monday the capital returned to normal. General Bridges found the streets empty at midday: "There is no hustling, but rather the calm of a university town and little conception of the need for haste."[28] The sleeping giant was emerging from its slumber, but the shape of America's involvement in the war was as unclear in Washington as it was in London. Confusion and uncertainty characterized the first days of American belligerency. The existing source of strategic advice and plans for mobilization, the understaffed and unprepared General Staff (the War College Division had only eleven officers), did not seem up to the great task. Bridges reported to Robertson: "There is at present in the War Department and the General Staff considerable confusion and lack of grasp of the situation." [29] Confusion certainly abounded within the hodgepodge of offices assigned to the War Department in the State, War, and Navy Building across from the White House, with no priorities being established or supplies allocated. But what surely concerned Bridges most was his discovery of the General Staff's strong opposition to bringing American power to bear in the trenches of the western front until an American army had been organized and trained. With not a single fully organized division in existence, much less corps and armies, significant American intervention in the land war appeared at least two years away.

Bridges's advice to his American comrades in arms was often as subtle as a cannonshot. His first approach was to argue that it was not possible for America to organize, train, and transport a force to Europe in time to influence military events there. Following Robertson's instructions, he bluntly asked for American recruits to man British divisions. After both houses of Congress accepted the Draft Bill on April 28 by large majorities, Bridges wrote Scott: "If you ask me how your force could most quickly make itself felt in Europe, I would say by sending 500,000 untrained men at once to our depots in England to be trained there, and drafted into our armies in France." After only nine weeks' training in England and nine additional days in France, Bridges claimed, these Americans could be killing Germans. He attempted to sugarcoat this extraordinary proposal by making an even more far-fetched suggestion. Given America's "enormous man power," he asserted, drafts dispatched to England might not prevent America from organizing its own army. "The drafts sent to us could eventually be drafted back into the U.S. Army and would be a good leavening of seasoned men." [30]

This letter was apparently seen by Wilson. Not surprisingly, Bridges discovered that "he was on the wrong path" and had had to "drop the proposal like a hot potato!" [31] When Bridges saw Wilson in person, he could make no impression on America's commander-in-chief. "He would talk to me of American labour problems, railways and even golf, but of war, not a word, and the hundred and one questions to which I had prepared answers remained unasked." [32]

The British, together with the French, were more successful in pressuring Wilson to send American units to France immediately so that the Stars and Stripes might boost Allied morale. This decision was prompted more by political than military considerations and was approved by Wilson and Baker over the American General Staff's opposition. Marshal Joseph Joffre, the head of the French military mission, had first broached the subject of immediately sending an

American force to Europe at a conference at the Army War College just
before Congress accepted conscription. Alarm rather than excitement
was the general reaction of the staff officers at the prospect of coming
to grips with the German army so soon. When the War College
Division submitted a memorandum on the possible organization of a
division for action in France, Kuhn emphasized that the early dispatch
of an American expeditionary force was unwise "from a purely military point of view." One of Kuhn's subordinates, Colonel W.H. Johnston, was more emphatic in his opposition. Johnston perceptively
argued that an expeditionary force, no matter how small, would serve
as a magnet to attract additional men and equipment to the European
theater, subverting attempts to develop a powerful, independent force
in America.[33]

The General Staff's opposition to depleting the small trained nucleus of its army through an expeditionary force was overcome by
intense Entente pressure on the president. The British and French
military representatives in Washington agreed that their first priority
should be to persuade the Americans to show the flag in Europe
without delay. Meanwhile, on the other side of the Atlantic, Secretary
of State for War Lord Derby, Robertson, and Haig personally lobbied
Slocum, the American military attaché in London.[34] Wilson, influenced by the potential psychological and political effects of the presence of American troops on European soil, bowed to this demand for a
symbolic demonstration of America's commitment to the Allies. He
told Marshal Joffre on May 2 "to take it for granted that such a force
would be sent just as soon as we could send it."[35] This pledge was
followed on May 14 by a formal agreement between Baker and Joffre on
the dispatch of an expeditionary force to train with the French army.[36]

Stressing common language ties, Bridges had initially lobbied for
placing American units with the BEF. Wilson, however, having already agreed to Anglo-American naval cooperation, wanted American
soldiers to assist the French on land. Bridges immediately conceded
this point—at least for the moment.[37] Reflecting the anti-French bias of
many senior British officers, he did not believe for a moment that
Americans would for long choose the French over the British.[38] If
anything, Bridges believed, the Americans' initial contacts with the
French would hasten the day they changed their minds. "There will be
friction and difficulties but the French will be saddled with them," he
wrote Robertson.[39]

As concerned as they were about their own worsening manpower
condition, some British leaders for the moment welcomed Wilson's
decision to commit the first American troops to the war-weary French.
Following the failure of Nivelle's offensive, the demoralized French
poilu needed encouragement more than the British Tommy. When

Slocum visited British headquarters in late April, Haig took him aside and urgently told him that America must come to the aid of the French, who were "flagging." With French politicians declaring that their country would not survive another winter, Haig thought it imperative that Washington take some action "to hearten them and stimulate them."[40]

Wilson's pledge to Joffre, however, did not at the time signify his acceptance of a major American role in the land war in Europe. Nor was his support of the draft related to any belief on his part of the inevitability of large-scale American military operations on foreign soil. As essential as these two decisions were to the defeat of Germany, they had not been made with long-range strategic considerations in mind. The French and British governments told him that they desperately needed a concrete display of American support to keep their peoples behind the war. In a face-to-face meeting with a famous French military leader, he had been unable to refuse this request, especially in the aftermath of the disastrous Nivelle Offensive (the Second Battle of the Aisne). But at this juncture, in correspondence with Baker, he agreed only to send one division while another was being formed in the United States, "ready to follow fairly shortly, so as to get the advantage of the training received by the first division and be able to supplement it should battle losses or sickness diminish its numbers."[41] That was all. It was by no means clear that Wilson had accepted the need for a massive commitment to the war of attrition in Europe.

It is true that the French version of Baker's formal agreement with Joffre on May 14 included the sentence "The secretary gives me to understand that, from now on, the efforts of the United States will be restricted only by transportation difficulties."[42] This statement, however, had little practical signficance. America's lack of preparation, even more than its "transportation difficulties," suggested that the U.S. Army could not take a meaningful part in the fighting until late 1919. Hence, Wilson can be forgiven for believing in mid-May that there was no pressing need to make a firm decision on the extent of the army's participation. Preparation for, rather than involvement in, the land war might be sufficient to enforce America's moral position in the event of peace negotiations and to demonstrate to Germany's military and autocratic leadership that it could not achieve a victor's peace.

With Wilson's oral approval, Baker selected John J. Pershing to command the American Expeditionary Force (AEF). Ramrod straight and extraordinarily self-disciplined, Pershing was every inch a soldier. Few World War I generals had greater presence, stubborn determination, or driving ambition. He stood only five feet and nine inches tall, yet his formidable bearing led many to think him above six feet. A Republican, Pershing initially had his doubts about Wilson's war leadership. When the president made his "too proud to fight" comment after the sinking of the *Lusitania*, Pershing had exploded: "Isn't that the damnedest rot you ever heard a sane person get off?"[43] Wilson's increasingly militant reaction to Germany's resumption of unrestricted submarine warfare, however, apparently changed Pershing's mind. Before becoming commander of the AEF, he wrote that Wilson "is going down in history as one of the three greatest presidents, if not the greatest. . . . It is also gratifying to a soldier to have such confidence in his leader."[44]

If Pershing admired Wilson, the president's opinion of his AEF commander came perilously close to blind faith. The two men met only once during the war: on May 24 Pershing and Baker called on Wilson at the White House. The possible bloody price of America's part in what had become a stalemated war on the western front was uppermost in Wilson's mind. House had just sent him a brief analysis of the siege trench warfare by an amateur strategist, George G. Moore, a retired New York businessman; he had made frequent visits to the British front as a guest of Sir John French, the British commander-in-chief who had been replaced by Haig in late 1915. Moore stressed the "impossibility" of breaking through the German defenses in 1917 and warned that "political urgency and the personal ambition of commanders have caused a hideous wastage of the man-power of England and France in attacks from which there was no intelligent hope of success." Rather than "rush troops" to France to engage in the senseless bloodletting, Moore wanted to delay American intervention in the land war until a well-equipped, 2,000,000-man force was created. Wilson wrote Baker on the day before his interview with Pershing that Moore's views had made "a considerable impression on me and I should very much like to discuss it with you when we have the next opportunity."[45] Now he told Pershing that the AEF should avoid repeating the bankrupt tactics of the Allied commanders. The president also talked about transporting American troops to Europe and Pershing's knowledge of France. He said nothing, however, about cooperation with the Allies or his conception of America's commitment to the land war, perhaps because in his own mind he had not yet decided.[46]

Although he had skillfully guided the draft bill through a hesitant Congress and adopted a forward, though by no means unlimited, policy in Europe by agreeing to send a token expeditionary force to Europe and dispatching destroyers to the war zone, Wilson was clearly uncomfortable discussing military matters with either American or foreign soldiers. He almost never talked with the bookish Bliss, who headed the General Staff throughout most of the last half of 1917. The evidence suggests that during the formative stage of America's involvement in the European land war, he relied on Baker, in whom he had absolute confidence, and amateur strategists such as Moore.

What Moore was saying, of course, was essentially what the American General Staff had initially urged: from a purely military point of view, the U.S. Army should not participate in the European war until it was capable of fighting as a large, independent force. Shipping American troops piecemeal to France to receive their training from the French army involved a considerable risk. With no independent American army operating in Europe, the Allied leaders would be encouraged to resume their demands for amalgamation, thereby undermining the significance of the American military role.[47]

On May 25 Bliss, who had become acting chief of staff when Scott was sent to Russia with the Root mission, painted an ominous picture of Allied intentions: "It seems to most of us that what both the English and French really wanted from us was not a large well-trained army but a large number of smaller *units* which they could feed promptly into their line as parts of their own organizations in order to maintain their man power at full strength." If the Allied leaders succeeded, a million Americans might fight as "parts of battalions and regiments of the Entente Allies" with "no American army and no American commander." When the war ended, Bliss suggested, America's contributions to victory might be obscured, with the Stars and Stripes not flying over a single mile of captured enemy territory. Bliss wanted his government "with all the force at its disposal" to urge the Anglo-French forces to "stand fast" until a great American force could be created to deliver "the final, shattering blow."[48]

Pershing was given a copy of Bliss's alarmist memorandum. He also received two sets of instructions. When he made his last visit to the War Department before sailing for Europe, Baker told him: "Here are your orders, General. The President has just approved them." This was not the only letter of instruction he received however, a state of affairs that mystified Pershing then and historians later. What apparently happened was that Bliss, as acting chief of the General Staff, signed one letter which had been prepared by Pershing and his chief of staff, Colonel James G. Harbord. But Bliss's May 25 warning that cooperation with the Allies might mean the destruction of the identity of American forces had apparently greatly alarmed Wilson and Baker. Hence, a second letter, with Baker's signature affixed, was written by Colonel Francis E. Kernan on instructions from the secretary of war, though it seems likely that its precise language about the protection of the "identity" of the AEF was added by Wilson and Baker. This second letter began with the words, "The President directs me to communicate to you the following." As in the other letter, Pershing was ordered to cooperate in the joint military effort against Imperial Germany and was given total control over the extent and timing of this military cooperation. Unlike the instructions over Bliss's signature, however, these orders used very direct language to insist that "the underlying idea must be kept in view that the forces of the United States are a separate and distinct component of the combined forces, the identity of which must be preserved." [49]

The powers conferred upon Pershing were truly remarkable. Wilson had kept soldiers in the background throughout his administration, allowing them no role in the formulation of national policy. Yet now he gave Pershing virtual control over America's contribution to the European war. No other American field commander in history has been given a freer hand to plan and conduct military operations. The fact that the United States was involved in a coalition war made Pershing's position all the more extraordinary.

Allied statesmen and soldiers soon despaired over Pershing's leadership of the AEF and sought his dismissal. A chief complaint was his refusal to accept the amalgamation of American units into Allied forces. But Pershing was following the orders of his political superiors in Washington to maintain the identity of American forces; a primary reason that the president continued to give Pershing such remarkable freedom is that his field commander's position on amalgamation mirrored his own. Nevertheless, if Pershing had accepted the Entente's dire view of the military situation during the first half of 1918 and recommended feeding American troops into Allied armies to save the Entente from defeat, it would have been extremely difficult for Baker and Wilson to overrule him.

Although the granite-willed Pershing became a major obstacle to providing the Allies immediate help through amalgamation, he played a pivotal role in developing the trickle of American soldiers crossing the Atlantic into a flood. Pershing did not want American arms to play a secondary role in Germany's defeat. He wanted a force large enough to fight as an independent army on its own front and with sufficient strength to deliver the death blow to the German war machine. Consequently, his demands on the War Department for more American soldiers escalated dramatically: first he wanted twenty divisions, then thirty, and finally more than a threefold increase to one hundred. If this last (and impossible) request had been met, the AEF would have easily outnumbered all other Allied armies on the western front combined. Pershing's demands for more men began as soon as he arrived in France. He wrote Bliss from Paris requesting "at least 1,000,000 men" by early spring 1918, with half that number on the line. This meant that the War Department would have to ship "the equivalent of at least four divisions per month between now and next May." [50]

By the time Pershing's letter arrived, the General Staff, following the lead of Baker, had abandoned its opposition to transporting American forces to Europe before they had been completely organized and trained in the United States. The General Staff now favored a continuous flow, with training on both sides of the Atlantic. Beginning on August 1, the War College Division contemplated "sending approximately 120,000 men with their equipment and paraphernalia per month." To relieve the "critical situation now existing in France," the General Staff had also begun a program to expand the army to a force of approximately 1,000,000 men within the next four months. "Manifestly," the War College Division asserted, "this force is being raised for the purpose of placing it, at the earliest practicable date, alongside the forces of other nations at war with Germany."[51]

What the president had initially approved, a symbolic show of force on the western front, had by early June in the planning of the General Staff become a million-man expeditionary force. Compelling military and political considerations were at the heart of this decision. As late as his interview with Pershing, Wilson was apparently reluctant to make a firm decision on deploying a massive American force in "the mechanical game of slaughter." Baker played the crucial role in getting the president to support a large-scale commitment of American manpower. The secretary of war had come to appreciate the time element: America simply did not have the luxury of following Moore's advice and organizing a great fighting force before shipping it to Europe.

When the president continued to equivocate, Baker sent him an unusually sharp letter on May 27. America, he noted, might not have any allies left by the time it was finally able to conduct great military operations of its own. Not only would delay prolong the war and make victory less likely, but important political considerations also had to be taken into account. The secretary of war warned that American inaction might demoralize Americans as well as citizens of the Entente nations, provoke harsh domestic as well as foreign criticism of Wilson's war administration, and make the president's claim that he sought to "make the world safe for democracy" a source of ridicule.[52]

Baker's arguments seem to have been decisive in shattering Wilson's illusion that he might be able to dominate the peacemaking without great loss of American lives. On June 14, the day the first units of the AEF embarked for Europe, Wilson proclaimed in his Flag Day Address: "We are about to bid thousands, hundreds of thousands, it may be millions, of our men, the young, the strong, the capable men of the nation, to go forth and die beneath [the flag] on fields of blood far away—for what?" The Wilson who delivered this address was not the same Wilson who had attempted in December 1916 to force on the

British a compromise peace that would have left Imperial Germany
and its allies in control of the heart of Europe and in a forward position
in Asia, able to resume the war at a time of their choosing. To justify
their coming sacrifices to the American people, Wilson now accused
the "military masters of Germany" of attempting to extend "a broad
belt of German military power and political control across the very
centre of Europe and beyond the Mediterranean into the heart of
Asia." If German expansionism should succeed, he warned, "America
will fall within the menace. We and all the rest of the world must
remain armed, as they will remain, and must make ready for the next
step in their aggression."[53]

Although Wilson's mid-June statement appeared to embrace the
British view of the war in many of its essentials, this appearance was
misleading. Potentially the most divisive question in Anglo-American
wartime cooperation was the threat posed to the future security of the
British Empire by the president's revolutionary diplomacy in the cause
of liberty and justice. During the British mission's visit to Washington,
Balfour and Wilson had circled Entente war aims rather than confront-
ing them directly. Contrary to Wilson's subsequent statements, Balfour did discuss British war objectives in Europe and the Near East
with both House and Wilson, later furnishing the president copies of
inter-Allied agreements. No mention was made, however, of the
British Empire's interest in the conquered German colonies, a matter
not covered by Allied secret treaties.[54] Whether Wilson chose to read
the secret treaties between Britain and its allies is not clear. What does
seem certain is that Balfour was reasonably forthcoming about the
Entente's territorial objectives as spelled out in those agreements.[55]
The British foreign secretary surely breathed a sigh of relief that Wilson
displayed no desire to make trouble over these annexationist treaties.

Apparently Wilson never considered making American support
conditional upon the Allies' modification of their war aims. The president may have understood that the secret treaties, acting as a guarantee of good faith, served to unify the Allied coalition, and that any
attempt he might instigate to revise them would be extremely divisive.
"If the Allies begin to discuss terms among themselves, they will soon
hate one another worse than they do Germany and a situation will
arise similar to that in the Balkan States after the Turkish War,"[56]
House cautioned the president. Britain might be divided from its
European allies, a wedge driven between London and Washington,
and the anti-German coalition generally weakened.

Wilson's tact on Allied war objectives in no way meant that he
planned to utilize American manpower to underwrite the imperialistic
secret treaties.[57] America's military involvement was designed to drive
Germany's "military masters" from power and to impose Wilson's

liberal peace program on victor and vanquished alike. As he wrote House in July, "England and France *have not the same views with regard to peace that we have* by any means." This would matter little if victory were obtained through ever increasing American assistance. Wilson could then dominate the peace conference and force the Entente powers "to our way of thinking because by that time they will, among other things, be financially in our hands."[58]

It is not surprising that Wilson stressed the Entente's financial dependence on the United States while American military power was still very much in its embryonic phase. The Balfour mission, although a great public relations success, had failed to convince Washington to accept emergency measures that could have provided immediate American assistance but were thought to be anathema to American interests. Understandably, the Americans had refused to serve as a recruiting ground for the French and British armies. Less defensible was the Shipping Board's refusal to respond to British requests for assistance in shipping.

As difficult as it was for America to create an army from scratch, the transportation of large numbers of soldiers to Europe presented even greater problems. The army had few troop transports capable of making the round trip to Europe. In April the U.S. Navy possessed one unseaworthy transport and the U.S.S. *Henderson*, yet to be commissioned.[59] But also in April, by adding to available American ocean-going tonnage confiscated German and Austrian ships that had been in American ports since 1914, the General Staff lowered estimates for the time it would take to transport an American force to Europe. Within seven months, the General Staff claimed, 500,000 troops (or roughly eighteen divisions) could reach France.[60] This proposal proved to be wildly optimistic.

The British had pressed the importance of shipping on the American government from the first. On the day that the United States went to war, London informed Washington that "the most vital thing for the Allies at present is the provision of shipping."[61] The shipping mission that accompanied Balfour hoped to spur American construction of merchant ships and to gain acceptance of Allied utilization of neutral shipping. William Denman, head of the United States Shipping Board, was wary of British intentions, however, suspecting that London hoped to use the war to steal a march on American merchant shipping.[62] He was especially concerned about previous British orders for ship construction in American shipyards; in Balfour's words, Denman feared that "the industry of the United States is to be upset in order that Great Britain may, at the end of the war, find itself in possession of a mercantile marine built in United States yards, by United States labour, with the assistance of the United States Government, and at the cost of the United States public."[63] Denman also believed that the British planned to continue their dominance over the United States as a merchant sea power by safeguarding their own shipping while putting American merchant ships in great peril of undersea assault.[64]

These anti-British views meant the "near total failure" of the British shipping mission. Denman refused to release the neutral shipping under his control for Allied purposes, demanded that Britain turn over British shipbuilding orders in United States shipyards to him, and chose a grandiose long-term plan, rather than immediate action, for the expansion of American shipping.[65] Nonetheless, the opening of American financial coffers provided some measure of relief for Allied shipping. The British were no longer forced to make shipping decisions based on considerations of national fiscal policy. Rather than transporting wheat from Australia, for example, the British Admiralty could save many sea miles by buying it from America.[66]

Alarmed by the submarine peril above all else, British political and naval authorities also wanted Washington to delay its ambitious capital shipbuilding program in favor of the construction of destroyers, which were vitally needed to conduct antisubmarine warfare. But the American naval establishment, with an eye to the postwar situation and especially the growing naval threat that Japan posed to American interests in the Pacific, initially opposed building destroyers instead of battleships.

A way out of this impasse was suggested by House on May 13 when he talked to Sir Eric Drummond, Balfour's private secretary. Could not the British, House suggested, promise to lend the United States battleships from its own fleet in the event of any near-term postwar Japanese threat? But the possibility that the German fleet would survive the war might make any such British promise inimical to British security, Drummond countered. One may surmise that House was speaking for Wilson up to this point in his discussions with Drummond, but he surely went beyond anything that the president had contemplated when he next proposed a startling solution to future American naval security concerns: a secret Anglo-American alliance whereby the two countries would agree to lend battleships to each other in an emergency.[67]

When Balfour was brought into these discussions, he was tremendously excited by the long-range potential of a defensive naval alliance with the United States. Such an arrangement, which would guarantee the Atlantic powers' domination of the postwar globe, was far beyond anything anticipated by his mission to Washington. But was House's suggestion too good to be true? When Balfour informed London of these unofficial discussions, he warned that both America's isolationist tradition and the U.S. Constitution made such an alignment unlikely.[68]

Balfour at first discounted the possibility that a naval alliance with the United States would destroy the Anglo-Japanese Alliance, which had supported British interests in the Far East for fifteen years. But the Foreign Office and War Cabinet did not. Believing that the prospects for the U.S. Senate's approval were remote at best, the War Cabinet was not prepared to pursue the chimera of an Anglo-American naval alliance at the risk of destroying the Anglo-Japanese agreement.[69]

Balfour, however, would not let the matter die. Immediately upon his return to London, he became the catalyst for renewed discussions within the War Cabinet of a possible defensive naval alignment that would encourage the United States to alter its capital shipbuilding program. Balfour now focused on a multilateral rather than a secret bilateral arrangement between London and Washington. To mollify Tokyo, Balfour suggested in a terse, one-sentence proposal that Japan be included in a defensive naval league with the United States, Britain, Italy, France, and Russia for a four-year period following the end of the war.[70]

Pressed to elaborate upon this plan, which included all of the world's major powers except Germany, Balfour prepared a more lengthy proposal, which was discussed by the War Cabinet on July 3. An Anglo-American naval alliance would have "the immense advantage of being both simple and adequate," he noted, "and I confess that, for reasons of high policy, there is nothing I should like more than a defensive Alliance with America, even for four years, as would be capable of extension and development, should circumstances prove auspicious." But he was forced to admit that coalition politics, especially Japanese sensibilities, made a bilateral treaty with Washington impossible. With little confidence that he would succeed, the War Cabinet authorized the foreign secretary to begin confidential negotiations with President Wilson for American participation in a multilateral naval alliance.[71]

When House received Balfour's proposal for a multilateral naval alliance, he passed it on to the president on July 8 with the comment, "That is not quite what we had in mind." After all, in the event of any conflict with Japan, the United States would receive no help from the other signatory powers, who would remain neutral. House wanted to return to "our first proposal," the British loan of battleships to the United States.[72] House's use of "we" and "our" suggests that the president was involved in his alter ego's initial unofficial feelers of May 13 to allow the United States to change its building program from battleships to destroyers without undermining its future naval position in the Pacific. It seems equally obvious that House had gone well beyond the president's intent when he had also advocated a secret Anglo-American naval alliance during his May 13 conversation with Drummond. All of Wilson's actions then and later indicate that he wanted no special relationship with the British, much less a secret naval alliance. Nor was he prepared to consider American participation in any naval league.

In a meeting with Sir William Wiseman in his study on July 13, Wilson sent a clear message to Balfour that he opposed any British initiative that would involve the United States in a collective naval security scheme. The president, who had already radically departed from American diplomatic tradition by dispatching ships and men to participate in a great European war, expressed a willingness for the United States to "take her place as a world-power." But in projecting its power abroad, America wanted to "play a 'lone hand,' and not to commit herself to any alliances with any foreign power."[73] A secret Anglo-American naval treaty so appealing to House and Balfour, or even a multilateral arrangement that included the United States, was obviously a nonstarter. David F. Trask, who devotes an entire chapter, "The Abortive Secret Treaty of 1917," to these confidential Anglo-American discussions, has read too much into this incident.[74] Every instinct of the president in 1917 was against a naval alliance with Britain. Equally, the War Cabinet recognized the great American constitutional and political obstacles to such an arrangement and was not prepared to sacrifice its valuable alliance with Japan. Happily for the Allied naval war against Germany, the United States soon decided on its own to emphasize destroyer over battleship construction.

Despite the unfeasibility of an Anglo-American naval alliance and the limited results of their negotiations to increase American shipping contributions, the British were encouraged by the apparent willingness of the United States to cooperate with the Royal Navy in European waters. Even before America entered the war, the president had sought close communications with the British Admiralty to protect American merchant shipping. Canadian-born Vice Admiral William S. Sims, known for his strong and independent thought, was sent to London as the Navy Department's representative abroad. While Congress was considering and passing a declaration of war, Sims, in civilian dress, was en route to Great Britain.

Unlike many in the Navy Department who viewed the Royal Navy as a future rival as well as a present ally, Sims thought that American and British naval interests were identical. He was soon at sixes and sevens with Admiral William S. Benson, the chief of Naval Operations, who was responsible for advising the government on the strategic deployment of the navy. Before Sims left for London, Benson told him:

"Don't let the British pull the wool over your eyes. It is none of our business pulling their chestnuts out of the fire. We would as soon fight the British as the Germans."[75] Germany's success with unrestricted U-boat warfare, however, provided Sims with a powerful argument for cooperation with the British Grand Fleet, even if circumstances demanded that American naval forces be given a subordinate role on the European maritime front.

One week after its declaration of war, the United States decided to send a flotilla of six destroyers to the European war zone to assist the British in protecting Allied shipping. Before the end of April the General Board recommended a major reinforcement of the American presence in European waters, a suggestion that was slow to be implemented.[76] Eventually Anglo-American naval cooperation saw a level of amalgamation never achieved by American land forces with the British and French, but not without serious disagreements over priorities and strategy.

Wilson, in contrast to his detachment toward the land war during the formative stages of the AEF, took a very active interest in naval matters. Favoring convoys, he was contemptuous of the British Admiralty's efforts to contain the U-boat threat. "In the presence of the present submarine emergency they are helpless to the point of panic," he told Sims. "Every plan we suggest they reject for some reason of prudence."[77] In opposition to the British, Wilson also favored an offensive policy against German submarine bases.

As the Balour mission, which had begun its return voyage on June 3, approached the Irish coast, it was escorted home by four American destroyers. This was an encouraging but misleading symbol of American participation. After three months of being at war, America's direct contribution to the defeat of Germany consisted of six destroyers in European waters and the crucial commitment, backed up by Pershing's arrival with a small staff in Liverpool on June 8, eventually to wage war against the main body of the German army in France. Despite Washington's acceptance of a forward policy on the land and maritime fronts in Europe, the Balfour mission had failed in its assignment of persuading the Americans to take the extraordinary steps that would have provided the Entente with immediate shipping and manpower assistance.

The precipitous decline of the French army was very much on the mind of the British government on the day Pershing arrived in Great Britain. General Sir Henry Wilson, who was at this time the chief liaison officer between the BEF and the French army, reported growing unrest in the French sector. At a meeting of the War Cabinet he "expressed grave doubts as to whether we could count on the continued resistance of the French army and nation until such time as effective military

"SWOOPING FROM THE WEST."

"It is the intention of our new Ally to assist us in the patrolling of the Atlantic." From *Punch*, April 18, 1917.

assistance could be received from the United States of America."[78] Lloyd George, who believed that Americans were too inclined to limit their war mobilization to "festivities and banner-waving," was inclined to pressure President Wilson. Sir Edward Grey, who was known to be admired by both Wilson and House, had been suggested as Balfour's successor in Washington. But Lloyd George was unenthusiastic; he feared that Grey and President Wilson "would be talking of peace when they ought to be preparing for War."[79] To the horror of the Foreign Office, the prime minister wanted to send the aggressive and unpredictable press proprietor Lord Northcliffe to the United States as Balfour's successor.[80] Fearing that the megalomaniacal Northcliffe might disrupt Anglo-American relations, Drummond warned of "deplorable consequences" if Northcliffe attempted "to hustle them [the Wilson administration] unduly."[81] Although Northcliffe was sent to Washington as head of a British war mission, many British leaders agreed with Drummond that the president must be handled with kid gloves.

America's reaction to the first Allied war missions in April and May has been interpreted quite variously. In Pershing's view, the United States freely offered the Anglo-French missions "not only all that we had but all we could hope to have, and it may be truly said that never did a nation engaging its resources and the lives of its citizens do less bargaining or show more complete response than we did on that occasion."[82] Conversely, it has been suggested that American aid during the first months of American belligerency was "deliberately rationed."[83] This wording gives a Machiavellian twist to the Wilson administration's response to Allied pleas for assistance. The actions of the president and most of his chief advisers, however, did not really reflect a deliberate and coordinated policy of rationing their country's military and naval assistance to place the Allies at the mercy of American political objectives. Rather, America's initially limited assistance was a result of its isolationist tradition, its almost total unpreparedness to fight on European soil, the Wilson administration's failure to appreciate that massive as well as early American involvement in the land war was required to thwart German expansionism, and a natural reluctance to accept extreme Allied positions (such as requests for amalgamating American units in Allied military formations) that were considered demeaning as well as detrimental to American national self-interests.

Russia's and France's decline in the spring of 1917 made Britain the cornerstone of the anti-German coalition. Difficult and critical decisions had to be made in London before the United States assumed a large part of the burden of fighting Germany. Lord Milner, who after the prime minister was the most influential civilian in formulating

British war policy, feared that his country would drift toward disaster during the coming months. He wanted a comprehensive strategic plan based on what might ultimately be expected from the United States. "The entrance of America into the war has introduced a new factor, of great ultimate promise but small immediate value," Milner wrote to the War Cabinet. "What are we doing to do to fill up the time before the weight of America can be thrown into the scale? How do we hope to get the greatest benefit from her assistance in the long run?"[84]

4

Britain as the Cornerstone

While the Balfour mission lobbied for American support in Washington, Entente fortunes took a serious turn for the worse. After bitter controversy with his high command, Lloyd George had succeeded in placing the BEF under the strategic direction of Nivelle, the French commander-in-chief, before the Allied spring offensive got under way on the western front. But Nivelle's offensive, which began on April 16, fell far short of achieving its grandiose objectives. On April 18 Robertson told the War Cabinet that "generally speaking, the French attack ha[s] not achieved apparently the results expected." More ominous than Nivelle's failure to drive through the German defenses in his promised twenty-four or forty-eight hours were reports of a new mood in France. With America as an ally, the French were inclining toward a defensive posture. News from Russia was equally depressing. The overthrow of the tsar had not revitalized the nation. Robertson believed that the Russian army had "fallen to pieces" and would be unable to maintain pressure on the Central Powers in either Europe or Asia.[1]

With the Russian army on the verge of collapse and the French hoping to defer action while waiting for America, the British were forced to reevaluate their war strategy.[2] Military events were increasingly shifting the burden of fighting the German army to Britain, placing even greater strain, both economic and military, on British manpower resources. On the same day, April 18, that the British leadership began its debate over the altered strategic landscape, Hankey finished a twenty-nine-page review of the war for the prime minister's private perusal. As he had done in the past, Lloyd George was substituting the advice of this former member of the Royal Marine Artillery, who has been described as "an intellectual in uniform," for that of the Imperial General Staff.[3]

Writing while the Balfour mission was on its way to America, Hankey was overly optimistic concerning the manpower help that the United States might provide in the near future, arguing that Russia's decline would be balanced by American participation: "The Allies will have great resources, not only of labour, but of *fighting* manpower to draw in the United States (to say nothing of coloured labour), *providing they can restore their failing maritime resources,* and the prolongation of the war, if we are to achieve the victory we desire, will be indefinite." Believing that the war might "last through 1918, and perhaps longer," Hankey linked Britain's staying power to the continued health of the British economy. If Britain were forced to wreck its economy by denuding its industry of workers, it might destroy national morale: "Man-Power is now the most difficult of the problems which the War Cabinet has to face under the economic head. . . . with the probability of a prolongation of the War, the Government feel it to be more and more dangerous to mortgage the future by reducing our man-power by any drastic steps."[4]

To Lloyd George's disappointment, Hankey did not rule out a major British offensive on the western front following the collapse of Nivelle's offensive. Unlike President Wilson, Lloyd George had an interest in defense policy and strategic questions that predated 1914.[5] Although his military experience was almost as limited as President Wilson's—a short and undistinguished stint in the pre-Haldane militia—he refused to give his generals a free hand in conducting the war against Germany, establishing himself as Britain's most important opponent of prolonged, costly, and, in his view, ultimately fruitless attacks against the ever more sophisticated German defenses of the western front. Lloyd George had been selected prime minister because of his commitment to total victory and the mobilization of British resources to that end, but he remained equivocal about the high cost and efficacy of any British effort to defeat the German army in France and Flanders. A common thread in his war strategy was limiting British casualties. At the conclusion of the war he did not want the BEF reduced to a second- or even third-rate force with a resulting loss of influence over the peace settlement.[6]

Another source of conflict between Lloyd George and the leadership of the British army was that the prime minister always considered the political ramifications of military action. His support for military operations was largely determined by their relationship to securing Britain's global position, their potential to limit British casualties and lift war-weary spirits on the home front, their prospects of forcing Britain's weaker foes to the peace table, and their role in holding the anti-German coalition together. He had given tentative—and temporary—support to the Somme offensive in 1916 to assuage French fears that the British were unwilling to do their fair share of fighting against the German army; pressed for sending guns and munitions to the eastern front to enable Russian manpower to wear down the enemy; lobbied for intervention in the Balkans to enlist the support of Balkan powers; urged attacks against Turkey that would serve to secure the British Empire against the Turko-German menace but not involve the same commitment of British forces as did the western front; and sought a diversion of British resources to the Italian front where the Italians would do most of the fighting and dying.[7] He had thrown his support to Nivelle's offensive in 1917 because the BEF was assigned a secondary and less costly role in the attack; moreover, he believed that a prolonged and futile attack would be avoided because Nivelle had promised that the success or failure of his operation would be known almost immediately.[8]

Lloyd George knew that the failure of the French offensive would revive Haig's plan of a gigantic offensive to clear the Belgian coast of German submarine bases. Rejecting the French desire to stand on the defensive and wait for America, Hankey told Lloyd George that Britain must not "sit still. We must do the enemy all the damage we can. This can best be done by fighting a great battle with the object of recovering the Flanders coast, which would be the most effective way of reducing our shipping losses," he wrote on April 18.[9] Nivelle's failure gave Lloyd George limited room in which to maneuver. His underhanded tactics in placing Haig under Nivelle had angered his generals, undermined his credibility in military affairs, and endangered his political support. France's and Russia's decline also presented a strong case for a more active BEF role on the western front to sustain the alliance. Hence Lloyd George's opposition to a major British offensive was initially muted. If he had been confident of early and substantial American military support on the western front, he would certainly have aggressively supported the French standstill policy until the Yanks arrived to share the burden of wearing down the German army.

Reports from the returning British mission confirmed earlier pessimistic British military estimates of the military significance of America's entry into the war. American belligerency did not seem to guarantee victory in either 1917 *or* 1918. In what Lord Curzon called "the most depressing statement that the Cabinet had received for a long time," General Bridges informed the civilians in mid-June that "it seems probable that America can have an army of 120–150,000 men in France by 1st January 1918, and of 500,000 men by the end of 1918." Significantly, Bridges stressed that this estimate left "all matters of sea-transport out of the question."[10]

America's inability to transport its own forces to Europe was now well known in the British government. In London, Pershing had emphasized America's lack of tonnage in discussions with Lloyd George and Robertson. Disappointed by their response, Pershing then and later viewed with considerable cynicism British explanations of why they had no tonnage to spare for the transport of American troops.

Britain's shipping crisis was real enough. The German submarine *guerre à l'outrance* continued to inflict heavy losses on Allied ships. A week after he talked with Pershing about shipping, Robertson wrote a fellow officer: "Generally speaking we are in a position probably never foreseen. Ever since I can remember and years before then it has always been assumed that we would have command of the sea and everything was based upon that hypothesis, and if anybody had thought it should be based on any other hypothesis they would have been classed as fools. As a matter of fact we have not got command of the sea. In every theatre we are suffering from shipping shortage."[11] If the British diverted scarce shipping to the transport of Pershing's raw troops, operations in other theaters would be placed in jeopardy. Furthermore, they would have to sacrifice their own supply of food, raw materials, arms, and munitions, thereby weakening the Allied war effort and lowering morale on the home front. And for what? Even if Pershing had the men, the British military authorities believed that he would not be able to organize them into effective divisions, corps, and armies for a long time to come. Only if American units were merged with existing Allied military formations with their sophisticated logistical systems did the diversion of British shipping to the transportation of doughboys appear to make military sense.

On May 1 Lloyd George almost certainly expressed his real views when he claimed to be playing devil's advocate at a meeting of the War Cabinet to discuss Britain's position at a forthcoming Allied conference in Paris. The French, he told the British leaders, would argue that the Entente did not possess "the superiority of men and material necessary for a successful offensive" in the West. "They would further urge that the blockade was telling on the enemy: that by 1918 the Russian situation would have cleared up definitely one way or the other, and that the United States of America would be able to put half a million men in the field. Even if the shipping conditions did not enable the American Army to be transported to the Western Front, it could be sent to Russia. . . . They would advocate that for the present our policy on the Western Front should be defensive, and that in the meantime we should use our surplus strength to clear up the situation elsewhere—in Syria, for example—and to eliminate first Turkey, then Bulgaria, and finally, perhaps even Austria from the War." Lloyd George admitted that these arguments "made some appeal to him."[12]

With the British Empire never far from the thoughts of the War Cabinet, Lloyd George took care to emphasize the political advantages of a peripheral strategy. "If Russia collapsed it would be beyond our power to beat Germany, as the blockade would become to a great extent ineffective, and the whole of the enemies' forces would become available to oppose the Western Allies. We could not contemplate with equanimity the prospect of entering a Peace Conference with the enemy in possession of a large slice of Allied territory before we had completed the conquest of Mesopotamia and Syria."[13]

Lloyd George's civilian colleagues, however, expressed little support for adopting a defensive position in the West in 1917; Anglo-French military inactivity against the Germans might allow Berlin to finish off Italy and Russia, and shipping losses might make impossible a great effort later. A decisive contribution to the discussion was made by Jan Christiaan Smuts, the South African soldier-statesman, whom Lloyd George would soon invite to become a member of the War Cabinet. Smuts argued that Britain had to apply pressure on the German army on the western front to prevent defeatism from spreading within the alliance. "To relinquish the offensive in the third year of the War would be fatal, and would be the beginning of the end," he warned. If the British could not break the enemy's front, "we might break his heart."[14] British losses were certain to be gigantic. And the British were naturally inclined to look to the United States eventually to replace these losses.

Lloyd George, with little confidence that he would be successful, was forced by the War Cabinet to press the French to continue their spring offensive. "We must go on hitting and hitting with all our strength until the German end[s], as he always [does], by cracking," he told an Anglo-French conference in early May.[15] The prime minister's fighting words, however, could not revive French morale, which was worse than even he suspected at the time. Without American and now French support, he believed that it would be disastrous for Britain to go it alone on the western front. To counter Smuts's argument that Britain must keep the pressure on Berlin until the United States became a major factor in the land war, he argued that it was even more important for Britain to maintain its staying power by limiting its losses. The minutes of the War Policy Committee (which had been created to assess the new military realities) reflect his anxiety about the political and economic consequences if Britain tried to fight Germany single-handedly in 1917: "The burden on us, therefore, was very great, and it was very important not to break the country. Yesterday the Committee had been considering the shipping situation, and there again the demand for men was more insistent every day. He wanted the country to be able to last. He did not want to have to face a Peace Conference some day with our country weakened while America was still over-whelmingly strong, and Russia had perhaps revived her strength. He wanted to reserve our strength till next year."[16]

If Lloyd George had dominated British strategy, he would have diverted Britain's military emphasis away from the West to the war against Turkey or to the Italian front (where, he argued, Austria-

Hungary could be forced out of the war). His colleagues, however, could not be persuaded to adopt this high-risk strategy. Britain needed its European allies more than they needed Britain. Imperial-minded statesmen such as Smuts and Curzon gave him no support for concentrating on areas such as Syria and Mesopotamia to gain negotiating chips for any peace conference. Only by maintaining its commitment to fighting the main body of the German army could Britain force the enemy to withdraw from Belgium and France, Curzon stressed. "If these two objects were made the subject of an offer by Germany at an earlier date, while her military strength and that of her Allies is still unbroken, it could only be at the price of conditions which Great Britain alone would have to pay and which would purchase the safety of our Allies by the acceptance of a grave peril to the future of the British Empire."[17] Despite the great loss of life in the trenches of the western front, Britain could not run the risk of losing its Continental allies by lessening its commitment to them.

After weeks of agonizing debate within the War Policy Committee, the civilians gave Haig permission on July 20 to proceed with the Flanders offensive that he had been preparing for months. Haig's optimism was in sharp contrast with the almost fatalistic mood of the civilians. He commanded five armies in France and Flanders, comprising sixty-two divisions, a total strength of some 1,500,000 men. Believing that the enemy he faced across no-man's-land was nearing the breaking point, he hoped to rupture the German line, take the Belgian coast, threaten vital rail communications, and perhaps force a general German retirement from Belgium.

C.R.M.F. Cruttwell, one of Britain's most distinguished World War I historians, has suggested "that Haig was obsessed with the determination to exhaust the enemy before the arrival of the Americans in such strength that their intervention might reduce Great Britain to a secondary role."[18] Haig unquestionably believed that the BEF was the best army in the world in 1917 and the only one capable of defeating Germany. But his papers provide no evidence that in 1917 he was worried that American intervention might deny the BEF the prestige of playing the leading role in the destruction of German militarism.[19]

As Haig's big guns pounded German defenses in Flanders in a prelude to his infantry assault, the British had their attention focused on developments in the East. Events there could be interpreted either in favor of or in opposition to Haig's campaign, which was certain to be costly to British manpower. Russia's feeble attempt to launch an offensive in July had resulted in the disintegration of its army. On July 29 Robertson reported to his government the results of an Austro-German counterattack: "The Russians broke, with the result that three

Sir Douglas Haig, Commander-in-Chief of the British Expeditionary Force. Courtesy of Special Collections, U.S. Army Military History Institute.

Russian armies comprising some 60 to 70 divisions, well equipped with guns and ammunition, are now running away from some 18 Austrian and German divisions."[20]

The Russian debacle and the deterioration of the French army (which was daily becoming clearer in London) forced the British leadership to think beyond the British offensive in Flanders. For the moment Haig's forces were capable of putting intense pressure on Germany. But what would be the situation in 1918 if Haig depleted his forces without decisive results? An Allied military conference attended by Pershing on July 26 considered the doomsday prospect that the Central Powers might be able to mass some 273 divisions in the West by June 1918. If every possible Allied division were concentrated in the West, the Allied inferiority would still be between forty and fifty divisions, giving the strategic initiative to the enemy unless America could fill this void.[21] Pershing promised to have twenty U.S. divisions in France by June 1, 1918, if transportation were made available; thereafter the United States would continue to furnish divisions "up to the limit of her resources," which Pershing believed to be between twenty-five and thirty additional divisions.[22] Robertson, however, informed the War Cabinet that he was certain there was no chance of America's deploying and maintaining fifty divisions in France "for two years or more."[23]

Lloyd George had argued during the debate over Haig's Flanders offensive in favor of a standstill strategy in the West until American units started arriving in force. But waiting for America while Britain collected imperial plums in Palestine and elsewhere might mean the political disintegration of the Entente, should Germany offer generous terms to Britain's European allies. Lloyd George's expectation that the war-weary Italians would either drive Vienna from the war or keep the German army occupied in 1917 was wishful thinking at best. A majority of the British leadership concluded that Britain, now the cornerstone of the Entente, had no choice but to apply pressure on the German army in 1917. Otherwise, the tottering anti-German coalition might collapse. Unlike Haig, however, the British civilians did not think that the German army could be defeated in 1917.

On July 31 Haig's infantry left the trenches to begin an assault against the German army that would last into November. The unanswered question for Lloyd George, who had rejected Haig's invitation to observe the launching of the British attack, was whether Britain could save the alliance in the summer and fall of 1917 without exhausting itself in the process. Because America's entry in to the war had thus far not lifted the heavy burden that the failing fortunes of the anti-German coalition had placed on the British Empire, a negative answer to that question remained a frightening yet real possibility.

Despite the many uncertainties of the military situation, the War Cabinet was determined to fight on. Smuts admitted in a paper for the War Cabinet that "the situation for us is going to be much darker than it is at present . . . the *nadir* of our fortunes has by no means been reached." Yet he thought that the "issues at stake are too vast for us to ever to contemplate a peace which will in effect mean a defeat." [24] Fearing that the war might continue into 1919 or even 1920, Lloyd George and other British civilians now saw their future salvation in what Smuts called "the incomparable resources in material and manpower of America." [25] On the day that Haig launched his controversial Flanders attack, it was noted in the War Cabinet that "eventually we might have to contemplate a situation in which the burden of the War was sustained entirely by the British Empire and the United States of America." [26]

With victory and a British peace being pushed further into the future, the politico-strategic conundrum for the British leaders was how to prop up their allies without eventually becoming totally dependent upon the United States, militarily as well as financially. A worrisome point continued to be Wilson's commitment to "peace without victory." The America leader almost certainly would oppose prolonging the war to secure the British Empire at Germany's and Turkey's expense. As Spring Rice reminded Balfour on July 27, "It must not be forgotten that this country is under no obligation to continue the war beyond the moment when it is America's interest to continue it or to wage war in any way which will not further first of all American interests alone." [27] Lloyd George might be prepared to trade conquered enemy territories for a favorable peace, but many of his Tory colleagues and the Dominions were not. [28]

As the strain on British resources continued to mount, the failure of the British mission to coordinate Anglo-American military efforts that would ease the future burden on the British Empire was very much on the minds of British leaders. The most important achievement of British (and French) diplomacy in Washington had been gaining the president's commitment to the land war in Europe. But since then the French had lost heart, and the Russian army was in headlong decline. With the AEF attached to the French army, the British were being forced to assume the primary burden of taking on the German army without any assurance that the BEF could count on American manpower to replace its losses. As July ended, an anxious Lloyd George told some of his colleagues that he wanted Wilson to come to Britain "and swear to support us." [29]

Although he was serious, Lloyd George did not know how to approach the president. Wiseman strongly resisted any proposal to invite Wilson to London. The president of the United States could not be summoned to London for discussions as if he were a Dominion prime minister. America leaders, Wiseman told London, "consider that Washington has become the diplomatic centre of the world." Another consideration for Wiseman was his belief that the chemistry between Wilson and Lloyd George and his Tory-dominated War Cabinet was wrong.[30]

Discouraged from inviting Wilson to London, Lloyd George— inclined to the grand gesture—decided to visit America, something no head of a British government had ever done.[31] Given his anxiety over the military situation and his political insecurity, this proposal was extraordinary, especially since such a visit would take him away from London for a long period. Yet Lloyd George was full of this idea during the first days of August and raised the possibility of a trip to Washington in the autumn.[32] Alas, the American government did not put out the welcome mat. House told Lord Northcliffe, the powerful British press baron who headed a special war mission to the United States, that a visit by the prime minister should "be reserved for an occasion when he would be very much needed."[33]

It is tempting to imagine a meeting between Lloyd George and Wilson, the two most powerful leaders of the anti-German coalition in the summer and fall of 1917. Both men sought dominance in foreign policy. Wilson, with the primary assistance of House, was his own foreign secretary on questions that he considered vital. He also kept his distance from his wartime partners as an "associate power." Lloyd George, his freedom of action in foreign affairs limited by his Conservative-dominated ministry, the Dominions, and the restrictions imposed upon him by alliance politics, did not enjoy the same independence as Wilson. Fearing to act directly against Balfour and the Foreign Office, Lloyd George nonetheless attempted to achieve his objectives with backstairs intrigue, the employment of personal representatives such as Smuts and Reading on foreign missions, and personal diplomacy. There were in reality two British foreign policies, the Foreign Office's and Lloyd George's.

If Anglo-American relations had been left largely in the hands of the Foreign Office and the State Department, the wartime partnership between London and Washington would almost certainly have been more congenial. Balfour and Cecil were convinced that the future peace and security of the British Empire depended upon postwar cooperation between the two great English-speaking democracies. House, Lansing, and the foreign policy establishment in the United States were also more inclined to link American to British security interests than was their nation's political leader. At times Lansing and House even worked behind the president's back to keep Anglo-American relations on an even keel. Hence, personal diplomacy as represented by a face-to-face meeting between the president and the prime minister was risky for both countries. Lloyd George, a born actor and a man of tremendous energy and personal charm, would have attempted to work his wizardry on Wilson. "The great bamboozler is now at work; the victim is being covered with saliva," was the way one of Lloyd George's secretaries described his technique.[34]

The president and the prime minister had some interests in common: both loved golf, a good joke, and singing. The president entertained his Cabinet with jokes in almost perfect dialect. Lloyd George enthusiastically sang Welsh hymns with Hankey and others, and Wilson once sang "Oh, You Beautiful Doll" to his second wife during their courtship. Both also had superb political instincts and were two of the best public communicators of their time.[35]

Their differences, however, were great and almost certain to lead to misunderstandings and conflict. Wilson often came across as aloof and cold; a journalist once likened his handshake to "a ten-cent pickled mackerel in brown paper."[36] He was deliberative and had the analytical mind of an academic. Lloyd George, both calculating and spontaneous, learned from people rather than books, put few of his thoughts on paper, and developed ideas from talking. The Welshman was opportunistic and explosive, a risk taker. It was said of him that he changed principles as frequently as others changed clothes. Lloyd George excelled in private negotiations and the art of compromise. Wilson's actions were more rooted in principle. His religion-inspired self-righteousness was reinforced by House's flattery. "America will not and ought not to fight for the maintenance of the old, narrow and selfish order of things. You are blazing a new path, and the world must follow, or be lost again in the meshes of unrighteous intrigue," House wrote Wilson on August 24.[37] Knowing where he wanted to go but cautious in the road he took, the president was not about to be rushed off his feet by Lloyd George or any other European statesman. With God as his compass and confident of America's exceptionalism, he proceeded at his own pace.

Wilson wanted to make the world safe for democracy—not for the British Empire. Lloyd George, however, saw no conflict between the lofty, humanitarian ideals he shared with Wilson and the protection of Britain's overseas position from the Turko-German menace. A crippled British Empire and the continued menace of Germany and its Asian ally Turkey to British global interests did not equal future world peace and stability in his mind.

The most immediate war objective that the British and Empire statesmen shared with the president was the necessity of defeating German militarism. But there were important differences as to how this might be achieved. In opposition to Lloyd George, Wilson hoped to achieve "peace without victory" and rejected the necessity of a crushing defeat of Germany. His war speeches carefully separated the German people from their government. His continued hope was that once it was understood in Germany that American participation made a victor's peace impossible, the liberal elements in that country would triumph over the autocratic and military clique, making it possible for the United States to be the peace broker between the Allies and a new, liberal Germany.

As Lloyd George's government began to link a British victory with an American role in the land war subordinate to British military and political objectives, the differences between the two countries' ends and means in war policy became more prominent. Lloyd George's proposed summit meeting with Wilson offered no better prospect than had the earlier Balfour mission of bridging this gulf during the formative stages of American participation in the European war. Second only to the defeat of German militarism, Wilson wanted to maintain his country's freedom of action in diplomacy. American independence was also the determining factor as the AEF leaders developed their tactical and strategic objectives for war against Germany.

5

Pershing's War Plans

The pace of the war was initially quite frenetic for Pershing. He had reported to the War Department on May 10 to be told officially that he would command the AEF. Eighteen days later he and his hastily selected staff were aboard the transport *Baltic* on their way to France. Their previous education and combat experience had not prepared them for the siege warfare of barbed wire and trenches. Nor did they appreciate how thoroughly high-explosive shells and rapid-fire weapons dominated the battlefield. Through its emphasis on the American Civil War, the Army War College had reinforced an image of nineteenth-century battle, stressing offensive and maneuver warfare. As junior members of the anti-German coalition, the American officers could have learned from the earlier mistakes of the British and French generals, who initially had been baffled by the stalemate. Certainly a serious examination of the evolution of tactics on the killing fields of the western front, 1914-17, would have been more informative about the effect of the new fire weapons than studying earlier wars and touring Civil War battlefields. Unfortunately, however, the president's 1914 admonition to his fellow countrymen about being "impartial in thought as well as in action" had encouraged the military professionals to adopt an ostrichlike position.

Although Pershing would be a commander without an army for many months to come, he never thought small. His mind focused on the expectation that America would play the dominant role in the war against Germany. As the *Baltic* crossed the Atlantic, he and his staff officers—many of whom had studied the Franco-Prussian War at the General Staff College at Ft. Leavenworth—took charge of future American military operations. Given freedom of action by his political superiors, Pershing at once made the theoretical "brain" of the army, the General Staff in the War Department, largely irrelevant in such critical areas as the AEF's theater of operations and offensive objectives.

The AEF's location in western Europe was crucial to both American and British political and military plans. The British military had been quick to make suggestions. When Slocum had visited Haig's headquarters in April, General John Charteris, chief of intelligence, had suggested that the Americans replace an isolated French division on the northern end of the British-Belgian front.[1] In Washington with the Balfour mission, Bridges had suggested to Scott that any American force, if not placed along the British front, should be located between the British and French forces, where it could be directed by the French and supplied by the British. When Bridges learned that the French wanted the AEF to be placed at the southern end of the line at Belfort,[2] he warned Pershing "not to get jammed up against the Swiss frontier," where American forces might be cut off if the French front disintegrated.[3]

Ignoring the British, Pershing pleased the French by selecting Lorraine, the area between the Argonne Forest and Vosges Mountains, as the American sector. He rightly suspected the British of attempting to harness American military power to their own. He wanted to control his logistics, which would not be possible if he used the British ports on the Channel; without his own supply lines he would never have a truly independent army. Proximity to the BEF would also increase the pressures and dangers of the amalgamation of American and British forces. Additionally, once Pershing succeeded in creating an independent American force, it would inevitably be assigned a secondary role if it fought alongside the British on the seaward side of their front or at the joint of British and French forces. The French, who sought to protect their great-power status through aligning American forces with their own, could be counted upon in the future to oppose British efforts to create any Anglo-American front.[4]

The war on the western front had in many ways become a war of railroads as well as artillery, and the importance of rail communications to his selection of a theater has been emphasized by Pershing and others. The Lorraine front would allow the AEF to utilize its own ports of supply along the southwestern French coast, and a railway network running south of Paris would permit American troops and supplies to flow along less-congested though distant lines of communication.

It was strategical and political rather than logistical considerations, however, that proved decisive in Pershing's decision. The commander of the AEF never discussed his plans to defeat Germany with President Wilson or with Baker, his civilian superior in the War Department. There was to be none of the civil-military debate that had preceded the massive British Somme and Passchendaele offensives. His instructions from Wilson and Baker had only assigned him the general objective of cooperating with Entente forces to defeat the German army. In Pershing's view, collective military action did not mean that the ever increasing number of Yanks crossing the Atlantic would play a secondary role in Germany's defeat. From the first, he wanted American arms to dominate the battlefield, and he planned accordingly.[5] President Wilson remained ignorant of the specifics of Pershing's strategy, but he could not have found (more by happy coincidence than by design) a military commander better suited to his political aims. Decisive military action by the AEF would, in all likelihood, give Wilson a controlling influence during the peace settlement.[6]

To understand Pershing's bold thinking, one has only to recall the caliber of his first troops to arrive in France. American soldiers were taller than their European counterparts, robust, and of excellent morale. But they were totally unprepared to take on the Imperial German Army. The First Division, the "Big Red One," though considered regular army, was dominated by citizen soldiers; half its company commanders did not have even six months' experience. Quite correctly, the General Staff had kept many of the regular army officers at home to train the mass conscript army being formed. Hence, most of the newly arrived American troops and many who followed knew little of military life and nothing of modern war. Only July 4 a battalion of the Sixteenth Infantry, First Division, paraded through Paris. The broad-brimmed hats they wore, designed for campaigns in the American west, delighted the enthusiastic crowd—"les hommes au chapeau de cow-boy." The hats as well as the men who wore them, however, were unsuited for trench warfare. Steel helmets could be purchased from the British, but preparing the AEF for siege warfare was another matter. One can well imagine what went through a French general's mind when he approached one of Pershing's men on sentry duty: the soldier handed the French officer his rifle, sat down, and rolled himself a cigarette. "This was not an army; this was a rabble," according to Pershing's most recent biographer, Donald Smythe.[7]

With his eyes fixed firmly on the future, Pershing ordered his operations section, headed by Colonel Fox Conner, to prepare a strategical appreciation that concentrated on the German defenses running from Verdun to the Swiss frontier.[8] The resulting memorandum, dated September 25, 1917, and titled "A Strategical Study on the Employment of the A.E.F. against the Imperial German Government," decisively shaped the American role in the land war for the remainder of the conflict. American officers echoed Wilson's view that American military operations, unlike those of their European partners, were not directed toward "territorial or economic aggression or indemnity." Contrary to what the shell-shocked German soldier might later believe on the Meuse-Argonne battlefield, the AEF planners also echoed Wilson's sentiment that the United States had no quarrel with the German people. As the title of the September 25 memorandum suggested, the AEF operations section believed that its primary mission was the "displacement" of the Imperial German Government.[9] The

American troops
march in Paris,
July 4, 1917.
Courtesy of
Special Collections,
U.S. Army Military
History Institute.

apparent harmony between the objectives of the president and his military leaders concealed one basic difference. Wilson, still believing that the peace elements in Germany might triumph over the Kaiser and the military leaders, was inclined toward limited military operations and still talked of "peace without victory," whereas the AEF leaders placed their faith in "peace through victory," or the total defeat of the German army.

Cooperation with the British in 1918 or 1919, even if the BEF found itself in dire straits, was firmly and specifically rejected with the possible exception of naval assistance along the Belgian coast. According to the authors of the AEF's strategic bible, "it seems out of the question for us to take over any section in the British line. If the British cannot hold, etc., their own line, certainly our entrance therein cannot produce any decisive results." Equally unattractive was placing American forces at the juncture of the British and French trenches, for this would also assign American arms "an indecisive part."

For the ambitious strategy of Pershing and his staff to be realized, American forces would have to be largely withheld from battle in 1918. As members of the operations section saw it, "Piecemeal waste of our forces will result from any other action and we will never have in France the power to accomplish our objective." Still, the AEF's leadership realized that American (as well as Allied) public opinion expected American troops to fight in 1918. Therefore, "minor offensive operations preparing for the 1919 offensive should be used for this purpose."

Pershing and his staff saw important strategic opportunities in Lorraine to the east and west of the extensively fortified city of Metz. The AEF's plan of September 25 aimed at the capture of German railway lines running laterally between the German right and left wings. It was anticipated that the loss of these vital communications would collapse the German southern defenses and force the enemy to withdraw beyond the Rhine or "at least to the eastern part of Belgium." Another advantage of an advance in this direction would be the possible capture of some of the enemy's important coal, salt, and iron resources, which would cripple—or so it was thought—the German economy.

The first phase, viewed by its designers as a minor operation in 1918, was conceived as prelude to a massive American offensive in 1919. The pronounced salient of St. Mihiel, southwest of Metz, was to be eliminated with the assistance of the French. With the AEF's line straightened at St. Mihiel and the threat of a German counterthrust from Metz neutralized, the AEF's war-winning offensive, with an anticipated army of five corps (or 1,272,858 men when line-of-communications troops were included), would be launched in 1919 to the east

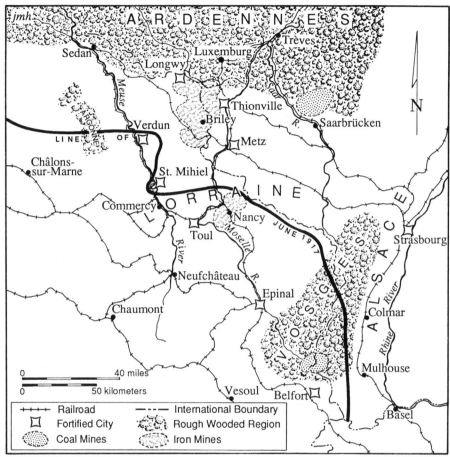

Source: American Battle Monuments Commission, *American Armies and Battlefields in Europe* (Washington, D.C., 1938)

Map 1. Strategic Features Influencing Selection of the Lorraine Front for the American Army

of that fortress city in conjunction with other Allied attacks against the German defenses on the French and British fronts.[10]

When asked by a reporter at a press conference in the fall of 1917 if he thought a breakthrough possible after three years of stalemate, Pershing retorted: "Of course the western front can be broken. What are we here for?"[11] His optimism was in sharp contrast to prevailing Entente military thinking. With a breakthrough and distant and important strategic objectives in mind, Allied generals had earlier launched massive preliminary artillery bombardments in an attempt to smash and destroy the enemy's trench system and neutralize its artillery. After a lengthy bombardment (the British preliminary bombardment on the Somme had lasted ten days), the infantry would be sent in waves across no-man's-land with the mission of occupying territory that supposedly had already been conquered by the high-explosive shells of the big guns. Once a gap had been opened along the enemy's front, the cavalry was expected to provide the advance into open country with the necessary momentum to prevent the retreating forces from regrouping and digging in once again. These offensives, which consumed massive amounts of material and numbers of men, saw real advances in preparation and execution in 1916-17. They succeeded in breaking *into* the enemy's ever thickening defenses but not completely *through* them. New fire weapons, especially the machine gun, served to strengthen the defense more than the offense. Meanwhile, the fortified positions became more difficult to penetrate when elastic defenses were adopted: "defense in depth" thinned the troops in the first lines, thereby reducing artillery-inflicted casualties.

Poison gas, flame throwers, grenades, airplanes, and other advances in weapons had not provided the solution to the deadly deadlock. The technology did not yet exist to maintain the momentum of the attack and prevent enemy reserves from being brought up by rail and new trench lines established. When the cavalry proved no match for machine guns and barbed wire, the British introduced tanks on the Somme in 1916. Though promising, these clanking iron monsters did not prove to be war winners. They struck terror in the hearts of German soldiers and helped capture enemy trenches, but in their primitive phase they were too unreliable and slow to turn the stalemate into a war of movement. The inability of the Allies to break through enemy defenses usually meant that ambitious and prolonged attacks cost the attacker more dearly than the defender.

The artillery's high-explosive shells (along with poison gas) in massive quantities and judicious and flexible use of infantry attacks increasingly became the tactics of choice. Success was seen in carefully prepared, limited attacks to destroy enemy divisions and the expenditure of metal rather than men.[12] What led to confusion and later recrimination between the British civilians and Haig during discussions of the Flanders offensive was that Haig, too, sought the destruction of German reserves and proposed what appeared to be a cautious step-by-step offensive against the German defenses in Flanders. He viewed this as the "wearing-out" phase, not an end in itself but a prelude to a breakthrough.[13] He thus blurred the distinction between his ultimate goal—breaking through the enemy's defenses with his infantry and cavalry—and limited attacks, which the civilians and the French high command saw as a means to maintain pressure on the enemy without exhausting their manpower.

When the French and British generals discussed future military operations in the immediate aftermath of Nivelle's failure at a breakthrough, they had agreed that "it is no longer a question of aiming at breaking through the enemy's front and aiming at distant objectives. It is now a question of wearing down and exhausting the enemy's resistance, and if and when this is achieved to exploit it to the fullest extent possible."[14] To Pétain (who replaced Nivelle) and the Anglo-French political leadership, this understanding represented an attempt to limit Allied losses in 1917. An unspoken hope was that the United States would eventually tip the scales in favor of the Allies—if the Allies could maintain their staying power in the interim. Ironically, the cautious Pétain was Pershing's favorite foreign general, but his soulmate for the single, deep-objective, and decisive offensive was Haig.

Central to the AEF planners' prolonged offensive with distant objectives was their assumption of American superiority in fighting men and tactics. To be blunt, Pershing believed that the Americans had almost nothing to learn from French and British officers, who had for three years paid dearly in "wastage" (as the British military called casualties) for their knowledge of siege warfare and the lethality of the new military technology. Repington's view of Pershing's staff in the fall of 1917 was harsh but not far off the mark: the famous British military correspondent for *The Times* found many American officers to be "keen, intelligent, and zealous" but "taken aback by the immensity of the problem before them"; he metaphorically characterized them as wearing "a child's suit among Allies completely armed in mail." Much could be imparted about the modern battlefield if Americans would only listen, but Repington was sure that they would not. Perhaps thinking of the contempt with which British senior officers viewed French practices of warfare, he noted: "No one in this world learns from the experience of anybody else. It will not do to try and force things on the Americans."[15]

Intense rivalry between national armies is commonplace, especially at the command level, and it was perhaps asking too much to expect the American military leadership to be any less nationalistic or parochial than their European comrades-in-arms. Pershing was convinced that the Anglo-French armies were spent forces whose offensive spirit had been destroyed by stalemated trench warfare. His answer to breaking the stalemate was the aggressive American rifleman, whose tradition of marksmanship and frontier warfare, he believed, made him uniquely suited for open warfare.

European general staffs had begun the war with a similar commitment to open warfare and an emphasis on the *élan* of individual soldiers. Their nineteenth-century image of warfare led them to believe that the soldier holding the weapon was more important than the weapon itself. The massive casualties inflicted by machine guns and artillery, however, had forced many European officers to adjust to the new technology of warfare. Pershing, although he had observed the trench warfare of the Russo-Japanese War in Manchuria, had yet to reconcile his deeply rooted traditional military values with the industrialization of battle. He recognized that the new military technology, especially rapid-fire weapons and improved artillery, had changed warfare; but in important ways, his prewar image of war was not altered by the new battlefield conditions. To him the valiant soldier and his trusty rifle, not the adaptation of the new weaponry to siege warfare, were paramount to success. As he explained, "Close adherence is urged to the central idea that the essential principles of war have not changed, that the rifle and the bayonet remain the supreme weapons of the infantry soldier and that the ultimate success of the army depends upon their proper use in open warfare." Training instructions for the AEF, published in October 1917, emphasized that "an aggressive spirit must be developed until the soldier feels himself, as a bayonet fighter, invincible in battle."[16]

What is remarkable is that Pershing, despite his extensive exposure to the siege warfare of the western front, never changed his belief in the rifleman's paramount role. "Ultimately, we had the satisfaction of hearing the French admit that we were right, both in emphasizing training for open warfare and insisting upon proficiency in the use of the rifle," he triumphantly proclaimed in his war memoirs. No such admission by any of the French war leaders, however, could be found by one of his research assistants assigned to the task.[17]

Pershing's strategy and tactics, however questionable, were designed to give America the leading role in the last phase of the great European civil war. Pershing feared that acceptance of Anglo-French strategy and tactics would force a subordinate role upon the United States, and in this respect the American field commander had the unequivocal support of his civilian superior in the War Department. When Colonel House expressed concern to Baker in July 1917 that the

AEF might repeat the costly blunders of the European armies, the secretary of war emphasized the link between military and diplomatic independence: "In order to avoid misunderstanding, it has seemed to me from the beginning, better for us to have our own doctrine, and be soon in a position to occupy an independent place on the line." This would enable the United States to be "a great power conducting *pro tanto* a war of our own, rather than having our force merged with that of one or the other combatants, and losing its identity."[18]

Long before the British took American land power seriously, Pershing had thus developed plans that profoundly shaped America's participation in the anti-German coalition until the end of the war. With unbending determination, Pershing and his staff sought the creation of an independent American army and the husbanding of the necessary resources for the elimination of the St. Mihiel salient in 1918 and a war-winning offensive in Lorraine in 1919. Pershing's ears were deaf to any British entreaties for assistance which impinged fundamentally upon this grand design.

As the AEF's leadership looked toward 1919, Haig's attack, often called the Passchendaele Offensive, was mired in mud. Buckets of rain turned the shell-churned Flanders battlefield into a quagmire. "Wounded men falling headlong into the shell holes were in danger of drowning," the commander of the Fifth Army, General Hubert Gough, later wrote. "Mules slipped from the tracks and were often drowned in the giant shell holes alongside. Guns sank till they became useless; rifles caked and would not fire; even food was tainted with the inevitable mud."[19]

Lloyd George's frustration knew no bounds. He had never believed in Haig's plan and feared that the BEF rather than the German army would be exhausted. Unlike Nivelle, however, Haig had not promised quick results; as long as he could claim that he was wearing down the enemy, his attack could not be deemed a failure. Lloyd George, uncertain of his political support, lacked the courage of his convictions: rather than issue a direct order to Haig to stop his attack, the prime minister chose indirect means to escape the mud of Flanders. Complicated and devious, his approach to political obstacles was as roundabout as his peripheral military strategy. As Smuts once told a British officer, "L.G. has the guerrilla war mind . . . entirely out of place in this war."[20] The prime minister's tactics ranged from seeking President Wilson's support in diverting military resources from the western front to considering a compromise peace with Germany at Russia's expense. The political risks of confrontation with the high command were great for his government, but he believed that the stakes for the nation were higher. Nothing less than the survival of Britain as a world power was at issue.[21]

Excited by a misleading report on August 26 of Italian progress during the Eleventh Battle of the Isonzo, the prime minister believed that if British assistance were quickly sent, the defeat of Austria-Hungary was in the offing. He considered ordering the BEF to divert guns and divisions south of the Alps. With new reports that the Italian army was stalled, however, and finding little support from his political colleagues, Lloyd George temporized. It is fortunate that he did because Italy was as war-weary as Austria-Hungary, and the Italian Army soon abandoned the offensive for the rest of the year.

Frustrated by his inability to win support for his indirect strategy in London and Paris, Lloyd George in late August looked to Washington for help. The Welshman had wisely abandoned his idea of attempting to strengthen Anglo-American ties by visiting President Wilson, but, unable to employ his political legerdemain in a face-to-face meeting, he still sought to enlist the support of the distant and aloof American leader through personal and unofficial channels. The route to redirecting Allied strategy might be through Washington. Hankey and Lloyd George's private secretary, Philip Kerr, were set to work drafting a letter, a task made difficult by Lloyd George's mercurial mood. "I drafted about 10 letters from Ll. G. for Reading to take to President Wilson," Hankey recalled, "but before we had finished one draft he would invariably get a 'brain wave' and want a new one."[22] In subsequent drafts, Hankey succeeded in toning down Lloyd George's attack on the idea of concentrating Allied military effort on the western front.

Hankey also persuaded the prime minister to read his letter to the War Cabinet and gain its approval. What Lloyd George apparently did not reveal to the War Cabinet was that he had in the meantime spoken more directly about his intentions with Wiseman and with Chief Justice Lord Reading, who was about to depart for the United States to discuss financial questions. After presenting his case for the necessity of knocking either Turkey or Austria-Hungary out of the war, Lloyd George asked them to seek American support for his position in inter-Allied councils. He felt that he could not do this himself without risking his influence at home and in the Allied countries, but the United States could do it with impunity," Wiseman reported to House. If the proposal was made by us and insisted upon, [then] he, George, would yield to our arguments and help force the other Allies into line."[23]

The nature of Lloyd George's private and personal letter, which Lord Reading handed to Wilson on September 20, did not surprise the president who had been forewarned by House. The persuasive Welshman had chosen his words carefully, coming as close as he dared to suggesting a special relationship between the English-speaking democracies in bringing the war to a close. He made the best case possible for shifting Allied emphasis away from the "solid and hitherto impenetrable" western front, arguing that the "whole enemy military edifice might fall rapidly in ruins" if one or more of Germany's allies could be forced out of the war. A satisfactory peace might be gained, he implied, without the bloody sacrifices required to destroy the German army through a frontal assault.[24]

The most delicate aspect of the prime minister's appeal was his suggestion that the British Commonwealth and the United States work together to direct the anti-German coalition's military and diplomatic efforts. "I fully appreciate the objections which the American people feel to being drawn into the complex of European politics," he wrote. "The British people have always attempted to keep themselves aloof from the endless racial and dynastic intrigues which have kept Europe so long in a state of constant ferment, and even to-day their main desire is to effect a settlement which will have the elements of peaceful pemanence in itself, and so free them and the rest of the world from the necessity of further interference." Lloyd George insisted that he had not "the slightest desire that the United States should surrender the freedom of action which she possesses at present." At the same time, he stressed that the coalition's success against the "German military oligarchy" would depend "more and more upon the British Commonwealth and the United States." The British and the Americans were destined to "supply that additional effort which is necessary in order to make certain of a just, liberal and lasting peace."[25]

The prime minister's attempt to coordinate British and American war policy was received coolly by Wilson and House. The British Foreign Office, especially Balfour and his deputy Lord Robert Cecil, was held in high regard by the White House, but the War Cabinet, dominated by Lloyd George and imperial-minded Tories such as Curzon and Milner, was not. Lloyd George's famous "knock-out blow" speech in response to Wilson's efforts at a compromise peace still rankled. "The entire British Government is honey-combed with reactionaries," is the way House expressed it.[26] Lloyd George in particular seemed an unscrupulous politician with ulterior motives. As the president's chief adviser in 1917 on the geopolitical and strategic aspects of the war, Colonel House warned Wilson of the link between Lloyd George's peripheral strategy and the British Empire's political interests: "The English naturally want the road to Egypt and India blocked, and Lloyd George is not above using us to further this plan. He is not of the Grey-Balfour type and in dealing with him it is well to bear this in mind."[27]

An awkward reality for Lloyd George and other British leaders who sought the forging of an Anglo-Saxon alignment was that the British Empire would never be an attractive partner for Wilson in achieving his world of liberty and justice. The president's enthusiasm for Anglo-Saxon political and legal institutions did not imply a similar affection for the far-flung British Empire with its millions of subject African and Asian peoples. As opposed to that of the British, American leaders viewed their country's expansion from coast to coast and overseas in the Philippines and elsewhere as the fulfillment of America's civilizing mission rather than conquest.

Nevertheless, Lloyd George's views on the futility of attempting to breach the German lines seemed to be confirmed by a paper just received by the president, "Memorandum on the General Strategy of the Present War between the Allies and the Central Powers," dated September 6, 1917.[28] The author, Major Herbert H. Sargent, had been recalled to active duty to serve briefly in the War College Division. Sargent was clearly a heretic on the General Staff, which he soon departed to become a professor of military science and tactics at Princeton. After the war he wrote a polemical account of its conduct and defended his view that the AEF should have concentrated its efforts away from the western front.[29] His attempt to reverse American strategy through a direct appeal to the president without going through the chief of the General Staff and Baker was curious indeed.

Sargent opposed sending more Americans to France to be chewed up by futile attacks against machine guns; American military power would be "simply bottled up" in western Europe. Sargent's alternative strategy was to maintain enough soldiers in the West to hold that front while deploying the main U.S. military effort elsewhere: either in the Balkans to "cut the Central Powers in two, much as Grant cut the Confederacy in two," or in cooperation with the British in Mesopotamia. Sargent made the mind-boggling proposal that American troops might be sent to the head of the Persian Gulf by way of the Pacific and Indian oceans.[30] A more difficult American theater, with its extreme heat and endemic noxious diseases, would be hard to imagine.

There is no evidence that Wilson approved of Sargent's suggestions. He obviously had no desire to help the British improve their position in Mesopotamia, nor were the proposed Balkan operations with their inevitable political complications likely to appeal to him. The United States was not even at war with either Bulgaria or Turkey. Yet Wilson could not ignore the humanitarian and domestic political considerations of pursuing a western front strategy that would kill or maim hundreds of thousands of Americans without decisive results. If the AEF suffered half a million casualties in a Somme-like offensive that brought victory no nearer, the American public might rebel. As Wilson told House in September, "The American people would not be willing to continue an indefinite trench warfare."[31] On September 22, then, at the very moment that Pershing's operations staff was putting the finishing touches on its ambitious offensive plans for 1918-19, the president suggested to Baker that the General Staff begin an inquiry into the "strategic considerations" that had led to choosing France as "the theatre of operations of our army."[32]

Wilson's request speaks volumes about the lack of coordination between the president and his military authorities during the formative phase of America's commitment to the land war in Western Europe. In May he had overruled the General Staff and ordered a small expeditionary force to be sent immediately to Europe. He had done this primarily to boost Allied morale and had agreed to expand this limited commitment only when pressed by Baker on May 27. Political rather than strategic aspects had been pivotal in the latter decision. Wilson's only apparent strategic interest in approving this forward military policy was the political leverage that might be gained in the peace settlement. Pershing, Baker, and the General Staff in the War Department had filled the strategical vacuum once Wilson decided to send American soldiers to Western Europe, and America's token commitment quickly grew to a massive military enterprise. Rather than showing the flag through limited operations with Allied forces, America's military leaders thought of playing the dominant role in Germany's defeat.

Prompted by the president's request, a War College Division committee did consider all possible theaters for American military action, not just operations in those proposed by Sargent but also intervention in Italy, in Russia, and on the coast of Asia Minor against Turkey. General Staff memoranda emphasized fundamental military principles, such as the interior lines of the Central Powers and concentration of forces against the main army of the enemy, to debunk the indirect or peripheral strategies of Sargent and, indirectly, those of Lloyd George. Military circumstances dictated that the war would be won or lost in France, the staff officers argued: "Let Germany once get the upper hand of or defeat France, or even let England and France get the idea that the United States proposes to embark on questionable, though highly desired operations elsewhere, and the war is won—by Germany."[33] Moreover, logistical considerations, especially shipping, made military operations more practicable in France than in other theaters: "The Western Front is the nearest to us; it can be most easily reached and with the least danger; . . . we can make our power felt on that front quicker and stronger than anywhere else."[34] Additionally, America would not become entangled in Allied political objectives in France as was bound to be the case in the Middle East and the Balkans. Finally, there was the obvious: America was not at war with Turkey, Bulgaria, or Austria-Hungary.

A WORD OF ILL OMEN.

Crown Prince (to Kaiser, drafting his next speech): "For Gott's sake, Father, be careful this time, and don't call the American Army 'contemptible.'" From *Punch*, June 13, 1917.

The American military elite, in opposition to Wilson's "peace without victory"—which implied something close to a military equilibrium between the Allies and the Central Powers—believed in total victory or the strategy of annihilation, rather than a more limited or indirect strategy that sought to gain a favorable peace through conquest on the fringes of enemy territory or destroying by attrition or blockade the will of the enemy to continue the struggle. The position taken in September by staff officers in Washington and France reinforces the thesis of Russell Weigley, who has observed: "The Civil War tended to fix the American image of war from the 1860s into America's rise to world power at the turn of the century, and it also suggested that the complete overthrow of the enemy, the destruction of his military power, is the object of war."[35] General Staff officers argued that Germany would be forced to concentrate its forces on the western front to counter the arrival of American divisions: "The contest will then narrow down to a tug of war like Grant had against Lee until, by means of our unlimited resources, we are enabled to force a favorable conclusion." The AEF's numerical advantage would compensate for inexperienced staff work. "We must make our superiority in men and materials so great that we can be certain of crushing the enemy in spite of misfortune and errors," Colonel F.S. Young asserted.[36]

The General Staff, then, did not obscure the potentially high cost of the strategy of annihilation. It advanced no limited or cheap way to defeat Germany. Victory was to be achieved by weight of numbers and material. In the view of Colonel P.D. Lochridge, acting chief of the War College Division, "While matters are now about a deadlock on the Western Front, a preponderance on this front on the part of the Allies of two or three million men, which we hope eventually to be able to provide, will make it only a question of time until they achieve success." If the AEF's experiences paralleled those of the Allied armies, it seemed inevitable that American casualties would run into the hundreds of thousands.[37] This was in marked contrast to Wilson's rigidly controlled and limited use of force as a tool to implement his Mexican diplomacy.

Baker sent Wilson the General Staff's strategic outlook on October 11.[38] In reality, without the president's full understanding, the shape of America's military role in the war had already been decided by Pershing, who by then was committed to his Lorraine plan, and the War Department, which focused its planning toward the development of a great army in Western Europe. "Our present plan has committed us to the western front in France. It is impossible to withdraw now," one of the General Staff's papers noted.[39] The best military opinion in the War Department, then, with Baker's warm endorsement, suggested to Wilson that the war was expected to last until American forces arrived in sufficient number to defeat the German army.

Only the briefest record exists of Wilson's reaction to the vital military questions being debated. With no American boys yet in combat, he remained strangely aloof from the titanic struggle, even neglecting to follow the course of the conflict on the war maps displayed in the Cabinet room.[40] Later, when Pershing sent him photographs of America's first assault at Cantigny in May 1918, he wrote in his reply that the pictures had given him his first opportunity of "visualising the circumstances of an action like that."[41] Before receiving the General Staff's weighty response to Sargent's strategical views, which he had requested, he did comment on a succinct General Staff defense of western strategy which had been prepared for (but never sent to) Senator George E. Chamberlain. But his response reflected little interest: "I have been able to give it only a cursory reading but I am glad to keep in touch with these things."[42] The more extensive views of the General Staff on Major Sargent's suggestions, which he received on October 11, apparently made no great impact on him either; a month later he was asking Baker about the validity of Sargent's strategic views. Baker's response was to send him once again the War College Department's strong defense of the American commitment to the western front.[43] On November 20 the president's response was noncommital: "I am glad to feel that all suggestions, good and bad, are being seriously studied."[44]

Despite his tepid interest in these strategic questions, Wilson obviously accepted Baker's and the General Staff's views. Two weeks after his terse note on the General Staff's western stance, he came to understand more fully the commitment that America was in the process of making. A cablegram that arrived at the War Department on December 5 reported the conclusions of a military conference involving Bliss, Pershing, Robertson, and Ferdinand Foch, the chief of the General Staff of the French army. Bliss informed his government that the United States had been asked as its minimum effort to send twenty-four divisions to France by the end of June. By the end of the summer, if the required men and ships could be found, the American contribution would rise to thirty divisions, or five complete corps—a figure which, not by chance, was precisely what Pershing's operations staff in September had deemed necessary for victory in the spring of 1919.[45] Pershing had in fact been the catalyst for the Allied request, and the Allied generals, who privately believed that this target was well beyond America's means, played along. Wilson, shaken by these numbers, asked Baker, "Is such a programme *possible*"?[46]

As the American military leadership embraced the policy of the "knock-out blow" against the German army and lobbied political authorities for the draftees to achieve this goal, Lloyd George, the author of that policy, began to waver. Uncertain that he could enlist Wilson's support for either the coordination of Anglo-American military resources or a peripheral strategy that would serve imperial interests, the prime minister began to wonder whether total victory would be worth the price if Britain were forced to continue bearing the brunt of the fighting on the western front in 1918. A negotiated peace with Berlin in 1917 would perhaps give the British Empire a better peace than a war-exhausted Britain might achieve in an American-dominated peace settlement.

6

The Knock-out Blow in Question

Before President Wilson acquiesced to his generals' western strategy, which Pershing believed would result in an American victory in 1919, Lloyd George began to equivocate on his policy of the "knock-out blow."[1] Significantly, the prime minister became interested in a negotiated peace with Berlin only after America came into the war. Setbacks to Britain's Continental allies, especially Russia's precipitous decline, and his pessimism about Haig's offensive weighed far more heavily on his mind in September than the question of American help during the last half of 1918 and 1919.[2] Russia was hanging in the war by a thread, with socialists there and elsewhere clamoring for peace negotiations. The Italian high command had stopped its offensive action for the remainder of the year. The French had twice postponed their offensive on the Chemin des Dames, intended to draw off German reserves from Haig's Flanders front. With American assistance still in the future and cracks appearing in the anti-German alignment, Haig's single-minded and single-handed concentration on the German army in the Ypres salient might be a prescription for national disaster.

As President Wilson considered and rejected Lloyd George's proposal for creating a special Anglo-American relationship to see the war against German militarism through to victory, the prime minister contemplated peace negotiations with Germany's warlords. In mid-September 1917 the startling news was received in London from Spain and France that Germany might be interested in negotiating a peace on terms generally favorable to Britain.[3] The first of these peace feelers was official. Initiated by the German secretary of state, Richard von Kühlmann, who believed that Britain would make peace if Germany did not establish itself on the English Channel, the message arrived in London by way of the Spanish Foreign Ministry. It made no mention of terms, expressing only the willingness to make a peace offer.

The second peace feeler was unofficial and its roots mysterious, as Balfour on September 24 tried to explain to the War Cabinet (which now included Sir Edward Carson, who had been added in July, and

George N. Barnes, who had replaced Henderson in August as the Labour party's voice). Baron von der Lancken, an official in the German occupation government in Belgium, had on von Kühlmann's instructions contacted Aristide Briand, a former French premier, through one of the Frenchman's acquaintances, a woman who was half French and half German. The suggested terms from the Lancken-Briand source, if genuine, represented substantial concessions by Berlin: Belgium and Serbia were to be restored, Alsace-Lorraine returned to France, Italy compensated with territory, and Britain given colonial concessions.[4] Just as important as what was said in these suggested terms was what was omitted. No mention was made of Britain's eastern allies, Romania and Russia.

The evidence strongly suggests that Lloyd George considered sacrificing Russia to achieve a peace that would generally satisfy the interests of Britain and her west European allies. He told the War Cabinet that he thought the Germans "proposed to acquire Courland and Lithuania, and to make some arrangement in regard to Poland as her spoils of war." This would mean that "two great Empires would emerge from the war, namely the British Empire and Germany."[5] If legitimate, the suggested German terms were at least as favorable to the British as those discussed by House in London during American mediation efforts in 1916.

Such a peace, however, would not destroy the menace of German expansionism. Lord Milner was quick to warn his colleagues that "it would mean Germany coming out of the war more powerful than she entered it, and another war in 10 years time." Lloyd George certainly recognized this danger, and he expressed a willingness to fight on, "but only provided that the Chief of the Imperial General Staff could advise that we could smash Germany, with Russia out of the war and the blockade gone. Germany would be able to supply herself in course of time with wheat, copper, tungsten and other metals."[6]

Lloyd George wanted to explore with the French the unofficial Lancken-Briand peace feeler, which could be quickly repudiated if discovered by the other Allies. Balfour, however, insisted that the American ambassador, Walter Hines Page, be informed, because President Wilson was "particularly interested in all matters connected with terms of peace."[7] Hankey recorded Lloyd George's disingenuous response in the secret minutes as follows: "*The Prime Minister* did not consider this necessary. At present we wanted the U.S.A. to fight and there was no need to discuss questions of peace with them."[8] The meeting ended with Lloyd George determined to confine discussions of the Lancken-Briand channel to his high command and French Premier Paul Painlevé.

A thoroughly alarmed Balfour emerged from the cabinet room.

Convinced that the German peace offer was genuine,[9] he feared that Lloyd George might explode the alliance. Wilson, if kept in the dark, would be understandably furious, and the Russians would probably defect. "I am not sure that I made it as clear as I ought to have done to the Cabinet this morning how dangerous I think it would be to hold any communications of an important kind with the Germans, without previously communicating the fact to the Russians," he wrote the prime minister later that day.[10]

This letter was not the end of Balfour's attempt to contain Lloyd George. Drummond (Asquith's former private secretary and Balfour's present one) told Asquith, who served as a de facto leader of the opposition in the House of Commons, of Lloyd George's interest in a peace that would sacrifice Russia. On September 26 Asquith issued a clear warning to Lloyd George in a speech on war aims at Leeds: "I assume as a matter of course the evacuation of the enemy of the occupied territories of France and Russia."[11]

During the early morning hours of September 25, Lloyd George and Hankey crossed the Channel for a meeting with the French leadership at Boulogne. Premier Painlevé proved to be adamantly opposed to pursuing the *pourparlers*, "not that the approach was *not bona fide* but that it was *bona fide*." Painlevé apparently believed that French support for the war would evaporate if the people discovered that the Germans were prepared to return most of Alsace-Lorraine and give up Belgium.[12]

The prime minister's next stop was the BEF's general headquarters (GHQ). At 9:30 A.M. on September 26 he met with Robertson and Haig. Lloyd George repeated the favorable peace terms that Baron von der Lancken had suggested to Briand. "We should not get our allies to continue fighting if it were known among them that the above offer had been made," he emphasized. There was therefore "a serious danger that the offer might be made public." It was a question not of making a peace offer to Germany but, rather of how Britain should respond if Germany publicly made a generous peace offer that sacrificed Russia. Robertson, who saw little prospect of serious American help in the land war in the near future, stated the prime minister's point a little differently: "Russia is practically finished for the purposes of the war. . . . The Italians are not fighting, and the French are not fighting. How, then, does the war look? We cannot singlehanded [*sic*] defeat the German army." Robertson himself admitted that the British could not win if the French refused to fight. Haig insisted that Britain could not abandon Russia. He attempted to penetrate the gloom with his usual shining optimism. The German army was "very poor stuff," and the German leadership realized that it could not prevent the BEF from capturing the Belgian coast. The general military situation on his front was "very favorable," he said, and would be "more favorable if only the French would fight." If the French army continued to decline, he offered the hope that the AEF could fill the void. The Americans were quick learners and would "probably make good fighters and be more valuable than the French," Haig suggested.[13]

When the War Cabinet resumed its discussion of the German peace moves on September 27, Lloyd George discovered strong opposition, especially from Balfour, Milner, and Curzon, to any peace that would leave a strengthened Germany in a position to start and win another war in the foreseeable future. Balfour, according to the minutes, "attached great importance to the deprivation to Germany of any Colonies, unless we could obtain guarantees that she would not break the peace, of which at present there appeared to be no prospect." Curzon and Milner were unprepared to accept a Germany enlarged by the acquisition of occupied Russian provinces and in a position to make Russia its "vassal." Germany would not only be the dominant power on the Continent but, through its control of Russia, pose a grave threat to Britain's Asian holdings.[14]

President Wilson was another consideration for the British leadership. George N. Barnes argued that America's opinion did not count: No great importance needed to be attached to the Americans' attitude, as they were "not as yet doing very much in the war outside of financial assistance to the allies." Lloyd George's comments suggested that he agreed with the Labour leader. The prime minister had already prevented Balfour from informing Washington of the German peace feelers; now he attempted to speak for the American people, arguing that they would "not continue fighting merely to prevent Germany from obtaining peace at the expense of Russia."[15] The opportunistic Welshman surely knew better. President Wilson was not prepared to sacrifice the new Russian democratic government to the clutches of German imperialism.

In contemplating a peace that would sacrifice Russia and reward German aggression, Lloyd George was standing on very precarious ground. A rupture of Anglo-American relations was only one of the dangers. In a sense he was a prisoner of his own often-expressed view that the war should be fought to a finish. There were posters in London of clenched fists, symbolizing his "knock-out blow" against Germany. The head of the Foreign Office and his strongest allies in the War Cabinet opposed a peace that would leave the British Empire menaced by a still powerful Germany. The Dominions also had to be considered. From Vimy Ridge to Gallipoli to Ypres to German East Africa, the Canadians, New Zealanders, Australians, and South Africans had made or were making vital contributions to the war effort. Their opposition to the German overseas threat could not be ignored. Walter

H. Long, secretary of state for the colonies, reminded Lloyd George that he could not proceed without consulting the Dominions.[16] Both national and Commonwealth unity on the war, then, might be destroyed by the issue of peace negotiations. The *Morning Post*, the influential Tory paper, spoke for the right in a leading article on October 4: "If our politicians were now to make a peace with an undefeated enemy, it would make our captains sick, and our dead would turn in their serried graves."

With Painlevé's opposition having effectively destroyed the Lancken-Briand channel, Lloyd George gave Balfour permission to reply to Madrid that Britain would be willing to receive an official German peace proposal. Balfour, however, refused to send this message until Lloyd George informed Britain's allies.[17] The prime minister relented, and on October 4 Balfour informed Washington for the first time of the German peace feeler.[18] When Britain's remaining allies were included in the peace discussions two days later, a joint note was sent to Berlin.

Berlin made no response through official channels, but von Kühlmann delivered his famous "no, never" speech to the Reichstag. Germany, he thundered, would "never" make any concession in regard to Alsace-Lorraine. "As long as a German fist can hold a rifle, the integrity of the German dominions, which we have received as a glorious heritage from our fathers, can never become the object of any negotiations or concessions." Meanwhile, Chancellor Georg Michaelis stated as Germany's war objective: "We must continue to persevere until the German Empire on the continent and overseas establishes its position."[19]

Once again German intransigence for the time being prevented any consideration of a compromise peace. If Germany had actually announced generous terms for the west European powers, as Lloyd George thought possible, the anti-German coalition would have been faced with a grave crisis: public support for the war in France and Italy would have been seriously eroded; in Britain national unity, along with Lloyd George's ministry (especially if he had spoken in favor of accepting the German terms), might have collapsed; and the Dominions almost certainly would have broken with London.

President Wilson would also have faced a great predicament if Germany had initiated general peace negotiations in the fall of 1917. Wilson believed that an essential starting point for his new order in international affairs was the removal of Germany's military-autocratic government.[20] On October 8 he publicly proclaimed that "the war should end only when Germany was beaten and Germany's rule of autocracy and might superceded by the ideals of democracy."[21] The prospect of a compromise peace at Russia's expense posed a disturbing truth: to avoid a disastrous peace, he needed the European democracies more than they needed him. Only if the Allies fought on, becoming more dependent on American resources in the process, would he be able to influence the outcome of the war decisively.

Germany's determination to achieve a victor's peace rescued Wilson from such a dilemma. Lloyd George, confronted with an uncompromising Germany, had no choice but to speak once again of "an overwhelming military defeat, which would absolutely compel the enemy to submit." But the prime minister thought that such a victory would not be obtainable until 1919 at the earliest, and he was determined to prevent Haig from sapping Britain's strength through ambitious and prolonged attacks against the German army. As Hankey reported his words on October 15, "A continuance of Haig's attacks might conceivably result in bringing Germany to terms in 1919. But in that case it would be the U.S. who would deal the blow and not we ourselves. If our Army was spent in a succession of shattering attacks during 1918, it would, indeed, be in exactly the condition that the French Army was in at this moment, with its numbers reduced and its morale weakened. He was particularly anxious to avoid a situation at the end of the war in which our Army would no longer be a first-class one. He wished it to be in every respect as good as the American army, and possibly a revived Russian Army, so that this country would be a great military power in the world." [22]

Confronted with an intransigent Germany, the prime minister's strategy for 1918 was to maintain pressure on the Germans in the West with "Pétain's tactics" and to detach Germany's allies or improve Britain's negotiating position through combined military-diplomatic campaigns in the outside theaters. With its army intact, Britain could then play a decisive role in the climax of the war in 1919. Rather than follow another course, Lloyd George told Hankey, he would step down as prime minister. [23]

The events of the last months of 1917 created a morass of uncertainty for the British leadership. The rains returned to Flanders in October, slowing Haig's advance toward the gutted village of Passchendaele, whose capture in early November brought an end to the offensive. A few miles of enemy territory were conquered and pressure maintained on the German army, but the price Britain paid for sustaining the anti-German coalition was great. In the aftermath of the Flanders operation, a surprise British tank offensive was launched on November 20 at Cambrai. Initially a great success, this attack raised hope of ultimate victory in the trenches of the western front: in one day the British penetrated the German defenses almost as far as a hundred days of heavy fighting had carried them in the Flanders action. The Germans launched a counterattack, however, recapturing most of the trenches they had lost. When the Battle of Cambrai ended on December 3, "the British and the Germans resembled two tired boxers, neither of whom was capable of doing the other any serious harm."[24]

Perhaps the most encouraging development in the West as the campaign season came to an end was that the French army was showing signs of recovering from its mutinous state: on October 23 the long-delayed French offensive to assist Haig's attack had been launched. But the good news that the French army might once again be an offensive force was immediately eclipsed by an unexpected Austro-German thrust against war-weary Italy. Supported by a massive barrage of artillery and poison-gas shells, the enemy smashed through the Italian lines near the town of Caporetto on October 24. General panic prevailed, and Italian troops fled the battlefield. If British and French divisions had not been quickly sent to stabilize the situation, Italy might have been driven from the war.

On the high seas, unrestricted German U-boat warfare continued to concern the British leadership. As former First Lord of the Admiralty Sir Edward Carson told the War Cabinet, the shipping situation might "improve slightly from time to time," but the amount of tonnage was "steadily going down and must disappear" if the war went on long enough.[25]

The fourth year of war ended as a year of defeats for the anti-German coalition. Only the British, assisted by the Dominions, had done more than hold their own against the Central Powers. Maintaining the strategical initiative, the BEF had played the major role in occupying the Germans on the western front. The cost in human terms was heartrending. Hankey provided the War Cabinet in mid-December with figures alleging that combined Dominion and British casualties on the western front in 1917 had amounted to 822,000.[26]

The War Office pressed the government to replace these massive losses with dire warnings of the consequences of not keeping the BEF up to strength. At every opportunity Robertson lobbied for drafting more young men into the infantry, where the BEF's deficiencies were most acute. The Army Council warned the government that "in view of the probable release of enemy Forces on the Russian front, the war may well be lost unless, while awaiting substantial American assistance, our field armies are quickly brought up to and maintained at full strength."[27] But Lloyd George's government was no longer prepared to accept the army's demands for men. "The generals are absolutely callous as to the gigantic casualties and order men to certain death like cattle to the slaughter," the prime minister once told a newspaper editor.[28] To wean GHQ from its propensity for prolonged and distant offensives and to force more effective use of men already in uniform, Lloyd George's government pursued a conservative man-power policy.[29]

In addition to humanitarian considerations, the civilians were mindful of the economic and political impact of providing Haig with all the men he requested to maintain his infantry. As Hankey advised the Man-Power Committee in December, "The problem that confronts the Committee . . . is to avert a military catastrophe without plunging us into an economic catastrophe equally fatal to the cause of the Allies."[30] The War Office demanded 600,000 "Category A" men—those deemed fit for combat—by November 1918; it got only a promise of 100,000 drafts to maintain all overseas forces in 1918. The navy, air force, shipbuilding, food production, and even timber-felling were given a higher priority than the field forces.[31]

Military operations in the Middle East in 1917, the "side shows" so denigrated by the British high command, had given Britain unprecedented influence from Egypt to India. The capture of Baghdad in March placed much of Mesopotamia under British control. Arabia had also fallen under British influence because of the heroics of Colonel T.E. Lawrence and his British irregulars. December brought the most heartening success: General "Bull" Allenby's capture of Jerusalem, which Lloyd George had wanted as a Christmas present to the British people. Although not sufficient to drive Turkey from the war, these successes strengthened Britain's position on the southern fringes of Germany's unbroken line of influence from the North Sea to the now diminished borders of the Turkish empire. Britain's forward position in Palestine also offered security for the Suez Canal and was of crucial strategic value for Africa's defense, should Germany triumph on the Continent.

British gains in Mesopotamia, on the other hand, were soon nullified by Russia's defection. On November 7 the Bolsheviks, committed to taking Russia out of the war, stormed the Winter Palace and overthrew the Provisional Government. The collapse of the eastern front that soon followed the Communist seizure of power dramatically altered the balance between the Entente and the Central Powers. Germany, if it massed its forces in Western Europe, would gain a numerical superiority over the western powers, a position that it had not enjoyed since the first months of the war. There was also the prospect (which never became a reality) that the Central Powers might neutralize the British blockade by extracting mineral and food resources from Russia.

Britain was most threatened outside of Europe by Russia's demise. The Turks, with their Russian Caucasian front moribund, could concentrate on the British in Palestine and Mesopotamia. Turkey also now posed a very real threat to Persia, the Caucasus, and Turkestan.

Germany, whose prewar ambitions in the East (reaching even to the shores of the Persian Gulf with the Berlin to Baghdad railroad) had helped plunge Europe into war, now might gain through its ascendancy in Russia a northern route to India by way of the Black Sea, the Caucasus, and the Caspian.

The continued stalemate in the West in combination with the emerging Turko-German threat to Britain's Asian position gave Lloyd George the support he needed from the imperial-minded War Cabinet to wrest the strategic control of the war from the high command. His maneuvers were as usual complicated and devious. Provoking Robertson's fury, he asked Lord French and Sir Henry Wilson, two generals who were not members of the Robertson-Haig camp, to review the course of the war and offer suggestions for future military policy. Wilson's and French's subsequent papers included direct as well as implied criticism of the high command's offensive strategy, if not emphasis, on the western front. Both supported Lloyd George's plan of a supreme war council to coordinate Allied military policy. They also found merit in his desire to defeat Turkey but argued that it was too late to put in train the necessary preparations for a winter campaign. French's paper could have been written by Lloyd George himself. The former leader of the BEF, whom Haig had replaced, concluded that "a *purely military* climax" could not be attained in 1918. He favored Pétain's cautious tactics until the United States had formed a great force on European soil.[32]

Given a chance to respond, Robertson characteristically came to the nub of the problem. Waiting for the Americans might be very dangerous indeed. "If by some miracle," he wrote, "we could suddenly pass over the next 18 months and in 1919 resume the war under present conditions, plus the reinforcement in France of, say, a million well-trained American troops, there would be no question as to the best policy. But unfortunately we cannot perform miracles, and therefore we have to consider whether, *all* things considered, the Entente may not, despite American assistance, be much weaker, and not stronger, in 1919 than in 1918."[33] The near collapse of Italy and the triumph of Bolshevism in Russia subsequently gave force to Robertson's words.

The philosophical Balfour also made his contribution to this strategic debate. In a memorandum circulated to the king and the War Cabinet, he attempted to debunk Lloyd George's view that Britain's ability to achieve its war objectives, some of which would be anathema to President Wilson, was dependent upon conserving British manpower. The foreign secretary argued that Britain's European allies were doomed if Britain, no matter what the condition of its land forces, withdrew from the coalition. Even the United States, despite its great

Sir William Robertson, Chief of the Imperial General Staff. Courtesy of Special Collections, U.S. Army Military History Institute.

economic power, would be reduced to military impotence in the European war without British participation. "What is true of us," Balfour went on to assert, "is still more true of America. Quite apart from her men and her ships, we have reached a stage in the war when American assistance in money and material is absolutely necessary for its continuance. It is therefore immaterial from this point of view whether our Armies be large or small: they cannot in either event carry on a great Continental war without American assistance. In other words, while America and Great Britain could fight without Italy and France, Italy and France could not fight without both America and Great Britain, nor could Great Britain support her French and Italian Allies without America." [34]

Robertson, then, saw no alternative to the continuation of heavy British casualties on the western front to save the alliance; and Balfour persuasively argued that Britain, no matter what the BEF's size, was already totally dependent upon the United States for victory on the Continent. Lloyd George, however, resisting these arguments, believed that he still might achieve a British peace without exhausting his country in the process. Determined to shift more of the burden of killing Germans to the Americans, he took advantage of the Italian disaster at Caporetto to gain his government's support for the creation an inter-Allied supreme war council with a permanent General Staff that would have advisory powers for Allied strategy and military policy. The prime minister had long argued that a central weakness of the conduct of the war against the German-dominated Central Powers was the lack of any unified command for the Allies. A comprehensive plan, taking in every theater and subordinating national interests to the general Allied cause, had not been devised. Allied military and political leaders in conference had effected only a " 'tailoring' operation in which different plans were stitched together." [35]

Lloyd George's argument was legitimate, but his motives were suspect. As later events were convincingly to demonstrate, the Welshman's primary aim was to undermine the Robertson-Haig combination and impose his own strategic views on the alliance. The Trojan Horse he chose to infiltrate the enemy camp was Sir Henry Wilson, whom Lloyd George planned to appoint to the inter-Allied General Staff.

General Wilson was as popular with the prime minister and the Unionist leadership as he was disliked by the leadership of the BEF, which considered him a political general—and indeed he has been called perhaps "the most accomplished intriguer produced by the British Army in recent times." [36] Senior British officers, however, wrongly suspected him of placing French interests over those of his own nation. Articulate, easygoing, amusing, and irreverent (he once claimed that if someone addressed a postcard to the ugliest man in

London, it would be delivered to him), Wilson was comfortable with politicians. Notwithstanding his opinion of them—and his private contempt as revealed in his diary knew no bounds—he conversed easily with the "frocks" about their strategical views, pretending to treat their ideas with respect. But it was his malleability on questions of strategy—in contrast to the granite-like firmness of Robertson—rather than his personality or political manipulation that best explains his ascendancy during this critical period of the war. Sir Henry agreed with Robertson that the war was ultimately going to be won or lost on the western front, but he was critical of Haig's strategy and tactics. He took a global view of the conflict, speaking in favor of military operations away from Western Europe for political purposes or for the containment of the Turko-German threat.

Wilson had long been on good terms with Lord Milner and his disciple, Lieutenant Colonel Leo S. Amery. Milner was the intellectual father of modern British imperialism with its emphasis on imperial federalism. Largely thanks to Milner, the prime ministers and leading ministers of the self-governing Dominions and representatives of the non-self-governing Empire of India had been invited to London at the beginning of 1917 to participate in meetings of the War Cabinet (called the Imperial War Cabinet when these leaders and representatives were present) to discuss the conduct of the war and possible peace terms. Milner had also used his considerable influence to include many of his disciples in Lloyd George's government; Amery, appointed to the new War Cabinet Secretariat, was the first. Although he held other positions—including head of the political branch of the British staff on the Supreme War Council—Amery's primary function became that of an imperial brain truster for the Milnerites, writing memoranda on geopolitical strategy. When Milner later became head of the War Office, Amery occupied a desk just outside the secretary of state for war's office. The troika of Wilson, Milner and Amery formed a hard core of support for Lloyd George in his efforts to redirect British strategy during the winter of 1917-18.[37]

Lloyd George's other key allies were Smuts and Curzon. Smuts had favored an active policy on the western front until becoming disillusioned with Haig when the latter continued his bloody bludgeoning in Flanders long after it was clear that his ambitious objectives were unobtainable. Now keen on military operations against Turkey, Smuts lobbied unsuccessfully for an attack from the sea against Syria. Curzon, a former viceroy of India, was especially concerned about a possible German march across the corpse of tsarist Russia. He could now be counted upon to support a forward policy in the East and a standstill policy in Western Europe.

Although he now enjoyed the War Cabinet's support, Lloyd

George was still restrained by the politics of coalition warfare from implementing his tripartite strategy: first, preserving British staying power through a conservative manpower policy; second, diverting British resources from the western front to outlying theaters; and third, gradually shifting the burden of fighting the German army from the BEF to the AEF. Lloyd George's campaign to employ America's emerging extra-Continental military role to further British interests started afresh with the month-long House mission to Europe in November and early December 1917.

7

The House Mission and Anglo-American War Aims

President Wilson had rebuffed Lloyd George's efforts in September 1917 to establish a special relationship between London and Washington. Having come around to the view that concentration on the western front served his country's interests best, he refused to advance the prime minister's strategic views in Allied councils. His apprehension about the Welshman had, if anything, been magnified by Wiseman's curious and disloyal actions. On several important occasions Wiseman, who might have been expected to represent the views of his prime minister to House and Wilson, assumed the role of an honest broker. Wiseman's distaste for Lloyd George's machinations, which served to undermine the influence of the Foreign Office, was no doubt genuine; but his frequently hostile analysis of Lloyd George's motives fed the suspicions of the American leadership, however much it may have increased their confidence in the British intelligence agent.

What especially shook Wilson was Wiseman's assertion that full American participation in Allied conferences might result in "shifting the center of gravity of the war from Washington to London and Paris."[1] In discussing British efforts to get him to send a political representative to Europe, Wilson emphasized to House that he would trust no other person to represent his views. "No one in America," he told the Texan, "or in Europe either, knows my mind and I am not willing to trust them to attempt to interpret it."[2]

Although Wilson was prepared to coordinate American military policy more closely with that of the Allies, he had no intention of creating the special Anglo-American alignment in military policy that Lloyd George wanted. To the contrary, he remained intensely suspicious of Lloyd George and the right-wing Tories in the War Cabinet. Moreover, perhaps influenced by Wiseman, he never did appoint a permanent political representative in Europe to speak for him. His only concession, then and later, to appeals for America's political participation in Allied councils of war was to send House, the individual whom he believed knew his mind best, to represent him for brief periods. As noted, Wilson declared that he had "no intention of loosening his hold on the situation."[3]

Before departing for Europe on October 29 as the president's special emissary, House discussed at length with Wilson "questions of strategy on each of the fronts," including "the campaign in Asia Minor, and the partition or non-partition of Turkey."[4] House's diary does not reveal the exact nature of this discussion, but the two men almost certainly agreed that the United States should not become involved in furthering the expansion of the British Empire in the Middle East.[5] To accompany House as the War Department's representative, and provide him with professional military advice, Wilson chose Bliss, who had earlier expressed alarmist views about Allied intentions to diminish the AEF's role through amalgamation. Chief of Naval Operations Admiral Benson, an Anglophobe, represented the Navy Department.

House arrived in London in the midst of a violent controversy over the powers of the new Supreme War Council, which had been created at Rapallo, Italy, on November 7.[6] Sir Henry Wilson's relationship to Robertson quickly became the central issue of the emerging political crisis. The military party charged that Lloyd George, rather than encouraging unity in military policy, had created a flawed system of dual military advice in his attempt to make General Wilson, as the British permanent military representative on the inter-Allied General Staff, independent of the British General Staff. "Dual advice can only lead to delay, friction, weakening of responsibility and lack of confidence amongst the troops," Robertson told Lord Derby.[7]

When Lloyd George returned to London from Paris on November 13, he was met with a barrage of press criticism. "Hands Off the British Army!" thundered the *Star*. Other papers warned that support for the concept of unity of command should not be confused with support for civilian meddling in military strategy. In Parliament there were ominous rumblings from both Unionists and supporters of Asquith. The beleaguered Lloyd George dined with House alone that night, asking for American support for the new Supreme War Council.

House, who had been lobbied by Robertson the previous day, was not about to be used in Lloyd George's attempt to divert British resources away from the western front to Palestine or elsewhere. On the other hand, he agreed with the prime minister that any further big attacks in the West should be delayed until America was prepared to "throw her strength on the Allied side or until Russia can recover sufficiently to make a drive on the Eastern Front."[8]

When House cabled Wilson for his opinion of the new Supreme War Council, the president immediately responded: "Please take the position that we not only accede to the plan for a single war council but insist on it, but think it does not go far enough."[9] House then issued a statement to the British press emphatically asserting that "unity must be accomplished if the great resources of the United States are to be used to the best advantage." Despite Wilson's strong stand for unity of command, however, his support for coordinating military resources and strategy was not always matched by his later actions. He was to prove extremely reluctant to allow the SWC to dictate to him in military or political questions. A consideration for Wilson in November may have been his hope that an inter-Allied body would facilitate the clear statement of the Entente's war objectives, for which he was then pressing.

Lloyd George survived this Parliamentary crisis, in part because of American support but more because of his brilliant but misleading performance before the House of Commons on November 19. The prime minister told the Commons that he sought only the "co-ordination" of Allied plans. He flatly denied any interest in an Allied supreme commander or the reduction of Robertson's authority.[10]

Lloyd George could afford to retreat because he had salvaged the Supreme War Council, headed by the prime ministers of Italy, France, and Britain. (House represented Wilson at the council's first meeting, but Wilson still rejected permanent political representation.) From Versailles, the headquarters of the inter-Allied General Staff, Sir Henry Wilson as British permanent military representative could still serve the prime minister as an alternative source for strategic advice. President Wilson's and Baker's choice for the American permanent military representative was Bliss.[11]

The American statement in support of the SWC had emphasized harnessing American power to the Allied cause through this inter-Allied body. To achieve his grand strategic objectives, however, Lloyd George was more inclined to bilateral negotiations with Washington because of the limitations imposed by coalition warfare. The French in particular were unlikely to support any strategy that diverted the flow of American soldiers from their war-weary army or limited the role of the British on the western front. In fact, French politicians were at this time putting intense pressure on the British to extend their front substantially by occupying trenches defended by the French army.

When Lloyd George had asked Haig and Robertson in October for their views on the military situation and their future plans to win the war, they had responded that the best policy, even if Russia fell out of the war, was to continue the offensive in the West.[12] In the face of Russia's decline and Italy's defeat at Caporetto, Lloyd George was prepared to resign rather than follow this advice. When the House mission arrived in London, he was eager to initiate a thorough re-evaluation of war plans for 1918 with emphasis on how American and

British military policy might be better coordinated. A procession of Britain's key war leaders soon passed through the library of Chesterfield House, where House was the Duke of Roxburghe's guest. These face-to-face confrontations did more to convince President Wilson's alter ego of the precarious military situation than did the confidential ministerial papers he was given.

According to the minutes for November 15, it was pointed out in the War Cabinet that "although the Departments generally had rendered every assistance in their power to the [House] Mission, it was beyond and outside their power to give information which depended on the decisions which might be arrived at as to our future war policy, as well as to the disposition of the United States troops, either on the Western front or in Russia, or whether they were to be asked, owing to the shortage of tonnage, to curtail their expeditionary forces and augment their supply to the Allies of food, munitions, &c."[13]

The suggestion that the Americans might be asked to "curtail their expeditionary forces" to alleviate the shipping crisis comes as a surprise. When these words were spoken, the consequences of the Bolshevik revolution were not yet in clear focus; the hope lingered that Russia might somehow be kept in the war, perhaps with American assistance. Also, just as the Americans desperately needed ships to transport their forces to Europe, Lloyd George and the Milnerites needed sea transport to give flexibility to their peripheral strategy. The men and equipment deemed necessary to defeat Turkey, for example, could not be diverted to Palestine or an attack made on the coast of Syria unless shipping could be found.[14] If the United States delayed military operations until it was capable of playing an independent role, any tonnage that might be squeezed from other sources during the winter to ship American soldiers and supplies would apparently have little impact on the 1918 campaign. At the beginning of November the AEF had a meager force in France of 87,000 men of all ranks. To place in Europe an independent American army capable of taking an important part in the fighting in the near future appeared out of the question.

But America had a vital resource that the British army desperately needed: fighting men. America's vast manpower was increasingly being viewed by the War Office as the reserve of the Entente, was in fact seen as the only means whereby the Allies could match or exceed German strength on the western front in 1918 if the German high command concentrated its forces there. A British General Staff memorandum, "American Assistance to the Allies," dated November 17, 1917, is noteworthy for its urgency and its fanciful proposals for the utilization of American resources.[15] Perhaps in an attempt to frighten its own government and enlist support from the United States, the

General Staff cast the military situation in the worst possible light. The British high command, it must be recalled, was at this time still contemplating a continuation of the offensive in 1918 rather than a defensive stance. Not until December 19, 1917, did Robertson assure the War Cabinet that it was "fully realised by Sir Douglas Haig that we must act on the defence for some time to come," and that he had "no offensive plans in mind at present."[16]

According to the General Staff memorandum of November 17, the Anglo-French reinforcements either sent to or contemplated for Italy and the planned cannibalization of French divisions on the western front to keep other divisions up to strength might mean a total reduction of Allied strength in the West by from twenty-four to thirty divisions. Meanwhile the Germans might be able to transfer as many as thirty divisions to France from the eastern front: "This may therefore mean an alteration in the balance of strength on the Western front in favour of the enemy by as many as 60 divisions." America's first priority, then, must be "to compensate England and France for the burden of supporting Italy." The British military also wanted the United States to assist the expansion of the Allied air forces and provide 20,000 to 30,000 workers, especially bricklayers and carpenters, to build Allied aerodromes and factories.[17]

The General Staff's wish list further included the employment of American resources beyond the western front, sowing the seeds of U.S. military intervention in Russia. In addition to the "re-organization and restoration of the transportation facilities of Russia," an idea earlier pressed upon President Wilson by the Allies, it was suggested that, "if shipping can be made available in the Pacific without reducing the tonnage available for transporting American troops and stores to France, then it is worth considering whether some of the enormous resources in man-power of the United States might not be utilised in sending a body of troops to Russia, where their presence might have a steadying effect on the political situation, and provide a nucleus round which the best elements in the country would rally." The British military also suggested that America might form a Georgian-Armenian army to keep alive the Russo-Turkish front and support the war in the Balkans by "aiding the re-constitution of the Greek Army" with food and money.[18]

Most of the proposals in the memorandum were obviously unlikely to appeal to American policymakers, whose first and *only* priority was the western front. The War College Division, as we have seen, had already considered and rejected sending expeditionary forces to other theaters. Baker had also just informed the president that "the tonnage question necessarily controls the strategy of this war so far as our participation in it is concerned whatever conditions there may be on the other side." To dispatch an expeditionary force across the Pacific in strength, for instance (and Baker argued that any U.S. force to assist Russia must number at least 500,000 men), was out of the question because "the length of the journey makes the whole plan inadmissible in view of the enormous tonnage necessary first to transport an adequate army, and second to keep it supplied."[19]

The question of shipping was a complicated one, involving conflicting and confusing figures, economic self-interest, and misconceptions frequently based more on mutual Anglo-American distrust than on fact. As previously noted, when the United States entered the war it did not possess the means to transport to Europe and supply a fraction of the men the country was capable of mobilizing. During the first months of the war, Washington failed dismally to expand its sea transport. The raising of an army received far more attention than shipping.

The British merchant marine, with some 16,000,000 gross tons at the beginning of 1917, remained by far the largest in the world. But during 1917 and the first months of 1918, German submarines sank British ships faster than new ships could be constructed. America's failures in ship construction consequently placed added strain on the British, who served as the merchant marine for the alliance. To transport grain to their allies (the French and Italian harvests had failed) and to meet their own military needs, the British planned further belt tightening, which would "involve some industrial disaster and the absolute cutting off of many articles of foodstuffs ordinarily regarded as essential."[20] Lord Curzon, who chaired the Shipping Control Board, warned the War Cabinet that the planned reduction of imports would "not only cause grave dislocation to certain trades, but also involve great hardships and drastic changes in the life of the people." Curzon predicted that the British people would accept the further war sacrifices "provided that some assurance can be given that our Allies are making equal sacrifices. At present we have only too much evidence that this is not always the case."[21]

Curzon did not mention the United States specifically, but he could have done so with justification. What emerges from the papers of Lloyd George and Wilson is that the president was much more motivated by commercial considerations in questions of shipping than was the prime minister. London, which saw its very survival hinging on the outcome of the war, was more inclined than Washington to sacrifice its commerce, both present and future, to the necessities of war.[22] Lloyd George stressed the economic damage done to British commerce when he addressed the House mission. "The trade of this country is largely an international trade," he told the Americans at a special meeting of the War Cabinet. "We manufactured for the world, and we carried for the world, and we did a good deal of financing for the world; all that is practically gone. *We have stripped to the waist for war. . . .* We have risked it all on this great venture."[23]

Not surprisingly, the British looked to American industrial might for assistance, especially since the American government had recently requisitioned ships (nearly 900,000 tons dead weight) being built in the United States for Britain. In December, however, they were shocked to discover that the United States planned to reduce its industrial target of constructing 6,000,000 tons dead weight to 2,000,000, just when the British were requesting an increase to 9,000,000.[24] "The United States shipbuilding programme," Lloyd George gravely told his colleagues on the Man-Power Committee, had broken down so badly that it would be impossible to "get the American troops over in American ships at the rate we had thought possible a short time ago."[25]

If anything, Lloyd George understated the seriousness of the failure of American transport in 1917. The American General Staff had discovered in October that it had only twenty-four ships with a gross tonnage of 338,000 to complete the transport of the thirty divisions that Pershing hoped to have in France by June 1.[26] While in London, Bliss asked the British General Staff to furnish its estimates of the tonnage required for four complete army corps of six divisions each by May 1. The director-general of Movements and Railways responded that the United States needed an additional 2,740,700 gross tons to convey twenty-four divisions, with auxiliaries and reserves, to France by that date. And this was considered a conservative estimate![27]

As Bliss pondered these truly staggering figures, the American General Staff discovered that "of more than fifty ships that have been commandeered on completion by the Government, only one has been placed available for the transportation of troops and equipment."[28] Clearly, more had to be done in employing seized German ships and requisitioned neutral shipping, not to mention diverting or constructing American vessels for the transport of American troops. No matter how great its sacrifice or its ingenuity, however, America was incapable of fully asserting its growing military power overseas without substantial British shipping assistance. American sea transport was so inadequate that Bliss, upon his return from Europe, bluntly informed Baker that unless means were found to expand and hasten the transportation of American soldiers to Europe, the United States would "be responsible for continued enormous destruction of wealth and of life and, to crown all, will have maintained an idle Army at home at a cost of billions of dollars for mere maintenance."[29]

As 1917 ended, the number of American soldiers in France had risen to 175,000, but only two combat divisions had been formed with two more promised in early 1918.[30] An additional 1,000,000 men were under arms in the United States. Not only had the United States no way to get them to Europe, but their clothing, equipment, and training were often woefully inadequate. The shortage of officers was especially acute. Some 200,000 officers were in uniform by the time of the Armistice, but when America entered the war, there were only 18,000 regular and National Guard officers available.

Lieutenant Colonel Gilbert W. Hall, a member of the British military mission to the United States who served as a machine gun instructor with the Eighty-ninth and Forty-second divisions at Camp Funston, Kansas, found American soldiers clothed in blue overalls, wearing inferior boots, and armed with inadequate equipment, "if it could be said that they were equipped at all. No rifles had been issued, wooden guns were being used, making the instruction of an infantryman in musketry almost impossible. . . . The machine gunners had old and obsolete Colt guns which could never be used with ammunition with any degree of safety."[31]

As the American military machine sputtered alarmingly, the House mission returned to the United States in mid-December. Meetings with British military and political leaders and the sharing of classified information had had a considerable impact on the Americans. Repeatedly, the British had impressed upon them that the alliance was faced with defeat unless the United States did more, and soon. "It is pitiful to see the undercurrent of feeling that the hopes of Europe have in the United States, pitiful because it will be so long before we can really do anything, although the very crisis seems to be at hand," Bliss had written his wife from London.[32]

The American representatives had also gained a greater appreciation of British sacrifices to keep the alliance intact. The reports of House, Benson, and Bliss, in fact, lent support to the "special relationship" between Washington and London that Lloyd George had advocated in his September message to the president. In his final report, Bliss recommended that Washington tilt its military policy in favor of the British. The French had diminished their military role in 1917 as the British had increased theirs. It seemed likely that the decisive blows would be delivered by Anglo-American forces, with the French playing a largely passive role. If this proved to be the case, Bliss cautioned, the location of Pershing's forces near the Swiss border, far removed from the BEF, was a grave strategical error: "We must take note of the deep, growing and already very strong conviction on the part of Englishmen, both military and the civil, that the war must finally be fought out by an Anglo-Saxon combination." If the French could be persuaded to accept a new arrangement, Bliss believed it would be good military policy to join the American and British forces at once.[33]

General Tasker H. Bliss,
Chief of Staff, U.S. Army,
at his quarters in
Versailles, May 13, 1918.
Courtesy of Special
Collections, U.S. Army
Military History Institute.

Admiral Benson, although he viewed British sea power as a threat to American interests, echoed Bliss's view that the war on land would be won by Anglo-American alignment. "From intimate contact with the actual war operations and from a knowledge of the European situation which is based upon secret and what I consider reliable information, I am convinced of the possibility of the burden of the entire war sooner or later devolving upon the United States and Great Britain—and this practically means the United States," he reported to his government. Benson's motives sprang from *realpolitik* considerations and certainly not from any Anglo-Saxon bias. The United States, he argued, had to support the Europeans to the hilt to keep the war from becoming almost totally an American-German conflict. "Every day that we can keep any of the European Allies in the war, just so much of the burden is being borne by that ally which otherwise would have to be borne by ourselves."[34]

House in his report made the questionable assertion that participation in a coalition against Germany had thus far cost Britain much more than it had gained. Acting alone, House argued, Britain could have avoided a land war in Europe, destroyed Germany's fleet, and conquered its colonies. Britain would consequently have gained in prestige and the "cost to her would not have been one-tenth of what she has already expended."[35]

America's obligations to its overseas war partners (and equally to its own national interests) seemed clear to the returning Americans. In the words of Bliss, "the one all-absorbing necessity now is soldiers with which to beat the enemy in the field, and ships to carry them." But putting more American troops in Europe was not the same as accepting amalgamation. House, who had cordially received such suggestions from the British, admitted that brigading "would be the most effective immediate help we could give the French and England, but it would be at great cost to us." U.S. soldiers once merged would "probably never emerge," and the United States would not receive credit for its sacrifices.[36]

On December 18 Wilson held a crucial war council in the White House with his most trusted advisers on the European war, House and Baker. Bliss, who had just presented to Baker a paper that emphasized ships, men, and unity of command, was also included.[37] Since America's entry into the war, the military situation had changed dramatically. The question now was not so much how to win the land war in Europe, as how to keep Germany from adding Western Europe to its conquest of eastern Europe. House, Benson, and Bliss had emphasized in their reports that the fate of the alliance hinged on America's ability to make a military contribution commensurate with its industrial and fiscal power. If the United States continued its leisurely pace of expanding the AEF and accepted Pershing's plan of concentrating his forces in the French sector, withholding American soldiers from battle, and waiting until 1919 for American arms to win the war, it might be too late. In Bliss's chilling words, "There may be no campaign of 1919 unless we do our best to make the campaign of 1918 the last." [38] Rather than marching in a victory parade, Pershing and his forces might be interned in German POW camps.

The only account of this meeting, House's diary, leaves the historian in the dark about what was actually said. "Bliss' advice was almost identical with what I had already given the President," House wrote, "and it was decided that Baker should draw up a cable to General Pershing indicating our decision." Wilson then decided that Baker's telegram to Pershing should also serve as his official response to British pleas for greater American military assistance. [39] It would in fact be read to all the Allied ambassadors simultaneously in Washington.

On December 21 the prime minister read in the War Cabinet a cable from Washington paraphrasing the telegram sent to Pershing. In his diary, House characterized Baker's cable as a "complete answer to their [British and French] requests." [40] Nothing could be further from the truth. On the question of amalgamation, Baker told Pershing that the administration desired to maintain the "identity" of American forces in Europe but that this consideration was "secondary to the meeting of any critical situation by the most helpful use possible of the troops at your command." Baker also suggested that Pershing consider positioning his forces "nearer the junction of the British and French lines." [41]

With House, Bliss, and Benson telling him that Germany might win the land war in 1918 unless America did more, Wilson's reaction was in many respects puzzling. The president of the United States in effect abdicated his responsibility as commander-in-chief. After either accepting or rejecting Pershing's advice, he should have given his own response to the Allied requests for assistance. Instead he turned over the vital question of American military cooperation (and any responsibility for failure) to his field commander in Europe.

Wilson apparently wanted it both ways. He was able to appear sympathetic to the British point of view without conceding anything. Having made a deep impression on the House mission, the British now had to deal with the one American leader who was least likely to support Anglo-American military coordination if it in any way undermined American efforts to create an independent army that waged its own campaign.

Wilson also implicitly rejected the British tilt in the reports of the House mission. He introduced the possibility that American troops might be amalgamated in *French* as well as British divisions; Baker's cable emphasized that the proposed location of the AEF at the Anglo-French juncture was designed to assist either army. Wilson may have been primarily motivated by a preference for a multilateral over a bilateral military arrangement. But by introducing coalition politics into the question, he effectively undermined British efforts to create a special relationship between London and Washington.

In response to Baker's cable, Pershing instructed his operations section, headed by Colonel Fox Conner, to make a confidential study "of the best place to employ the AEF on the Western front," placing emphasis on the possibility of American divisions training with the BEF.[42] The letter requesting this study is printed with the policy-forming documents in the AEF's official history. Perhaps significantly, his operations section's response is not.

That response gave political factors equal standing with strategic considerations. Strategically, Conner argued in January 1918 as he had in September 1917 that an American offensive in Lorraine offered the best hope of bringing the war to a successful conclusion in 1919. To parcel out American forces in 1918, he asserted, "and use them up prematurely in piecemeal means eliminating the possibility of launching a great Allied offensive in 1919." As for political considerations, Conner was quick to admit that war-weariness had grown in Britain since the burden of fighting the main German army had shifted to the British; American cooperation with the BEF would unquestionably raise British morale. Conversely, French morale would just as surely plummet. The suggestion that the AEF be placed at the joint of the British and French forces to assist either war partner was not, in Conner's view, a workable compromise: "It is difficult for us to avoid friction now and to place our forces between those of our Allies would increase our difficulties," he wrote. "We are on French soil, and must use French facilities and it would appear that we must get along with the French unless we should decide to turn all our forces over unreservedly to the British. The natural conclusion appears to be that from a political standpoint nothing is to be gained by changing our present plan."[43]

The operations section's reevaluation was really a foregone conclusion. Pershing and his staff had from the beginning decided that any American force fighting alongside the British would be given a secondary role. The dramatically altered military landscape did not change one iota Pershing's strategy of concentrating his forces in the Lorraine theater. The only concession that he and his operations section were prepared to consider was the placing of American troops behind the British front for training, if additional British shipping could be found to transport them. But Conner emphasized that "in no case should we consent to putting units of less strength than a division with the British. Otherwise we will never develop the necessary higher commanders and staffs."[44]

Pershing had an ace up his sleeve in rejecting direct assistance to the BEF: the unequivocal support of the French. Pétain, determined to pressure the British government to reinforce the BEF with soldiers of its own, had agreed with Pershing on December 23 that "there can be no thought given to Americans' entering the front at the junction of the British and French armies. This entrance can be made only on the French front."[45] Pershing believed that the location of the American theater had been "practically decided" by that December 23 agreement with the French.[46] This would not be the last time Pershing found the French a useful ally in undermining the efforts of the British to co-opt American military intervention for their own purposes.

Perhaps Wilson's refusal to take an unambiguous position on collective military action can best be understood by his steadfast determination to force his political objectives upon his war partners. His Flag Day speech in June 1917 had emphasized Germany's global threat, but nine months of war with Germany had not yet shaken his conviction that peace should be negotiated among equals. In his mind, for example, there was no difference between British objectives in Mesopotamia or Palestine and German designs on Courland or the Persian Gulf. He was blind to any strategic interest the British might have in protecting imperial lines of communication from German or Turkish encroachment. What seemed to the British essential to the maintenance of a stable and peaceful world was viewed by Wilson as selfish colonialism and discredited power politics. Having failed to get a joint American-Allied statement of moderate war objectives out of the Supreme War Council, his thoughts in mid-December were turning increasingly to a bold American statement on war aims to effect his radical reconstruction of the international system.[47]

The grave military crisis faced by his European partners presented Wilson with opportunities as well as risks. The growing dependence of the Allies upon American resources, now manpower as well as financial and material resources, raised America's international voice, and he was reluctant to sacrifice any political leverage by diminishing the identity of America's military role in the war through either amalgamation or interference with Pershing's war plans. He thereby ran the risk of losing the land war in Europe. By specifically rejecting a special Anglo-American alignment to see the war through to victory, he also unknowingly risked losing Britain as a war partner if Lloyd George once again considered a separate British peace with Germany.

As 1918 began, the War College Division painted a dark picture of America's global position should Germany triumph in Europe and then consolidate a great Eurasian empire. Reflecting the suspicion of

Japan that ran deep in American military and political circles, the War College Division in its review of the strategic situation expressed the fear that Tokyo might switch sides if Berlin controlled the world's heartland. The result might be a Berlin-Tokyo axis "to divide the world" between them.[48] War-depleted Britain, still a great naval power but with its manpower and economy exhausted, might remain America's only important ally in this global struggle. A Wilsonian peace in that event would be most unlikely. Without the British Empire's assistance, America's world position would be precarious in the extreme.

That the British might seek a satisfactory peace through negotiations with Berlin and not through the military assistance of Washington was, to be sure, an unlikely possibility. Lloyd George argued with genuine conviction that Germany must suffer military defeat to demonstrate that militarism did not pay. As the war went from bad to worse during the last months of 1917, however, many British leaders, the prime minister included, began to doubt that destroying the German army was possible without undermining Britain's status as a great power in the process. Lloyd George had attempted to square this circle by putting his faith in two premises: Germany would *not* launch an all-out offensive against the BEF in 1918 which would force Britain to commit its remaining military resources without reservation to the land war in Western Europe; and, of equal importance, America could be persuaded to begin providing manpower relief to the BEF in 1918 and assume the primary responsibility for fighting the German Army in 1919. His failure to convert Wilson and Pershing to a special Anglo-American alignment, consequently, was a cruel disappointment to him.

As London experienced another war Christmas, the British leadership considered a unilateral and moderate statement of war aims. Lloyd George had resisted House's attempt to elicit a joint American-Allied statement of war aims at the first meeting of the SWC, arguing that such a statement would weaken the alliance and encourage the Germans to believe in ultimate victory. Increasingly, however, it appeared that general peace negotiations might ensue from the wearing military stalemate and the widespread war-weariness on the European home fronts.

Lord Lansdowne, who had earlier privately urged the Asquith government to seek a compromise peace, went public with a request for the liberalization of Allied war objectives and the beginning of general peace negotiations. His letter, printed in the *Daily Telegraph* on November 29, struck a responsive chord with some British Socialists and elements within the non-Socialist left. "There are gradually accumulating in the country a great many wounded and crippled men

who are not of a very cheery disposition; there are others who are mere
wasters and without patriotism; and finally, there are the various
Labour Unions etc. On the whole there is a fairly formidable body of
discontented or half-hearted people," was Robertson's uncharitable
description of this anti-war sentiment. Yet Robertson concluded that
"on the whole the majority are quite sound."[49]

What is really surprising is that the massive casualties suffered by
the BEF in 1916-17, the increased war sacrifices demanded from the
civilian population, and the Russian Revolution did not have a greater
impact on support for the war. Beginning in mid-April 1917 the War
Cabinet received frequent and extensive reports on the mood of the
workers.[50] These reports reflect a surprising steadfastness on the part
of the working classes, despite the strain of protracted conflict. Mus-
cular patriotism rather than pacifism or defeatism motivated most
workers. As J.M. Bourne has remarked, "Perhaps Britain's greatest
asset in a war against Germany was Germany herself. The Germans
were in many ways the perfect enemy." Recent works by Bourne, John
N. Horne, and Trevor Wilson support Robertson's conclusion that
support for the war within the labour movement remained strong.[51]

International and geopolitical considerations, more than any concern about morale on the home front, in all likelihood influenced Lloyd
George to seek a liberalization of British war objectives. The Bolsheviks
signed an armistice on December 15 and issued an appeal for general
peace negotiations at the Polish fortress town of Brest-Litovsk. The
Central Powers accepted this invitation and falsely gave the impression that they were prepared to begin peace discussions on the Bolshevik formula of no annexations or indemnities. Concurrently with the
Brest-Litovsk peace discussions, secret British negotiations with the
Austrians in Switzerland suggested that a moderate British statement
of war aims would encourage Vienna toward peace and might even
result in Germany's acceptance of a moderate settlement.[52]

On January 5, 1918, before a Trades Union Congress in Caxton
Hall, Lloyd George delivered a speech on war objectives which in
some respects could have been written by President Wilson. Prevailing
opinion is that Lloyd George's intent was to respond to the liberal
challenge posed by the America president, the revisionist demands of
the English left, and the peace offensive of the Bolsheviks (which
included the publication of Allied secret treaties that seemed to make a
mockery of the Allies' claim that they were fighting to resist German
imperialism). Much has been made of his choice of audience, a packed
gathering of trade unionists. Arno Mayer argues that the prime minister's speech before workers provides "conclusive proof" that the War
Cabinet's intent was to placate the moderate left.[53] Overlooked by
Mayer and others, however, is the fact that Parliament, which the War

Cabinet generally agreed was the proper setting for a speech of such import, was not in session.

Lloyd George's motives were more complex than have generally been recognized. He was greatly influenced by geopolitical and strategic considerations, especially his hitherto unsuccessful efforts to use American intervention in the war to guarantee a British peace and the survival of the economic and military capacity that would ensure Great Britain's status as a great power. Germany's militant position following his tentative exploration of peace feelers in September and October had made the prime minister doubt that the German military masters would consider terms satisfactory to the western powers, particularly as the war began to turn in their favor. Russia's abandonment of the Allies and the beginning of peace negotiations at Brest-Litovsk, however, might present Britain with both the opportunity and pretext to make peace at Russia's expense.

Just before the Labour party's December 28 program of opposition to imperialist war objectives, Jan Smuts, whose advice carried more weight with the prime minister than did that of Foreign Secretary Balfour,[54] suggested that the British must be prepared to "suddenly" find themselves "confronted with a peace situation for which we have made no adequate preparations. Questions of peace will rush to the fore very rapidly at the end, and it is conceivable that the end may come as early as next spring or even earlier." The catalyst for negotiations might be a "peace with Russia which may amply compensate Germany and Austria for all possible sacrifices in the West." Such a peace might "convince the enemy that the war is not worth continuing, and that it would be better to concede to us most of our legitimate war aims."[55]

Lloyd George certainly understood the advantages of delineating his country's peace terms to prevent Britain's remaining European allies or President Wilson from dominating the peace agenda at the expense of Britain's global interests. Lloyd George also wanted to signal Berlin that he would not reject outright a peace that sacrificed Russian interests—especially if Germany largely confined its eastern objectives to the non-Russian Baltic provinces—in return for generous German concessions to the western allies.

During the War Cabinet's discussion of the draft of his war aims speech, Lloyd George candidly asserted that it was "necessary to give warning to the Bolsheviks that we [do] not any longer consider ourselves bound to fight on in Russian interests, so that there [will] be no misunderstanding on the subject in the future"; he also wished "to give a hint to the enemy in the same direction."[56] A Germany able to dominate central Europe without a strong Russia as a counterweight would destroy the European equilibrium. A Germany that also dominated Courland and Lithuania and was in league with an Asian power, Turkey, would be a positive danger to Britain's world position. Lloyd George had grave reservations about any peace that would leave Germany unhumbled and in a stronger imperial position. Given the increasing strain on British manpower and the economy, however, he apparently hoped to keep his options open in the event of a rush to peace because of general war exhaustion among Britain's European allies. Clearly, he did not want his country's national interests to be defined by other powers, especially the United States.

In his famous speech Lloyd George redefined British war aims, going, in his own words, "to the extreme limit of concession."[57] The author of the "knock-out blow" did not now call for the destruction of Germany or even the elimination of its navy. He did, however, demand the restoration of Belgium, Serbia, Romania, Montenegro, and occupied Italy and France. Beyond supporting the revival of an independent Poland, he ignored Germany's conquest of other Russian territories. Lloyd George thus seemed prepared to accept Britain's military failure to demote Germany from the position of great, almost certainly the greatest, Continental power.

His definition of war objectives was designed to thwart Germany's overseas threat to the British Empire. Lloyd George also understood the political requirement that Britain needed some territory as compensation for its sacrifices. He told Lord Riddell, as his press proprietor friend noted in his diary, that "we should have to secure some territory to compensate us for what we had expended—the greater part of the German Colonies, Palestine and Mesopotamia." The Germans could recoup themselves with a large slice of Russia. The Russians had acted badly and must take the consequences."[58] Turkey, which served as Germany's bridge to Asia, was to be stripped of Arabia, Armenia, Mesopotamia, Syria, and Palestine through the recognition of their "separate national conditions." There was no talk of annexing Germany's colonies; instead, Germany's overseas possessions were to be "held at the disposal of a Conference whose decision must have primary regard to the wishes and interests of the native inhabitants of such colonies."[59] The principle of self-determination in Turkish- and German-ruled territories was thus employed to mask British determination that any peace settlement would dismantle the Turkish Empire and reduce Germany to a Continental—not global—power.[60]

In the unlikely event that Germany accepted these terms, Britain would emerge from the war with its political independence and great power status intact. Haig, who now believed that America would not be a "serious military factor even in 1919," probably spoke for many British war leaders when he told Smuts, following Lloyd George's war aims statement, that so far the British Empire had "got most out of this war, certainly a good deal more than even Germany"; according to Smuts, Haig "doubted whether we would gain more by continuing the war for another twelve months. At the end of that period we would be much more exhausted and our industrial and financial recovery would be more difficult, and America would get a great pull over us."[61]

No American was more interested in Lloyd George's January 5 statement than President Wilson. The prime minister talked of a peace of "reason" and "justice," the "sanctity of treaties," a territorial settlement based on the "right of self-determination," and the creation of an "international organisation to limit the burden of armaments and diminish the probability of war." Wilson was pleased that these views resembled his own and did not place him publicly in a confrontation with London over war objectives. But he was skeptical that the imperial-minded British war government had been truly converted to his world view and feared that his preeminent role as peacemaker had been undermined, not just by the British but by Lenin's peace offensive as well.

House raised Wilson's sinking spirits by insisting that the president's views on the peace settlement "would so smother the Lloyd George speech that it would be forgotten and that he, the President, would once more become the spokesman for the Entente, and, indeed, the spokesman for the liberals of the world."[62]

On January 8 Wilson delivered his famous Fourteen Points address to a joint session of Congress.[63] In discussing territorial questions, he made it clear that he opposed any peace that would allow Germany's domination of Eastern Europe. Accusing Berlin of seeking the conquest and subjugation of the Russian people, Wilson made his first territorial point the demand that all Russian territory be evacuated by the Central Powers. Wilson's rhetorical stand on containing Germany's eastern expansion appeared to move him closer to accepting the necessity of a crushing defeat of the German army as the only means of preventing Berlin's domination of Europe.

Lloyd George was moving in the other direction. As he told the editor of the *Manchester Guardian*, "to defeat the impending great German attack in France and Italy, or wherever else it may take place, would in itself constitute military victory."[64] Unlike Wilson's, Lloyd George's speech was not delivered primarily with the threat posed by Lenin and public opinion in mind. His moderate stance on British and especially Allied war aims had the effect of bringing British political objectives more in line with his conservative views on British manpower and his and the Milnerites' peripheral strategy, which would serve to strengthen Britain's defensive and bargaining position in the event of an inconclusive end to the war.

8

Before the Storm

The War Cabinet's strategical focus prior to Hindenburg's gigantic offensive on March 21, 1918, has an unreal quality about it. As Germany prepared for a war-winning offensive on the western front, the British prime minister and the imperial-minded members of his government increasingly looked eastward, alarmed by the potential Turko-German threat to Britain's Asian position following Russia's collapse. Robertson's repeated warnings that Britain had no choice but to concentrate its military effort in the West to counter the growing German threat were greeted with considerable skepticism by the civilians. Often with a numerical superiority of more than three to two, never less than five to four, the British and French during the last three years had launched massive and prolonged attacks to break through the German defenses. These costly and ultimately unsuccessful attacks had driven the French army to mutiny and almost exhausted the BEF. The Germans, equally, had paid a heavy price in 1916 during their ten-month offensive at Verdun.

Despite the alarmist tone that he had taken with the House mission in requesting American manpower, Lloyd George simply could not accept the War Office's dire warnings. On extracts from one of Robertson's memoranda predicting a German offensive, he wrote: "By all means. Nothing would suit us better—but unfortunately he has learnt his lesson."[1] At the very time he pressed House to accept the amalgamation of American with British units, he was confident that the Allies had sufficient manpower to withstand a German attack, even one reinforced by "all their serviceable divisions from the Eastern front."[2]

Haig's testimony to the War Cabinet on January 7, 1918, reinforced Lloyd George's conviction that existing Allied forces were sufficient to withstand any German assault in the West. "If you were a German Commander," Haig had been asked, "would you think there was a sufficient chance of a smashing offensive to justify incurring the losses which would be entailed?" Haig had responded that a policy of limited attacks "seemed to him to be the more probable course for the enemy to adopt, because an offensive on a large scale made with the object of piercing the front and reaching Calais or Paris, for instance, would be very costly." If the Germans gambled for victory and failed, Haig accurately predicted, their position "would become critical" by August, when the Americans were expected to have a sizable force in Europe.[3] "L.G. is convinced by the figures generally that we are all right on the W. Front," Amery wrote Sir Henry Wilson at Versailles following Haig's appearance before the War Cabinet, "& nothing will budge him."[4]

Rather than reinforce the BEF, Lloyd George and the Milnerites were determined to limit Britain's casualties in the continued stalemate on the western front. On the eve of the Bolshevik revolution, Milner had written to warn the prime minister about the danger of "tying ourselves up more than ever in France. . . . The great point is that if, next year at any rate, we cannot make that force strong enough to break through, it is waste to keep it stronger than is necessary for a lively defensive. The force we could afford to withdraw from France *should be the mobile force of the alliance*[,] the strategic reserve, wh. we have never had & without wh. we can never win."[5]

Russia's subsequent collapse gave added force to Milner's words. If the war now ended in mutual exhaustion, Britain might, through military operations away from the western front, both contain Germany's global threat and improve its bargaining position in peace negotiations. "We might find it possible if Damascus were in our possession," Lloyd George told the War Cabinet on February 21, "to persuade the French to be content with something less than the whole of Alsace-Lorraine in return for compensation in Syria."[6]

The War Cabinet's interest in diverting British military resources from the West to advance Britain's global strategical and political objectives made it even more essential that Washington be persuaded to increase its commitment to the western front, especially in or adjacent to the British sector. This consideration, more than the fear that the Germans might achieve a breakthrough, prompted the British political leadership's resumption of its campaign to win the American military and political leadership over to amalgamation.

The War Office, although for different reasons, lent its enthusiastic support to brigading Americans with the BEF. The civilians had been pressing Haig for months to reduce his battalions per division from twelve to nine, which would allow him to maintain the number, though not the size, of his existing divisions. Robertson, unable to change his government's manpower priorities, wanted to employ some of the approximately 1,000,000 Yanks being trained in America for the maintenance of BEF divisions at full strength.

The General Staff argued that the BEF could absorb one American regiment (or three battalions) per division, some 150,000 riflemen or, if reinforcements were included, about 200,000 American soldiers. The General Staff's position was that Americans serving with the BEF would be introduced to combat six months earlier than those serving under Pershing's command. Moreover, since the British were asking only for soldiers not organized into divisions, Pershing would not be prevented from forming an independent army. On the other hand, the General Staff did not favor reducing British imports in order to accelerate the arrival of American soldiers destined for Pershing's command, which the General Staff thought incapable in its present organization of absorbing more than an additional 250,000 men before the end of April. The anticipated temporary loss of 450,000 tons of imports which would be entailed in transporting 200,000 Americans to maintain the twelve-battalion British divisions was, however, clearly worth the economic sacrifice. Robertson cabled Haig: "The War Cabinet are very desirous of carrying out the first proposal [using surplus American battalions to reinforce British divisions], as it undoubtedly offers the best prospect of making additional American troops available quickly."[7]

The British high command apparently had more success convincing the House mission than its own government of the possibility of an Allied disaster in the West in 1918. A concerned House consulted Pershing. The American field commander agreed that a big German offensive was likely and expressed uncertainty that the Allies had sufficient troops to hold on until he had created a powerful army of his own. "The situation is liable to become grave and dangerous," he informed House in a confidential memorandum.[8]

Pershing's words may have been intended to frighten the American administration into doubling its efforts to supply him (certainly not the British or the French) with the men he was requesting, along with ships to carry them. Discovering that House had discussed America's military role with the Allies (he learned from Pétain, for example, that the AEF was planning an offensive to clear the St. Mihiel salient in 1918), Pershing felt that his position was being undermined.[9] And indeed it was; House had left the British with the impression that he had "cordially received" their proposal for amalgamation.[10] The president's response (via the Baker-to-Pershing cable of December 18, 1917) to Britain's renewed pleas for amalgamation left the utilization of American manpower squarely in Pershing's hands, however.[11] Both Baker and Wilson were confident that their field commander in Europe would protect America's national military identity and not, in the words of Pershing, "scatter regiments for service among French and British, especially under the guise of instruction."[12]

On January 9 Robertson began direct negotiations with the American commander. The cards held by both men were face up on the table. America had the men. Britain had the ships to transport them to Europe. Robertson argued that battalions could be brought over five times faster and placed in the line sooner than complete divisions. The rugged and plain speaking Chief of the Imperial General Staff (CIGS) made it clear that Britain was not prepared to "run the risk of going short of food" to supply Pershing with two or three additional divisions (plus their many noncombat personnel such as cooks, typists, and supply clerks) that might see no action until late 1918 or perhaps even 1919. The Americans, Robertson darkly warned, did not have the luxury of building toward 1919. The Germans had been able to cripple one or another of the allies each year—Russia (in 1915), France (in 1916) and Italy (in 1917). In 1918 it might be the British if America could not help "in the way suggested."[13]

With his operations section opposed to placing any American unit smaller than a division with the BEF for training, Pershing downplayed the German threat and continued to urge British transport for complete American divisions. The British military authorities were furious with what they saw as Pershing's obstinacy. "General Pershing is looking older and rather tired, and I doubt if he has yet an intelligent and considered view of the nature of his task, or how to set about it," Robertson reported to the War Cabinet.[14]

On January 10 Pershing appeared more flexible when discussions of Robertson's so-called 150-battalion program resumed. But his distrust of British motives remained.[15] Robertson fed his suspicion that the British wanted to use American manpower for their own purposes when he admitted that he had no intention of allowing Pershing to reclaim before 1919 any U.S. troops brigaded with the BEF. Still, the British were ultimately in a superior negotiating position because of America's inability to provide shipping for its forces. American troops that otherwise would remain in the United States could be gotten to Europe only with British help. Hence, Pershing agreed to send Robertson's proposal on to the War Department and to "add a recommendation to the effect that as this scheme was only proposed as a help to win the war, it should be given consideration if other schemes do not appear suitable."[16]

Robertson, believing that the war would reach a climax perhaps as early as the spring and early summer, emerged disheartened from these negotiations. Pershing's lukewarm and conditional acceptance of brigading reinforced his view that the American's driving interest was the creation of a great and independent army. To Robertson's disgust, Pershing proceeded as if he "had years in which to prepare." Given the limited progress of the AEF, Robertson concluded in his report to the War Cabinet, "America's power to help us to win the war—that is to help us to defeat the Germans in battle—is a very weak reed to lean upon at present, and will continue to be so for a very long time to come unless she follows up her words with actions much more practical and energetic than she has yet taken."[17]

The civilian leaders however, continued to be positive about Washington's willingness to assist the British. Wilson, they convinced themselves, really wanted to fall in with British policy. The president was just being restrained by American public opinion and an unco-operative Pershing. When amalgamation was discussed by the War Cabinet on January 14, Smuts thought that the president "desired to be fortified, in making his decision, by a recommendation from his Mili-tary Advisers." Lord Reading, who had been chosen to replace Spring Rice in Washington, blithely assumed that ultimately Wilson "must be guided by the English view."[18]

Nothing could have been further from the truth. Wilson was both surprised and concerned when Pershing, although he later denied it, did in fact recommend the acceptance of Robertson's 150-battalion plan as a temporary measure.[19]

Pershing's recommendation, seconded by Baker,[20] could not have come at a worse time for the Wilson administration. A serious political crisis had erupted because of the snail-like pace of American war preparations. When Congress reassembled in December 1917, the War Department's alleged mismanagement soon captured its attention. More than a million men were in uniform in the United States, but only one U.S. division was at the European battlefront. On January 18 elements of the First Division took over a quiet section of French trenches, the first time that Americans had held a part of the front on their own. National security considerations kept the American public in the dark about the small number of Yanks trained and deployed in the trenches, but breakdowns in mobilization on the home front were receiving extensive press coverage.

Following several weeks of hearings, the Democratic chairman of the Senate Military Affairs Committee, George E. Chamberlain, who had aspired to be secretary of war in 1916, issued a violent attack against Wilson's and the War Department's management of mobiliza-tion. In a speech in New York on January 19 to a joint meeting of the American Defense Society and the National Security League, with Teddy Roosevelt and other super-patriots cheering him on in the audience, Chamberlain acidly proclaimed, "The military establish-ment of America has fallen down." The very survival of the United States was at stake, he went on to assert. The following morning, newspapers across the country emphasized these dramatic charges against the Wilson administration. Chamberlain's solution, which was endorsed by the *New York Times* and many Republican newspapers, was a proposed Senate bill that would create a three-man war cabinet of "distinguished citizens of demonstrated ability" to oversee preparations for war. This proposal was a direct hit at Baker's and Daniels's leadership. Even if such a war cabinet reported directly to Wilson, its creation would represent a deep humiliation for him as well.[21] Wilson led a vigorous counterattack against his Capitol Hill critics, and Baker, who dared not reveal the persistent Allied pleas for American manpower assistance, promised Congress that American troops would arrive in France in time to prevent a German victory. The war cabinet bill was never put to a vote.

Doughboys fighting under the Union Jack would be a telling demonstration of the truth of the charges being made against his administration. Pershing had been careful to demand that American battalions be transported in British bottoms not already allocated to the shipping of his complete divisions, but Wilson feared that his field commander had been hoodwinked by the British.[22] An impressive display of independent American power in Europe, which would silence his critics, was being pushed into the distant future. Wilson had the War Department immediately cable Bliss, who had just returned to Europe to take his new position on the SWC, to exercise the "utmost care" to reach "an explicit understanding that these battalions and their transportation are contingent upon the supply of tonnage to us for our agreed minimum military effort."[23]

Wilson's position, that the British had agreed to take up the slack in shipping required to fulfill the American program of having a minimum of twenty-four divisions in Europe by mid-July, was without foundation. In November the Allied generals, as previously noted, had supported Pershing's request with little or no expectation that the United States could fulfill it. Pershing himself had informed Robertson on January 9 that the maximum number of divisions he expected to have by the end of June was fifteen. The British General Staff thought even this figure quite unobtainable. And then there was the matter of preparing these newly arrived Yanks for trench warfare, which would require an additional six months' training.

The Anglo-French military leadership was convinced that if dramatic changes did not occur in the pace and shape of America's involvement in the European war, the AEF would have little impact in 1918 and would probably not even be an important factor in offensive operations in 1919. A French General Staff memorandum (reviewed by the British government) estimated that Pershing's forces by mid-1919 would still be unable to undertake and carry out "offensive action on a large scale."[24]

The British were currently supplying shipping for approximately 12,000 Americans a month, less than half the strength of a complete American division. Yet although their construction continued to fall short of replacing their shipping losses,[25] the British now agreed to reduce vital imports, including food, in order to allocate additional shipping for some 150,000 Americans under Robertson's 150-battalion plan. Hence, there was no basis for Wilson's assumption. Far from undertaking to make up the deficit in the tonnage required to fulfill the American program (which had been caused in large part by the failure of American ship construction to live up to expectations), the British, with the creation of the Allied Maritime Transport Council in December, had anticipated an expanded American merchant marine in 1918 to assist *them* in supplying the tonnage needs of Italy and France.[26]

On January 25, fortified by Wilson's suspicions of the British, Pershing told Robertson and Bliss in Paris that he had never approved of Robertson's 150-battalion program. He returned to his demand that six complete American divisions be transported in British bottoms. These troops would train with the British prior to becoming part of an American force. Robrtson protested. Pershing's plan would provide the British with only 72 instead of 150 infantry battalions.[27]

Pershing's about-face placed Bliss in an awkward position. More than any other American soldier, Bliss accepted the necessity of coordinating emerging though still limited American military power with the British, even if this meant assigning American arms an inferior, some might say demeaning, national role. He agreed with Robertson that he transport of American infantry for incorporation in British divisions was the quickest and most practicable means of countering the expected German offensive. On January 25 he did not support Pershing against Roberton. This difference of opinion between America's two four-star generals in Europe created a potential crisis for the American military role in the land war.

On January 29, in Sir Henry Wilson's private room in the offices of the SWC, the British leadership confronted Pershing over his change of heart. Lloyd George, Lord Milner, Wilson, Robertson, Hankey, and Haig, who joined the discussions after they had begun, presented a solid British phalanx against Pershing, his principal aide, Carl Boyd, and Bliss. The atmosphere was tense, the discussion heated. When Lloyd George tried to exploit the apparent differences between Bliss and Pershing, the former surprised him by responding, "Pershing will speak for us and whatever he says with regard to the disposition of the American forces will have my approval."[28] Suspecting political motives, Haig recorded in his diary that Americans "were criticising their Government because there seemed to be no results to show for the money which America has been spending! No troops in the field, no aeroplanes, no guns, no nothing yet in fact!"[29]

Faced with a united American command, the British on the following day capitulated. Pershing's six-division plan, which called for the British transport of the personnel of six complete American divisions by June for training with the BEF, replaced Robertson's 150-battalion plan.

Pershing had won a victory for the political objectives of his president. Additional British shipping had been gained without accepting brigading, which would have diminished the American role in the war and provoked political opposition at home. President Wilson's unjustified interpretation of British shipping obligations to the AEF helped carry the day. Bliss wrote Baker that, following his president's instructions, he had pressed the British to "give us additional tonnage to carry out our 24 division program." His failure to get such a pledge fom London, along with Pershing's renewed and determined opposition to amalgamation, had led him to join Pershing in opposing Robertson's proposal.[30]

Although Lloyd George had been completely outmaneuvered, he did not realize it until later. The prime minister, having given in to Pershing's six-division plan, still believed that the new understanding placed a large body of Americans on the British front. The promised six American divisions at full strength would equal twelve British divisions. Lloyd George also believed, or so he told the War Cabinet, that the American troops arriving at the British front would be available for combat as well as training. Moveover, there was "no limit as to numbers [available for cooperation with the BEF], other than the limit imposed by the amount of shipping available and the rate at which we [can] equip the American divisions with material."[31]

President Wilson's soothing words also initially encouraged British civilians to believe that they might soon gain relief for their depleted divisions and endangered front, which was being extended by a controversial agreement to take over more of the French line.[32] Wilson, over lunch with Wiseman on February 3, emphasized that domestic political considerations militated against his brigading American soldiers with the BEF. "The placing of American troops in small bodies under foreign leaders would be taken as a proof that the recent criticism of the War Department was justified and that the American military machine had broken down." Be assured, however, Wilson told Wiseman, that no matter how adverse the public pressure, he would not resist the coordination of Anglo-American arms, even brigading, if the military need arose.[33]

Wilson sounded an ominous note, however, in warning the British not to make transport of the six U.S. divisions conditional upon their serving with the British.[34] On February 4 he made his intentions clearer in a letter to Baker. He accepted Pershing's six-division plan but emphasized that only a "sudden and manifest emergency" should be allowed to "interfere with the building up of a great distinct American force at the front, acting under its own flag and its own officers."[35]

It was thus wishful thinking by the War Cabinet that the six-division plan promised real assistance to the BEF and the creation, even on a temporary basis, of a front line manned by Anglo-Americans. Wilson said as much once he had gotten the British to accelerate the shipment of complete American divisions rather than battalions to Europe. On February 15 he told Lord Reading, as the latter reported to London, that American opinion was "unanimous that it would be a grave error to send American troops under any bargain or understanding with British Government that these should be used to supplement British army instead of for purpose of forming an American army."[36]

Wilson's opposition to the BEF's partial absorption of American forces abroad is certainly understandable. Nationalistic and political considerations alone provide a strong defense of his actions. His continued rejection of close military cooperation with the British, however, has been seen by some historians as a reflection of his preference for multilateral cooperation as opposed to any special Anglo-American military and political alignment.[37] At first glance, Wilson's wartime actions do suggest strong support for international cooperation in military matters. He vigorously backed the creation of the SWC, strongly supported the creation of an inter-Allied General Reserve, and looked with favor upon the creation of a supreme Allied commander-in-chief.[38]

Wilson's support of collective security, however, was more ambivalent than those facts would indicate. Lloyd Ambrosius has demonstrated that he was torn between universalism and unilateralism in his approach to the League of Nations.[39] The same appears true in his reaction to cooperative military efforts. His support for unity of command came easy because he initially saw in it no conflict with American national objectives. Since his field commander in Europe commanded only a phantom force, compared with the other Allied armies, he did not have to subordinate America's military role to a supreme Allied military authority. Wilson also deflected Anglo-French suggestions that the Americans serve as the Allied reserve, favoring instead the formation of an inter-Allied General Reserve, which would not require the armyless Pershing (as it would the French and British commanders-in-chief) to lose control of his reserve divisions.

At this point the Americans apparently had little to lose and much to gain from unity of command. The creation of the SWC served to enhance the American leadership's "western front" posture in the discussions of future Allied military policy while undermining the concept of a special Anglo-American relationship. Bliss, although American arms had played no part yet in the land war, was given a strong voice at the SWC. His participation in Allied military decisions, however, involved potential responsibility and commitments and were bound to have political undertones. Wilson, attempting to maintain America's political independence, artificially separated military and political decisions. He seems to have believed that Allied unity of command, whatever its form, should pertain only to decisions directly related to the American policy of fighting the war in Western Europe. When he came to realize that military operations such as those proposed in the former tsarist empire, although connected by their advocates to the defeat or containment of Germany, had possible political ramifications inimical to American goals, he sought to withhold American cooperation.

Wilson's views on his country's military role continued to be shaped decisively by his ultimate political aims. He proved as ready as any European statesman to put national objectives over those of America's partners in the war. America's military and political policy often spoke the language of unilateralism rather than multilateralism. In this Wilson apparently saw no inconsistency. Unlike Lloyd George and his imperial-minded colleagues in the War Cabinet, his motives in international affairs, at least in his own mind, were to further the interests of humankind, not the interests of a particular country. The British political leaders were no less convinced that their peripheral strategy during the winter of 1917-18 was directed toward the future peace and stability of the world. Unless German expansion in Eurasia could be contained, the national security of the United States as well as Britain would remain imperiled.

It is usually assumed that Lloyd George's and the War Cabinet's "eastern" or indirect strategy was essentially political in nature with little strategical value, as opposed to the "western" strategy of the British high command, which sought the defeat of the Imperial German army. This assumption proves misleading, especially when the precarious military situation of the Allies is viewed in broad perspective. As 1918 began, the British—with one major European ally out of the war and the other two in serious decline—were on the defensive. It was no longer a question of either turning Germany's flank (the "easterner" solution) or the destroying of the German army (the British high command's formula for victory). Germany, which now controlled all of Eastern Europe, Belgium, and a considerable part of northern France, was on the verge of dominating Europe and advancing across Asia, perhaps even threatening India. Allied victory, it was thought, depended upon the still unproven ability of the United States to substitute its military power in the land war in Europe for Britain's fading or lost European allies. Under these circumstances the British had reason to be concerned about their capacity to contain the emerging German-Turkish threat in the East, which was directed more against the national and strategical interest of the British Empire than that any other Allied state. Thwarting German and Turkish imperialistic ambitions rather than expanding the British Empire was at the heart of the War Cabinet's geopolitical strategy. There was an element of desperation in its attempts to implement its peripheral policy, especially in the chaotic situation that existed in the lands of the former tsarist empire.

Following the Bolshevik *coup d'état* on November 7, 1917, the British government had been advised by soldiers on the spot that token military intervention might result in the establishment of a pro-Ally, anti-Bolshevik regime that would keep Russia in the war. Lieutenant General Sir Charles Barter, the head of the British military mission at Russian military headquarters, telegraphed the War Office that the "mere announcement of the landing of foreign troops . . . would bring about the total collapse of the Bolshevists."[40]

The fundamental problems for British advocates of military intervention in Russia were where Allied soldiers could be located for an expeditionary force, and what armed force could be constituted in Russia that would favor the continuation of the war. Lieutenant General Sir George Macdonogh, with an eye toward the Romanian army, which still remained in the war despite Russia's collapse, believed that he had found the answer to both questions. The usually level-headed chief of intelligence on the General Staff submitted a memorandum to Robertson on November 20 that crossed the line into cuckoo land. Macdonogh suggested that General A.M. Kaledin, an anti-Bolshevik Don Cossack leader who expressed loyalty to the Allies, could rescue southern Russia from the clutches of Germany.[41] If an Allied force of "say two American divisions" were able to lend support to Kaledin, Macdonogh wrote, it would be possible to create an army of pro-Ally elements in the East consisting of "500,000 Poles, 400,000 Cossacks, 80,000 Czechs and Slovaks, 300,000 Rumanians, 15,000 Serbians, 105,000 Armenians and 25,000 Georgians, etcetera." In another flight of fantasy, Macdonogh suggested that 575,000 Knights of St. George, storm battalions, volunteers, and loyal elements from the Russian army could also be collected, making an army of an even 2,000,000 men.[42]

On December 3, with the Bolsheviks engaged in armistice negotiations with the Central Powers at Brest-Litovsk, the War Cabinet took a concrete step toward involvement in Russia by deciding to extend financial aid to Kaledin.[43] But money alone was thought unlikely to serve as the impetus for a pro-Allied force in southern Russia. Allied soldiers and supplies were even more essential. On December 7 Robertson advocated landing a "police force" composed of Japanese and perhaps Americans at Vladivostok, Russia's Asiatic port of entry and the terminus of the Trans-Siberian Railway. An important consideration for Robertson was that it might eventually be possible to control this vital railway and open communications with Kaledin's forces.[44]

With momentum building in Paris and London for military as well as financial intervention in Russia to rescue the Allied cause, the British sought to coordinate their policy with that of the French at an Anglo-French conference at the Quai d'Orsay on December 23. The British hoped to maintain their blockade of the Central Powers by denying the enemy access to the food and mineral resources of southern Russia. Important strategical considerations were also at stake. Lord Milner told the French that if Germany and Turkey were given free rein in southern Russia, there would exist no "barrier against the development of a Turanian movement that will extend from Constantinople to China and will provide Germany with a weapon of even greater danger to the peace of the world than the control of the Baghdad railway."[45]

As the British and French at Paris drafted a convention that divided southern Russia into spheres of Allied operations—the British in southeast Russia; the French in Bessarabia, the Crimea, and the Ukraine—the SWC addressed the problem of linking up with national groups who wanted to resist Germany's *Drang nach Osten*. In their Joint Note No. 5, dated December 24, 1917, the permanent military representative advocated the establishment of direct communications with Kaledin either along the Trans-Siberian Railway or through military operations against Turkey.[46]

Increasingly, the Milnerites related southern Russia and the war with Turkey, which had become a British affair, to the collapse of the Russo-Turkish front. Amery, now head of the political branch of the British staff on the Supreme War Council, emphasized the "intimate connection of the South Russian problem with the Turkish problem" in a letter to the prime minister on December 29, 1917. "The control of South Russia is in fact for the Germans the only condition on which they can put Turkey on its legs again, check our advance, and carry out their scheme for linking up the Turks of Asia Minor with the Turkish populations of the Eastern Caucasus, North-Western Persia, and Turkestan in a Pan-Turanian combination which would be a most serious threat to our whole position in the East." Turkey's defeat, Amery argued, could "turn the tables upon the Germans in that part of the world" by establishing direct contact with southern Russia through the Dardanelles.[47]

Although skeptical about British involvement in the confused Russian situation, Lloyd George welcomed any argument that strengthened his case for concentrating on Turkey in 1918. He intended to outflank Robertson and the General Staff by working through Sir Henry Wilson and Amery at Versailles; they now took the approach with the other permanent military representatives, that British military operations against Turkey were intimately connected with the south Russia situation.[48]

Lloyd George also briefly considered placing his ally Smuts, who would report directly to the War Cabinet instead of to the War Office, in charge of all naval and military operations against Turkey.[49] "With Wilson at Versailles & the East delegated to Smuts," Amery gleefully wrote Lloyd George, "I don't think the old gang can give too much trouble—if they do you can deal with them."[50]

Britain's war partners presented almost as great an obstacle to British concentration on Turkey as did Robertson's opposition. After considerable British politicking, the military representatives at Versailles in their Joint Note No. 12, titled "1918 Campaign," approved of a campaign to remove Turkey from the war. The Allied political leaders at a meeting of the SWC, although not without some unpleasant Anglo-French wrangling and opposition from Robertson, then ratified the decision. This success for Lloyd George and the Milnerites was tempered by conditions insisted upon by the French. Britain was expected to maintain its forces on the western front and not divert any of its military resources there to the war against Turkey.

The United States played the bystander during this debate over the advisability of attempting to knock Turkey out of the war in 1918. Since the United States was not at war with Turkey, no direct American involvement in this conflict was requested or expected. Hence Bliss took only a passive part in the discussions and did not affix his signature to Joint Note No. 12.

Standing aside from the Russian situation, however, was not so easy for the Americans. When the British military authorities had first discussed possible Allied military intervention, they included the use of American as well as Japanese soldiers in their calculations.[51] Although President Wilson was hostile to Bolshevism and had initially considered providing secret support to the Cossacks in Southern Russia, he decided on a policy of nonintervention in the emerging civil war in Russia, a position strongly supported by Baker and the General Staff, who opposed diverting any American military resources from the western front.[52] The British War Office consequently turned its attention increasingly toward enlisting Japanese rather than American manpower to further British policy in Russia.

The military authorities exercised their influence primarily through the Russia Committee, an interdepartmental group composed of representatives of the Foreign, War, and Treasury offices. This body had been reluctantly created by the Foreign Office at the beginning of

1918 to develop a common policy for organizing resistance to Germany in Russia. George Russell Clerk, a senior Foreign Office official, issued a warning that the government later ignored to its detriment: "The scanty information which reaches us as to the progress of events from Vladivostock to Jassy is so confused and so constantly shifting that it is almost hopeless to attempt anything like a constructive scheme for establishing our position in South-Eastern Russia, giving Romania the essential support due to her, and denying the wealth of the Ukraine, the Don, the Caucasus, and Siberia to Germany." [53]

In mid-January the Russia Committee ignored this sound advice and produced a proposal involving Japanese intervention, which was already popular with British and French officers in the Supreme War Council at Versailles. To prevent German domination of Russia, it was suggested that a largely Japanese force be deployed some 3,600 miles from Vladivostok along the Trans-Siberian Railway to Cheliabinsk. From this town, just to the east of the Urals, a branch line ran to the edge of Cossack country. [54]

On January 24 the War Cabinet discussed this far-fetched proposal. Representing the military were General Macdonogh and Brigadier General A.W.F. Knox, the British military attaché who had just returned from his post in Russia. These military authorities, along with Milner and Balfour, spoke in favor of the plan. Opposition came from Deputy Foreign Secretary Robert Cecil, Curzon, and Lloyd George. "The proposal now made," Cecil proclaimed, "would probably result in the domination of the Japanese over the whole of Siberia, and would have far-reaching results upon the world's history, as it would make the Japanese a prodigious Power in Asia, including the virtual domination of China." [55] Curzon expressed concern about giving the Japanese a military role that would impinge upon the "racial ascendancy and international prestige" of Europeans. [56] Lloyd George argued that Bolshevism might prove to be a more effective barrier against German expansionism than Japanese intervention. "Any attempt of the Germans to interfere in Russia," he stressed, "would be like an attempt to burgle a plague-house." Although of a mixed mind, the War Cabinet still decided to urge its war partners to support the Japanese takeover of the Trans-Siberian Railway from Vladivostok to Cheliabinsk as a mandatory of the Allies. [57]

By mid-February Balfour began to experience serious second thoughts about the advisability of Japanese intervention. There seemed little likelihood that strong Russian native resistance could be initiated against Germany. Only the French gave their enthusiastic support to armed intervention. The Italians dragged their feet, and President Wilson raised weighty objections, arguing that since the Japanese would not advance as far as West Siberia, they would pose little threat to the Germans; the only effect of their intervention would be to turn the Russians against the Allies.

Wilson's opposition made Balfour pause. The American president, he informed the War Cabinet, would "yield only under the strongest pressure from the Allies, and I feel very reluctant to take any share in exercising this pressure unless we are certain that the Japanese will carry out their allotted role." Balfour was "extremely doubtful" that they would.[58] Another consideration was that Kaledin had committed suicide. By late February the only anti-Bolshevik force in all of European Russia was the Volunteer Army, a small band of three to four thousand men, which had succeeded Kaledin's broken movement. It was no longer "a question of bringing help to the Cossacks by means of Japanese intervention," Balfour told the War Cabinet on February 20, because it had become clear that the Cossacks were no longer "an efficient fighting force."[59]

Despite Balfour's strong reservations, the proponents of Japanese intervention—especially the Milnerites, who were desperate to protect the now exposed British position in Asia—pressed on. On February 21 Sir Henry Wilson, who had just replaced Robertson as CIGS, noted in his diary: "Russia is falling to pieces and I suppose Roumania will follow and then we may lose the Caucasus and must watch Persia."[60] To Milner, the most influential civilian advocate of Japanese intervention in Siberia, it was nonsense to argue as Balfour did that Japanese intervention might drive the Bolsheviks into the waiting arms of Germany. He had written off northern Russia and believed that the Bolsheviks were puppets of Berlin. "In the future Russia [will] have a German-controlled Government at Petrograd, either under the Bolsheviks or a pro-German Czar," he told the War Cabinet. Concerned about the prospect that the Germans might one day dominate Siberia if no country stepped in to stop them, he desired rather than feared Japanese domination of Siberia as a counterweight to German influence. Although Lloyd George was absent, the War Cabinet on February 25 decided to try once again to gain President Wilson's support for Japanese intervention.[61] British advocates of the plan, however, dared not mention their true fears to Wilson: the possible future German threat to India. "It would be most unfortunate if the idea prevailed here that we are encouraging Japanese occupation of Siberia in order to protect our own interests in India," Wiseman cautioned from Washington.[62]

Despite the War Cabinet's February 25 decision, which was subject to the prime minister's concurrence, the government remained badly divided on the question of Japanese intervention. Smuts, whom Lloyd George had sent to the Palestine theater to ensure that the General Staff did not sabotage British offensive plans there, raised powerful objections to Japanese intervention in Siberia when he returned to London. "I profoundly distrust Japan," he wrote the prime minister, "whose attitude leads me to think that she either has or is contemplating an understanding with Germany; and in that case her position in Siberia at our invitation would be the worst possible business for us."[63]

Lloyd George, probably believing that President Wilson would continue to resist, made no move to reverse the War Cabinet's decision. Imagine his surprise when on March 4 Balfour made the dramatic announcement to the War Cabinet that "the United States [has] agreed to Japanese intervention in Siberia."[64] Wilson's apparent volte-face could not have come at a better time for the British leaders concerned with the Empire's vulnerable Asian position. On the previous day the Bolsheviks had signed the Treaty of Brest-Litovsk. A German peace treaty with Romania, which would place the Germans above the Black Sea, seemed certain to follow.

Panic prevailed among the Empire-minded statesmen. "I am seriously concerned about the Eastern front," Milner wrote Sir Henry Wilson. "Russia has gone & we must set up a barrier somewhere to stop the Bolshevik flood, carrying German influence with it, or paving the way first, from sweeping right over Asia. . . . We have to draw a line from the Persian Gulf to the Trans-Siberian—nearer west or further east as we best can."[65] On March 8 Curzon expressed concern in the War Cabinet about a Romanian peace: "Germany would be supreme on the Black Sea, and also in Turkish territory in this part of the world, with possibilities of penetration into Persia and through Turkestan towards India." Prompted by Balfour, the concerned civilians requested a study from the General Staff on Berlin's prospects of sending troops across the Black Sea from Odessa to Batum and then by rail to Baku on the Caspian.[66]

Just as the need for Allied intervention in Russia had never seemed greater from an imperial perspective, Wilson again disappointed the British. Lord Reading cabled from Washington: "United States Government have never been favourable to policy of intervention. The most they said was that they had no objection to His Majesty's Government making request to Japanese Government."[67]

Wilson's renewed opposition, and the inability of London to exact a commitment from Tokyo to advance beyond eastern Siberia, for the moment frustrated the interventionists, who realized that Britain could not afford to alienate the American president. "There was a possibility of a rift on a matter of cardinal policy between ourselves and the United States of America, to secure which was one of the aims of German policy," it was noted in the War Cabinet minutes. "Japan in any case would not go far West, as she had ceased to feel confident that her Allies were on the winning side."[68]

If not for the important imperial strategical considerations being stressed by the Milnerites and the military authorities, the War Cabinet would probably have abandoned the rash and impractical plan of drawing a line with Japanese soldiers to limit German influence in the East. Sir Henry Wilson's domination of the General Staff strengthened the interventionists. The choice of the Milnerites, he believed that the drive for world dominance might eventually place Germany on Russia's Pacific coast. The British response, he argued, "must be to establish an effective barrier to German progress eastwards." [69] As CIGS, Wilson gave free rein to the military professionals who were considered experts on the Russian situation: Knox, Major General F.C. Poole, who had served as chief of the British artillery mission with the Russian army, and Captain Alex Proctor, another experienced Russian hand. If the attempt to gain Japanese intervention failed, Knox argued in appreciations for the War Cabinet, Britain must be prepared to accept "the definite passing of all European Russia, Caucasia, Northern Persia, Western Siberia and Turkestan into Germany's political and economic sphere of influence." [70]

These officers joined General Wilson in developing plans to check Germany in Russia and to protect British imperial interests. The cornerstone of their plans continued to be a Japanese advance along the Trans-Siberian Railway to the Urals. A Japanese presence on the eastern border of European Russia supposedly would place Siberia under the control of the Allies and provide shelter for anti-Bolshevik elements. To the south, the War Office also wanted the Nipponese to cross the Urals and advance to Samara on the Volga, thereby protecting railway communications to the Afghan frontier from the northwest. A benefit of encouraging the Japanese, the military argued, was that they would be drawn into full membership in the league against Germany; otherwise, the military feared that Japan might make an alliance with Germany to exploit Asiatic Russia. While Siberia and Samara were being occupied by Japanese forces, the western Allies would secure control of the northern ports of Archangel and Murmansk, from which they could exercise influence in northern Russia and possibly link up with the Japanese at Volgoda, the junction of the Trans-Siberian Railway. In the Caspian area, the government was advised by General Wilson to conduct "an energetic policy on [the] Persian frontier, so as to open the road to the Caucasus." [71]

The Japanese were contemplating intervention, but only to fulfill their own imperialistic designs; they were as unlikely to prop up the British position in Asia as were the Americans. President Wilson recognized this, along with the unrealistic nature of attempting to erect a new eastern front with Japanese or any other Allied soldiers. The British, however, clung to the hope that Wilson could, if carefully handled, be persuaded to support their plans in Russia. As Wiseman had reported, "President Wilson may be led but certainly not driven." [72]

This British preoccupation with events in the East, on the eve of the titanic German effort to impose a peace on the Allies by victory in Western Europe, makes strange reading. As the field-gray German divisions deployed for their massive assault on the British front, the War Cabinet's attention was fixed on such troubling omens as the German occupation of Kiev on March 16 and a report that Austrian prisoners had shown up in northeastern Persia.

On March 20, the day before the Germans attacked, the prime minister received a "very anxious" letter from Milner. "Persia, wh. we are to discuss to-morrow, is *only an incident*. The question is really very much larger than that. We have a new campaign, wh. really extends from the Mediterranean shore of Palestine to the frontier of India. . . . Whether or not Japan takes on Northern Asia—I doubt her doing it— we alone have got to keep Southern Asia, and we are lucky if our line only extends from the Mediterranean to the Caspian & does not have to double back from the Caspian to the Himalayas. Note that, according to one report, some Austrian prisoners have already turned up near Meshed in North-*Eastern* Persia! That shows what comes of the collapse of the Power, wh. used to cover our whole Asian flank. . . . How right was the instinct, wh. led you all along to attach so much importance to the Eastern campaigns & not to listen to our only strategists, who could see nothing but the Western front. If it were not for the position we have won in Mesopotamia & Palestine & the great strength we have developed on that side, the outlook would be black indeed." [73]

Just before dawn broke on March 21, some 6,000 German big guns unleashed their torrent of steel and poison gas against the British line west of St. Quentin. As the British and Germans locked in a fierce battle that would not be equaled until May 10, 1940, when Hitler invaded France, Belgium, and Holland, the War Cabinet continued to focus on Germany's eastern threat. With Sir Henry suggesting that there was the "possibility" that the German attack might constitute only a "big raid or demonstration," the civilians at their regular midday meeting discussed Siberia and Persia. If the Germans were to gain control of Siberia, General Wilson ominously warned, "their influence would extend south into Turkestan, and our whole position in India would be imperilled." It was part of the same problem as the danger to Persia. It was a question of "pulling Siberia out the wreck, in order to save India." Balfour suggested violating the neutrality of Persia by sending a small force of some 1,300 men with armored cars into that vital area. [74]

The War Cabinet decided to establish the Eastern or Vigilance

Committee, "ready to warn the War Cabinet and furnish advice on the Eastern area of operations." Curzon was asked to chair this committee, which included Balfour, Smuts, and Sir Henry Wilson.[75]

Prior to the colossal German drive against the BEF, the British had failed to gain President Wilson's support for their plans to maintain their position in France with American manpower. Nor was the War Cabinet successful in gaining American involvement in Russia to shore up Britain's deteriorating position in Asia, which had been made vulnerable by the collapse of the eastern front from the Baltic to the Black and Caspian seas. President Wilson had seemed ready to offer a helping hand during negotiations over the utilization of American soldiers on the British front (which might give the British a freer hand on the periphery) and Japanese intervention in Siberia, but in the end he had withheld American cooperation. More dependent than ever on American good will and power, the British feared to press him hard, especially if their pressure seemed designed to protect Britain's overseas possessions.

Saving the alliance from defeat in Western Europe, however, was another matter. The great German threat provided the British with a powerful argument for using American manpower on the British front and in Russia. During the next few months, with Berlin coming dangerously close to winning a German peace on the battlefield, the Americans no less than the British confronted their deepest military crisis of the war.

9

The Western Front Imperiled

General Erich Ludendorff, the German army's de facto commander, rejected a defensive policy designed to achieve a negotiated peace. Instead, he gambled on victory in Western Europe in 1918 through battles of annihilation against the Anglo-French forces. His all-or-nothing strategy depended upon delivering a knock-out blow before the Americans arrived in sufficient strength to change the balance of forces decisively in favor of the Entente. The BEF was his initial target.

On March 21, called by Hankey "one of the decisive moments of the world's history,"[1] the main German blow fell on General Sir Hubert Gough's Fifth Army, which had been weakened by continuous fighting in the Flanders quagmire. British defenses were beached in two places, and attempts to plug the gaps failed. The Fifth Army started to disintegrate. On the first day of the battle, Haig requested three French divisions as reinforcements. On the following day he issued a panic-stricken plea for twenty. Yet the French initially responded by withholding their forces from the great battle. By Saturday, March 23, the shape of the military catastrophe was becoming clear to the civilians in London.

Lloyd George, who had spent the night at his home in Walton Heath, rushed back to London. "The news is very bad. I fear it means disaster," he told his newspaper friend Lord Riddell.[2] Canceling a meeting of the War Cabinet, he took charge in the War Office, seeking to locate and send every available rifleman to France. At 4:00 P.M. the other members of the War Cabinet joined him to review the military situation. The deputy director of military operations on the General Staff, Walter Kirke, who had just arrived by plane from Haig's head-quarters, presented a report that mirrored the approaching gloom of a March evening in London. The British had been thrown back twelve miles, lost some 40,000 men, and abandoned not less than 600 guns. After hearing Kirke's report, General Wilson spoke bluntly: The British army was now under attack by "a large proportion of the German Army" and was "menaced with a possible attack by the whole."[3]

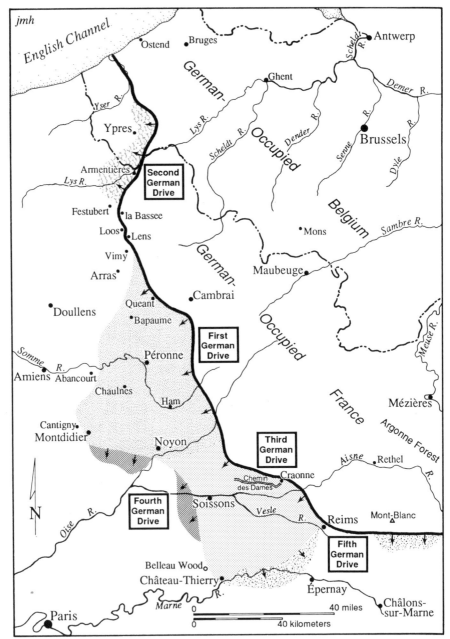

Map 2. Five German Offensives, March 21 – July 17, 1918

Lloyd George's plan of conserving British manpower by gradually shifting the burden of the fighting to the United States lay in ruins. As Robertson had forecast, Germany now confronted the British with a life-or-death struggle on the western front. There no longer seemed any way of preserving Britain's staying power with a prudent manpower policy that protected industry and maintained morale on the home front.

In time, British forces could be transferred from other theaters— Italy, Palestine, perhaps even Mesopotamia—but Haig needed reinforcements immediately. All available men in uniform in Britain were rushed across the Channel. There were 88,000 members of the BEF on leave. An additional 50,000 trained boys, over eighteen and a half but under nineteen years of age, could be sent into combat earlier than previous practice had permitted. More soldiers could be found by diverting drafts for other theaters and advancing the orders of drafts to go overseas. In all, the War Cabinet discovered 170,000 men who could be sent to Haig within the next three weeks.[4]

But the vast majority of these reinforcements were not new men to add to Haig's existing or anticipated numbers. They were already either a part of Haig's establishment (those on leave) or boys who would soon have been sent to join the BEF anyway.

On March 25 the War Cabinet held one of its most painful meetings of the war. Extraordinary suggestions were advanced to find additional soldiers. The eyesight test for recruits could be modified. Conscientious objectors could be used as non-combatant workers behind the front. Men released from the Territorials "on compassionate grounds" might be recalled, along with men who had been discharged because of wounds. Coal miners, munitions workers, and even ministers of religion were considered as possible recruits.[5] Many of these measures were impractical, politically dangerous, or potentially ruinous to the economy. "We might almost as well recruit Germans," H.E. Duke, the chief secretary for Ireland, exclaimed when the proposal was made to impose conscription on rebellious Ireland.[6]

These manpower discussions provide convincing evidence that no "secret army" existed in Britain. The French had long believed—and never missed an opportunity to tell the Americans—that the British were hoarding vast numbers of soldiers at home. It is true that Lloyd George's government, believing that the war would go into 1919 and perhaps beyond, had denied Haig the number of draftees he demanded. But Lloyd George and his civilian colleagues were not responsible for withholding men already in uniform from the BEF.

As London agonized over manpower, Ludendorff, concentrating seventy-one divisions against twenty-six British divisions, piled on the pressure. The Fifth Army melted away. It could "no longer be regarded as a fighting unit," Sir Henry Wilson told the War Cabinet on March 27. He even doubted whether any of the corps in this army could be considered fighting units.[7] The Fifth Army's destruction constituted the BEF's worst defeat of the war, a setback even more alarming than its panicky retreat in 1914 after the Battle of Mons.

The British military and political leadership, however, believed that the situation on the Continent could be saved. Lord French, the commander-in-chief of the Home Forces, told the War Cabinet that it was too soon to consider abandoning the French army and retreating to the Channel ports, a desperate act that would almost certainly destroy the Anglo-French alignment and signify defeat in Europe.[8] While Lord French spoke with guarded optimism in London, an important step was taken at Doullens to strengthen the cohesiveness of the anti-German coalition. On March 26 Ferdinand Foch was granted "coordinating" power over the Anglo-French armies on the western front.

Although the Doullens agreement made no mention of Pershing's forces, the American field commander visited Foch's headquarters on March 28 and assured him of his support: "Infantry, artillery, aviation, all that we have are yours; use them as you wish. More will come, in numbers equal to requirements."[9] Within the week the AEF was officially placed under Foch's command through an inter-Allied resolution at Beauvais that extended Foch's control to strategy on the western front. Pershing wanted it that way. "I think this resolution should include the American Army," he asserted at the Beauvais Conference on April 3. Intending to create an independent army at his first opportunity, Pershing proclaimed: "The arrangement is to be in force, as I understand it, from now on, and the American Army will soon be ready to function as such and should be included as an entity like the British and French armies."[10]

Pershing supported his words with an offer to put all four of his available divisions into the line as a corps. Such a deployment, of course, would constitute a giant step toward creating an independent American army. It would also mean turning over a section of the French front to inexperienced soldiers. For this reason Pétain rejected the offer. Although Pershing's best division, the "Big Red One," was moved from Lorraine to Picardy, no American combat units were committed to stopping the first German offensive. Two American engineer companies working on railways behind the British front, however, found themselves in the path of the German advance and suffered seventy-nine casualties.

Pershing's dramatic "all that we have" pledge to Foch actually had little practical value. The Americans had no planes or artillery of their own to commit to battle, only men. Lloyd George hoped that the tightening of the anti-German alignment at Doullens and Beauvais, in combination with the dire military situation, would force Washington to accept brigading with British and French divisions. Milner, fresh from the Doullens Conference, wrote him in no uncertain terms that even if the German drive stalled, other attacks would follow: "If they do not break us now, they will break us later, unless we can keep on sending substantial reinforcements." All too aware of Pershing's iron determination to create an independent army, Milner believed that "it must be a year at least before the Americans can make their weight felt."[11]

Lloyd George thought that more British soldiers must be found for Haig, but he rejected Milner's pessimistic view of American assistance in 1918. He was much encouraged by two recent events. First, Bliss on March 27 had gone against Pershing's wishes and joined the other permanent military representatives at Versailles in approving Joint Note No. 18, which asked Wilson to ship only infantry and machine gun units during the present emergency.[12] Second, news from America suggested that the United States, shocked by the force of the German assault, now recognized that the Entente—especially Britain—was "standing between her and German militarism," according to Lord Reading. Americans "realized as it were in a flash their own military shortcomings and the time they have lost since they entered the war. This has already produced an outburst in the Press and Congress which naturally enough takes the form of an attack on the Administration."[13] Believing that Wilson was in a vulnerable political position, Lloyd George planned to press him hard on the issue of brigading. If he got his way, Pershing would be forced to suspend building his army, and most of the American troops arriving in Europe during the next three or four months would serve with the French and especially British armies.[14] To outflank Pershing, Lloyd George thought that he had the backing of Baker, who was on an inspection tour of the western front, and the Allied military advisers (which included Bliss) at Versailles.[15]

Wilson was surprised and perplexed by the powerful German offensive and the collapse of the western front at the juncture of the British and French armies. As late as February he had clung to the hope that the peace factions in the Central Powers would triumph over the war elements and make possible general peace negotiations based on his liberal war aims. Including the Central Powers in the making of a new world order might serve to moderate Allied war objectives. War-weary Austria-Hungary appeared especially vulnerable to his liberal diplomacy. He had been furious with the Entente leaders when they had resoundingly rejected peace discussions with an unhumbled Berlin and Vienna during a meeting of the SWC in early February. "There is infinite stupidity in action of this sort. It stiffens every element of hatred and belligerency in the Central Powers and plays directly into the hands of their military parties," he had written his secretary of state. "These people have a genius for making blunders of the most serious kind and neutralizing each thing that we do. Do you think that anything can be done to hold them off making fools of themselves again and again?"[16]

In British eyes, Wilson—who in Curzon's words, "aspires to become the great figure in the peace negotiations"—was the loose cannon.[17] London had been exploring peace feelers from Vienna. As opposed to Wilson, who sought general peace *pourparlers*, the War Cabinet sought a separate peace with Austria-Hungary in order to isolate Germany. On March 1 the British leadership spoke bluntly about its differences with Wilson. The prime minister expressed apprehension that the president, having failed as a war leader to mobilize his country effectively, "might want to end the war, and might agree to conditions that we could not accept." Speaking for the Dominions, Smuts warned against "entrusting our interests to the United States."[18] These discussions made it clear that the British were adamantly opposed to allowing Wilson to define their interests in Europe or elsewhere. In Hankey's words, it was "preposterous" to let Wilson dominate peace discussion with Vienna because "we have all at stake; Wilson very little."[19]

The massive German attack in March ended all talk of a negotiated peace. The future of Europe and perhaps even of the world order was being decided in the trenches of France and Flanders. The British told President Wilson that they were "engaged in what may well prove to be [the] decisive battle of [the] war."[20] That Wilson grasped the danger posed to American interests (although it must be noted that he stressed economic rather than strategic considerations) is suggested by a comment he made to Edward Hurley, the new tsar of American shipping: "Unless we send over every man possible to support the Allies in their present desperate condition, a situation may develop which would require us to pay for the entire cost of the war to the Central Powers."[21]

Domestic criticism of his war leadership and the prospect of a German victory forced Wilson to devote greater attention to military affairs in Europe and to broaden his circle of advisers on military questions. With the Cabinet's time being devoted more and more to jokes, storytelling, and insignificant matters, the president in March created an informal war cabinet or war council which met separately on Wednesday mornings. Chaired by Wilson, this inner committee had a fluctuating membership. Frequent participants were Baker, Daniels, and Secretary of the Treasury William Gibbs McAdoo. Heads of the primary war agencies were also included in these discussions, which focused primarily on mobilizing the economy for war but also included questions of military cooperation with the Allies.[22]

Confronted with critical inter-Allied matters such as amalgamation, shipping, and military intervention in Russia, Wilson also regularly looked to soldiers for help. He had always worked hand in glove with Baker, with whom he met almost daily; he now included Bliss and Peyton C. March, Pershing's former chief of artillery, who had become chief of staff on March 4, 1918, among his intimate advisers. March's elevation to the leadership level brought needed stability to that body and enhanced its influence on national policy. Since April 6, 1917, Scott, Bliss, and Major General John Biddle had been involved in an astonishing merry-go-round: during the first eleven months of American belligerency, these three men had been rotated as chief of staff no less than seven times. It is small wonder that the General Staff remained in the background during the formative phase of America's extra-Continental commitment. Wilson respected March's straightforward and almost always sensible advice. The president also valued the frequent and comprehensive assessments of inter-Allied politics and military matters which Bliss forwarded from Versailles. Viewing Bliss as "remarkable" and a "real thinking man,"[23] Wilson frequently issued instructions based on specific and minor details contained in these reports.[24]

The president's now intimate involvement in such questions as shipping did not mean that he was prepared to march in step with British plans to save the military situation. When Lloyd George urged him to abandon Pershing's six-division plan in favor of transporting infantry battalions to serve with Allied military formations, he temporized and looked for advice from Bliss and Pershing, who were close to the sound of the cannons. But no matter what their counsel, he was most reluctant to accept amalgamation, which would delay the creation of an American army, undermine America's political influence, and give ammunition to those who were attacking his war leadership.[25]

As the British intensified their pressure, his irritation mounted. On March 27, Lord Reading, appearing at the Lotos Club in New York, delivered a message to the American people from the prime minister. Lloyd George's words echoed those spoken earlier to the American military attaché by authorities in the British War Office: "For God's sake, get your men over!"[26] Wilson reacted with fury, believing that he was being blamed for the destruction of the Fifth Army. It was intolerable that Lloyd George should speak directly to the American public, expressing sentiments that seemed to pass judgment on their president. Momentarily he thought of having Reading recalled. On March

28 he acidly told the British ambassador, as Reading reported to Lloyd George, that there "was no need to press these matters upon him as he was only anxious to do all he could."[27]

London's response was to escalate its demands. The British government planned to draft an additional 400,000 or 500,000 men, but these new recruits could not be trained for at least four months. Hence, Lloyd George asked Wilson for 120,000 men a month for the next four months to be brigaded with British divisions.[28] It was suggested within the War Cabinet that a special meeting of the SWC be called to pressure Wilson "should there be any reluctance on the part of the American Government to comply with the proposal put forward."[29]

The carrot as well as the stick was used to persuade Wilson. Wiseman cautioned London: "Expediency demands that we should help the President in order that he will help us."[30] When House suggested to Reading that London could bolster the president in his political difficulties by praising American contributions to the Allied cause, Lloyd George immediately issued a public statement on April 1, 1918, which asserted that Wilson had done "everything possible to assist the Allies" and had "left nothing undone which could contribute thereto."[31]

Wilson welcomed these generous words of praise and believed that he had neutralized the unpredictable and volatile Lloyd George, who he had feared might attempt to make him the scapegoat for recent German successes. But he was uncomfortable with the heavy responsibility for the success or failure of the Allied cause that the urgent British requests for help placed upon him. Clinging to his prebelligerent role of the honest broker, he had hitherto maintained his distance from his war partners. The powerful German attack—which followed on the heels of Berlin's annexationist Treaty of Brest-Litovsk with Russia—was now forcing his hand. To save the alliance, he was under intense pressure to make military and perhaps even political decisions that threatened to impinge upon American independence. A nagging thought was that London's assessment of the conflict was more nearly right than his own. An objective reading of the facts indicated that the British view of a predatory Germany was correct.

On April 1 Wiseman recorded a revealing statement from the president: "If then the Allies became exhausted, what should we do? He supposed we should have to make a compromise-peace, but we could not deceive ourselves—it would be a German peace, and mean in effect a German victory. The Germans would no doubt be prepared to deal generously with France and Belgium, and other questions, providing she was allowed practically a free-hand in Russia. . . . He could not help being aware (he said) of the position of America. She was now supplying a large part of the material support of the war, and she was also the potential military factor. It meant, he said, that the decision as to whether the war should continue would rest in his hands. It was, he said, a terrible responsibility, and a question which he certainly would not regard from solely an American point of view: he must consider it also from the point of view of the Allies and indeed the whole world."[32]

On April 6, the first anniversary of the American entry into the war, Wilson gave public expression to his fears of German world domination. Before a large, enthusiastic audience he delivered his strongest attack yet on German expansionism. "Their purpose is undoubtedly to make all the Slavic peoples, all the free and ambitious nations of the Baltic peninsula, all the lands that Turkey has dominated and misruled, subject to their will and ambition and build upon that dominion an empire of force upon which they fancy that they can then erect an empire of gain and commercial supremacy,—an empire as hostile to the Americas as to the Europe which it will overawe,—an empire which will ultimately master Persia, India, and the peoples of the Far East."[33]

Wilson's emphasis on Germany's eastern ambitions encouraged London to believe that he might now cooperate with British efforts to contain German influence in northern Russia and elsewhere in the East. On April 12 the War Cabinet asked the General Staff and Foreign Office to draft a strategic appreciation for Wilson that treated Europe and Asia as a single front. With some trepidation, the War Cabinet decided that this communication should express in direct language the British concern about Germany's threat to their imperial position.[34]

Still, it was the hope of Wilson's cooperation on the question of amalgamation rather than American assistance in containing Germany in the East that remained uppermost on the minds of the British in April. American combat deaths after one year in the war equaled 163; British casualties from March 21 to April 7, 1918, excluding the sick, were 115,868.[35] Not surprisingly, the British believed that the United States should do more—no, had to do more. Haig had written Lord Derby on April 7 that "in the absence of reinforcements, which I understand do not exist," the situation would "become critical unless American troops fit for immediate incorporation in my Divisions arrive in France in the meantime."[36]

As bleak as Haig's position appeared, it was about to become even more tenuous. Ludendorff, having seen his first drive stall in late March, shifted his attention to the north of the British front to the Ypres salient. On April 9-10 twenty-seven German divisions tore a gap in the British line in Flanders and advanced along a twenty-four-mile front. This German success disturbed the British leadership even more than the earlier German breakthrough at the Anglo-French juncture.

Vital rail communications and perhaps even the Channel ports were endangered.[37] Every line of the assessment of the situation prepared by the head of intelligence on the British General Staff spoke the language of panic. "Germany is endeavoring to destroy the British Army and decide the war by concentrating all her available reserves against the British front," Macdonogh wrote. Unless France and the United States sent massive reinforcements and most of the British troops were withdrawn from the periphery, Britain was faced with "decisive defeat."[38]

There was an unjustified though understandable tendency to assign much of the blame for this rout in progress to the American leadership, especially Wilson. On several previous occasions the president had seemed ready to accept amalgamation, the only realistic method of providing immediate American relief, but he had always stopped short. Lloyd George feared that Wilson would disappoint again. "We have so often had large promises in past which have invariably been falsified in result that I am sincerely apprehensive that this last undertaking may not be carried out in actual practice," he cabled Reading.[39]

The British this time went to the limit in pressuring Wilson, stressing that the Entente's survival depended upon immediate American reinforcements. Reading was a frequent and increasingly unwelcome visitor at the White House. His Lotos Club speech had put him on thin ice with the president. Now Lloyd George ordered him "to step outside his ambassadorial functions and to satisfy himself that every possible step is being taken to fulfil the President's pledge."[40] The "pledge" that Lloyd George believed Reading had extracted from the president on March 30 was a commitment to send to France, for brigading, 120,000 infantry a month for the next four months. Wilson had indeed accepted the "principle" of brigading, but he had no intention of making this commitment open ended.[41] The number of troops actually brigaded was to be left to the American military leadership in Europe. Although London sought to use President Wilson's attempts to reassure Lord Reading as a stick with which to beat the AEF's leadership into line, its pressure tactics were futile, for Pershing's operations section believed that acceptance of the British position would destroy "any hope of forming even a single army corps this year, if indeed it does not end all hope of seeing an American army in this war."[42]

As the initial German offensive of March 21 ground to a halt, Wilson began to retreat even from his qualified commitment to brigading. He had March cable Bliss that he had made no specific agreement with the British; in response to the SWC resolution he had only agreed to "send troops over as fast as we could make them ready and find transportation for them. That was all."[43] In Wilson's view, then, neither Pershing's theatrical promise of "all that we have" nor American cooperation with Joint Note No. 18 constituted an American commitment to parceling out the newly arrived American units to the Allied forces. Indeed, that was very much Pershing's position as well, as the British were all too aware.

At the Beauvais Conference on April 3, where Foch's authority was extended to the "strategic direction of military operations" of the Allied forces, including the Americans, Pershing had resisted any form of amalgamation in preference for building an American army. "The man's an ass. I think—he doesn't mean business—what Bliss calls the God-damned American programme is going to f—— up the whole show," was the way Major General Sir Charles Sackville-West, the Britain's permanent military representative at Versailles, expressed the British military's rage over Pershing's intransigence.[44]

America's continued hedging on amalgamation, especially when the new German offensive on April 9-10 renewed the prospect that the BEF faced annihilation unless doughboys served as its reserve, provoked identical fury (though not expressed in such earthy terms) in London. The War Cabinet rejected the suggestion that the House of Commons be asked to pass a resolution of thanks for President Wilson's cooperation, and Lloyd George fired off another cable to Reading which pointedly noted that building an independent American army must be subordinated to meeting the present military crisis.[45]

To his shock, Reading found that Wilson, who believed the British had lost their nerve and resented their pressure tactics, was unwilling to see him at first. He did eventually meet with the British ambassador, but he was extremely reticent and refused to make any commitments until he had conferred with Baker, who was en route home from Europe. Such a defensive and cool reception convinced Reading that his government had pushed the president too far."I beg of you not to regard this report as indicating a change of view of President," he reported to London.[46] The dynamic and irrepressible Lloyd George was unconvinced. He furnished more ammunition to Reading to use in the forthcoming discussions with Wilson and Baker. His message was direct: "We can do no more than we have done. It rests with America to win or lose the decisive battle of the war."[47]

Differing perspectives had plunged Anglo-American relations to their worst depths since December 1916. The British demanded that America forgo an independent military role for the near future. If it did not and the war were lost, the responsibility would rest with Washington. Wilson was naturally loath to accept the British position. His irritation knew no bounds. He exploded, "[I] fear I will come out of the war hating [the] English."[48]

On April 19 Wilson canceled a Cabinet meeting to confer with Baker, who had just returned from Europe. The outcome of their discussions has been rightly characterized as a "masterpiece of studied ambiguity."[49] The American response was handed to Reading on the evening of April 19 and received in London on April 21.[50] Although this much qualified document appeared to support amalgamation, its real intent, as Baker wrote Pershing on April 29, was to retain American freedom of action and to avoid a "definite and obligatory promise as will permit representatives of the British Government to feel that they have a right to watch what we do and sit in judgment on our action."[51] This sentiment, surely as much Wilson's as Baker's, was intended to be the last word on the subject. House informed the War Cabinet through Reading that the American position "should be accepted, not only without raising any objection, but also without having any in mind."[52]

At this point the tense Anglo-American discussions of amalgamation took another twist. Pershing had been conducting his own negotiations in London with Sir Henry Wilson and Milner, who had just replaced Derby as secretary of state for war. The resulting London Agreement of April 24 represented a return to Pershing's six-division plan, the major differences being that only the infantry and machine gun units of six divisions were to be shipped and that these doughboys could be used for combat as well as for training in the British sector. A decisive moment for the British in these negotiations occurred when Pershing implied on April 22 that the war would be won with "an American army fighting side by side with the British" on the Flanders front.[53]

There were now two understandings, the London Agreement of April 24 and the so-called Baker-Reading understanding of April 21. Pershing naturally preferred his arrangement with Milner, which gave him more freedom of action, limited the American commitment to ship combat elements to one month instead of four, and generally impinged less on the creation of an independent American fighting force. In opposition to his civilian superiors in Washington, Pershing stood by the London Agreement at a Supreme War Council meeting on May 1 at Abbeville.

Believing that the French had a virtual monopoly on American troops, Clemenceau was enraged when he learned that the London Agreement apparently gave the British control of the American infantry being shipped in May. Neither his government nor the new Allied supreme commander had been consulted. Foch's command was not "a mere decoration," he thundered at the Abbeville meeting. If the British got 120,000 Yanks in May, the French must get their 120,000 in June.

As the British and French squabbled over the division of American manpower, Pershing erupted. Surely his comrades-in-arms were not saying that "the American Army is to be entirely at the disposal of the French and British commands." From that point on, the discussions rapidly went downhill. When Foch asked Pershing if he were prepared to see the French forced behind the Loire, the grim-faced American responded: "Yes, I am willing to take the risk. Moreover, the time may come when the American Army will have to stand the brunt of this war, and it is not wise to fritter away our resources in this manner." The meeting concluded when Pershing pounded the table with his fist, declaring, "Gentlemen, I have thought this program over very deliberately and will not be coerced." [54]

On the following day, with the Allies threatening to go over his head directly to Wilson, Pershing retreated but not by much. He agreed to accept the extension of the London Agreement into June but no further. The resulting Abbeville Agreement provided for British shipping of a minimum of 130,000 American infantry and machine gun units in May to serve with Haig, and 150,000 in June for service with either the British or French. In return for this commitment, Pershing got the SWC's formal approval for the creation of an independent American arm. [55]

A puzzling aspect of this whole episode is that Lloyd George initially kept the War Cabinet in the dark about the London Agreement. The ministers were thunderstruck when they learned that the Baker-Reading understanding of April 21 had been abandoned. By their calculations the London Agreement provided the infantry-starved BEF with only 72,000 combat troops for its immediate use. Moreover, by emphasizing American divisions rather than battalions to serve with the British, Pershing had undermined British efforts to revive their forces with American manpower. Two weeks earlier, for example, the War Cabinet had discussed using American manpower to restore shattered British divisions and perhaps then exchanging these divisions for British divisions in Italy. Now, the ministers pondered, how could Lloyd George, who had practiced brinkmanship in pressing Wilson to accept amalgamation, accept such a half-loaf? On the other side of the Atlantic, Reading was equally "mystified and disturbed." [56]

When he returned from Abbeville, the prime minister gave his explanation, which was, in a word, Pershing. Lloyd George probably believed that renewed pressure on Washington to overcome its field commander's intransigence would do more harm than good. Pershing's so-called divisional program still seemed to provide the British front with tens of thousands of doughboys and, just as important, the prospect of joint Anglo-American operations. Pershing had told Lloyd George that he would supply 170,000 (instead of 120,000) infantry and machine gunners in June if the British found the necessary shipping. [57]

Meanwhile, in Washington, Wilson and Baker assessed the results of Abbeville. Baker, encouraged by Pershing to believe that the Abbeville solution represented a true meeting of the minds of the Allies rather than capitulation to his intransigence, expressed delight in an agreement "which relieves us from any possible embarrassment due to a misunderstanding of our execution of the resolution [Joint Note No. 18] of the Permanent Military Representatives at Versailles." Wilson, too, thought the "agreement entirely satisfactory." The president was especially relieved that this SWC decision would, or so he believed, "dispose of further indefinite discussions of the particular views of any single government."[58] He meant Lloyd George's unilateral appeals for British utilization of American soldiers.

The prime minister returned from Abbeville to find his war leadership under serious assault in the press and by a combination of Asquith's supporters and right-wingers led by Sir Edward Carson. The catalyst for this political crisis was the publication of a sensational letter by Major General Frederick B. Maurice, the director of military operations on the General Staff. Central to Maurice's accusations was the damaging charge that Lloyd George, having failed to maintain the BEF's effectives, had misinformed Parliament about the strength of Haig's forces prior to March 21, wrongly claiming that the BEF was stronger in January 1918 than it had been a year earlier.[59]

Maurice's letter threatened to destroy Lloyd George's coalition ministry. The climax came when the Welshman defended himself brilliantly, though not always truthfully, in the House of Commons.[60] "I have never seen such a complete collapse as Asquith's yesterday," one M.P. commented. "You couldn't find him with a magnifying glass."[61] Lloyd George's parliamentary triumph secured his political position for the rest of the war, but his rhetorical genius did not solve the BEF's shortage of infantry. Even Clemenceau had come to realize that the British were telling the truth about their manpower difficulties. There was no large secret reserve being held back in Britain.[62]

On May 9, the day that the prime minister defended his conduct of the war in Parliament, Milner informed the War Cabinet that the BEF had suffered 310,000 casualties (including 130,000 missing in action) since March 21.[63] French casualties during this period were estimated at 90,000. Sir Henry Wilson believed that the first two German attacks on the British front would soon be followed by a third, with disastrous consequences. With nine divisions already knocked out, the CIGS predicted that Haig's effective divisions might be reduced to about half of what they had been on the eve of the German attack on March 21.[64] The dramatically increased flow of Americans across the Atlantic offered Haig his only realistic hope of immediate relief—that is, if Pershing gave his genuine cooperation to the training and *service* of Yanks with the BEF.

Lloyd George exploited his politial triumph to increase his control over strategy and military questions. He had replaced Robertson with the more malleable Wilson as CIGS. Lord Derby, the soldiers' friend, had also been cast aside; Milner replaced him as head of the War Office. The prime minister now consolidated his position by creating the so-called "X" Committee, composed of himself, Milner, Sir Henry Wilson, Hankey, and (after the first two meetings) the imperialist braintruster Leo Amery. Officially, Hankey and Amery were secretaries, but they both enjoyed influence far beyond their position. Lloyd George hoped to use this imperial-minded committee (which met just before the regularly scheduled meeting of the War Cabinet) to chart future grand strategy. When weather permitted, these five men often conducted business while walking abreast on the flagged terrace just outside the Cabinet's meeting room.

American reinforcements dominated the "X" Committee's first meetings. Major General Robert Hutchison, director of organization in the War Office, whom Lloyd George had sent to America in April to assist the War Department in accelerating the transport of American troops to their embarkation ports, gave a disheartening report on American shortcomings in providing clothing and equipment for draftees. He deemed American war mobilization in general and Peyton C. March (the new head of the General Staff) in particular "inadequate" to the task.[65]

No doubt there was some truth in Hutchison's critical analysis of America's war machinery. His evaluation of General March, however, could not have been further from the mark. Tall and erect, March was a soldier who meant business, as reflected by his steely eyes and direct, decisive ways. His forceful personality had at once energized the General Staff. "He took the War Department like a dog takes a cat by the neck, and he shook it," was one staff officer's analogy. "I am going to get the men to France if they have to swim," March once exclaimed. Under his leadership, the War Department transported 1,788,488 men to France during the last eight months of the war.[66]

The flow of American troops after March 21 rapidly exceeded all expectations. In convoys of fast transports, three men to a bunk, sleeping in shifts, doughboys poured across the Atlantic. Lord Reading raised spirits in London when he reported that as many as 250,000 troops of all kinds might be ferried across the Atlantic in May. The British, who provided the additional shipping, were initially the prime beneficiaries of the dramatic increase in the American presence in Western Europe. At the beginning of May there had been only 1,341 combatant troops (along with 3,417 Engineer Corps, 426 Signal Corps, and 763 Tank Corpsmen) training with the British.[67] All the stripped-down U.S. divisions, composed only of their combat elements, were with one exception placed behind the British front.[68] No less than ten U.S. divisions, without their transport and artillery, composed roughly of 12,000 infantry and 3,000 machine gunners per division when at full strength, were in the process of being formed, fed, equipped, and trained by the British. One of these huge four-infantry-regiment American divisions, designed by the War Department in part to overcome the shortage of trained command and staff officers, was the equivalent of two British divisions.

Believing that only trained U.S. soldiers were arriving in Europe, Lloyd George wanted these Americans in the line as quickly as possible. Yet Haig informed him that by June 1 (by which time the Germans might have resumed their offensive), there would be only three American battalions in the line, and then only for "instruction." Lloyd George was incredulous. How was this possible? Was Haig responsible? Pershing? To whom should be protest?[69]

The answer was no one. In its eagerness to assist the Allies, the Wilson war administration sent recruits to France before they had received their prescribed five months' training. In the Seventy-seventh Division, for example, 10,000 men were on their way to France five weeks after being drafted; another 4,000 were on the high seas within a week after donning a uniform.[70] Both British and American military authorities recognized that it would be tantamount to murder to introduce these raw troops to combat.

General Sir H.S. Rawlinson, commander of the British Fourth Army, was greatly impressed with the quality of the individual American soldiers and the enthusiasm of their officers, but he thought that none of the American divisions training behind his line were ready for the trenches: "At present they are helpless, they cannot feed themselves, they cannot move, and the art of getting into and out of billets is strange to them. They are about what our Territorials were before the war but much better material." As for their tactics, "Rawly" reported to Sir Henry Wilson, "Pershing's 'Schedule of Training' is shocking. Nothing in it!!"[71]

Rawlinson's critical assessment of the AEF's doctrine and staff work had merit, yet it is by no means certain that the doughboys would have fought better under British tutelage. Major Lloyd Griscom—who had just left the Seventy-seventh, the first American division assigned to the British front, to take up a new assignment as Pershing's personal representative to Lord Milner in the British War Office—reported to House: "It took only two weeks to develop the fact that our men do not like being with the British or in fact with anybody else but their own people."[72]

Pershing clearly indicated to the British that American divisions were being placed with the BEF for service if necessary. But did he really mean this? The square-jawed and stubborn Missourian was showing himself "very obstinate regarding their employment," Rawlinson reported to Sir Henry Wilson on May 19.[73] On this day, without the knowledge of the British, Pershing reached an agreement with Pétain to transfer his divisions then with the BEF to an American front in the Lorraine theater as soon as their training was complete and the present military emergency terminated.[74]

London's best leverage over Pershing was its control of the lines of supply for the British front.[75] As Hutchison told the "X" Committee, Pershing could not "feed more troops than those provided in his original programme," so the American troops attached to British units could not be fed unless they remained with the British. Realizing this weak link in collecting all American divisions under his command, Pershing joined forces with the French to lobby for pooling supplies.[76] He was "abetting the French in their aims by his scheme for a pooling of all resources," General Wilson told Milner and Lloyd George. Because the number of troops he could supply through the southern French ports was limited, he wanted "to get a part use of the Northern ports for the American Army, in order that he might hereby avoid putting American troops in the British Army and increase the strength of the American Army."[77] Since the supply of all of the armies in France depended upon shipping, the British held the whip hand. There was not going to be any pooling of supplies, despite pressure from the French and Americans in that direction.

Germany's massive assaults had forced the Allies to create unity of command in March and April to prevent military collapse, but Foch's powers should not be exaggerated. His position as Allied commander-in-chief or, more accurately, persuader-in-chief did not truly represent the machinery for effective military coordination. Foch's position, for example, cannot be compared with General Dwight Eisenhower's during World War II. No Allied Joint Chiefs of Staff or Supreme Headquarters Allied Expeditionary Force (SHAEF) existed in 1918. Foch (as suggested by the British) could have utilized the permanent military representatives at Versailles as an Allied general staff, but instead he chose to rely on his own staff. His essentially personal command often failed to inspire confidence in the British military and political authorities. Even Sir Henry Wilson, a friend of Foch and widely thought to be the most pro-French general in the British army, talked with Milner on May 9 about "the French absorbing us, our

Army, our Bases, our Merchant Marine, our Food, Italy, Salonica, etc."[78]

Lloyd George initially resisted sinister interpretations of French designs. The prime minister's priority was "to win the battle." Nothing should be done to handicap General Foch in that respect. An important British consideration in supporting unity of command at Doullens had been to encourage the French to commit their forces to battle. Believing that the next German offensive would destroy a "large part" of the BEF, the prime minister wanted the French to take on the German army during the summer until the burden might be shifted to the Americans in the fall. As he told Milner and Wilson, he hoped that the French would "take a very big share in the battle"; he did not want the British army to be "so reduced that next year we should find ourselves the third Military Power on the Western front."[79]

German pressure on the British front in March and April had not forged the closer Anglo-American military ties that Lloyd George had hoped for. President Wilson and the American General Staff under March's forceful leadership did respond handsomely to desperate British appeals for help by dramatically increasing the flow of American troops across the Atlantic, but the tug-of-war between Lloyd George and the American political and military leadership about the employment of these Yanks provoked mutual recriminations. The underlying cause of these disagreements remained the differing strategic and political perspectives. Pershing, supported by his civilian superiors, wanted to build an army capable of playing the leading role in defeating Germany in 1919. The result would be an American victory not only on the battlefield but perhaps at the peace table as well.

Lloyd George and the Milnerites saw no hope of victory over the German army in 1918 and perhaps not even in 1919. Their immediate objective was to stave off defeat on the western front through American reinforcements. Their next priority was to take the military initiative against the enemy on the periphery in order to ensure a successful political outcome to the war if the main German force could not be crushed in Western Europe. Without significant American assistance they feared that they would not have the means to secure both their position on the Continent and their imperial possessions in the East against the Turko-German menace. They were further concerned that the BEF, unless substantially reinforced by American troops—through either brigading or joint military operations in Flanders with an American army—would be reduced by the end of the year to a second-rate force with a consequent loss of influence in any peace negotiations. These fears continued to dominate London's relations with Washington as renewed German assaults in late May and June confronted the anti-German coalition with the specter of defeat.

10

A New Strategic Landscape

During Germany's two powerful offensives against the BEF in March and April, the bludgeoned British front had bent but not collapsed. But it was a near thing, and there was anxiety in London over the alliance's ability to withstand further German attacks. During the lull between the second and third German offensives, the British leadership addressed future military prospects. The catalyst for this discussion was a paper by Leo Amery titled "Future Military Policy." If the Central Powers defeated Italy and France, Amery asserted, Britain and the United States would have to "concentrate our whole military effort on the East, confining our operations in Europe to action by sea and air." Even if Ludendorff's campaign ultimately failed, eastern operations still offered the Allies their only realistic opportunity to "take the strategical initiative" before 1920, when a great American army would be assembled in Western Europe. Amery proposed a two-pronged strategy for the next eighteen months: an attack on Turkey in Palestine and Mesopotamia, and "the salvage of Great Russia from Vladivostok and Archangel."[1]

Sir Henry Wilson looked to 1919 rather than 1920 when he talked with the prime minister on May 27 about future military policy. The next few months were to be anxious ones, Wilson contended, but by the end of September the West might be relatively secure. The Allies could then build their forces toward a "tremendous and crushing blow." But this would take many months, and Sir Henry expressed opposition to engaging in "operations of the Passchendaele type" during the interim. He professed to favor a forward policy in one of the outlying theaters during the time-consuming military buildup in the West.[2]

The increased flow of American troops across the Atlantic encouraged Lloyd George to believe that any "tremendous and crushing blow" against the German army would largely be delivered by Yanks rather than Tommies. During the meeting of the War Cabinet that immediately followed his conversation with General Wilson, he placed the "greatest importance" on America's "having an army available and ready for operations in 1919." When the CIGS was asked how much

U.S. manpower Foch believed necessary for victory in 1919, Wilson shocked those present with his answer: one hundred American divisions. When augmented by proportionate corps and army troops, replacements and supply units, one hundred American divisions could equal as many as 5,000,000 men, an enormous army that would dwarf the combined Allied forces on the western front. How was this possible, a puzzled Lloyd George wanted to know. Present arrangements, the prime minister noted, called for forty-two American divisions to be in France by June 1919, of which twenty-eight would be combatant divisions and fourteen replacement divisions.[3]

On May 27, the same day that Lloyd George and Wilson discussed future military policy, Ludendorff wrenched the British back to the present with his third offensive, this time against the French along the Chemin des Dames. His purpose was to lure British reserves southward to rescue the French. He then planned to finish off the British army in either June or July.

On the first day of the battle, German shock troops swept forward thirteen miles. After three days their advance covered thirty miles. On the fourth day, May 30, German forces reached the Marne River. With the Germans within fifty miles of Paris, Sir Henry Wilson noted in his diary: "I find it difficult to realize that there is a possibility, perhaps a probability, of the French Army being beaten. What could this mean? The destruction of our Army in France? In Italy? In Salonica? What of Palestine and Mesopotamia, India, Siberia & the Sea? What of Archangel & America?"[4]

The Supreme War Council reassembled at Versailles on June 1-2. Paris was in a state of great agitation. As the noise of the big guns to the east drew closer, hundreds of thousands of Parisians fled. Bliss requisitioned trucks and prepared to abandon his offices at Versailles if necessary. "Our plans are all made in case we should have to leave and in that event we will probably go to Tours," he wrote his wife. "A few days more will probably decide."[5]

Tempers were on edge, especially within the French delegation, which emotionally criticized the British as well as the Americans: the former (who had suffered some 350,000 casualties since March 21) because they would not promise to maintain fifty-nine divisions on the western front, and the latter because they would not feed their men into French divisions. On this latter point there was unanimity between Paris and London. Pershing was the organizer of defeat because of his stubborn determination to put an independent American force into the field, no matter what the consequences to Allied military fortunes.

President Wilson, vulnerable to the charge that he had given Pershing too much latitude on the question of amalgamation,[6] had

recently instructed Baker to order Pershing to adopt a more "sympathetic" attitude toward the Allies. He also had just informed Wiseman
that "if PERSHING really stood in the way, he would be ordered to
stand out of the way."[7] Yet Pershing proved as immovable as ever
when it came to wholesale amalgamation and introducing Americans
to trench warfare before he deemed them ready for combat. The
following exchanges at Versailles most certainly did not reflect a "sympathetic" attitude:

Foch to Pershing: "You are willing to risk our being driven back to
the Loire?"
Pershing: "Yes, I am willing to take the risk."
Lloyd George to Pershing: "Well, we will refer this to your President."
Pershing: "Refer it to the President and be damned. I know what
the President will do. He will simply refer it back to me for recommendation and I will make to him the same recommendation as I have
made here today."[8]

Pershing correctly gauged the support he enjoyed from Wilson, Baker,
and March.[9] Their acceptance of any Allied military policy infringing
upon the distinctiveness of the American role was given with extreme
reluctance and lasted only as long as the latest military crisis. In his
defense, Pershing did recognize the gravity of the military situation
and was prepared to help, but only on terms that would not destroy his
program of forming complete divisions and creating an independent
American army during the last half of 1918. He conditionally offered
Foch the loan of U.S. divisions and enthusiastically supported the
SWC's appeal to Washington to have one hundred U.S. divisions in
Europe by 1919. No less than the Allies, he demanded "men, men, and
still more men" from Washington.
     The most recent German offensive had provided American troops
an opportunity to demonstrate their combat effectiveness, a matter
very much on the minds of both the Germans and the Allies. On May
28, the second day of the German offensive, a regiment of the First
Division launched a previously planned and meticulously organized
local attack against Cantigny. Several days after this village was captured, the Third Division engaged the advancing Germans on the
Marne at Château-Thierry. West of Château-Thierry the Second Division attempted to block the road to the French capital. On June 6 a marine brigade made its famous and costly advance into Belleau Wood,
with Gunnery Sergeant Dan Daly exhorting his troops in the immortal
words: "Come on, you sons-o'-bitches. Do you want to live forever?"
     A year and two months after declaring war, at Cantigny, Château-
Thierry, and Belleau Wood, Americans were entering combat. Thou-

sands more were moving toward the front. "They are coming fast," the *New York Times* reported on June 6. "In passenger trains, in freight cars, or hiking along dusty roads, they arrive from the seaports and pour into camps behind the battlefront." The military impact of these limited American engagements should not be exaggerated. The psychological consequences, however, were profound.

No American was more elated by the good showing of the doughboys than Pershing. He believed that his program of hoarding American military resources for a gigantic American offensive effort in Lorraine in 1919 had been vindicated. "The allies are done for," he wrote House, "and the only thing that will hold them (especially France) in the war will be the assurance that we have force enough to assume the initiative. To this end we must bend every possible energy, so that we may not only assume the offensive, but to do so with sufficient force to end the war next year at the latest." [10]

Not surprisingly, British perspective differed from Pershing's. More dependent upon America's emerging military power than ever, they continued to link the British Empire's survival with the integration of the American military role their own. Uncertain of France's staying power and fearing that Foch might use his position as generalissimo to protect Paris at the expense of the British front (with its Channel ports), the British leadership began to panic.

Foch's recent actions gave the British real cause for anxiety. At the SWC meeting just concluded he had suggested that some of the American divisions behind the British front be moved south to inactive sectors in Alsace to relieve French divisions for action. Sir Henry Wilson had been miffed at the time, believing that Foch wanted "to pinch all our American Battns & send them to Alsace." [11] Pershing, who had already made arrangements with Pétain for the formation of an American army in this sector, accepted with alacrity Foch's subsequent proposal to transfer five American divisions training with the BEF. Haig was angered. Just as his American divisions were becoming "fit for battle," they were being taken from him. [12]

Foch had previously claimed four French divisions that were part of Haig's reserve. Now he ordered three British divisions moved from the north to a position astride the Somme, west of Amiens, to serve as a reserve for either the French or the British front. Foch's handling of American divisions and British reserves served to shift the Allied center of gravity southward, away from the beleaguered British front. Paris, not the Channel ports, seemed to be Foch's priority. A worried Haig released his British divisions but not without issuing a formal protest.

Foch's leadership was discussed in alarmist terms on June 5 at a meeting of the "X" Committee. Sir Henry Wilson insisted that the

British, who were being denuded of their reserves, must go against Foch's wishes and shorten their front at its northern end toward the sea. The CIGS was "absolutely convinced" that they were not in a position to hold the present line against the attack of Prince Rupprecht, who still had forty-eight reserve divisions. Ominously, the British, fearing that the French were about to crack, began making secret plans to withdraw their army from France in that event.[13]

Anxiety over Pershing's leadership explains the most extraordinary proposal yet made by a member of the British war leadership for Anglo-American military integration. "I fear very much that with the present Higher Command," Smuts wrote Lloyd George on June 8, "the American Army will not be used to the best advantage; and victory for us depends on squeezing the last ounce of proper use out of the American Army." Pershing, Smuts argued, was "overwhelmed by the initial difficulties of a job too big for him" and unlikely to cooperate loyally with any Allied strategy. The South African's astonishing solution was to propose himself as the "fighting" commander of American forces. Pershing's duties would be confined to "all organisations in the rear."[14] A more unattractive request of President Wilson would be impossible to imagine—the handing over of American forces in Europe to one of the most prominent spokesman for British imperial interests. Not surprisingly, the prime minister kept this proposal to himself.

Lloyd George, more than any other member of the government, was exercised about the shift of American troops from the British to the French front. It would be August before British draftees could be trained and sent; Haig needed his Americans at least until then. Lloyd George believed that one of his greatest achievements had been to persuade the Americans to place ten of their divisions with the BEF. Now Foch, supported by Pershing, was rapidly undoing what he had accomplished.[15] The volatile Welshman concluded that the French were involved in machinations to force the British to find replacements from their own manpower resources to maintain the British front. Pershing was Foch's willing instrument because the French seemed more inclined than the British to allow him to create an independent army.

On June 7 Milner and Sir Henry Wilson confronted the French in Paris at a meeting characterized by plain speaking on both sides. The French continued to demand that the British maintain their divisions at fifty-nine. The British complained about Foch's placement of Allied reserves, especially his ordering the five American divisions away from the British zone. Foch, understanding that his future authority was at stake, was conciliatory in that he proclaimed no intention of withdrawing any more American divisions from the BEF.[16] He emphasized, in response to a query by Sir Henry Wilson, that his primary objective as generalissimo remained keeping the British and French forces joined. He also assured the British that he assigned equal weight to the defense of Paris and the Channel ports.[17]

Rather than strengthening the alliance, this meeting served as a warning that more trouble lay ahead. Lloyd George, believing that the American troops arriving in June would replace the divisions just moved by Foch, was greatly agitated to discover in mid-June that Pershing had no intention of sending any of his newly arrived divisions to the British sector to substitute for those ordered southward.[18]

Faced with Pershing's granitelike determination, BEF headquarters finally accepted as inevitable the creation in the near future of an independent American force with its own front. The British military authorities thus shifted their focus from lobbying for amalgamation to persuading Pershing to cooperate with the BEF rather than the French army, which they feared was on the verge of being routed. On June 14 Colonel Griscom, Pershing's liaison officer with the British War Office, dined at GHQ with Haig. "He said," Griscom informed Pershing, "the sooner we had American Corps and Armies operating the better he would be pleased and he had told General Foch that it was folly to send two of our good divisions to the Vosges to relieve second-rate French Divisions. He said he would do anything he could to help get an American Army together, and that geographically he thought the place for our concentration now was in or opposite Belgium in view of the immediate crisis."[19]

With Foch as generalissimo, however, the French retained the upper hand in putting American forces into the line. Two of the American divisions withdrawn from the British sector, the Fourth and the Twenty-eighth, were stopped on their move southward to the Vosges front and established on the west side of the Marne salient not far from Château-Thierry. They joined the Second, Third, Twenty-sixth, and Forty-second divisions, which were already in the area, giving Pershing the nucleus for an independent army and strengthening the defense of Paris at the same time.

When Lloyd George discovered what had happened, he erupted, suggesting that Foch had, "intentionally or unintentionally, 'done' us in the matter."[20] Pershing also incurred his anger. A protest was cabled to the American War Department. When Baker attempted to discover the circumstances of the transfer of the American divisions from the BEF, Pershing replied that he was only following Foch's instructions and that the British had no legitimate claim to these divisions. The president, brought into this discussion on June 19, exploded: "If the English continue to maneuver around and about, this way and that, to have their own way, I shall speak very plainly."[21]

On June 9 Ludendorff had resumed his offensive, his fourth of 1918, attacking a twenty-mile section of the French front between Montdidier and Noyon. This fresh onslaught was quickly checked by French counterattacks, however, and the Germans now paused. Time was running out for Ludendorff. His initial successes against the French had led him to concentrate on them instead of launching his strike against the British in Flanders as he had originally planned. With his forces exposed in vulnerable salients that had been punched into the Allied front, his casualties, which could not be replaced, continued to mount.

German numerical superiority, although being fast reduced by the arrival of the Americans, still seemed to give the strategical initiative to the enemy. Ludendorff's fourth attack had achieved little, but there was no doubt in London that he would try again, and concern about France's staying power continued as strong as ever. On June 19 the prime minister tried to suppress the reporting of parliamentary speeches that advocated a British withdrawal from France.[22]

Preying on British minds was the fear that France's collapse would put Germany in control of the Continent and in a position to expand against the British Empire in Asia and Africa. Sir Henry Wilson asked Lloyd George if "he meant to go on with the war if the French fell out." The prime minister's prompt response: "Yes if America will stick to it."[23] At a time when Anglo-American military cooperation never seemed more vital, the British leadership was confronted with a deteriorating relationship with Washington and the AEF's leadership.

Uncertainty about American intentions continued to plague the formulation of imperial military policy. The CIGS urged Lloyd George to get in touch with President Wilson to learn what he was prepared to do if the French lost Paris and the general situation became critical. It was "essential" to know if the United States was "prepared to go on in all circumstance."[24]

As July began, the "X" Committee learned that the infantry and machine gun units of seventeen American divisions were now in France. Seven of these divisions were in the line, complete with their artillery. But British civilians remained in the dark about American plans to employ these unbloodied soldiers. Lloyd George emphasized his ignorance of how General Pershing was using the large forces being brought over from the United States in British shipping.[25]

America's role in the war was also uppermost on the minds of the imperial leaders, who reassembled in London in June to join the War Cabinet in taking stock of the military and diplomatic situation. The Empire statesmen included Robert Borden for Canada, William Hughes for Australia, W.F. Massey for New Zealand, and Sir S. Sinha and the Maharaja of Patiala for India; Smuts, already a member of the

War Cabinet, represented South Africa. The mood differed sharply from that of their first meeting in March 1917. There was no talk this time about the British Empire's being the premier power in the world. Rather, Britain's ever increasing dependence on the United States, both in checking Germany's drive toward global domination and in achieving a decent peace, was an important theme running through the discussions.

On the eve of the first meeting of the Imperial War Cabinet, Milner urged the prime minister to tell the Empire statesmen "what they really are up against." Milner wrote: "We must be prepared for France & Italy both being beaten to their knees. In that case the Germans-Austro-Turks-Bulgar bloc will be master of all Europe & Northern & Central Asia up to the point, at wh. Japan steps in to bar the way, *if* she does step in. . . . In any case it is clear that, unless the only remaining free peoples of the world, America, this country & the Dominions, are knit together in the closest conceivable alliance & prepared for the maximum of sacrifice, the Central bloc, under the hegemony of Germany, will control not only Europe & most of Asia but the whole world. . . . The fight will now be for Southern Asia & above all for Africa (the Palestine bridge-head is of immense importance)." To Milner, the war was now a "new war." The United States held the key to the British Empire's salvation. "One thing more—intimately connected with the above. Of course all this depends on what America may do. Is not the time approaching, when we should try to find out, what she *will* do in case of a collapse of the Continental campaign against Germany? . . . Unless he [Wilson] can be shaken out of his aloofness & drops 'co-belligerency' or whatever half way house he loves to shelter himself in, for out & out alliance. . . . I don't see how the new combination can have sufficient cohesion & inner strength."[26]

Milner's disciple Amery also emphasized that the war had entered a new and ominous phase. "You asked me the other day to say what I thought of the situation," Amery had written the prime minister on June 8, "and I ventured to sum it up by saying that as soon as this 'little side show' in the West is over, whether the line gets stabilised or disappears altogether, we shall have to take the war for the mastery of Asia in hand seriously, and that in that quarter we can call a New World into being to redress the balance of the Old—if the Old should go wrong, which I am not yet prepared to admit."[27]

With charges and countercharges still reverberating between the civilians and the military party over responsibility for the BEF's setbacks, Lloyd George's opening statement to the Imperial War Cabinet was calculated to defend his war leadership. Russia's collapse was partly responsible for creating the precarious military situation, but the slow buildup in Europe of American forces ready to enter combat was termed Britain's "worst disappointment." The Americans had "promised us 450,000 men in the field by the spring" but had fallen far short. "If we had had reasonable ground for believing that the Americans would have failed us altogether, we would have risked our industries and would have cut down our rations to one-half, and done all sorts of things in order to put the very last man into the field, but as the battle was going to be a battle of endurance we did not feel justified in doing that when we were expecting American aid to that extent." Lloyd George conveniently omitted mention of the War Office's repeated warnings that serious American military assistance could not be counted on until the last half of 1918 at the earliest, and perhaps not even until 1919.

The prime minister also vigorously defended military operations away from the western front, especially British successes in Palestine and Mesopotamia. Germany had "thought of the Baghdad Railway as a means of getting to the East; they thought of the railway through Palestine as a means of getting to Egypt, and through Egypt to Africa. There we have cut them off, and these two successes which occurred during last year, although, for the time being, they have not loomed as large as the gigantic events which have taken place in the West, may turn out to be even more eventful than those great battles." Control of the world's shipping lanes and these strategic overland lines of communication might, in the nightmarish event of a German triumph on the Continent, allow the rim powers—the British Empire, America, and Japan—to continue the struggle as Britain had done a century earlier against Napoleon.

Significantly, Allied misfortunes made Lloyd George reject any thought of peace negotiations with an unrepentant Berlin. The prospect of a confident and expansionist Germany dominating the Continent, with a free hand to challenge Britain in Africa and Asia, was too horrible to contemplate. Any German effort to buy a German peace in the East with concessions to Britain's allies in the West must be rebuffed. "They would be selling out at the top of the market," he told the Imperial War Cabinet, leaving Germany "strong," "triumphant," and in a position to menace the British Empire. "Unless Germany is beaten now, there [will] be another war."[28]

During the following weeks the Imperial War Cabinet sought to formulate a military and political strategy that would harmonize the Empire's declining manpower resources with a favorable peace won on the battlefield. Wilson's world view and liberal war aims constituted an obvious barrier to Anglo-American cooperation in bringing the war to a successful conclusion from the British perspective. London and Washington had hitherto successfully avoided an open confrontation over Britain's secret treaties with its allies and the British

Empire's determination to eliminate the Turko-German threat. Wilson's and Lloyd George's January war aims statements had had much in common, but the British knew enough about Wilson to fear any peace settlement that he dominated.

On August 13 Lloyd George read to the Imperial War Cabinet the remarks Wilson was alleged to have made in April to foreign journalists about the position he planned to take at any peace conference: "Gentlemen of the Conference, we come here asking for nothing ourselves, and we are here to see you get nothing." Lord Reading immediately interjected that Wilson might not have used those exact words, but the president had "refused to let the Ambassadors have it [a copy of his statement]. . . . it was not a prepared thing." Lloyd George remained unconvinced. He had it on good authority that these had been Wilson's exact words. In any event, he stressed, "I think it is very much like what President Wilson would say."[29]

Balfour, Lloyd George, and many of the Empire statesmen were opposed at this stage of the war to extending the already vast holdings of the British Empire unless vital economic and strategic interests were involved. Their primary motive in advocating any expansion of British rule in Africa, Asia, and the Pacific was the future security of the British Empire. The oil fields of Mesopotamia and the phosphate-rich German Pacific island of Nauru, in fact, were the only territories sought chiefly for economic gain.[30]

When Lloyd George suggested that Wilson's opposition to the annexation of territory might be lessened by sharing captured territory with the United States, the reaction was strong skepticism. British statesmen who had firsthand experience with Wilson doubted that the president could be persuaded to go along with any form of territorial aggrandizement. Lloyd George was engaging in wishful thinking to argue that Wilson, for altruistic motives, might accept American administration of Palestine, thereby providing the Suez Canal with a shield from any future threat from the north. Equally unrealistic was Borden's view that Wilson's radical departure from American isolationism formed the basis for a new Anglo-Saxon world order. "The more we can induce the United States to undertake its just responsibilities in world affairs, the better it will be for the world and the better also for the British Empire," he suggested. "I put the future welfare and peace of the world first, but I think this purpose is equally essential for the security of our huge and scattered empire which we believe to be perhaps the greatest influence for the welfare of humanity and the advancement of civilisation that has yet been established. . . . The more we can get the United States to realise her great responsibilities for the peace and welfare of the world the better it will be for us and for all mankind."[31]

No conflict over war strategy demonstrated the differing Anglo-American geopolitical objectives and the difficulty of any integration of their military resources more than British efforts to promote U.S. military intervention in Russia to thwart long-range German designs in European Russia and protect the British position in Asia from German and Turkish encroachments. Much ink has been expended on the origins of Allied intervention in Russia to prove, on the one hand, that this controversial enterprise was motivated largely by ideological considerations and, on the other hand, that military factors rather than fear of Bolshevism were the root cause. A detailed discussion of the argument is obviously beyond the scope of this book. Suffice it to say that the voluminous British government records now available to the historian strongly suggest that the advocates of intervention who were in a position to determine British policy during the first half of 1918 were motivated far more by fear of German and Turkish expansionism than by any threat, real or imagined, posed by Bolshevism. The designs of President Wilson, who almost single-handedly determined America's Russian policy, are less clear. Carl J. Richards identifies no less than six theories concerning his motives.[32] But Wilson, too, seemed much less influenced by fear of Bolshevism than by other factors.[33]

Ludendorff's campaign in the West, in combination with what the British interpreted as a forward German policy in the East,[34] eventually gave the upper hand to British advocates of action over caution in dealing with Russia. Suspicion of Japanese aggrandizement was overcome by the apparent need to forge closer relations with Tokyo in the event of defeat in Western Europe. Lloyd George, who shared President Wilson's belief that armed intervention, especially by Japan, would fail to revive the eastern front and would succeed only in driving the Russians into the waiting arms of Berlin, was put on the defensive by the Milnerites' concern over the security of the British Empire. When Sir Henry Wilson, standing before a large map in front of the Imperial War Cabinet on June 18, took stock of the war, his pointer beat an ominous tattoo of German menace in Asia. "It seems to me we have to get a position on *this* side (the east) as well as on the west. If that is so, we have got to get everybody to help, and we must get the Japanese. I can see no other way out of it. No military decision, as far as I can see, that we can get *here* now will settle the east. It is for that reason that I think that between the days when all anxiety is past, this autumn, and the time when we throw down the glove *here* for a final clinch, we ought to exploit the outside theatres as much as we can, so that at the Peace Conference we, the British anyhow, will not be so badly off."[35]

German pressure on the western front, however, prevented the

British from diverting sizable military resources to the East. Meanwhile the president's opposition on political and military grounds thwarted both Japanese and American involvement in Russia. In yet another effort to win Wilson's support, Balfour cabled Reading that America's "western front" strategy could not by itself achieve a Wilsonian peace. "No military decision in the Allies' favour can ever be expected as the result of operations on the Western front alone; nor will such a measure of equality as may be looked for in that theatre in any way secure objects for which the allies are fighting, unless combined with the maximum military effort that can be made in the East." [36]

At the beginning of June, Wilson had bent a little in his opposition to armed intervention in Russia, accepting with a marked lack of enthusiasm the Allied military argument that American troops were necessary to keep the north Russian port of Murmansk out of German hands. General March opposed this and all other American military involvement in Russia, but the president overruled the General Staff (for only the second time, the first being his decision to send the AEF to Europe immediately). The suggested military commitment appeared limited (although Sir Henry Wilson actually expected the United States to assume the "chief burden" of maintaining the Allied position in North Russia);[37] Japanese imperialism was not an issue; and the strategical objective seemed clearly linked to the war with Germany. An additional consideration for Wilson, especially with Generalissimo Foch supporting the venture, was that he was weary of being portrayed as an obstructionist in the implementation of Allied strategy. Hence, a small contingent of American troops (mostly from Michigan and Wisconsin) who were destined for the trenches of the western front was eventually placed under British control for intervention in northern Russia.[38]

Persuading Wilson to employ Yanks in Siberia proved much more difficult. Unconvinced by military arguments that dared not speak directly to London's primary concern, the use of American and Japanese manpower as a shield for the British Empire, the president continued to stymie Allied intervention in Asiatic Russia. British diplomats fared little better with the president than did the soldiers. "There remains only the Czechoslovak complication to use as a lever," lamented John D. Gregory, a member of the Russia section of the Foreign Office.[39]

Some 50,000 Czechs (mostly Austro-Hungarian deserters and prisoners of war who had formed the Czechoslovak Legion to fight with the Allies on behalf of Czechoslovakian independence) were about to become central characters in the saga of Allied intervention in Siberia. Spread along the Trans-Siberian Railway, this body of troops was in the process of being transported to ports for shipment to the western front. British advocates of intervention, however, with their country dominant in shipping, sought to use the Legion's control of this vital rail artery to form the nucleus of a pro-Allied force in Asiatic Russia.

Wilson's military advisers in Washington, March and Baker, were both strong "western fronters"; if they got their way, the United States would pursue a hands-off policy in Asiatic Russia.[40] When the president asked him about the efficacy of armed intervention, the chief of staff on June 24 dictated a memorandum emphasizing the impracticable nature of Allied proposals to revive the eastern front by means of the Trans-Siberian Railway. "To make a substantial diversion of German forces," he informed the president, "would require the occupation of the Trans-Siberian Railroad to Russia proper, and the maintenance of a force in Russian territory entirely beyond the possibility of the present resources of the United States to maintain."[41] Or any other great power, he might have added. What is not usually appreciated is that many British statesmen agreed with March on this point. It was frankly admitted within the War Cabinet that no military authority had yet devised a believable plan for erecting an active front in the East that would threaten the Central Powers and force them to divert troops from the western front.[42]

Emphasis on the reconstitution of Russia, or the revival of the eastern front as it had once been, misses the point. The British Empire now confronted, in Milner's words, a "new war," which might mean defeat in Europe, a prolongation of the war into 1920 or later, and increasing German concentration in the East. The Empire statesmen were intent on filling the vast vacuum created by Russia's collapse. In Curzon's panicky utterance, the whole of Russia was "laid out prostrate and impotent at the foot of an advancing Germany."[43] Without the military means themselves, Empire statesmen sought to block Germany's eastern expansionism with a polyglot force of Czechs, Japanese, Americans, and native elements. If the war went wrong in Europe, it appeared absolutely essential to have Japan and the United States committed to Asiatic Russia.[44]

With Wilson's approval considered essential to any military action in Siberia, the Imperial War Cabinet had suggested on June 20 that a direct British request be made to the White House. Foreign Office officials, however, knew that unilateral British action would fall on deaf ears. "What would really appeal to him is a message from the Supreme War Council backed by Foch," Drummond wrote Hankey.[45] On June 27 the Imperial War Cabinet decided to pressure Wilson through the Supreme War Council.

On July 2, the SWC sent Wilson an urgent appeal for armed intervention in Siberia. A new and insincere argument, calculated to appeal to the president's idealism, was that intervention was necessary to rescue the Czechoslovak Legion, which was reportedly in a life-and-death struggle along with the Bolsheviks, and Austrian and German prisoners of war.

This Allied request finally forced Wilson's hand. On July 6 he met with Baker, Lansing, Daniels, March, and Benson at the White House. Although the president agreed with his military advisers' criticism of the military justifications for this intervention, he nevertheless overruled them on the employment of American troops beyond the western front. When March vigorously shook his head and expressed his fears of the consequences of armed intervention in Asiatic Russia, Wilson retorted, "Well, we will have to take that chance."[46] He decided to send 7,000 soldiers to join with an equal number of Japanese troops to assist the Czechs.[47]

Wilson's motives for this decision remain murky. It has been suggested that he sought not to rescue the Czechs but to use them to block further German inroads in Russia.[48] The president may have believed that national sentiment would not be aroused if a Slavic contingent, the Czechoslovak Legion, constituted the core of anti-German resistance in Siberia, around which loyal native forces might rally. Political questions aside, Wilson probably saw little risk in his conception of armed American intervention. Determined to keep the American presence limited and under his tight control, he almost certainly saw no conflict with America's commitment to the western front.

The president's reaction to the appeal by the SWC was generally consistent with his previous responses to British efforts to coordinate the American military effort with their own. He did not hesitate to reject an Anglo-American military alignment, but finding it difficult to refuse outright a proposal for collective military involvement in Siberia if it came ostensibly from Foch and the SWC, he was prepared to give the appearance if not the substance of American cooperation. Wilson quickly emphasized that any American participation was to be on his terms. On July 17 he delivered to the Allied ambassadors his famous *aide-mémoire*, in which he disclaimed any intention of intervening in Russia's internal affairs. The heavy-handed implication was that America needed to protect Russia from both the Central Powers *and* the Allies. Wilson, echoing his generals, also took a strong "western front" position, arguing that only in Western Europe could the United States conduct large-scale military operations. "The American Government, therefore," he noted, "very respectfully requests its Associates to accept its deliberate judgment that it should not dissipate its force by attempting important operations elsewhere."[49]

The British were furious. Wilson's position of moral superiority annoyed them, and his desire to limit American and Japanese involvement to 7,000 men apiece, if adhered to, would effectively destroy British efforts to create a barrier to German expansionism. In short, the British viewed Wilson's actions as another example of American uni-lateralism—which indeed they were, for his response had little in common with Allied interventionist plans. The prime minister sar-castically compared Wilson's "half-fledged" acceptance of the SWC's appeal to Prime Minister William Gladstone's failure to send relief to "Chinese" Gordon at Khartoum.[50]

The ray of hope for the British was that American and Japanese intervention, once launched, would inevitably grow. Believing that the war would not end until 1919 or later, their most prudent policy seemed to be one of patience. Pressing Wilson, who at this time was bitter about what he thought were British-inspired articles in the American press favorable to intervention, was certain to be coun-terproductive.[51]

Rather than integrate their military resources with those of the British to bolster Britain's position in Europe and Asia during the grave military crisis of June and early July, American policy-makers clearly wanted American arms to make a big, essentially independent splash in Western Europe. On July 7 Baker wrote Pershing a confidential and personal note stressing two points: "(1) I want the Germans beaten, hard and thoroughly—a military victory. (2) I want you to have the honor of doing it."[52]

Before Baker's letter arrived, Pershing was already moving in this direction. On July 10 he talked with Foch about forming an American army with its own theater of operation. In short, he wanted indepen-dent objectives as well as an independent force. To give him the necessary military muscle, he pressed the War Department hard to achieve the impossible: one hundred American divisions in France by July 1919, which would more than quadruple the size of his existing forces.[53]

The British hoped that Pershing would employ some of his in-creasing military strength alongside the BEF, putting the five remain-ing American divisions into a corps that would take its place in the line, if not in Flanders, perhaps at the joint of the British and French forces.[54] An incident on July 4, however, destroyed any chance that Pershing would ever allow a sizable American force to fall under British influence or control. Companies C and E, 131st Infantry, and A and G, 132nd Infantry, of the American Thirty-third Division (National Guard,) participated in an attack by the Fourth Australian Division on the village of Le Hamel.

The Battle of Le Hamel, although a minor engagement, was a brilliant success. Following an opening artillery bombardment, which some Americans described as better than "any previous Fourth of July

demonstration they had ever heard," a well-coordinated thrust captured 41 German officers, 1,431 other ranks, several big guns, 171
machine-guns, and 26 trench mortars. The Australians lost 51 officers
and 724 other ranks; the Americans, 6 officers and 128 other ranks. In
ninety-three minutes the attack achieved its objectives. The untested
Americans fought well, impressing the Aussies: "United States troops
are now classified as Diggers," an Australian company commander
reported to his superior. On the following day, Lloyd George and
Milner visited soldiers from the Thirty-third Division. After saluting
the American flag as he reviewed American troops marching by, the
prime minister stood on an automobile and spoke of the common
struggle against Germany. Across the globe there was talk of the new
Anglo-American alliance; American flags flew in Toronto, Sidney, and
Wellington in recognition of America's Independence Day.[55]

Behind the scenes it was a different story. Rawlinson had intentionally chosen the Fourth of July for the first American offensive
action in the British zone. Despite its clear success, Pershing seethed.
In his view the United States was still struggling for its independence
from the British. Earlier he had vetoed American participation in this
Australian attack, and Haig had passed on his instructions to Rawlinson, with whom the Thirty-third was training. Rawlinson then duti-
fully informed Lieutenant General John Monash, an unconventional
Jewish officer who was a genius at meticulous preparation for infantry
assaults. Receiving these orders at 4:00 P.M. on July 3, Monash was
aghast: if he withdrew the American companies, the resulting gaps in
his orchestrated attack would force cancellation. He protested and was
given permission to proceed. Rawlinson was at the same time greatly
relieved that the attack had been a great success with small American
losses ("If things had gone wrong I suppose I should have been sent
home in disgrace!!") and furious with Pershing. "Pershing is a tire-
some ignorant and very obstinate man as we shall find later on when
he begins to try conclusions with the Boche 'on his own,'" he wrote the
assistant private secretary of George V.[56]

Pershing's apprehension over British ulterior motives would have
been even greater if he had been privy to the discussions taking place
in the "X" Committee. On July 1 Lloyd George discussed 1919 military
operations with Major General P. de B. Radcliffe, the director of
military operations, and Major General Charles H. Harington, the
deputy CIGS. These generals explained that the Americans, who were
expected to have their own front in 1919, would play a key role along
with the British in offensive operations. Predictably, the prime minister sat uneasily in his chair when big attacks on the western front
involving heavy British losses were discussed. He suggested that if the
Americans were to concentrate "a great Army on the Western front

next year, it might be possible for our Army to follow out its traditional *rôle* of operating on the outskirts of the war area."[57]

In his attempt to implement a strategy so favorable to the political interests of the British Empire, Lloyd George ran afoul of unity of command. Central to his conflict with Robertson had been his determination to limit British casualties on the western front. In an effort to undermine Robertson's stranglehold on strategy, he had been the motive force in creating the SWC, which he planned to use as an alternative to his own General Staff's advice. Foch's position as generalissimo had evolved out of this first hesitant step toward unifying Allied military policy. But Foch, no less than Robertson, opposed any reduction of the British commitment to France.

The War Cabinet refused to march in step with Foch for two reasons. First, the ministers did not believe it either economically or politically feasible to make the draconian demands on depleted British manpower resources that would be required to replace Haig's losses. Second, Lloyd George hoped to gain strategical flexibility for the British Empire, freeing some of Haig's divisions for theaters where their use would directly further imperial interests; the United States would replace Britain as the linchpin of the anti-German coalition in Europe. Foch, however, checkmated him by placing almost all the AEF divisions behind or in French defenses, at the same time insisting that Britain was not providing its fair share of infantry to the western front.

A meeting of the Supreme War Council, July 2-4, gave Lloyd George the opportunity to confront the French. First he took on André Tardieu, the high commissioner for Franco-American affairs, for meddling with the British transport of Americans across the Atlantic.[58] Next he attacked the French for unilaterally changing the orders of the Allied army in the Balkans, which was commanded by a French general, from a defensive to an offensive position. Trouble would arise "the moment General Foch came to be considered merely as the servant of the French Government," he blustered. For the present, the SWC "trusted him absolutely," but if it was thought that he was "taking instructions from one Government more than from another, this feeling of complete confidence would disappear."[59]

One suspects that Lloyd George confronted the French to put them on the defensive. To prevent Foch from unilaterally deciding Allied strategy in 1919, he moved that the permanent military representatives, who had largely been made superfluous by Foch's enhanced position, study future military operations.[60] If Lloyd George and Milner got their way, they intended to transfer some of Haig's divisions to Palestine once the western front was secure.[61] British plans to reduce their commitment to the western front, of course, could not be revealed to either the French or Americans.

When Foch threatened resignation over any effort to diminish his authority, Lloyd George firmly stood his ground. According to General Wilson's diary, he told both Foch and Clemenceau that "there was a d—— sight too much of these Generals threatening to resign & that if they were private soldiers they would be put up agst. a wall & shot."[62] Lloyd George's resolution stood, with some change in the wording.

This contentious meeting set the stage for a showdown over shipping between London and Washington. The tottering of the European side of the anti-German alignment confronted Lloyd George and the Milnerites with the inescapable conclusion that the British Empire's salvation rested in the hands of Wilson, who had become the world's most powerful political figure. The president's uncooperative Russian policy, along with Lloyd George's maneuverings to shift the primary British military contribution to the periphery for political reasons, widened the gulf between London and Washington, not to mention Paris. Unable to persuade the president to cooperate with British military and political policy in Europe or in Asia, Lloyd George confronted the American political and military leadership with his only remaining bargaining chip: shipping.

11
Disunity of Command

It has often been remarked that America in World War I had almost no strategic role to play in the land war because the principal theater of the war, the western front, had already been well established by the course of military events prior to April 1917. This argument assumes that Anglo-French strategic policy constituted a monolith, which was far from being the case, especially during the last phase of the war. The political leadership of Great Britain and the Dominions, more concerned than their primary war partners about the Turko-German threat to Asia, sought strategic flexibility to meet this menace. The War Cabinet's imperial focus, which threatened to diminish the British commitment to the western front, placed it on a collision course with France, especially with a Frenchman as Allied supreme commander. With Paris and London at sixes and sevens over Foch's growing control of Allied military policy in Western Europe, the Americans held the balance of power.

The wide divide between the American "western front" view and the British imperial strategy is abundantly demonstrated by the differing perspectives of Bridges and Bliss. General Tom Bridges, who had returned to Washington in July, vigorously lobbied Baker to increase America's military role in Siberia, arguing that it was essential to an Allied victory. After an especially frustrating encounter with the American secretary of war, Bridges, never one to mince words, charged that advocates of the single-minded "western" approach "must take the responsibility of prolonging the years of war, millions of American casualties, the expenditure of billions of treasure, and in fact the heavy additions to the sum of human misery that we shall hereby incur, as well as a great risk of an inconclusive peace."[1] President Wilson in particular was incensed by this tough talk, and the Foreign Office was subsequently warned not to send Bridges to Washington again.[2]

In opposition to Bridges, Bliss argued that Britain's emphasis on the outer theaters was a political rather than a war-winning strategy. On August 14 he cabled Baker and March that the war could be ended in 1919, but only if the Allies were prevented from shifting the burden of the fighting in Western Europe to the United States, while they squandered their military resources elsewhere to guarantee themselves a favorable peace. "If sufficiently favorable military situations are not created on certain secondary theaters by beginning of Autumn next year," he warned Baker, "the Governments of our Allies may be willing to continue through 1920 and at the cost of United States troops and money a war which may possibly be ended with complete success for us by operations on the western front in 1919."[3]

Following the fourth German offensive of 1918, June 9-13, there was yet another pause, the last such lull in military operations. With hope of a knock-out blow waning, Ludendorff's gamble for total victory took on an even more desperate note. If his next move failed, he knew that his declining numbers would not allow yet another throw of the dice. Ludendorff planned to threaten Paris with an attack around Rheims on July 15 (thereby encouraging Foch to weaken further the British position in Flanders) and then shift his reserves north to drive the BEF into the sea.

Foch, as early as June 28, had learned of the German plan to attack the French front and made his preparations accordingly, provoking anxiety in London. Anticipating a great German push at any moment against their forces, the British civilians feared another March 21 disaster. German preparations across no-man's-land suggested (correctly) that Ludendorff ultimately planned to seek a German victory against the British rather than the French. Although Lloyd George's government had survived the destruction of the Fifth Army, it would be down and out if confronted with another military debacle of that magnitude.

On July 8 General Wilson told the War Cabinet that "the Germans could now put in a bigger attack than they did on the 21st March." Although British defenses were stronger, the BEF's position "was weaker in the respect that we [are] not in a position to give ground, as was possible on that occasion."[4] Foch's placement of Allied reserves in a position to counter any German move against Paris especially concerned the civilians. On July 11 the War Cabinet instructed Lloyd George to remind Clemenceau that Foch was "an *Allied* and not merely a French Commander-in-Chief, and that he must treat the Allied interests as a whole, making his dispositions on this basis and not mainly from the point of view of French interests."[5]

The prime minister saw sinister motives in the actions of Clemenceau and Foch. As frequently as a cloudy day in England, the French had pressed him to maintain the strength as well as the number of Haig's divisions. He was convinced that Foch's deployment of American troops was designed to force the British to provide their last man to the killing grounds of Western Europe. The infantry and machine gun units of thirty American divisions would be in France by the end of the month, yet the BEF apparently would have only five American divisions on its front. Lloyd George told the "X" Committee on July 12 that the French had "secured the bulk of the American divisions for themselves." Clemenceau had "more than hinted" that he was "getting hold of the American divisions in order to compel us to re-fill our own," which was "an unjustifiable attempt to put pressure upon us."[6]

The following day, Lloyd George took on the French in preemptive fashion. Speaking on behalf of the Imperial War Cabinet, he wrote Clemenceau (copy to Foch) that the generalissimo's deployment of divisions to meet the German threat must not give Empire statesmen the impression that "their armies have been let down by the united command." At the very least, Foch must reinforce the reserves behind the British sector "by a much larger proportion of the American troops brought to France during the last two or three months." The British Empire, in fact, had a "special claim" to many of these troops. At "great sacrifice" the British had brought some 582,000 doughboys across the Atlantic since March 1, yet only 100,000 were now training behind British lines. Lloyd George concluded his letter with a threat and a demand. If Foch's allocation of American manpower resulted in the BEF's being "overwhelmed by superior numbers," it would "undoubtedly be fatal" to unity of command; therefore Clemenceau should apply pressure on Foch and Pershing to deploy more American divisions in the British sector.[7]

On Sunday, July 14, a crisis atmosphere existed within the ruling political circle in Britain. Discovering the exact hour of the German attack, Foch ordered Haig, who still believed that his forces were Germany's primary target, to send four divisions from the British reserves south of the Somme to an area south-east of Chalons.[8] Previously he had moved the last six French divisions of the Detachment de l'Armée du Nord, the French army group in Flanders, south to Beauvais, where they could reinforce either the French or British front. At the very time Lloyd George was demanding that the British sector be reinforced, Foch was thus moving its reserves southward.

The prime minister convened an emergency council of war in Sussex at Danny Park, Hurstpierpoint, where he was Lord Riddell's guest. He dispatched Hankey to Canterbury to fetch Milner. "Yesterday you saw the letter I wrote to Clemenceau," the prime minister wrote the secretary of state for war. "I fear that it may not suffice with that queer tempered old gentleman. When so much depends upon his decision—his immediate decision—we must take no chances."[9] The Welshman wanted to send Smuts and Canadian Prime Minister Borden, who "I am told will have special influence with Pershing," to France to back up his earlier appeal to Clemenceau.[10] Meanwhile, Smuts arrived at Danny Park from Oxford, Robert Borden from London, and Sir Henry Wilson from Henley.[11]

Believing that British forces were about to be "overwhelmed," Lloyd George lost his nerve, threatening to destroy the unity of command which he in large measure was responsible for creating. He was prepared to veto Foch's transfer of the four British divisions unless Haig could guarantee that Germany would not attack his forces. Neither Haig nor any other general could give such rash assurance. Milner and Wilson, however, urged against any precipitous action on Britain's part until German intentions were clearer. They persuaded the prime minister to rely on Haig's judgment; Wilson telephoned BEF headquarters, instructing the field marshal to appeal to his government Foch's handling of Allied reserves (which he had the right to do under the Beauvais Agreement)[12] if he thought that his front was in danger or believed that "political reasons" were behind the movement of reserves from the British sector. Smuts followed this telephone message with a visit to GHQ to ascertain whether the British commander-in-chief "was satisfied with the evidence on which General Foch was acting."[13]

Significantly, Lloyd George's obsession with acquiring American troops to replace those moved to the French front was in no way modified when the Germans attacked the French front on July 15. Smuts, who left for France just as this fifth German offensive began, was instructed to enlist Haig's support in pressuring Foch to allocate more doughboys to the BEF. To Lloyd George, much more was at stake than the battle in progress. Without substantial American support in the British sector, he feared that the British would never have the strategical flexibility to protect British interests outside of Europe and establish the territorial basis for a favorable political settlement. Consequently, he continued to press Clemenceau on the "undiminished importance to the training of additional American divisions behind our lines."[14]

Germany's assault on July 15 was quickly repulsed, with heavy losses to the attackers. On July 17, recognizing his defeat in the Second Battle of the Marne, a disappointed Ludendorff called off his attack. On the following day Foch launched a counteroffensive, the Aisne-Marne Offensive, to eliminate the Marne salient. America began to flex its new military muscle. Eight American divisions (equal in infantry to some sixteen Allied divisions) were involved in the Franco-American advance. American divisions also fought for the first time in larger military units. When the offensive formally concluded in early August, the former front of the French Sixth Army in the Marne sector was manned by the American First and Third Corps. Ludendorff's gamble had failed. His five offensives had cost him 800,000 casualties. Numerical superiority (given the Allies by the arrival of U.S. forces) and the strategical initiative passed from his hands to Foch.

Foch's steadfast direction of the Second Battle of the Marne and the counteroffensive that followed earned him a marshal's baton. Lloyd George, however, continued to believe that Clemenceau was taking unfair advantage of the British through his manipulation of the generalissimo. Nothing could alter this view: not Foch, who promised to protect the British front;[15] not Milner and Wilson, who argued that there was "no proof that General Foch had let the British Army down";[16] and not Haig and Chief of the General Staff Sir Herbert Lawrence, who expressed the view that "the presence of the Americans" had had "a remarkable effect in stimulating the French *moral.*" Haig went so far as to tell Smuts that he "doubted if the French army would have had any offensive spirit left" without American support.[17]

The prime minister's anxiety was to a large degree a result of Britain's worsening manpower situation, which Lloyd George linked to "the part that this country would take on the Western front and the part that America would take next year, a matter closely connected with questions of our future war policy, which [is] now under consideration by the Military Representatives at Versailles, by the General Staff, and by a Committee of Prime Ministers set up by the Imperial War Cabinet."[18] The Committee of Prime Ministers, which Lloyd George had just initiated, included the political leaders of Canada, New Zealand, Australia, and Newfoundland, and Smuts, who represented General Louis Botha, the prime minister of South Africa. Milner, as secretary of state for war, was given a seat on this committee; and Sir Henry Wilson, as the government's chief adviser on strategy, was usually in attendance. This subcommittee of the Imperial War Cabinet quickly came to overshadow its parent organization. Chaired by Lloyd George, it was dominated by military and political leaders who believed that the war in Asia was as important, if not more so, than the war in Europe.

To his chagrin, however, Lloyd George discovered that the deliberations of the Committee of Prime Ministers had been rendered largely irrelevant by the powers of the generalissimo. Having broken the stranglehold of the "westerners" on British strategy with the dismissal of General Robertson in February, Lloyd George found that the means to that end, unity of command, presented a formidable obstacle to implementing his peripheral strategy. Shielded by Foch's position, the "western" generals had greater ability than ever to plan and conduct military operations, free from Whitehall's interference.

The determination of Pershing and his staff to launch a great American offensive in Lorraine in the direction of Metz also undermined Lloyd George's plans. The creation of an independent American army was the first step toward that goal. On July 10, in a conference with Pershing at Bombon, Foch had proclaimed: "The day when there are one million Americans in France, America cuts a figure in the war. America has a right to an American army; the American army must be."[19] Gaining acceptance for the AEF's Lorraine strategy was more difficult, for Foch wanted the Americans to participate in 1919 in Allied attacks from the Argonne Forest to Arras, which would shift American emphasis away from Metz. Fox Conner spoke for the leaders of the AEF when he wrote: "A campaign limited to the front planned by General Foch carries with it no reasonable prospect of final victory during 1919. This final victory can only be had by reaching the vitals of Germany and by destroying her armed forces. Since her vitals are in Lorraine the simplest method is to take the most direct road to that region."[20]

On July 24 Pershing and the other Allied commanders-in-chief on the western front, Haig and Pétain, met with Foch. It was probably Pershing's most enjoyable meeting yet with the other commanders. With some 1,200,000 Yanks in Europe and his forces engaged on a large scale with the enemy, he believed that he had earned a position of equality with the Allied generals. Three days earlier he had reached an agreement with Pétain to establish American armies on two sections of the French front, one active and the other a quiet sector for battle-weary and untrained American divisions. With the expectation of an American offensive there later in the year, the southern side of the St. Mihiel salient was chosen as this "rest" sector. Pershing then dined with Haig and gained his support for the formation of an independent American army. Significantly, as he slyly admitted in his memoirs, he omitted any mention of "the probable early recall of our units from his front."[21]

The results of Pershing's lobbying, which reached fruition at the July 24 meeting, could not have been more satisfactory from the American point of view. Pershing joined the Allied generals in embracing a policy of maintaining offensive pressure on Germany, with the AEF being given responsibility for a future campaign at St. Mihiel. Pershing immediately issued orders, to go into effect on August 10, creating the American First Army in the Marne sector. Earlier, with the bulk of his forces attached to the French army, Pershing had received his orders through Pétain. As head of the First Army, he now stood equal with the French and British commanders-in-chief.

As Pershing anticipated the prospect of achieving an American victory in 1919, Lloyd George plotted to get his fair share of Yanks in the British sector. Britain's dominant shipping position represented the only leverage left to the prewar's premier global power. Responding to an American request for assistance in fulfilling its hundred-division program by July 1919, the British agreed to provide additional transport. The British share (with some Italian assistance) was 180,000 men a month; 120,000 would be transported by the Americans and French.[22] Thereupon, on July 24, Washington informed London that although additional British transport was still required, the fulfillment of the hundred-division program was impossible.[23]

With Washington retreating from that program, Lloyd George saw an opportunity to hedge on his promise to provide shipping for some 180,000 troops a month. He sent Hankey to visit Sir Joseph Maclay "to 'rig' him in regard to an American application for tonnage to help in their military programme in France." The minister of shipping was instructed to manipulate British sea transport figures "to force Foch to put some of the American divisions to train behind our line and to take over part of our line in winter."[24]

On the same day that Lloyd George prepared the ground for pressuring the Americans and French through Britain's dominant shipping position, Foch cabled Sir Henry Wilson his decision immediately to create two American armies, situating them both on the French front. Foch also ominously suggested that Pershing might "ask for the divisions now in the British zone to go to the American zone when fully trained, if they are left holding back lines, but that if it is proposed to use them in active operations General Pershing will probably not ask for them."[25]

Lloyd George was thunderstruck at this news. Despite his pressure tactics, the BEF, rather than having additional American divisions allocated to it, was in danger of losing all its American troops. Greatly agitated over this "French plot," he launched into a tirade during a meeting of the "X" Committee on July 26. He accused the French of a "political game" that General Foch was playing "at M. Clemenceau's instigation." As reported in the "X" Committee's minutes, he went on to say that "the whole object of it was, by depriving us of the support of the American troops, to force us to keep up our present total of 59 divisions regardless of the effect upon our industries and national life generally. It was intolerable that the French should attempt to put the screw upon us in that way and he was determined that if this continued he would ask the authority of the Cabinet to refuse the French any ships for the conveyance of American troops to France. . . . He was determined to call a halt to this process of putting the screw on us. He would have to give the reasons quite plainly to M. Clemenceau though not to the United States."[26] Lloyd George followed up his angry words with decisive action, gaining the War Cabinet's approval to use British shipping "as a lever to secure a fair redistribution of Allied forces in the line on the introduction therein of the American divisions."[27]

On August 2 the prime minister sent a bombshell message to Paris which emphasized that Washington, although unable to fulfill its one hundred-division program, still required further British shipping to achieve its reduced eighty-division program. "Owing to the serious character of this intimation I immediately made a preliminary examination of the question with the Minister of Shipping, Sir Joseph Maclay. I regret to say that we shall be unable to render further assistance in cargo tonnage, and will probably have to reduce our troop transport tonnage."[28]

Logistics took center stage in the Anglo-French tug-of-war over Allied war policy. The British controlled sea transport, but the French were in the process of centralizing in Paris all land transportation authority under M. Albert Claveille, the chairman of the Inter-Allied Transportation Committee. Lloyd George, warned by First Lord of the Admiralty Sir Eric Geddes, a leading authority on rail transportation, that Foch's consolidation plan would allow him "to control the detailed strategy of the Allied Armies' Commanders [more] than any number of Conventions," attempted to counter the French move by centering all shipping decisions in London.[29]

With this Anglo-French power struggle as a backdrop, the British civilians took stock of the improved military situation that followed the checking of the Germans on the Marne.[30] Their conclusions on the future direction of British military policy were in sharp contrast with the growing optimism of GHQ BEF. From 1916 on, approximately two-thirds of the British and imperial divisions had been committed to the western front.[31] If imperial troops such as Indian soldiers (who played the major role in Britain's war with Turkey) are omitted from the calculation, the percentage of the British contribution to the Continental war is even greater. Haunted by Britain's massive losses since the Battle of the Somme in 1916, the politicians' perspective was shaped by the country's manpower resources. They needed to realise that they were "passing from the time of enlisting 75,000 men a month to 20,000," Milner stressed within the War Cabinet, which meant moving from "an army of big to one of moderate dimensions."[32] In 1916 the nation had provided 1,200,000 recruits; in 1917, 800,000; in 1918, an estimated 700,000; and in 1919, a projected 300,000 (of these, 90,000 would go to the air force and 40,000 to the navy, leaving only 170,000 for the army.) Lloyd George clearly spoke for his government when he talked of limiting British "strategy to our income."[33]

The catalyst for these important discussions by the Empire statesmen was the memorandum, "British Military Policy 1918-1919," dated July 25, which had been prepared by the CIGS on the prime minister's instructions. No soldier had expressed a greater interest in military theaters "over the salt water," as he expressed it, or tailored his strategic advice to fit more closely the geopolitical goals of the Milnerites than Sir Henry Wilson. These views, in fact, had been largely responsible for his becoming the government's primary strategic adviser. This latest strategic appreciation, however, seemed to indicate that he had been a closet "westerner" all along. Stressing General Robertson's familiar though no less valid argument of the German advantage of interior lines of communication, Sir Henry came down hard on Lloyd George's and the Milnerites' formula for achieving a satisfactory peace. Rather than British concentration on the periphery, he favored limited military operations in the West as a prelude for a decisive victory over the German army in 1919.[34] General Wilson's change of heart was, in all likelihood, due to the improved Allied position and his probable knowledge that the higher commanders on the western front had in great secrecy adopted an offensive strategy for the last half of 1918, with the now rested BEF initially assigned the leading role. This information, if known to him, he dared not share with his civilian superiors.

"Wully redivivus," was the shocked prime minister's bitter remark (alluding by nickname to Sir William Robertson) when he read Wilson's memorandum.[35] With enemy troops pouring out of the Marne salient under Franco-American pressure, Lloyd George recognized that the immediate danger of a German victory was over. Britain's position outside of Western Europe also looked better. There were reports of German soldiers being withdrawn from Palestine, and the swirling chaos of the borderlands of the old tsarist empire was proving to be quicksand for the Germans. "Russia merely absorbed some 30 German divisions," the Welshman reported to the Committee of Prime Ministers, but the Germans "were in despair there and did not know quite what to do."[36]

Notwithstanding these encouraging developments, Lloyd George, Smuts, and Milner vigorously attacked General Wilson's proposal to concentrate the British Empire's remaining military resources on the western front. The following sentiments appear in the minutes of the Committee of Prime Ministers meeting on July 31.

Milner: "In his view the Western front was a candle that burned all the moths that entered it."

Smuts: "He did not question that the Western front was the decisive front, but from the beginning of the War it had always proved the fatal front."

Lloyd George: "The enemy had only done it [attacked on the western front] twice since the very first onslaught, namely, at Verdun and in the present year. If the enemy had gone eastward or made an attack on Italy in the present year we should now be in a most difficult position."[37]

To Milner, Lloyd George, and Smuts, Britain's exhaustion meant that the western front must be a secondary theater until Pershing had the weight of numbers and trained troops to overwhelm the German army. It was "out of the question," Milner stressed, that the British could ever again "play the great *rôle* on the Western front." In Lloyd George's view, the nature of Britain's military effort during the last phase of the war would determine "the position of the British Empire when ultimate victory" was achieved. He gave a graphic prognosis of what would happen if Sir Henry's advice were followed: "We might batter the enemy, and possibly they might have to sue for peace. What would be the conditions when that occurred? America would have an Army equivalent to 120 divisions, France perhaps 40, and the British Empire perhaps 23. When Australia said she wanted the Pacific Islands, or Palestine, President Wilson would look down his nose and say: That he had entered the War with quite different ideas in view, he would say he had his 120 divisions ready to continue the War, and he would ask what assistance we could give." Before deciding "to put our Army on the table next year and get it smashed to pieces" said Lloyd George, "this consideration ought to be very carefully weighed."[38]

Although Hughes, the Australian prime minister, strongly dissented, the Committee of Prime Ministers favored deploying a good part of Britain's remaining military strength away from the West, both as a guarantee of a settlement in the interests of the British Empire and as a protection against Germany if it stood on the defensive in the West and concentrated on the East in 1919.[39] If Lloyd George had his way, Hankey recorded in his diary, the British commitment to the western front would be halved by 1919, with the surplus divisions employed in Italy, in Salonika, or against Turkey. "This of course will get us into great difficulties with our allies," Hankey admitted.[40]

While his political superiors were discussing diminishing his force for use in other theaters, Haig, in consultation with Foch, moved forward his preparations for a surprise attack against the Germans at Amiens. The government received its first indication that something was afoot on August 1, when Borden, the Canadian prime minister, informed the civilians that he had been "told in confidence and great secrecy" that the Canadian Army Corps was being deployed for an offensive.[41]

The ministers were shocked, especially when the CIGS denied any knowledge of a forthcoming operation. The last time he had seen Foch, Sir Henry insisted, the generalissimo had talked of a German attack rather than any Allied offensive. The worried statesmen then discussed their ability to control Haig, who was under the strategic control of Foch. As Smuts had exclaimed the previous day, if Foch planned a great offensive, "the British Government should have a very serious talk with him." It was agreed that the government could not stand by helplessly if Foch countenanced large-scale attacks.[42]

Instructed by the ministers to discover Foch's intentions, General Wilson reported on August 6 that "it was difficult to say exactly what General Foch's forthcoming operations would be." The Frenchman said he planned to keep the pressure on the retreating Germans, but so far as Wilson knew, "General Foch did not intend to undertake any considerable operations."[43]

Two days later, at 4:20 A.M., 2,000 big guns opened fire in the Amiens salient. Rawlinson's Fourth Army jumped off, assisted by French troops on its right. The forces of the British Empire swept forward in a dense mist, with the Canadian Corps on the right, the Australian Corps in the center and the British on the left. Supported by massed tanks and air cover, the BEF took 16,000 prisoners and 200 guns within two hours. By noon the advance had surged forward nine miles. It was the BEF's best day of the war, the German army's worst.

Haig's triumph at Amiens did not go unrecognized in London. Sir Henry Wilson delivered glowing reports on the BEF's progress. Milner tried to put British losses in correct perspective, telling the Committee of Prime Ministers that after four days' fighting Haig reported only 20,000 casualties out of some 150,000 men engaged against the Germans. The British had actually captured almost as many Germans as they had suffered casualties.[44]

Always the optimist, Haig thought his success suggested that the war could be ended in 1918 if the Allies continued their offensive pressure into the fall. He told Winston Churchill, then minister of munitions that "[we] ought to do our utmost to get a decision this autumn. We are engaged in a 'wearing out battle,' and are outlasting and beating the enemy."[45] Lloyd George was unconvinced. Fearing that the BEF would wear out along with the German army he told Hankey that he did "not take a very sanguine view of our military prospects, in spite of recent success."[46] Haig's resumption of the offensive had not only seized the strategical initiative fom Ludendorff; it also threatened to dictate war policy to the civilians for the remainder of the war. If Haig continued his offensive, the BEF's losses were bound to be huge—and irreplaceable. With Haig's casualties for August exceeding 100,000, the prime minister believed that his fears were coming true.[47] The inevitable result, even with ultimate victory, which he did not think possible in 1918, would be that the British Empire would see its political influence shrink along with its army.[48]

The prospect of massive casualties weighed heavily on the minds of the Empire statesmen as they discussed future war plans in mid-August. Their preliminary policy draft was overwhelmingly Lloyd Georgian in tone. It emphasized military operations away from the western front and opposed Sir Henry Wilson's advocacy of limited attacks in the West in 1918 as prelude to a decisive victory in 1919: "If we are to enter upon a great offensive next year we should conserve our Army for that purpose, give it rest, and bring it to the highest possible pitch of training, in order that it may combine with the American Army which is now being built up in whatsoever operations it is decided to utilise." It also noted that "the husbanding of our man-power has become a consideration on which the whole future of our Empire depends."[49]

When this preliminary draft was discussed by the prime ministers on August 16, Hughes, the blunt-speaking Australian, said what was on everyone's mind. If the draft were adopted, "the position would be very delicate as regards our Allies. It would be difficult to tell France and our other Allies that we now preferred to look after ourselves and to draw the line as to the number of troops we would place at stake."[50] It was equally true that Britain, by withholding her military resources if military events took a decisive turn in the favor of the Allies, might prolong the war. Lloyd George had to admit that if the Allies were on the verge of defeating the German army, the British could not hold back. But at this time, he obviously did not believe that Haig's steady advance on the Somme in August portended victory in 1918, and perhaps not even in 1919.[51] The formidable Hindenburg Line, with its ten-mile deep defensive system, remained to be conquered.[52]

The checkmating of Germany on the Marne might in fact endanger the Empire if Ludendorff adopted a defensive posture in the West and concentrated on expansion in the East. "Nobody concerned in this war except ourselves has any interest in Asia," is the way Smuts expressed this fear. The South African leader also warned against fighting the war "to the absolute end, because I think that, although that end will be fatal to the enemy, it may possibly be fatal to us too." In that case, the United States and Japan would be the great winners.[53]

By linking the indirect strategy favored by Lloyd George and the Milnerites to a compromise peace that would leave German power intact in Europe, Smuts was being logical. The prime minister and many other British leaders, although determined to prevent the British army and economy from being reduced to second-rate status, paradoxically clung to the hope of military victory. Only American manpower could prevent their war policy from being impaled on the horns of this tormenting dilemma. In desperation, Lloyd George sought to revive amalgamation, which to Pershing was akin to lighting a match in a room full of gas. Washington, which had emphasized the shipping of men rather than their supplies, was amassing a vast force in Europe yet did not have the required cargo transport to supply this force. If the Americans could not maintain the eighty divisions, Lloyd George told the Imperial War Cabinet, "it would be better to fit them into our organisation."[54] He had in mind an American army of from fifty to sixty divisions with the surplus assigned to Anglo-French forces and becoming a part of their existing logistical systems.[55]

The War Office and GHQ BEF, quite sensibly, had long since abandoned any thought of feeding American troops into British divisions. Radcliffe, the General Staff's director of military operations, argued that "it would be a most shortsighted and mistaken policy to put any obstacle in the way of General Pershing [in creating his own army]."[56] When brought into the Imperial War Cabinet's discussions, he bluntly told the civilians that "it would be wrong to give the Americans the impression that we were trying to tie them to our apron strings." Yanks cooperating with the BEF offered the British their best hope of receiving direct American assistance. The War Office, in fact, was at this time discussing with Griscom the possibility of Britain's assuming responsibility for supplying, from Dunkirk, an American army in the British sector. Any American force so dependent upon British supply lines would, of course, be under Haig's strategic control.[57]

This was the field marshal's hope and expectation. He agreed with Foch's conception of a broad Allied offensive stretching from Verdun on the Meuse River to the North Sea.[58] Instead of a series of limited blows by each army against separate German salients (Foch's conception), however, Haig wanted to go for the jugular. "The eccentric was to be made concentric," Brigadier General John Charteris has explained.[59] Haig wanted the French and the American First Army to treat the front from Verdun almost to the North Sea as one great salient, attacking it on its flanks or shoulders.

Haig's ambitious strategic goal for the BEF was to rupture the lateral German rail communications, through either their capture or their neutralization under artillery fire. Without these vital rail communications, the German army would be unable to maintain its position in France and Belgium.

The Scotsman was willing to risk an attack against the hitherto impregnable Hindenburg Line because he believed that his forces represented the best chance the Allies had for victory over the German army in the near future. He gave no thought to a war prolonged until 1920; on one of Sir Henry Wilson's memoranda that talked of future military operations, he commented, "What rubbish! Who will last till 1920—only America?!"[60]

Although Haig accepted that the Empire must bear the brunt of the fighting, he knew his government could not replace his losses. An integral part of his offensive strategy was the utilization of at least one American corps on his front. He was thus unable to conceal his exasperation when Pershing informed him on August 12 that as soon as the Amiens offensive, in which only one American regiment had participated, was over, he was probably going to withdraw his five divisions still training with the BEF. Curiously, Haig initially kept this unhappy information to himself. On August 22 Lord Milner learned informally from General Rawlinson that Pershing had begun to move American divisions out of the British zone. He was furious, telling Griscom that their removal was "premature and the manner of removal without consultation showed want of consideration" for both him and the prime minister. Sir Henry Wilson was, if anything, even more upset, "so angry that he can hardly speak civilly to me," Griscom reported to Pershing.[61]

The prime minister was having no better success in using shipping as a weapon in his negotiations with the French. On August 18 he received an uncompromising letter from Clemenceau which expressed concern over actions "tending to show that British Empire has arrived at end of sacrifices which it could make in common cause." Did not Lloyd George realize, Clemenceau stressed, that a satisfactory political settlement depended upon the British Empire's doing its fair share? Otherwise the American military effort would give Wilson the upper hand in the peace settlement.[62]

Having joined the battle, Lloyd George was not inclined to retreat. He ordered the War, Shipping, and Foreign offices to make no new pledges on American troop and cargo transport. He also emphasized that existing arrangements to ship American troops lasted only through December 1918.[63] Since early August, the American government had known of Lloyd George's threat to reduce the flow of American troops and supplies across the Atlantic. The French had given Pershing a copy of Lloyd George's August 2 letter to Clemenceau. Believing his 1919 war-winning Lorraine strategy imperiled, the American field commander immediately cabled Baker requesting "an early and complete understanding with the British Government on this subject." Informed by Baker that Lloyd George's shocking letter was possibly not a final decision, but rather a negotiating ploy with the French, President Wilson agreed with Pershing that shipping arrangements with the British must be resolved, and soon. "This is serious," he wrote Baker, "and how characteristic after urging the 100 division programme! We must now insist that the decision be definite and final as to what they can do. Would that we were dealing with responsible persons!"[64]

Lloyd George's threat to reduce shipping, if serious, would gravely undermine American military prospects for 1919, in part because of continued setbacks in American merchant ship construction. Not until the last months of 1918, when some hundred hulls were being completed every day, did American shipbuilding hit its stride.[65] The British estimated that it would be March 1919 at the earliest before America would have the shipping to supply eighty divisions in Europe.[66]

The American leadership, with Wilson's war cabinet reviewing the Allied advance on maps at the War Department, sensed victory in mid-August. Bliss reported from Versailles: "Everything now points to favorable conditions for launching a conclusive campaign on the western front next year, and if enemy's resistance is crushed on this front it will cease everywhere." Believing that victory would come through American "troops, supplies and money," Bliss urged Washington to put pressure on the British through Foch. "If Marshall Foch will state that the 80 division program gives reasonable assurance of a final campaign next year I feel sure that United States can demand and secure the necessary tonnage."[67] Unless the British promised to make up for American transport deficiency, the future American military role would be plunged into uncertainty.

"There must be a show-down on this subject," Baker wrote the president, who accepted the suggestion that his secretary of war go to Europe to make possible the implementation of the eighty-division program.[68] On August 31, Baker left for France on a troopship.

As Baker departed the United States, Lord Reading served as Lloyd George's emissary to the French. Having finally abandoned any hope of amalgamation, the prime minister focused on getting the Americans to take over part of the British front, and his heavy-handed approach to Foch and Clemenceau seemed to be having some effect.[69] Pershing had removed only three of the remaining five American divisions training behind British lines, and Foch agreed to place the two divisions left under Haig's command on the "active Battle front."[70]

When Lloyd George received this encouraging news, he took the extraordinary step of having the CIGS instruct Haig to make prudent use of these American forces. As he told Milner and Sir Henry Wilson, "If the Americans got badly smashed up it would be as bad as in the case of the Canadians [during Passchendaele], since in that case General Pershing would never send any more men to the British line."[71] Lloyd George was convinced that in 1919 the American army would "take a large slice of the front now occupied by our troops."[72] But until he had a firm commitment on this, he was, as he informed Reading, prepared to withhold "further assistance in the matter of shipping" beyond December.[73]

Reading had taken with him to Paris a letter from the prime minister that made a strong defense of Britain's contributions to the Allied war effort. "I venture to believe that history will record that no nation engaged in this war has made a more complete or unreserved use of their resources in man-power and material for the Allied cause than the people of Great Britain," Lloyd George asserted. He stressed that the "reserves of the Allied army are in America."[74] The French, however, continued to argue that Britain had to maintain its existing divisions in France, if not in ration strength, at least in total number.[75]

Pershing was only dimly aware of this controversy that separated the British and French political leadership during Reading's visit to France from August 31 to September 8. He had a more important matter on his mind, the launching of his long-planned offensive to reduce the St. Mihiel salient. He shifted First Army headquarters to Ligny-en-Barrois— about twenty-five miles southeast of St. Mihiel— and began to mass his scattered divisions, collecting three corps of fourteen divisions, or some 550,000 troops, for the first all-American offensive of the war.

On August 30, however, the generalissimo in person showed up at Ligny with an abrupt change of plans. As Sir Henry Wilson explained to Milner and Lloyd George in London, Foch planned to "employ part of the American forces with the British and part with the French, leaving only one Army under General Pershing's command."[76] This scheme, of course, would divide Pershing's forces and undermine his plan to win the war in 1919 with a great attack in Lorraine, especially if the initial phase of this American offensive, the reduction of the St. Mihiel salient in 1918, was abandoned. In the Haig-Foch plan, American forces would combine with the French on the right shoulder of this bulge, driving northwest between the Meuse and Aisne rivers toward Mézières and Sedan, with the British on the left shoulder in the area of Cambrai.[77] To Allied generals, who had high praise for American troops but disdain for American staff work, this plan offered the best prospect for victory. As General Wilson told Lloyd George and Milner, if General Pershing insisted on attacking with only American troops, he would either "meet the Germans in large numbers in strongly fortified positions, and suffer heavy casualties," or his advance would collapse "at a relatively early stage, owing to inadequate staff work."[78]

Pershing was stunned. "But Marshal Foch," he said with feeling, "here on the very day that you turn over a sector to the American Army, and almost on the eve of an offensive, you ask me to reduce the operation so that you can take away several of my divisions and assign some to the French Second Army and use others to form an American army to operate on the Aisne in conjunction with the French Fourth Army, leaving me with little to do except hold what will become a quiet sector after the St. Mihiel offensive." When Foch asked him soldier-to-soldier if he wished to "take part in the battle," Pershing shot back, "Most assuredly, but as an American Army and in no other way." At one point, Pershing became so angry that he thought of striking the generalissimo.[79]

On September 2 Pershing, Pétain, and Foch effected a compromise. Pershing was allowed to launch his St. Mihiel offensive, but as soon as it was concluded, he had to extend his front to the Argonne Forest, a distance of approximately sixty miles. With most of the American forces in Europe under his command, he would then participate in the converging Allied attacks with an offensive scheduled for late September in the Meuse-Argonne sector.[80]

Pershing's understanding with Foch has been criticized on several grounds. It was asking too much of Pershing's green corps and army staffs to launch a great attack, immediately disengage, and then in some two weeks assemble a powerful strike force many miles to the north for a second big offensive. Moreover, Pershing chose a theater, the area between the Argonne Forest and the Meuse River, which had limited road communications and was deemed by Colonel Hugh Drum, the First Army's chief of staff, the "most ideal defensive terrain I have ever seen or read about."[81] But Pershing took these considerable risks because his objectives were as much political as they were military. He was determined to keep most of the doughboys under American command in American-dominated operations, rather than utilize them in joint operations where the AEF's accomplishments would be blurred. As he told Marshal Foch on August 30, "Give me a sector anywhere you decide, and I will take it over at once."[82] Nor had he abandoned his conception of a war-winning American offensive in the direction of Metz, to which the reduction of the St. Mihiel salient would be a prelude.

On September 12 Pershing finally got his chance to fight in his own sector with his infantry-rich army. He had struck a hard bargain with Foch over the support the French would provide the American First Army: Foch agreed to assign some 110,000 French troops to his command. Allied material support for the AEF was even more impressive. Breakdowns in American industrial mobilization and the decision to ship infantry and machine gun units without their artillery meant that Pershing was dependent upon the Allies for his modern weapons. The First Army's 3,010 artillery pieces, airplanes, and 267 tanks came from the Allied arsenal.

The timing of the AEF's attack could not have been more opportune. The Yanks fell on the Germans just as they were in the midst of a planned withdrawal. In some thirty hours the battle was over except for local operations that flickered on until September 16. Two hundred square miles of French territory were liberated, 450 guns and 16,000 prisoners captured.

On September 13, Pershing and Secretary of War Baker met near the village of St. Mihiel to celebrate a great American triumph, both political and military, which has been characterized as "the stroll at St. Mihiel" or as "the sector where the Americans relieved the Germans." Victory had indeed come with deceptive ease against a greatly out-numbered and retreating foe. Nonetheless, an independent American force under its own commanders, with its own tactics and its own strategic objectives, had met and defeated elements from what was still the world's greatest fighting force. The AEF, fighting 3,000 miles from home, had made dramatic progress since its regiment-sized attack against the village of Cantigny in May.

Pershing later argued that a great opportunity was lost when the AEF stopped its advance at St. Mihiel to cooperate with Foch's and Haig's concentric attacks, which shifted American resources north-ward. "Without doubt, an immediate continuation of the advance would have carried us well beyond the Hindenburg Line and possibly into Metz" he wrote in his memoirs.[83] Pershing's creation of an inde-pendent American force at least six months earlier than Allied generals had thought possible was a remarkable achievement that should not be understated. But the First Army was a fighting force still in its formative stages. American troops could not move or fight effectively with massive traffic jams occurring, coordination of infantry and artil-lery lacking, and command and control problems abounding. The commander of the I Corps at St. Mihiel, Hunter Liggett, later provided a realistic appraisal of Pershing's forces in September. "The possibility of taking Metz and the rest of it, had the battle been fought on the original plan, existed in my opinion, only on the supposition that our army was a well-oiled, fully coordinated machine, which it was not as yet."[84]

Germany had begun September in occupation of more French and Russian territory than it had held in 1917, with an army of over 2,500,000, all its Allies still in the war, and its formidable defensive position, the Hindenburg Line, intact. Defeat followed defeat, how-ever, as the month progressed. Daily, Berlin's position became more hopeless. In the Balkans the Allies collapsed the Bulgarian front with a powerful offensive on September 15. Four days later "Bull" Allenby launched a spectacularly successful British attack against Turkish de-fenses near Megiddo. Supported by air power, horse soldiers main-tained the momentum of the attack as the Turkish and German forces fell to pieces in Palestine. Even before these dramatic successes on the periphery, the War Office had assured the Eastern Committee on September 11 that it would not be possible for the Germans "to take advantage of the comparative cessation of military operations on the Western front during the winter months to indulge in any big cam-paign in the East."[85]

The war news from Haig's command was also extremely good. General Wilson told the War Cabinet of captured documents showing that the Germans were "in a bad condition." As the British attacks at Havrincourt and Epéhy began on September 12 against the outer defenses of the Hindenburg Line, the CIGS suggested that given "the evidence of the last few weeks," no defensive position could "be regarded as impregnable."[86] On his own initiative, Haig visited the War Office to persuade Milner that his continuous attacks constituted the *"beginning of the end"* for the German army.[87]

Milner had heard similar expressions of confidence too many times in the past not to be skeptical. He left London to inspect the war up close. He found Foch full of praise for Haig's generalship. This was no longer the Haig of the mud and blood of Passchendaele, Milner reported to Lloyd George. Instead of "hammering away at a single point" with distant objectives in mind, the new Haig had launched "a series of successive attacks, all more or less surprises & all profitable" with an economy of losses.[88]

British casualties mounted, however, as Haig's forces pressed forward. From the Battle of Amiens, August 8, to the Armistice, November 11, the BEF incurred some 350,000 casualties.[89] Back in London, Milner told Sir Henry Wilson that Haig was "ridiculously optimistic." The lanky Irishman agreed, writing in his diary, "The Man Power is the trouble & D H & Foch & Du Cane *can't* understand it."[90]

With the British secure in the East, Lloyd George no longer thought of transferring divisions from the BEF to the outer theaters.[91] The embarrassing Draft Report of the Committee of Prime Ministers that was so at variance with American war policy (and the current military situation!) was not signed but allowed to die a quiet death. Instead, Foch's and the Americans' "western" strategy for the autumn of 1918 and 1919 was ratified by the military representatives of the SWC.[92] When March gave Wilson a copy of this Joint Note No. 37, dated September 10, 1918, the president responded, "I have read it carefully and with not a little satisfaction."[93]

Lloyd George still did not expect the war to end in 1918, however, and was no less concerned than before about the political conse- quences should the British Empire enter peace negotiations with a battered and diminished army in Western Europe. The British had carried the weight of the war in 1918, while the role of the French was reduced by the addition of American forces on their front.[94] By the time of the Armistice the French in fact held only forty miles of "active front."[95]

With his thoughts on 1919, Lloyd George was prepared to con- front Baker over the necessity of having more Yanks in the British sector. As Bonar Law said of Lloyd George at this time, "He will only see one side of a question when he has made up his mind."[96] In negotiations with Reading and the Inter-Allied Maritime Council, Baker had been discussing future British shipping obligations to the AEF, especially cargo tonnage to supply the American troops, and these talks—although delayed when Reading became ill with gout— were nearing conclusion.[97]

On September 29 Lloyd George, who was himself recuperating from influenza at Danny Park, reminded Maclay that he had the full authority of the War Cabinet behind him and that he was acting as the "trustee of the interests of the British soldier." He ordered that during the discussions of the Inter-Allied Maritime Council, the shipping controller pursue "relentlessly" the placement of more American troops with the BEF.[98] When Lloyd George sent Milner a copy of this letter, he noted, that "the American Army is not to be used merely for the relief of the French line whilst our men are left in an exhausted and depleted condition to hold the mud through the winter."[99]

The American "show-down" with the British on the matter of shipping finally occurred when Baker, at the prime minister's invitation, drove to Danny Park on September 30. Although Griscom's secondhand account is the only record of this confrontation, it has the ring of truth in its essentials. After lunch, Lloyd George bitterly complained about the small number of American troops in the British sector.[100] As far as Great Britain was concerned, he exclaimed, the American army was "perfectly usless, and the shipping devoted to bringing it over utterly wasted." In the face of the Welshman's violent outburst, Baker did not blink. How could the prime minister say that the American Army was "useless?" He had just returned from France, where he had studied war maps showing that the AEF was opposed by a considerable part of the German army. Baker then called Lloyd George's bluff. "If you decide to withdraw your shipping," he coolly told the Prime Minister, "I shall cable immediately to Washington to cease sending troops on British ships, which may then be released at once." Baker's message was crystal clear as his voice rose and his fist thumped the table. Pershing's control and use of American forces was nonnegotiable.[101] The massive Meuse-Argonne Offensive, the largest battle in American history, which had begun on September 26, gave added force to his words.

On the way back to London, Reading told Baker: "Oh, by the way, Mr. Secretary, the Prime Minister sent for me before we started and asked me to excuse his not saying good-by. Incidentally, he also asked me to say to you that you should think no more about the matter which he raised for discussion after lunch."[102]

Subsequently, the Allied Maritime Transport Council, meeting at Lancaster House October 1-2, recommended that no reduction in

American troop transport take place for the remainder of the year, "in spite of the grave condition of the import programmes." An additional 500,000 tons (which included 200,000 tons that had already been arranged for in discussions between Baker and Reading)[103] was diverted from imports to the American program from October through December.[104] On October 6 a triumphant Baker cabled Wilson: "Tonnage situation favorably cleared up."[105]

The single-minded determination of America's leaders to defeat the German army in Western Europe had served to hold the alliance together, simultaneously increasing Wilson's potential political influence. While Baker thwarted British efforts to place more American troops on their front, President Wilson gave unequivocal notice that he would send no more troops to northern Russia or cooperate with any Allied effort to launch military operations in South Russia.[106] Lloyd George, playing what he thought was his trump card, British dominance in shipping, had been completely routed in his efforts to harness the American military role to British political and strategic objectives.

Just as American's shipping problems seemed resolved, Germany cracked. On the night of October 3-4 the German government, accepting the Fourteen Points as a basis for peace, appealed to President Wilson for an armistice. Wilson told his secretary Joseph P. Tumulty and Colonel House, "This means the end of the war."[107] Serious fighting still lay ahead—the German army remained capable of waging a tenacious defensive struggle—but Wilson was right. With victory in sight, attention increasingly shifted from the battlefield to the peace settlement.

12

Pax Americana?

The war's unexpected conclusion in November could not have been more advantageous to the British Empire's geopolitical goals. Nor could the results from the worldwide battlefields have been more surprising. As late as August the British political leadership, believing that the war would not reach a climax in Western Europe until 1919 at the earliest, had favored a conservative Continental military policy designed to further imperial interests.

British arms in the outer theaters gave Lloyd George the strong negotiating position he sought. Following the Battle of Megiddo in Palestine in mid-September, Allenby's cavalry pursued the broken enemy, advancing 350 miles in thirty-eight days. In the Mesopotamian theater the British Empire's forces pushed north of Baghdad to Mosul. Meanwhile, Baku was reoccupied and a British position established on the Caspian Sea. With a peace settlement in mind, the War Cabinet urged its eastern generals to secure control of as much Turkish territory as possible before the end of hostilities.[1]

To the initial discomfort of the Imperial War Cabinet, the BEF also assumed the leading role in the Allied counteroffensives after the Second Battle of the Marne. Lloyd George and most of the Empire statesmen accepted the necessity of defeating the German army to get a durable peace but were determined to husband British manpower. If Foch's position as generalissimo had not protected Haig from London's political interference, the BEF would not have been given permission to launch its series of successful offensives. On the same day, October 5, that President Wilson told House and Tumulty that Germany's bid for peace through Washington meant an end to the war, the BEF achieved one of its most dramatic successes, the breaching of the final defenses of the famous Hindenburg Line. Some 35,000 prisoners and 380 guns were taken in a nine-day drive. This victory was only one of the nine successive defeats inflicted upon the German army by the BEF from August 8, the Battle of Amiens, to the last British drive of the war, the Battle of Sambre, November 1-11. During this glorious Hundred Days' Campaign, Haig's forces captured 2,840 guns and 188,700 prisoners.

These victories in both Europe and the Middle East had come without employing a large American force in the British sector. Haig advanced with the support of only two American divisions, organized into a corps. When Pershing refused to replace American casualties (some 13,182 men), Haig had to withdraw this corps from the line on October 20. Although Pershing subsequently promised reinforcements on October 23, he rejected the plea to bring Haig's American Corps up to four divisions. This rationed American assistance to the BEF continued to rankle the prime minister, who told the "X" Committee that with "250,000 men . . . being brought over every month, and British ships alone . . . carrying from 160,000 to 190,000 men a month," it was "preposterous that only 2 divisions were given to the British Army."[2]

As British arms in September and October surpassed all expectations in Europe and elsewhere, the American First Army between the Meuse River and the Argonne Forest proceeded at a crawl with heavy losses. To reach the key German rail communications in the Sedan-Mezieres region, the Americans had to overcome determined defenders manning sophisticated and extensive fortifications along a narrow front. "There was no elbow room," Drum, one of the AEF's most able staff officers, has written. "We had to drive straight through."[3]

The First Army's staff hoped to exploit the AEF's material and numerical superiority to achieve a breakthrough. Encouraged by the easy American victory at St. Mihiel, AEF planners expected to advance ten miles within the first twenty-four hours of the attack. On September 26 nine divisions, organized into three corps, attacked along a twenty-mile front. Facing these double-strength American divisions were five under-strength German divisions. With only four of the nine American divisions ever having served in the line, however, the AEF's offensive soon faltered. Inexperienced units lost their cohesion when faced with stiff German resistance. American logistics bordered on total collapse. "Whether because of incompetence or inexperience or both," Donald Smythe has asserted, "the First Army was wallowing in an unbelievable logistical snarl. It was as if someone had taken the army's intestines out and dumped them all over the table."[4]

The First Army tried again with a renewed offensive on October 4-5. Rather than the open warfare with "bayonet fighters" that Pershing had envisaged, the conflict resembled the attrition battles that had characterized most of the earlier fighting on the western front. The AEF advanced eleven kilometers on September 26. During the next three weeks, the advance covered only five kilometers. The combination of limited advance with mounting casualties took its toll on Pershing. Driving near the front, he momentarily broke down, holding his head and uttering his dead wife's name. "Frankie . . . Frankie . . . my God, sometimes I don't know how I can go on."[5]

Before the autumn of 1918 the United States had succeeded brilliantly in fitting its political objectives to its role in the land war. Wilson's political and Pershing's military independence had been maintained, goals that were intimately connected with dominating the peace settlement. In September and October, however, America's growing political and military influence was in some respects being neutralized by the march of military events.

Yet President Wilson conducted peace talks as if he held Britain's fate as well as Germany's in his hands. Despite the enormous casualties that the British had suffered in wearing down the German army, they were not consulted before Wilson responded to Germany's entreaties for peace. Colville Barclay, the British chargé d'affaires in Washington, reported to the Foreign Office that during a dinner in honor of Sir Eric Geddes the president had given no hint of the response he planned to make to the first German note. Smiling, he had only suggested that his "position was a difficult one, as the Central Powers were professing to be accepting his own terms."[6]

And the Allies would, too, if Wilson had his way. Urged by House to "try to commit the Allies to some of the things for which we are fighting" before victory was in their grasp,[7] Wilson had delivered an important speech on war aims on September 27 at a Liberty Loan drive in New York city. The European nations were warned that the United States wanted a "permanent" peace that could only be made without "any kind of compromise or abatement" of Wilson's liberal principles. The Allies were invited to join the president in making a peace that would reflect the "final triumph of justice and fair dealing."[8]

In responding to Berlin's peace feeler, Wilson knew that he was walking through a political mine field, both at home and abroad.[9] His powerful enemies Henry Cabot Lodge and Theodore Roosevelt were campaigning hard for German "unconditional surrender," a position that had considerable popular appeal with the war-aroused American public. Wilson feared that he might damage Democratic chances in the forthcoming congressional elections if he were successfully portrayed as favoring a soft policy toward the Hun. The Allies were no less concerned that weakness on his part might alter the whole military and political situation that seemed to be turning so dramatically against Berlin.

These considerations, however, were almost certainly outweighed in Wilson's mind by what appeared a heaven-sent opportunity to impose his peace program on the Allies as well as the enemy. Hoping to create a balanced environment for a liberal peace, Wilson resurrected his formula of stopping the war short of the total victory. "He

Woodrow Wilson leads the victory parade. "All together now, boys!"
From *Life*, December 5, 1918.

wants," Lodge correctly charged in the Senate, "to be the great world
figure in making the peace. If Germany surrenders unconditionally,
he will only share in making the peace with the Allies. His hold over
the Allies is the German Army in existence, which makes our Army
and our alliance indispensable."[10] Wilson's *realpolitik*, however, was
faulty. What the president did not grasp was that the war's prolongation would make America supreme in the land war. If the AEF delivered the final and decisive blows as Pershing planned, the war would
end with America dominant militarily as well as economically.

The president's tentative response to Berlin on October 8 probably reflected House's advice: "delay without seeming so." [11] Berlin was asked to accept his peace plan, spelled out in the Fourteen Points and subsequent speeches, and to limit any further discussion to the "practical details of their application." Wilson also insisted upon stiff conditions for agreeing to an armistice: Germany's withdrawal from all conquered territory. [12]

Lloyd George had retired for the night on October 12 when Germany's response to Wilson's queries was received in Britain. Returning from having delivered the news, the prime minister's private secretary, Philip Kerr, was quoted as reporting: "There is awful language going on upstairs. I can tell you! He thinks that the Allies are now in a devil of a mess. Wilson has promised them an armistice." [13] Lloyd George was especially annoyed by Wilson's arrogant and unilateral approach to peacemaking.

On October 14, after breakfast, the president and House discussed America's response to the German peace note of October 12. House had never seen Wilson "more disturbed. He said he did not know where to make the entrance in order to reach the heart of the thing. He wanted to make his reply final so there would be no exchange of notes. It reminded him, he said, of a maze. If one went in at the right entrance, he reached the center, but if one took the wrong turning, it was necessary to go out again and do it over." [14] Believing that he was on the verge of reshaping the world, Wilson responded positively to Berlin but insisted on even tougher terms for an armistice: the existing military supremacy of the United States and the Allies must be guaranteed.

Wilson's effort to define the basis for a good peace forced London to confront the unhappy prospect that British influence on any peace settlement might be considerably diminished. [15] The British deeply resented any implication that the president represented the forces of light against the forces of darkness in international affairs. When *The Times* correspondent in Washington, for example, in his October 19 comments on Wilson's political offensive, noted that the American leader stood "for peace with justice" and a peace "free from any taint of an old-fashioned, secret and revengeful diplomacy," the War Cabinet reacted with indignation. The British, Lloyd George stressed, had taken the lead in 1918 in redefining Allied war objectives. Wilson's Fourteen Points address echoed much of what Lloyd George had already expressed three days earlier on January 5. [16]

Two issues that threatened to divide London and Washington were Wilson's precise interpretation of the freedom of the seas—the second of his Fourteen Points—and his views on the fate of the German colonies, which was of particular concern to the Dominions.

Freedom of navigation on the seas would be fiercely resisted if it undermined the security of the British Isles and communications with the British Empire. As for Germany's overseas territories, Cecil expressed the British dilemma succinctly: "While undoubtedly a great case" had been made against returning the colonies, it was "not so easy to make out the case for our keeping them."[17]

British imperialists, it must be remembered, were convinced that their Empire was the world's greatest civilizing force and the foundation of future global stability. In the summer of 1918, when Allied fortunes were uncertain, the Imperial War Cabinet had divided roughly into two camps over how the British Empire should deal with America's emergence as a global power. Lloyd George, Lord Reading, Borden, and others had wanted to enlist American support for the Empire's civilizing mission (and its future security) by giving Washington the administration of some Turkish and German territories: for example, Palestine and German East Africa. "The more it [is] possible to get the United States to undertake responsibility in world affairs," Borden had asserted, "the better for the world as a whole and for the British Empire."[18] Curzon, Hughes, Amery, and other avid imperialists, however, were opposed to allowing Wilson to dictate to the British in imperial matters. Their position was generally summarized by Curzon: "My view is that the salvation of the dark places consists in having them under British rule. It is rather unpopular to state this, and at a Peace Conference it may even be impossible to state it, but I deprecate the idea that when the time comes we are to sit still and take what President Wilson offers us. If he says: 'I cannot have you British there,' I am not prepared to say: 'All right, we are quite willing to disappear from the scene, you take our place.'"[19]

British fears of a serious Anglo-American division over the future of conquered German and Turkish territories were somewhat allayed by Wilson's comments to Wiseman on October 16. The president expressed opposition to returning the captured colonies to Germany and suggested that he would be happy to see them administered by the British, "whose Colonial government [is] in many respects a model for the world." The only catch was that the British should administer these territories as a trustee for the proposed League of Nations, a cover for controlling the enemy's former territories that already had support in London.[20]

The peace process accelerated when Berlin accepted Washington's latest and tougher terms. On October 22 Wilson candidly informed his Cabinet that he planned to force the Allies to discuss peace on his terms. Wilson and others believed that if the war continued until Germany was beaten flat, the Allies would be encouraged to demand harsh and vindictive terms.[21] An unanswered question, of course, was whether America's contributions to the land war really gave Wilson the commanding position he sought over the Allies. As Wilson conferred with his Cabinet, House was on his way to Europe to bind the Allies to a Wilsonian peace.

With matters coming to a head, the British struggled with two difficult and related questions. First, should an armistice be accepted that would save Germany from experiencing invasion and total defeat? Second, how could Wilson be prevented from gaining a preponderance of influence on the peace settlement? Understandably, the British believed that they had earned the right to a peace in the interests of the British Empire. At the same time, London wanted to avoid a split with Washington that would jeopardize the peace and stability of the postwar world.

Lloyd George once again embraced his full-blooded version of a "knock-out blow" and was inclined toward invading the German fatherland and dictating terms. "At the first moment when we were in a position to put the lash on Germany's back she said, 'I give up,'" he contemptuously noted. The question was "whether we ought not to continue lashing her as she . . . lashed France."[22] Given the later Nazi "stab in the back" myth, there was, in fact, a good deal to be said for the Allied invasion of Germany that would convincingly demonstrate the defeat of the German army.

Lloyd George, however, found little support for his hard-line position. Haig, supported by the CIGS, told the civilians that the Germans were not yet decisively defeated.[23] "In my opinion the German Army is capable of retiring to its own frontiers and holding that line against equal or even superior forces," he told the "X" Committee on October 19, 1918. According to Haig, the French Army was war-weary; the AEF was hopelessly disorganized; and the BEF, taking into account its heavy losses, was incapable of smashing what was left of the German army on its own. If an armistice were not signed, Germany would be able to "hold the line which [it] selects for defence for some time after the campaign of 1919 commences."[24]

The pessimism of Haig, who is often criticized for being foolishly optimistic about the German army's decline in 1916-17, is puzzling at first glance. The General Staff's "Battle Situation Reports," which the government received both before and during Haig's visit to London, do not suggest that the resistance of the German army was stiffening or that the steady British advance was slowing.[25] On the other hand, Haig realized that his tired and depleted forces were nearing the end of their tether. His assessment of the military situation was apparently intended to discourage unreasonable armistice terms that might provoke the Germans to fight on.[26] Within the next few weeks the arrival of rain and mud might deny his troops victory in 1918. If a 1919 campaign proved necessary, Haig's forces, whose losses could not be replaced, would take second place to the AEF, an army now larger than the BEF and continuing to grow. With the AEF delivering the final and decisive blows to the Kaiser's army the magnificent advance of the BEF during the last months of 1918 would be forgotten; instead, the glory and added political influence would fall to the Americans. On several occasions in 1918 Haig had expressed the belief that it would be to the British Empire's advantage to stop the fighting while the BEF still had the best fighting force in the anti-German coalition; otherwise, the Americans might be in a military position to dominate the peace settlement.[27]

Haig's nightmare was in fact Pershing's dream. The AEF's leadership had long been building toward 1919. Once the Americans dominated the battlefield, Pershing contemplated replacing Foch as generalissimo; he told a staff officer in October that the "command should go to an American."[28] Pershing's faith in his 1919 plans, bolstered by the enormous increase in his forces after the German offensives began in March, almost certainly explains his unexpected and shocking stand on October 30 at an inter-Allied meeting to consider armistice terms. The American field commander submitted a letter to the SWC that emphasized America's growing military presence in Europe and advocated continuing the war until Germany accepted unconditional surrender.[29]

Baker and Wilson were enraged at Pershing's attitude, so at variance with the administration's desire for a moderate armistice before Berlin's armed forces lost all power of resistance. "Too much success or security on the part of the Allies will make a genuine peace settlement exceedingly difficult if not impossible," the president had just cabled House.[30]

It has been suggested that Pershing's intent was to guarantee harsh armistice terms rather than to seek unconditional surrender on the battlefield.[31] It is much more likely that Pershing, sensitive to Allied criticisms of the performance of his forces, still wanted the war to end through an American offensive in Lorraine. Attempting to justify his position to House, he wrote: "I am of the opinion that we shall not be able in case of an armistice to reap the benefits of a decided victory which has not yet altogether been accomplished."[32] Certainly if hostilities had ended on October 30, when Pershing submitted his letter to the SWC, the AEF would have shown a marked lack of accomplishment in its Meuse-Argonne Offensive.

On November 1, however, the greatest American force ever assembled broke through the German defenses. During the next ten days, in what Pershing grandiosely called "probably the most important operation that has been undertaken by the allies on the Western front," the Yanks advanced farther than they had during the previous month.[33] When the fighting ended on November 11, Griscom discovered a curiously deflated Pershing at Chaumont. Minutes before the Armistice went into effect at 11:00 A.M., Pershing, using a map on his office wall, talked about the precise details of the American plan to take Metz, which now would never be implemented. "What an enormous difference a few days more would have made!" he exclaimed.[34]

If Wilson was angered by Pershing's opposition to the armistice, considering him "glory mad,"[35] Lloyd George was no less taken aback by Haig's pessimism. As he told Lord Riddell, "If the Commander-in-Chief is tired out, what must the Army be?"[36] Sir Henry Wilson's newly completed plan for a campaign in southeastern Europe to defeat Austria-Hungary and then invade Germany, however, may have momentarily encouraged Lloyd George to hold out for Germany's decisive defeat.[37] If Sir Henry's plan for an Allied invasion through Germany's back door ended the war, the prime minister's controversial "eastern" strategy would be completely vindicated. But Lloyd George found no support within his government for prolonging the war in order to "crush" Germany and obtain "better security for peace for the future."[38] His colleagues now believed that they possessed a negotiating position beyond anything anticipated a few months earlier.

General Smuts's views apparently proved decisive. In a memorandum circulated to the king and the war cabinet, he argued: "The salient fact to remember is that, *as matters now stand*, this great result has been achieved largely by the unexampled war effort of the British Empire. On land and sea and in the air the great turn of the tide of war in the summer and autumn of this year has been due to the supreme British effort. If peace comes now, it will be a British peace, it will be a peace given to the world by the same Empire that settled the Napoleonic wars a century ago." Conversely, if the war were prolonged for another year, the "centre of gravity" would shift to the United States, which would become the "diplomatic dictator of the world." Lord Reading strongly supported this position during a meeting of the War Cabinet on October 26: "At present it [is] in the main America and the British Empire that [are] dominating the situation, and we [are] in a position to hold our own. . . . by continuing the War it might become more difficult for us to hold our own."[39]

With no other great power in the world did Britain find such a commonality of interests as with the United States. Yet the British wanted to speak for themselves and not have President Wilson assume, as Lloyd George expressed it, that he was "the great arbiter of the war."[40] The British had sacrificed too much blood and treasure not to expect that their relations with Wilson should be based on political

equality. This attitude best explains the increasingly derogatory remarks made by British political and military leaders about the AEF's
contributions to the land war in Europe. The American army, Haig told
the political leadership on October 19, "is disorganised, ill-equipped
and ill-trained with very few N.C.O.'s and officers of experience. It has
suffered severely through ignorance of modern war and it must take *at
least a Year* before it becomes a serious fighting force."[41] For his part,
Lloyd George characterized the AEF as an "amateur army" suffering
enormous casualties because of poor leadership. Under these circumstances, the Americans' view that they were winning the war was
especially galling. The American Press were sending out "the most
absurd accounts of the prowess of their Army," and Wilson was
"probably being misled." In his last note, he had spoken of "the
supremacy of the troops of the United States of America and their
Allies, or some such phrase."[42] If the Germans sued for peace, Lloyd
George insisted, it would be because of the "splendid" Grand Fleet
that had "provided the essential foundation of victory," and the victories of the BEF, which was now "the finest fighting force in the field."[43]
The only credit the British were prepared to give Pershing in October
was that his offensive on the strategically important southern end of
the front had pinned down German forces that could not then be used
against the Allies.[44]

The British leadership pressed Clemenceau and Foch to make the
limited success of the AEF an issue with the American political leadership—ostensibly to ensure that the AEF would in the future "pull its
proper weight."[45] Just as important, however, the British were not so
subtly making the point that Germany sought an end to the fighting
more because of British than American military power. Clemenceau
apparently needed no urging to speak his mind about Pershing. He
had already sent a letter to Foch, dated October 21, accusing the
American commander of "marking time" since the beginning of the
Meuse-Argonne Offensive. "Nobody can maintain that these fine
[American] troops are unusable; they are merely unused," he harshly
noted.[46]

This was hardly fair. The AEF earned a measure of redemption in
November with its long and rapid advance as German resistance
crumbled on the battlefield and on the home front. During the Meuse-
Argonne campaign, from September 26 to November 11, the AEF,
committing twenty-two of its twenty-nine combat divisions, advanced
thirty-two miles to the north and fourteen miles to the northeast in
forty-seven days of continuous assault. Suffering a loss of 120,000
casualties (25,000 killed in action), the AEF captured some 26,000
prisoners, 874 guns, and 3,000 machine guns.[47]

America's greatest contribution to victory, however, was its extraordinary response to the German bid for victory in 1918. With over 2,000,000 troops in Western Europe by November, the United States had surpassed all Allied expectations, and the psychological consequences of the rapidly expanding American presence in Western Europe were immense. As Vera Brittain writes in her recollections of the war: " 'Look! Look! Here are the Americans!' I pressed forward with the others to watch the United States physically entering the War, so god-like, so magnificent, so splendidly unimpaired in comparison with the tired, nerve-racked men of the British Army. So these were our deliverers at last, marching up the road to Camiers in the spring sunshine." [48]

But the American land and naval part in bringing Germany to its knees should not be exaggerated. The British believed that any comparison based on numbers was in their favor. Ships controlled by the British had transported more than half of the Americans sent to Europe. At sea the Royal Navy enforced the blockade and dominated the antisubmarine war; American warships could claim only four certain "kills" of enemy submarines. In the air the U.S. Army Air Service (which was dependent on foreign aircraft) constituted only 10 percent of the air forces of the victorious powers on the western front. On land the heaviest fighting in 1918 had been done by the British in absorbing the first German blows in March and April and leading the counteroffensive in September and October. The AEF's successes during only 110 days of extensive combat suffered by comparison. Doughboys also had to rely on the Allies for modern armament, including tanks, high-explosive shells, and (until the last weeks of the war) their automatic weapons. According to Lieutenant General Hunter Liggett, who succeeded Pershing as commander of the First Army during the Meuse-Argonne Offensive, his artillery (except for some 14-inch naval guns) was totally dependent upon the Allies for its 4,000 big guns. Nor had any of the shells expended been manufactured in America for the AEF. [49]

The British confidently confronted President Wilson's spokesman, Colonel House, in Paris on October 29 at a conference at the Quai d'Orsay to discuss peacemaking. Lloyd George and Balfour had been instructed by the War Cabinet to "make it perfectly clear to the Conference that we do not accept the doctrine of the Freedom of the Seas, and that a notification to this effect must be made in some form to Germany before we entered into peace negotiations." [50] Lloyd George chose to make this point in dramatic fashion. When House threatened the British with a separate peace, Lloyd George did not flinch. If the United States made a separate peace, the British would be "sorry" but could not give up the blockade, which enabled them to live. "As far as the British Public is concerned, we will fight on." [51]

Source: American Battle Monuments Commission, *American Armies and Battlefields in Europe* (Washington, D.C., 1938)

Map 3. American and Allied Attacks on the Western Front September 26 – November 11, 1918

Lloyd George clearly relished calling House's bluff and forcefully making the point that London was not to be dictated to by Washington. Nevertheless, his government overwhelmingly believed that Britain would never again be in a better position militarily to advance British interests at a peace conference. Hence he was not about to torpedo the peace progress, prolong the war, and cause an irreparable schism with Washington *if* the British Empire's position in the postwar settlement was protected.

The following day, the conference considered Lloyd George's draft of the Allied reservations to the Fourteen Points. In addition to its objection to the freedom of the seas, this document included a second reservation concerning indemnities. Lloyd George stressed that Germany was expected to pay for nonmilitary damages, which included shipping losses. The prime minister also privately took up with House the question of the British acquisition of enemy territories. Although the president had already indicated to Wiseman that he would accept a solution that gave Britain control of the German colonies, the Empire statesmen pressed Lloyd George on this point. India and the Dominions had provided 2,500,000 men to defend the British Empire. One fifth of Haig's forces were Dominion troops, and imperial forces had sustained the war on the periphery.[52] Lloyd George therefore told House that unless the Dominions were satisfied on the question of certain German overseas territories, "Great Britain would be confronted by a revolution." He also declared that Britain "would have to assume a protectorate over Mesopotamia and perhaps Palestine."[53]

Having noted their reservations, the British were prepared to accept the Fourteen Points as a basis for the peace settlement. Wilson, however, was loath to give an inch of freedom of the seas. This Anglo-American impasse was broken when Lloyd George accepted a solution that saved face for Washington. On November 3 he addressed a note to House that expressed readiness to discuss freedom of the seas at the forthcoming peace conference.[54] Following the formal Allied acceptance of Wilson's peace plan with the exceptions of reparations and freedom of the seas, House exuberantly cabled Wilson: "I consider that we have won a great diplomatic victory in getting the Allies to accept the principles laid down in your January eighth speech and in your subsequent addresses. . . . I doubt whether any other [of the] heads of the governments with whom we are[55] have been dealing [quite] realize how far they are now committed to the American peace programme."[56]

On this same day Lloyd George gave a strikingly different version of the pre-armistice negotiations to the Imperial War Cabinet: he told the Empire statesmen that he had refused to accept the American proposal on the freedom of the seas. Furthermore, having carefully studied the Fourteen Points and subsequent statements by President Wilson, he said that he had not discovered "a single point which we wanted that was not amply covered, with the exception of the points regarding the freedom of the seas and indemnities, and of our position in regard to these matters notice had been duly given."[57] In sum, the prime minister argued that the pre-Armistice discussions set the stage for a peace settlement that was as much British as it was American. The vagueness of Wilson's Fourteen Points, along with his apparent willingness not to make trouble about Britain's territorial objectives, certainly helped in this respect. In the few cases where clear disagreement surfaced, the British firmly stated their dissent. On the eve of the Paris Peace Conference, then, the British had committed themselves to nothing in the president's liberal peace objectives which threatened the strategic interests of the British Empire.

The end of the war on November 11 found Britain with impressive military achievements in Western Europe to match its triumphs in the Middle East. The AEF's role in finishing the war seemed modest by comparison. No Americans, only French and British officers, were included when the German delegation signed the Armistice agreement in Foch's railway car in the forest of Compiègne. If not for the unexpected achievements of British arms during the last hundred days of the war, the United States would have eventually achieved the military dominance over Britain that it already enjoyed in the economic realm. Whether Wilson's revolutionary diplomacy in that event would have succeeded in creating a more stable world remains an argument without end.

The British Empire seemed to have emerged from the war stronger than ever. It had acquired vital overseas territory, and its only strategic rival, Germany, had been vanquished. By default, the British Empire was the world's only true global power. Yet although Great Britain seemed destined to maintain its premier global position, time soon proved that the British had been exhausted by the war, in spirit as well as in its economy. Nationalistic unrest in Egypt, India, and Mesopotamia, in addition to Arab-Jewish violence in Palestine, also brought the last days of empire closer.

Despite America's and Britain's common struggle against Germany, Wilson's substitution of moral for traditional diplomacy and his self-appointed role as the peoples' spokesman militated against the creation of a postwar Anglo-American partnership to maintain the future peace and stability of the world. Wilson talked about international law and universal rights, but his actions, even when the success of collective security was at stake, were essentially designed to enable the United States to control its own destiny. He placed the maintenance of American freedom of action second only to the defeat of

Germany. The imperial orientation of the British government and Lloyd George's machinations also created a gulf between the two Atlantic powers. President Wilson, naturally enough, did not link his new world order to the furthering of the British Empire.

Although the United States had become a prodigious economic power, its citizens favored a retreat into political isolation following President Wilson's setbacks as a global peacemaker in 1919-20. The political leadership looked inward and sought to defend American interests independently of other powers. Yet American strategic and political interests continued to parallel those of Great Britain more closely than those of any other great power. The failure to achieve a true Anglo-American partnership during and after the war thus represented a great setback to world stability, greater than the collapse of the flawed League of Nations that emerged from the peace settlement. With the European balance of power destroyed by the Great War, the British government drew back from participation in another great Continental war without the prospect of American assistance. Such assistance was not forthcoming as Germany once again threatened world peace in the 1930s.

Notes

Abbreviations

Cab	Files of the Cabinet Office, Public Record Office, London
FO	Files of the Foreign Office, Public Record Office, London
IC	Files of International Conferences, Public Record Office, London
IWC	Imperial War Cabinet records (in Cab)
MPC	Man-Power Committee records (in Cab)
RG	Record Group, National Archives, Washington, D.C.
WC	War Cabinet records (in Cab)
WO	Files of the War Office, Public Record Office, London
WPC	War Policy Committee records (in Cab)
WWP	Arthur Link, ed., *The Papers of Woodrow Wilson*, vols. 30-51 (Princeton, 1979-85)

Prologue

1. Foster Rhea Dulles, *America's Rise to World Power, 1898-1954* (New York, 1963).

2. See, e.g., Kathleen Burk, *Britain, America, and the Sinews of War, 1914-1918* (Boston, 1985); Lloyd C. Gardner, *Safe for Democracy: The Anglo-American Response to Revolution, 1913-1923* (New York, 1984); W.B. Fowler, *British-American Relations 1917-1918: The Role of Sir William Wiseman* (Princeton, N.J., 1969); Sterling J. Kernek, *Distractions of Peace during War: The Lloyd George Government's Reactions to Woodrow Wilson, December 1916-November 1918* (Philadelphia, 1975); Edward B. Parsons, *Wilsonian Diplomacy: Allied-American Rivalries in War and Peace* (St. Louis, 1978); Laurence W. Martin, *Peace without Victory: Woodrow Wilson and the British Liberals* (New Haven, Conn., 1958).

3. See David F. Trask, *Captains & Cabinets: Anglo-American Naval Relations, 1917-1918* (Columbia, Mo., 1972): and Trask, *The United States in the Supreme War Council: American War Aims and Inter-Allied Strategy, 1917-1918* (Middletown, Conn., 1961).

1. From Rapprochement to the House-Grey Memorandum

1. For an informed discussion of Great Britain as the "preeminent great power" in 1914, see Keith Neilson, " 'Greatly Exaggerated': The Myth of the Decline of Great Britain before 1914," *International History Review*, November 1991, pp. 695-725.

2. During the summer of 1916 the United States did sign a treaty with Denmark to purchase the Virgin Islands in order to prevent Germany from utilizing these strategic islands as a submarine base.

3. A.E. Campbell, *Great Britain and the United States, 1895-1903* (Westport, Conn., 1974), p. 195.

4. P.A.R. Calvert, "Great Britain and the New World, 1905-1914," in *British Foreign Policy under Sir Edward Grey*, ed. F. H. Hinsley (Cambridge, 1977), p. 383.

5. Zara S. Steiner, *Britain and the Origins of the First World War* (New York, 1977), p. 12.

6. Robert A. Huttenback, *The British Imperial Experience* (New York, 1966), p. 90.

7. Avner Offer, *The First World War: An Agrarian Interpretation* (Oxford, 1989), p. 90.

8. Bradford Perkins, *The Great Rapprochement: England and the United States, 1895-1914* (New York, 1968), p. 7.

9. For a standard "realist" critique of American foreign policy, see Hans J. Morgenthau, *In Defense of the National Interest: A Critical Examination of American Foreign Policy* (New York, 1951).

10. Norman A. Graebner, *Foundations of American Foreign Policy: A Realistic Appraisal from Franklin to McKinley* (Wilmington, Del., 1985), p. 314.

11. Ibid., p. 354.

12. Quoted in Arthur S. Link, *Wilson the Diplomatist: A Look at His Major Foreign Policies* (New York, 1974), p. 5.

13. Ibid., p. 10.

14. *WWP*, 30:307.

15. For a recent revisionist work on Wilson's pro-British sympathies and their effect on American neutrality, see John W. Coogan, *The End of Neutrality: The United States, Britain, and Maritime Rights, 1899-1915* (Ithaca, N.Y., 1981). Wilson's views toward the British government, however, underwent a dramatic change in 1916.

16. Herbert Bruce Brougham, "Memorandum of Interview with the President," 14 December 1914, *WWP*, 31:458-59.

17. Woodrow Wilson, "An Appeal to the American People," 18 August 1914, *WWP*, 30:394.

18. To defend Wilson against criticism from the realistic school of thought, Link argues that the president's idealism was in reality a form of "higher realism" in foreign affairs; see Link, "The Higher Realism of Woodrow Wilson," *Journal of Presbyterian History*, March 1963, pp. 1-13.

19. For a perceptive analysis of America's emerging economic power, see Paul M. Kennedy, "The First World War and the International Power System," in *Military Strategy and the Origins of the First World War: An International Security Reader*, ed. Steven E. Miller (Princeton, 1985), pp. 7-40.

20. See Frederick S. Calhoun, *Power and Principle: Armed Intervention in Wilsonian Foreign Policy* (Kent, Ohio, 1986), pp. 30-31. See also the succinct summary in Daniel M. Smith, "Robert Lansing, 1915-1920," in *An Uncertain Tradition: American Secretaries of State in the Twentieth Century*, ed. Norman A. Graebner (New York, 1961), pp. 101-27.

21. See John Milton Cooper, Jr., *The Warrior and the Priest: Woodrow Wilson and Theodore Roosevelt* (Cambridge, Mass., 1983), p. 293.

22. See Mary R. Kihl, "A Failure of Ambassadorial Diplomacy," *Journal of American History*, December 1970, pp. 636-53.

23. An excellent introduction to House's controversial role in American diplomacy, 1914-19, can be found in Inga Floto, *Colonel House in Paris: A Study of American Policy at the Paris Peace Conference, 1919* (Princeton, 1980), pp. 11-24.

24. See Charles Seymour, *The Intimate Papers of Colonel House*, 4 vols. (Boston, 1926-28).

25. Quoted in Alexander L. George and Juliette L. George, *Woodrow Wilson and Colonel House: A Personality Study* (New York, 1956), p. 130.

26. [Edward Mandell House], *Philip Dru: Administrator: A Study of Tomorrow, 1920-1935* (New York, 1912).

27. Cooper, *Warrior and the Priest*, p. 245.

28. Spring Rice to Balfour, 5 January 1917, Balfour Papers, BM Add 49740.

29. See the perceptive comments in Max Beloff, "The Special Relationship: An Anglo-American Myth," in *A Century of Conflict, 1850-1950: Essays for A.J.P. Taylor*, ed. Martin Gilbert (New York, 1967), p. 155.

30. On Anglo-American considerations of a League of Nations, see George W. Egerton, *Great Britain and the Creations of the League of Nations: Strategy, Politics, and International Organization, 1914-1919* (London, 1979).

31. Grey is usually portrayed as not taking seriously House's mediation proposal. To the contrary, Grey attempted to persuade Paul Cambon, the French ambassador in London, of Wilson's sincerity. He wrote the British ambassador in Paris that he had told Cambon he "was convinced that President Wilson really was prepared, if the Allies desired it, to take the action that Colonel House stated. I believed that the Allies could, if they desired it, have a Conference now, presided over by President Wilson, on the lines described by Colonel House in Paris and here; and that, if Germany refused such a Conference, President Wilson would intervene on the side of the Allies." See Grey to Francis L. Bertie, 22 February 1917, Grey Papers, FO 800/181.

32. For recent studies of British strategy, see David R. Woodward, *Lloyd George and the Generals* (Newark, N.J., 1983), and "Britain in a Continental War: The Civil-Military Debate over the Strategical Direction of the Great War of 1914-1918," *Albion*, Spring 1980, pp. 37-65. See also David R. French, *British Strategy & War Aims, 1914-1916* (London, 1986).

33. Robertson, "Memorandum by the Chief of the Imperial General Staff regarding the Supply of Personnel," 21 March 1916, Cab 42//11/8.

34. This hostile interpretation of the American terms is given in a letter from the financial secretary, who was close to the prime minister: Edwin S. Montagu to Herbert H. Asquith, 18 March 1916, Asquith Papers, I, vol. 16, fols. 95-106.

35. E.g., Fritz Fischer, in his *Germany's Aims in the First World War* (New York, 1967), finds many links between the expansionist designs of Imperial Germany and the later Hitler regime.

36. Andrew Bonar Law, the Conservative leader and then colonial secretary, circulated an intelligence report from Canada that portrayed the president as committed to a "peace at any price" policy for political reasons. Spring Rice also consistently expressed the view that "the American people want to keep out of war and will avoid it at all hazards." Memorandum by L.C. Christie, 27 January 1916, circulated to War Committee by Bonar Law, 14 February 1916, Cab 42/8/9; and Spring Rice to Grey, 12 February 1916, Grey Papers, FO 800/86. Lloyd George, writing in the 1930s and perhaps reflecting the widespread disillusionment of that time over the cost and outcome of the war, blamed Wilson and Grey for the failure of the House-Grey agreement. Contrary to what he writes, Lloyd George opposed American mediation. See David Lloyd George, *War Memoirs of David Lloyd George* (London, 1938), 1:412-13; and War Committee, 22 February 1918, Cab 42/9/3.

37. See David R. Woodward, "Great Britain and President Wilson's Efforts to End World War I in 1916," *Maryland Historian*, Spring 1970, pp. 45-58; John Milton Cooper, Jr., "The British Response to the House-Grey Memorandum: New Evidence and New Questions," *Journal of American History*, March 1973, pp. 958-71; and Michael G. Fry, *Lloyd George and Foreign Policy*, vol. 1, *The Education of a Statesman: 1890-1916* (Montreal, 1977), pp. 215-30.

38. Lord Hankey, *The Supreme Command, 1914-1918* (London, 1961), 2:480.

39. Asquith Papers, I, vol. 16, fols. 95-106.

40. Hankey, "Addendum to the Proceedings of the War Committee on March 21, 1916," Cab 42/11/6.

41. For an enlightening discussion of Wilson's attempt to balance his foreign objectives with American public opinion, see J.A. Thompson, "Woodrow Wilson and World War I: A Reappraisal," *Journal of American Studies*, December 1985, pp. 325-47.

42. See Steven Roskill, *Hankey: Man of Secrets*, vol. 1, 1877-1918 (London, 1970), p. 295.

43. Squier, "Memorandum for the Ambassador, Subject: Interview with Field Marshal Earl Kitchener, Secretary of State for War, London, April 27, 1916," Baker Papers.

44. Apparently no copy of this report has survived. See John A.S. Grenville and George Berkeley Young, *Politics, Strategy, and American Diplomacy, 1873-1917* (New Haven, Conn., 1966), p. 334.

45. Entry of 24 May 1916, Hankey Diary, 1/1; since no minutes were taken of this decision by the Army Council, Hankey's diary remains the only record of the military's position. See also David R. Woodward, "Britain's 'Brass Hats' and the Question of a Compromise Peace, 1916-1918," *Military Affairs*, April 1971, pp. 63-68.

46. See Fry, *Education of a Statesman*, p. 219.

47. William Bayard Hale, "Growing up in Georgia," in *Woodrow Wilson: A Profile*, ed. Arthur S. Link (New York, 1968), p. 2.

48. Interview with Frank I. Cobb, 19 March 1917, quoted in full in Link, *Woodrow Wilson: A Profile*, p. 129.

49. Ray Stannard Baker and William E. Dodd, eds., *The New Democracy: Presidential Messages, Addresses, and Other Papers (1913-1917)* (New York: 1926), 2:171.

50. Calhoun, *Power and Principle*, pp. 37, 65.

51. Wilson to Bernhardt Wall, 8 July 1918, WWP, 48:557. See also Ernest R. May, ed., *The Ultimate Decision: The President as Commander in Chief* (New York, 1960), pp. 3-4, 111-13; and the enlightening essay by Arthur S. Link and John Whiteclay Chambers II, "Woodrow Wilson as Commander in Chief," in *The United States Military under the Constitution of the United States*, ed. Richard H. Kohn (New York, 1991), pp. 317-75.

52. See Edward M. Coffman, "The American Military and Strategic Policy in World War I," in *War Aims and Strategic Policy in the Great War, 1914-1918*, ed. Barry Hunt and Adrian Preston (London, 1977), pp. 67-83.

53. Marvin A. Kreidberg and Merton G. Henry, *History of Military Mobilization in the United States Army, 1775-1945* (Washington, D.C., 1955), pp. 215-16.

54. The Naval War College, however, had drawn up War Plan Black for defensive naval operations against the German High Seas Fleet to prevent it from conveying an army to the United States or the West Indies.

55. These war plans against Britain and Japan were apparently destroyed. See Grenville and Young, *Politics, Strategy, and American Diplomacy*, pp. 317-19, 335. For mention of the incomplete plans to defend the east coast against Germany, see Kreidberg and Henry, *History of Military Mobilization*, p. 236.

56. Memorandum by Scott, 18 February 1915, RG 165/6966-116; and Memorandum by M.B. Mercer (chief clerk, War College Division), 31 January 1916, RG 165/6966-176.

57. "A Memorial to the President of the United States by the American Union Against Militarism," c. 8 May 1916, WWP, 36:644.

58. See John Whiteclay Chambers II, *To Raise An Army: The Draft Comes to Modern America* (New York, 1987), pp. 112-14.

59. War Committee, 22 February 1916, Cab 42/9/3.

60. War Committee, 5 August 1916, Cab 42/17/3.

61. War Committee, 10 August 1916, Cab 42/17/5.

62. Ibid.

63. Wilson to Baker, 26 December 1916, Baker Papers. See also Arthur S. Link, *Wilson*, vol. 5, *Campaigns for Progressivism and Peace, 1916-1917* (Princeton, 1965), pp. 165-219.

64. Lloyd George, *War Memoirs*, 1:413.

65. See V. H. Rothwell, *British War Aims and Peace Diplomacy, 1914-1918* (Oxford, 1971), pp. 38-58.

66. Montagu, "The Problems of Peace," 29 August 1916, Cab 42/18/7; Crawford, "Conditions of an Armistice," 17 September 1916, Cab 42/20/2.

67. Quoted in Fry, *Education of a Statesman*, p. 219.

68. For the text of this speech, see John Grigg, *Lloyd George: From Peace to War, 1912-1916* (Berkeley, Calif., 1985), pp. 424-28. I am much indebted to Bentley Brinkerhoff Gilbert for allowing me to read in typescript his section on the Howard interview in the forthcoming second volume of his Lloyd George biography.

69. Grey to Lloyd George, 29 September, and Lloyd George to Grey, 2 October 1916, Lloyd George Papers, E/2/13/5-6.

70. War Committee, 5 October 1916, Cab 42/21/2.

71. Spring Rice to Balfour, 5 January 1917, Balfour Papers, BM Add 49740.

2. From Mediator to "Associate Power"

1. "The General Review of the War," 31 October 1916, Cab 42/22/14.

2. Memorandum by Robertson, October 1916, Cab 42/22/15.

3. Memorandum by military members of Army Council, 28 November 1916, Cab 37/160/25.

4. Runciman, "Shipping," 9 November 1916, Cab 42/23/11.

5. For the text of the Lansdowne memorandum, see Lloyd George, *War Memoirs*, 1:514-20; for British liberals' views of Wilson's peace diplomacy, see Marvin Swartz, *The Union of Democratic Control in British Politics during the First World War* (New York, 1971), pp. 130-41.

6. Wilson to House, 24 November 1916, *WWP*, 40:62.

7. Spring Rice to Balfour, 19 January 1917, Balfour Papers, BM Add 49740.

8. "An Unpublished Prolegomenon to a Peace Note," c. 25 November 1916, *WWP*, 40:68.

9. Speech at Shadow Lawn, New Jersey, 4 November 1916, in Baker and Dodd, *New Democracy*, 2:391.

10. See Burk, *Britain, America, and the Sinews of War*, pp. 80-88.

11. War Committee, 28 November 1916, Cab 42/26/2; *WWP*, vol. 40, pp. 62-63.

12. For the most recent account of the "December Crisis," see John Turner, *British Politics and the Great War: Coalition and Conflict, 1915-1918* (New Haven, Conn., 1992), pp. 112-51.

13. For the view that the fall of Asquith brought the New Imperialists to power, see Paul Guinn, *British Strategy and Politics, 1914 to 1918* (Oxford, 1965), pp. 191-208. A cautionary note on Guinn's thesis is sounded by Max Beloff, *Imperial Sunset*, vol. 1, *Britain's Liberal Empire, 1897-1921* (New York, 1970), pp. 214-17, who argues that "the idea of an imperialist takeover is too sweeping." As will be shown, however, the British approach to war policy and military relations with the United States was decisively influenced by imperial considerations.

14. On Lloyd George's position toward Wilson's peace initiative in December, see Sterling Kernek, "The British Government's Reactions to President Wilson's 'Peace' Note of December 1916," *Historical Journal*, December 1970, pp. 721-66.

15. See Turner, *British Politics and the Great War*, p. 437.

16. See J.M. Bourne, *Britain and the Great War, 1914-1918* (London, 1989), pp. 199-224.

17. Entry of 15 November 1916, House Diary, *WWP*, 38:658.

18. WC, 21 December 1916, Cab 37/162/3.

19. Massingham to Lloyd George, 22 December 1916, Lloyd George Papers, F/94/1/41. Not long after this the foreign circulation of *The Nation* was suppressed by the government.

20. *WWP*, 40:536.

21. David R. Woodward, ed., *The Military Correspondence of Field-Marshal Sir William Robertson, Chief Imperial General Staff, December 1915-February 1918* (London, 1989), p. 130.

22. *WWP*, 40:307-11; and John Milton Cooper, Jr., *Walter Hines Page: The Southerner as American, 1855-1918* (Chapel Hill, N.C., 1977), pp. 358-59.

23. Quoted in Barbara W. Tuchman, *The Zimmerman Telegram* (New York, 1958), p. 141.

24. See, e.g., the comments in John J. Pershing, *My Experiences in the World War* (New York, 1931), 1:16-17, 78. Though a very important and generally accurate record, Pershing's account of his wartime leadership was not—as it purported to be—a history of the AEF organized around his diary entries; rather, it was a combination of his wartime diary with other headquarters records.

25. The General Staff was forced to expand from nineteen officers in April 1917 to 1,222 by the end of the war.

26. Frederick Palmer, *Bliss, Peacemaker: The Life and Letters of General Tasker Howard Bliss* (New York, 1934), p. 103.

27. Scott to Charles B. Rushmore, 6 February 1917, Scott Papers, Box 27.

28. Russell F. Weigley, *History of the United States Army* (New York, 1967), p. 352.

29. Scott to editor of *Philadelphia Bulletin*, 4 January 1931, Pershing Papers, Box 181.

30. Paolo E. Coletta, "The American Naval Leaders' Preparations for War," in *The Great War, 1914-1918: Essays on the Military, Political, and Social History of the First World War*, ed. R.J.Q. Adams (College Station, Tex., 1990), p. 177; John Patrick Finnegan, *Against the Specter of a Dragon: The Campaign for Military Preparedness, 1914-1917* (Westport, Conn., 1974); and Edward M. Coffman, *The War to End All Wars: The American Military Experience in World War I* (New York, 1968), pp. 5-19.

31. Memorandum by Kuhn, 3 February 1917, RG 165/9433-4.

32. At least one imperial strategist in London, Jan Christiaan Smuts, argued that the British should not automatically lobby for American involvement on the western front. Smuts wrote the prime minister: "If the war goes on till America can come in in 1918 she will become a factor of decisive military importance. The most careful forethought should, therefore, be given as to the form her military effort should take and where her army, which will be our fresh strategical reserve, could be utilised to best advantage. For this it may be necessary to review our whole military and naval strategy for the future, as it may be found that none of the existing fronts should be allowed to absorb this our final reserve force." See Smuts to Lloyd George, 24 May 1917, Lloyd George Papers, F/45/9/2.

33. Kuhn to Davis, 5 February 1917, RG 165/9910-6.

34. See the reports by Davis of 17, 18, 27 November, and 18 December 1916, RG 165/9910-1,2,3, and 4. See also Ronald Spector, "'You're Not Going To Send Soldiers Over There Are You!': The American Search for an Alternative to the Western Front, 1916-1917," *Military Affairs*, February 1972, pp. 1-4.

35. WC (115), 6 April 1917, Cab 23/2.

36. Memorandum by Kuhn, 2 February, and Scott to Kuhn, 3 February 1917, RG 165/10050-6.

37. Arthur Walworth, *Woodrow Wilson*, vol. 2, *World Prophet* (New York, 1958), p. 108; and Trask, *Captains & Cabinets*, p. 73.

38. Trask, *Captains & Cabinets*, p. 51.

39. *WWP*, 41:227-29; Daniel R. Beaver, *Newton D. Baker and the American War Effort, 1917-1919* (Lincoln, Neb., 1966), pp. 25-26.

40. For an excellent account of Wilson's role in the adoption of the draft, see Chambers, *To Raise an Army*, pp. 125-51.

41. "An Unpublished Prolegomenon to a Peace Note," c. 25 November 1916, *WWP*, 40:67-70.

42. Ibid., p. 69.

43. Quoted in Link, *Wilson*, 5:414. For Wilson's motives, see also Ernest R. May, *The*

World War and American Isolation, 1914-1917 (Cambridge, Mass., 1966), pp. 416-37; and Robert H. Ferrell, *Woodrow Wilson and World War I, 1917-1921* (New York, 1985), pp. 1-12.

44. Serious questions have been raised about the authenticity of this interview, which figures prominently in most treatments of Wilson's decision for war. The account of the interview was not published until 1924, after both Cobb and Wilson were dead. Moreover, it was not written by Cobb but based on what the editor of the *World* told two of his fellow journalists, Maxwell Anderson and Laurence Stallings. Arthur S. Link, although he places this conversation on March 19 rather than April 2, does not—as do some others—consider it an invention of Anderson and Stallings. See Jerold S. Auerbach, "Woodrow Wilson's 'Prediction' to Frank Cobb: Words Historians Should Doubt Ever Got Spoken," *Journal of American History*, December 1967, pp. 608-617; and "Interview with Frank I. Cobb," 19 March 1917, in Link, *Woodrow Wilson: A Profile*, pp. 127-29.

45. Link, *Woodrow Wilson: A Profile*, p. 128.

46. [Lansing], "Memorandum of the Cabinet Meeting, 2:30-5 p.m., Tuesday, March 20, 1917," *WWP*, 41:436.

47. On this point, see Robert Endicott Osgood, *Ideals and Self-Interest in America's Foreign Relations* (Chicago, 1953), pp. 252-56.

48. See Daniel M. Smith, *Robert M. Lansing and American Neutrality, 1914-1917* (Berkeley, Calif., 1958). For a succinct discussion of the role of national security interests (and other factors) in the decision for war, see John Milton Cooper, Jr., *Causes and Consequences of World War I* (New York, 1972).

49. [Lansing] "Memorandum of the Cabinet Meeting, 2:30-5 p.m., Tuesday, March 20, 1917," *WWP*, 41:436-44.

50. See "A Study of Conditions Affecting Possible Operations in the Macedonian Theater in Case of War With Germany," "Study of the Possibility of Holland Becoming Involved in the Present European War, through the Sinking of Her Ships in the North Sea, and Permitting the Invasion of France in Rear of the Western Germany Army," and covering memorandum by Kuhn, 29 March 1917, RG 165/10050-6.

51. Ferrell, *Wilson and World War I*, p. 5.

52. Kreidberg and Henry, *History of Military Mobilization*, p. 324.

53. Kuhn, "Memorandum for the Chief of Staff: Subject, Studies prepared in the Army War College relating to possible operations in certain European theatres of war," 29 March 1918, RG 165/10050-6.

54. *WWP*, 41:519-27.

55. Ibid.

56. Cabinet Paper G.T. 623 of 13 April 1917, Cab 24/12.

57. *WWP*, 41:462-64.

58. In a different context this conflict between Wilson's unilateralism and universalism is the theme of Lloyd E. Ambrosius, *Woodrow Wilson and the American Diplomatic Tradition: The Treaty Fight in Perspective* (Cambridge, Eng., 1987).

59. House to Wilson, 19 March 1917, *WWP*, 41:429.

3. The Balfour Mission and Americans Abroad

1. Woodward, *Military Correspondence of Robertson*, p. 149.

2. General Staff memorandum, 5 February 1917, WO 106/467.

3. Memorandum by Barclay, 7 February 1917, WO 106/467.

4. Ibid.

5. Page to Secretary of State, 11 February 1917, Department of State, *Papers Relating to the Foreign Relations of the United States, 1917, Supplement I, The World War* (Washington, D.C., 1931), p. 44.

6. See Woodward, *Lloyd George and the Generals*, pp. 116-59.

7. IWC (1,3), 20 and 23 March 1917, Cab 23/40.

8. Ferrell, *Wilson and World War I*, pp. 12-13.

9. On the British position toward negotiations, see Rothwell, *British War Aims and Peace Diplomacy*, pp. 65-66.

10. IWC (1), 20 March 1917, Cab 23/40.

11. WC (103), App. II, 23 March 1917, Cab 23/2.

12. Balfour Papers, BM Add. 49740.

13. Balfour Papers, FO 800/208.

14. Robertson Papers, I/33/76.

15. Slocum's report of 26 April 1917, RG 165/8690-580.

16. Frederick B. Maurice (director of military operations on Imperial General Staff) to Balfour, 3 April 1917, Balfour Papers, FO 800/208.

17. Memorandum by Percy, 4 April 1917, Balfour Papers, FO 800/208. Not surprisingly, Wilson and Lord Percy did not hit it off. Wilson called him "one of the most slippery and untrustworthy of the men we have had to deal with here." See Wilson to House, 31 August 1918, House Papers, Box 121, fol. 4286.

18. Wiseman to Eric Drummond (Balfour's private secretary), 25 January 1917, Balfour Papers, BM Add 49741.

19. House to Wilson, 19 March 1917, WWP, 41:429.

20. My discussion of the draft is largely based on Chambers, *To Raise an Army*, pp. 125-51. See also Beaver, *Baker and the American War Effort*, pp. 28-33; and David M. Kennedy, *Over Here: The First World War and American Society* (New York, 1980), pp. 147-49.

21. Notes by Bliss relating to Roosevelt-Baker correspondence, n.d. but apparently April 1917, Baker Papers.

22. Wilson to Newton Baker, 11 April 1917, Baker Papers.

23. House Papers, Box 121, fol. 4274.

24. Woodward, *Military Correspondence of Robertson*, p. 169.

25. For Balfour's instructions, see WC (116), 10 April 1917, Cab 23/2. See also Burk, *Britain, America, and the Sinews of War*, pp. 99-136; and Sir Tom Bridges, *Alarms & Excursions: Reminiscences of a Soldier* (New York, 1938), pp. 170-88.

26. Spring Rice to Balfour mission, 13 April 1917, Balfour Papers, FO 800/208.

27. Entry 22 April 1917, Thomas Brahany Diary, WWP, 42:121.

28. C. à Court Repington, *The First World War, 1914-1918* (London, 1920), 1:582.

29. Bridges to Robertson, 3 May 1917, WO 107/467.

30. Bridges to Scott, 30 April 1917, WO 106/467.

31. Repington, *First World War*, 1:583. "It is practically certain that we shall not be allowed to recruit American subjects for the British Army," Bridges wrote Robertson. Believing that Britain would soon be "shouting for men," however, Bridges did make one last attempt through Balfour to get American drafts. Balfour with great diplomacy pressed this question upon the American government just before he departed. See Bridges to Robertson, 3 May 1917, WO 106/467; Bridges to Balfour, 21 May 1917, Balfour Papers, FO 800/208; and Balfour's confidential report (copy to Lansing), 23 May 1917, FO 371/3073/158660.

32. Bridges, *Alarms & Excursions*, p. 175.

33. See War College Division memoranda of 10 and 11 May 1917, RG 165/10050-8.

34. Slocum to War Department, 4 May 1917, RG 165/10050-12; and Kuhn, "Memorandum for the Chief of Staff: Cablegram [from Slocum] relative to cooperation of the United States," 30 April 1917, RG 165/10050-5.

35. Wilson to Baker, 3 May 1917, Baker Papers.

36. Minutes of conference with Baker, 14 May 1917, transmitted to French Ministry of War, Department of the Army (Historical Division), *United States Army in the World War, 1917-1919* (Washington, D.C., 1948), 2:5.

37. Bridges reported to Robertson that the French expected any American expeditionary force to serve with them; being less than candid with the French, Bridges had told Marshal Joffre that it was "a matter of indifference to us where they went as long as they came over soon." See Bridges to Robertson, 29 April 1917, Balfour Papers, FO 800/208.

38. When Slocum had asked Haig's chief of intelligence, General John Charteris, about the prospect of American forces serving with the French, he had been told: "There would be a row in a month." See Slocum to War Department, 27 April 1917, RG 165/10050-9.

39. Bridges to Robertson, 3 May 1917, WO 106/467.

40. WC (126), 25 April 1917, Cab 23/2; and Slocum to War Department, 27 April 1917, RG 165/10050-9.

41. Baker to Wilson, 8 May 1917, and Wilson to Baker, 10 May 1917, Baker Papers.

42. Minutes of conference with Baker, 14 May 1917, transmitted to the French Ministry of War, Department of the Army, *United States Army in the World War*, 2:5.

43. Quoted in Ferrell, *Wilson and World War I*, p. 50.

44. Pershing to Mrs. Dickins, 29 April 1917, Pershing Papers, Box 64.

45. Moore to House, 17 May 1917, and Wilson to Baker, 23 May 1917, *WWP*, 42:373-74, 377.

46. Pershing, *My Experiences*, 1:37; and Frank E. Vandiver, *Black Jack: The Life and Times of John J. Pershing* (College Station, Tex., 1977), 2:693.

47. Baker to Wilson, 8 May 1917, Baker Papers.

48. Bliss to Baker, 25 May 1917, confidential copy for Pershing, Pershing Papers, Box 123.

49. Baker to Pershing, 26 May 1917, *WWP*, 42:404-5; Frederick Palmer, *Newton D. Baker: America at War* (New York, 1931), 1:170; Pershing, *My Experiences*, 38-40.

50. Pershing to Bliss, 2 July 1917, Pershing Papers, Box 26.

51. Memorandum by Kuhn, 7 June 1917, RG 165/10050-30.

52. Baker Papers.

53. *WWP*, 42:498-504.

54. Lloyd George's primary war objective at this time remained the destruction of German militarism, but there was strong sentiment among the Dominions that the future security of the British Empire depended upon the destruction of Germany's overseas empire. Unless Wilson added his moral force to any peace settlement, Lloyd George had earlier told the president, "Great Britain, who wants nothing for herself, will be prevented from returning the German colonies" because of Australian and South African fear of Germany. Page to Lansing, 11 February 1917, Department of State, *Foreign Relations, 1917, Supplement 1*, p. 44. See also Rothwell, *British War Aims and Peace Diplomacy*, pp. 67-75; and Wm. Roger Louis, *Great Britain and Germany's Lost Colonies, 1914-1919* (Oxford, 1967), pp. 77-116.

55. Seth P. Tillman, *Anglo-American Relations at the Paris Peace Conference of 1919* (Boston, 1961), pp. 9-11.

56. House to Wilson, 22 April 1917, House Papers, Box 121, fol. 4274.

57. Responding to an August 1917 peace appeal from Pope Benedict XV, Wilson spoke out against "punitive damages, the dismemberment of empires, the establishment of selfish and exclusive economic leagues." As he told House, he had not been more specific because he did not for the moment want to provoke either France or Italy. See Link, *Wilson the Diplomatist*, pp. 100-101.

58. Wilson to House, 21 July 1917, House Papers, Box 121, fol. 4277.

59. Kreidberg and Henry, *History of Military Mobilization*, pp. 234-35.

60. See memorandum by Kuhn, 13 April 1917, RG 165/9433-24. More than half the soldiers transported by America were carried in ships formerly belonging to Austria and Germany. See Ferrell, *Wilson and World War I*, p. 39.

61. Burk, *Britain, America, and the Sinews of War*, p. 110.

62. For Anglo-American conflicts and misunderstandings on maritime policy, see Jeffrey J. Safford, *Wilsonian Maritime Diplomacy, 1913-1921* (New Brunswick, N.J., 1978).

63. Balfour to Lloyd George, Balfour's confidential report enclosed, 23 June 1917, FO 371/3073/158600.

64. Burk, *Britain, America, and the Sinews of War*, p. 112.

65. Ibid., pp. 111-14.

66. On this question, see Trevor Wilson, *The Myriad Faces of War: Britain and the Great War, 1914-1918* (Cambridge, Eng., 1986), pp. 431-33; and WC (150), 30 May 1917, including App. V, Cab 23/2.

67. Seymour, *Intimate Papers of Colonel House*, 3:66-67.

68. Spring Rice to Foreign Office, Balfour to Lloyd George enclosed, 14 May 1917, *WWP*, 42:296.

69. See WC (142), 22 May 1917, Cab 23/2; Foreign Office to Spring Rice (Cecil to Balfour enclosed), 19 May, and Cecil to Spring Rice, 4 June 1917, *WWP*, 42:354, 450-51.

70. WC (165), 19 June 1917, and note by Balfour, 19 June 1917, in App. II, Cab 23/3.

71. WC (174), 3 July 1917, and memorandum by Balfour, 19 June 1917, in App., Cab 23/3.

72. House to Wilson, Balfour to House enclosed, 8 July 1917, *WWP*, 43:123-26.

73. [Wiseman], "Notes on Interview with Ajax [Wilson] Friday, July 13th," *WWP*, 43:172-73.

74. Trask, *Captains & Cabinets*, pp. 102-25.

75. Ibid., p. 55.

76. For the formative stages of American naval policy, see ibid., pp. 61-101. Parsons has argued that American naval policy was designed to achieve American dominance over the British by withholding American naval resources. It is much more likely, however, that America's naval leadership was reluctant to commit the bulk of its destroyer strength to European waters until it had a better reading of the U-boat threat in home waters. Wilson was also reluctant to make any wartime agreements that might impinge upon his freedom of action during the peace settlement. See Parsons, *Wilsonian Diplomacy*, pp. 33-55. For a balanced discussion of Anglo-American naval corporation, which inevitably assigned the U.S. Navy a secondary role in the eastern Atlantic and the Mediterranean, see Dean C. Allard, "Anglo-American Naval Differences during World War I," in *In Defense of the Republic*, ed. David Curtis Skaggs and Robert S. Browning III (Belmont, Calif., 1991), pp. 239-51.

77. Wilson to Daniels (Wilson to Admiral Sims enclosed), 3 July 1917, *WWP*, 43:79-80.

78. WC (159 A), 8 June 1917, Cab 23/16.

79. WC (140 A), 16 May 1917, Cab 23/13.

80. The Northcliffe press, in control of approximately half of London's newspaper circulation, had often sided with the military camp against the civilians. Hence Lloyd George's motive may have been to get Northcliffe out of London.

81. Drummond to Hankey, 27 May 1917, Balfour Papers, BM Add 49704.

82. Department of the Army, *United States Army in the World War*, 12:7.

83. See David Stevenson, *The First World War and International Politics* (Oxford, 1988), p. 170; and Parsons, *Wilsonian Diplomacy*, pp. 1-78.

84. Milner asked the right questions but furnished the wrong answer. He suggested that "an overwhelming effort in the air" might be "the quickest and the most effective contribution which America could make to the termination of the war." It is indeed fortunate that Britain didn't base its plans on American air support; American airplane production was one of the greatest fiascos of the war. See Note by Lord Milner, 7 June 1917, WC (159 A), App., 8 June 1917, Cab 23/16.

4. Britain as the Cornerstone

1. WC (122), 18 April 1917, Cab 23/2; Robertson to Monro, 19 April 1917, Woodward, *Military Correspondence of Robertson*, pp. 177.

2. For the impact of Russia's demise on British strategy, see Keith Neilson, *Strategy and Supply: The Anglo-Russian Alliance, 1914-17* (London, 1984), pp. 249-304.

3. For a recent discussion of Hankey's indirect strategic ideas and his Atlantic orientation, see Offer, *First World War*, pp. 4, 246-49, 266-69, 317.

4. Memorandum by Hankey, 18 April 1917, Cab 63/20.

5. See Fry, *Education of a Statesman*, pp. 1-181.

6. An extreme example of Lloyd George's view on casualties is his response to criticism of his support of intervention in the Balkans, which until late 1918 resulted in tying down valuable Entente military resources with little to show for it. The "Salonican diversion," he argued, had "probably saved hundreds of thousands of men from being engulfed in the mud of the Western front." Committee of Prime Ministers (27 A), 31 July 1918, Cab 23/44.

7. His argument in favor of emphasizing the Italian theater over the western front is a striking illustration of Lloyd George's attempt to limit British casualties at the expense of British allies. Even if the Germans used their interior lines to transfer divisions to assist Austria-Hungary, he told his colleagues, "you would be fighting them and wearing them out. But this could be taking place at the expense of the Italians and not of our men. . . . It would be the first time that the Italian resources of man-power had been properly utilised to pull their full weight in the War." WPC (10), 21 June 1917, Cab 27/6.

8. For a detailed account of the development of Lloyd George's ideas on strategy, see Woodward, *Lloyd George and the Generals*.

9. Memorandum by Hankey, 18 April 1917, Cab 63/20.

10. Memorandum by General Bridges, 14 June 1917, WP 5, Cab 27/7; and Repington, *First World War*, 1:581.

11. Robertson to General Sir C.C. Monro, 19 April 1917, Woodward, *Military Correspondence of Robertson*, p. 177.

12. WC (128 A), 1 May 1917, Cab 23/13.

13. Ibid.

14. Ibid. See also David R. Woodward, "The Imperial Strategist: Jan Christiaan Smuts and British Military Policy, 1917-1918," *Military History Journal*, December 1981, pp. 131-45, 148, 153.

15. Anglo-French Conference, 4-5 May 1917, Cab 28/2/IC-21.

16. WPC (7), 19 June 1917, Cab 27/6.

17. Cabinet Paper G.T. 703 of 12 May 1917, Cab 24/13. Curzon had earlier warned the Imperial War Cabinet's subcommittee on territorial desiderata in the terms of peace that if Britain's allies failed to achieve their war objectives, "they might press us to give up our overseas conquests in order to help them out of their difficulties." Subcommittee of IWC (4), 23 April 1917, Cab 21/77.

18. C.R.M.R. Cruttwell, *The Role of British Secretary in the Great War* (Cambridge, Eng., 1936), p. 72.

19. This point has been confirmed in correspondence with Gerard J. De Groot, the author of *Douglas Haig, 1861-1928* (London, 1988).

20. Cabinet Paper G.T. 1549 of 29 July 1917, Cab 24/21.

21. Military Conference of 26 July (attended by Cadorna, Robertson, Pershing, Pétain, and Foch), Cabinet Paper G.T. 1533 of 26 July 1917, Cab 24/21.

22. "Addendum to the Military Conference of July 26th," ibid.

23. Robertson, "Policy to Adopt Should Russia Be Forced Out of the War. Report of Military Conference on 26th July, 1917. Covering Note by C.I.G.S., July 26, 1918," ibid.

24. Cabinet Paper G.T. 1573 of 31 July 1917, Cab 24/21.

25. Ibid.

26. WC (200 A), 31 July 1917, Cab 23/13. Two weeks later (14 August) Page reported this new mood to Wilson: "The probability that is generally accepted is that the war, unless Germany collap[s]e during the next six months by reason of economic exhaustion or by the falling-away of Austria or Turkey or both, will become a war between Germany and the English-speaking nations, all which except the United States are partially exhausted." WWP, 43:464.

27. Balfour Papers, BM Add 49740.

28. At the first meeting of the Imperial War Cabinet in March 1917, Lloyd George told the political leadership of the Dominions that some German colonies might have to be restored. See Rothwell, British War Aims and Peace Diplomacy, p. 127.

29. Roskill, Hankey, p. 418.

30. Fowler, British-American Relations, 1917-1918, pp. 65-66.

31. In 1927 Ramsay MacDonald, during his second term of office, became the first British prime minister to visit the United States.

32. J.M. McEwen, The Riddell Diaries, 1908-1923 (London, 1986), p. 193; Wiseman to House, 12 August 1917, House Papers, Box 123, fol. 4325.

33. House to Wilson, 13 August 1917, House Papers, Box 121, fol. 4278.

34. See the comment by Philip Kerr in McEwen, Riddell Diaries, p. 197.

35. Wilson's declining health apparently altered his behavior during his last years, adversely affecting his political skills. See Edwin A. Weinstein, Woodrow Wilson: A Medical and Psychological Biography (Princeton, 1981).

36. Quoted in Walter LaFeber, The American Age: United States Foreign Policy At Home and Abroad since 1750 (New York, 1989), 254.

37. House Papers, Box 121, fol. 4278.

5. Pershing's War Plans

1. Slocum to War Department, 27 April 1917, RG 165/10050-9.

2. Translation of telegram from Major James A. Logan (U.S. military attaché in Paris), 17 May 1917, RG 165/10050-19.

3. Bridges to Scott, 30 April 1917, WO 106/467; Repington, First World War, 1:584.

4. For the French position, see André Kaspi, Le temps des américains: Le concours américain a la France en 1917-1918 (Paris, 1976), pp. 24, 100-105, 124.

5. Pershing, My Experiences, 1:81-86.

6. The pioneer study of American strategic/political policy during World War I is Trask, United States in the Supreme War Council. For other enlightening discussions of American strategy in the war, see Allan R. Millett, "Over Where? The AEF and the American Strategy for Victory, 1917-1918," in Against All Enemies: Interpretations of American Military History from Colonial Times to the Present, ed. Kenneth J. Hagan and William R. Roberts (Westport, Conn., 1986), pp. 235-56; Timothy K. Nenninger, "American Military Effectiveness in the First World War," in Military Effectiveness, vol. 1, The First World War, ed. Allan R. Millett and Williamson Murray (Boston, 1989), pp. 116-56; and Coffman, "American Military and Strategic Policy."

7. Donald Smythe, Pershing: General of the Armies (Bloomington, Ind., 1986), p. 30.

8. Memorandum by Pershing, dated 3 September 1917 on reverse, G-3, GHQ, AEF, Secret General Correspondence, File 1003, No. 681, Pt. 2, Box 3112, RG 120.

9. Prepared by Fox Conner, LeRoy Eltinge, and Hugh Drum, G-3, GHQ, AEF, Secret General Correspondence, File 1003, No. 681, Pt. 2, Box 3112, RG 120.

10. Ibid.

11. Quoted in Smythe, Pershing, p. 239.

12. Robertson's statement on meeting of Nivelle, Robertson, Haig, and Pétain, Anglo-French Conference, May 4-5, Cabinet Paper G.T. 657 of 5 May 1917, Cab 24/12.

13. For a critical examination of Haig's three-or four-stage structured battlefield, which he had learned at Staff College, see Tim Travers, *The Killing Ground: The British Army, the Western Front, and the Emergence of Modern Warfare, 1900-1918* (London, 1987).

14. Cabinet Paper G.T. 657 of 5 May, 1917, Cab 24/12.

15. Repington, *First World War*, 2:89-90.

16. James W. Rainey, "Ambivalent Warfare: The Tactical Doctrine of the AEF in World War I," *Parameters*, September 1983, p. 34. See also Russell Gilmore, "'The New Courage': Rifles and Soldier Individualism, 1876-1918," *Military Affairs*, October 1976, pp. 97-102; and "Final Report of General John J. Pershing, September 1, 1919," Department of the Army, *United States Army in the World War*, 12:22.

17. Smythe, *Pershing*, p. 235.

18. Baker to House, 18 July 1917, Baker Papers.

19. Sir Hubert Gough, *The Fifth Army* (London, 1931), p. 215.

20. Quoted in entry of 8 August 1917, H. Wilson Diary.

21. See Woodward, *Lloyd George and the Generals*, pp. 190-220.

22. Hankey, *Supreme Command*, 2:694.

23. Entry of 16 September 1917, House Diary, *WWP*, 44:200-203.

24. Lloyd George to President Wilson, 3 September 1917, Lloyd George Papers, F/60/1/1.

25. Ibid.

26. Entry of 16 September 1917, House Diary, *WWP*, 44:202.

27. House to Wilson, 18 September 1917, ibid., p. 213.

28. Memorandum enclosed in Wilson to Baker, 22 September 1917, Baker Papers.

29. See Herbert Howland Sargent, *The Strategy on the Western Front, 1914-1918* (Chicago, 1920).

30. Wilson to Baker, 22 September 1917, Baker Papers.

31. Entry of 16 September 1917, House Diary, *WWP*, 44:203.

32. Baker to Wilson, 22 September 1917, ibid., p. 239; Colonel P.D. Lochridge (acting chief of War College Division), "Memorandum for Committee Consisting of the Chairmen of the War College Division Committees," 22 September 1917, RG 165/10050-111.

33. "Possible line of action from the head of the Persian Gulf," 25 September 1917, App. III, RG 165/10050-111.

34. "Possible lines of action in the Eastern Mediterranean," 28 September 1917, App. I, ibid.

35. Russell F. Weigley, *The American Way of War: A History of United States Military Strategy and Policy* (Bloomington, Ind., 1973), p. xxi. See also Weighley, "To the Crossing of the Rhine" in *In Defence of the Republic: Readings in American Military History*, ed. David Curtis, Skaggs and Robert S. Browning III (Belmont, Calif., 1991), pp. 255-73.

36. Colonel F.S. Young, "Strategy of the present war. Line of Advance through Russia," 28 September 1917, RG 165/10050-111.

37. See Lochridge, "Strategy of the present war," n.d., with three enclosures: "Possible lines of action in the Eastern Mediterranean," 28 September 1917, App. I; Possible line of Action through Russia," n.d., App. II; and "Possible line of action from the head of the Persian Gulf," 25 September 1917, App. III, ibid. See also Colonel F.S. Young, "Strategy of the present war. Line of Advance through Russia," 28 September 1917, ibid. These strategic appreciations amount to twenty-eight single-spaced pages.

38. Baker to Wilson, 11 October 1917, *WWP*, 44:361. Baker sent Colonel P.D. Lochridge's memorandum with its three enclosures.

39. See Colonel F.S. Young, "Strategy of the present war. Line of Advance through

Russia," 28 September 1917, RG 165/10050-111. This memorandum, perhaps significantly, was not included with the ones Baker forwarded to Wilson.

40. See Warren W. Hassler, Jr., *The President as Commander in Chief* (Menlow Park, Calif., 1971), p. 101.

41. Wilson to Pershing, 24 July 1918, Pershing Papers, Box 213.

42. Wilson to Baker, 4 October 1917, Baker Papers.

43. Baker to Wilson, 11 November 1917, ibid.

44. Wilson to Baker, 20 November 1917, ibid.

45. Bliss to War Department, sent 4 December, received 5 December 1917, ibid. See also Pershing, *My Experiences*, 2:105.

46. Wilson to Baker, n.d., Baker Papers.

6. The Knock-out Blow in Question

1. Robertson discovered Lloyd George's secret efforts to win Wilson over to his indirect strategy when Bliss told the French military attaché in Washington that efforts were being made to employ American soldiers in theaters other than Western Europe. Robertson immediately made it clear that "no pressure of any kind has been brought to bear on America by Chief of the Imperial General Staff to send troops elsewhere than to France." Some of Robertson's subordinates, however, had considered giving the United States limited military responsibilities elsewhere. In late July an officer of the operations section had approached Slocum and inquired about the possibility of America's sending a small military mission to the Caucasus to organize an Armenian force, the first such attempt by the British military to involve the United States in a military role in the old Russian empire. On July 27 Slocum forwarded a General Staff paper, "The Organization of an Armenian Corps in the Caucasus," dated 25 July, to the War Department. See Maurice (DMO) to Colonel Edward Spiers, French War Ministry, Paris, 3 October 1917, and Brigadier General James Douglas McLachlan (attaché to British Embassy in Washington) to War Office, 5 October 1917, WO 106/468; and Slocum to War Department, 27 July 1917, RG 165/10050-93.

2. Although the British now anticipated that 500,000 American troops would be in France by June, they were concerned about Pershing's willingness to commit these green troops to battle. London pressured Wilson to put American troops in the line prior to the forming of an American army. Concerned about France's decline, Wilson assured Reading that America had no "settled" policy regarding the circumstances in which American soldiers would be committed to battle. WC (227), 3 September 1917, Cab 23/4; and Reading to Spring Rice (for transmission in cipher to Foreign Office), 21 September 1917, Reading Papers, Eur F. 118/114.

3. For accounts of these peace feelers, see David R. Woodward, "David Lloyd George, A Negotiated Peace with Germany, and the Kuhlmann Peace Kite of September, 1917," *Canadian Journal of History* (March 1971), pp. 75-93; Rothwell, *British War Aims and Peace Diplomacy*, pp. 105-110; Fischer, *Germany's Aims*, pp. 410-428, and L.L. Farrar, "Opening to the West: German Efforts to Conclude a Separate Peace with England, July 1917-March 1918," *Canadian Journal of History*, April 1975, pp. 73-90.

4. WC (238 A), 24 September 1917, Cab 23/16.

5. Ibid.

6. Ibid.

7. Hankey's original minutes (ibid.) had Balfour saying that "otherwise there might be a difficult position. There was a feeling in the United States that we were keeping things back." Balfour marked out these passages when he corrected the minutes.

8. Ibid.

9. Entry of 24 September 1917, Hankey Diary, 1/3.

10. Lloyd George Papers, F/3/2/30.

11. Quoted in Rothwell, *British War Aims and Peace Diplomacy*, pp. 106-7.

12. Lloyd George's description to the War Cabinet of his meeting with Painlevé. WC (239 A), 27 September 1917, Cab 23/16.

13. Hankey's minutes are in Cab 1/25. Most of this paragraph relies on two pages in Hankey's handwriting, dated 26 September 1917. The comment about the Americans is from typewritten minutes apparently prepared after Hankey returned to London; they are dated 29 September 1917.

14. WC (239 A), 27 September 1917, Cab 23/16.

15. Ibid.

16. Cabinet Paper G.T. 2172 of 29 September 1917, Cab 24/27.

17. Entry of 28 September 1917, Hankey Diary, 1/3.

18. Foreign Office to Sir William Wiseman, 4 October 1917, Balfour Papers, FO 800/201.

19. *The Times* (London), 11 October 1917; Erich von Ludendorff, *Ludendorff's Own Story: August 1914-November 1918* (New York, 1919), 2:134.

20. Wilson was alarmed by reports that Germany was prepared to give up Belgium and Alsace-Lorraine. This would still leave Berlin "impregnable" in Mitteleuropa and would not "restrict German power for evil in the future." Entry of 13 October 1917, House Diary, *WWP*, 44:379.

21. News Report: "Wilson Sees End of War Only When Enemy Is Beaten," 8 October 1917, *WWP* 44:325.

22. Hankey, *Supreme Command*, 2:705-6.

23. Ibid., 706-7.

24. James E. Edmonds, ed. and comp., *Military Operations, France and Belgium, 1917,* (London, 1948), 3:305.

25. WC (266), 6 November 1917, Cab 23/4. The convoy system reduced British submarine losses. Still, British war and marine losses during the last quarter of 1917 amounted to 783,000 gross tons, twice the 389,000 gross tons added to the register. See Hankey, *Supreme Command*, 2:741.

26. WC (300), 17 December 1917, Cab 23/4.

27. Cabinet Paper G.T. 2849 of 3 December 1917, Cab 24/34. The War Office wanted 250,000 Category "A" men recruited in November, and 50,000 each month from December to June 1918. See Cabinet Paper G.T. 2751 of 24 November 1917, Cab 24/33.

28. Trevor Wilson, ed., *The Political Diaries of C.P. Scott, 1911-1928* (London, 1970), p. 324.

29. In an unusually candid memorandum in April, Hankey had written that the government's recruiting policy was designed to "compel the soldiers to adopt tactics that will reduce the waste of man-power" and make better use of men already in uniform. See Hankey's memorandum, 18 April 1917, Cab 63/20.

30. Hankey, "Note by the Secretary," 8 December 1917, MPC 2, Cab 27/14.

31. For a study of this controversy, see David R. Woodward, "Did Lloyd George Starve the British Army of Men prior to the German Offensive of 21 March 1918?" *Historical Journal* (March 1984), pp. 241-52. See also Keith Grieves, "'Total War'?: The Quest for a British Manpower Policy, 1917-1918," *Journal of Strategic Studies*, March 1986, pp. 79-95.

32. WP 60 and WP 61, 20 October 1917, Cab 27/8.

33. WP 62, 26 October 1917, Cab 27/8.

34. Memorandum by Balfour, 24 November 1917, Lloyd George Papers, F/160/1/14.

35. WC (259 A), 30 October 1917, Cab 23/13.

36. A.M. Gollin, *Proconsul in Politics: A Study of Lord Milner in Opposition and in Power* (New York, 1964), p. 243.

37. When Wilson left London to join the inter-Allied staff of the SWC, Milner told him, "Our hopes are now centered on you—at this 11th hour." Meanwhile, Amery prepared a working paper on giving flexibility to Allied strategy. See Milner to Wilson, 3 November 1917, and Amery, "The Turning Point of the War," 31 October 1917, Milner Papers, dep. 354 and 372.

7. The House Mission and Anglo-American War Aims

1. Wiseman to House, October 10, 1917, *WWP*, 44:354.
2. Entry of 13 October 1917, House Diary, *WWP*, 44:378.
3. Ibid., p. 380.
4. Ibid., p. 379.
5. When the Bolsheviks published secret Allied annexationist treaties, Wilson cabled House, who was then discussing peace terms with the British leadership: "Our people and Congress will not fight for any selfish aim on the part of any belligerent, with the possible exception of Alsace-Lorraine, least of all for divisions of territory such as have been contemplated in Asia Minor." Wilson to House, 1 December 1917, Department of State, *Foreign Relations of the United States, 1917, Supplement 2, The World War*, 1:331.
6. See Woodward, *Lloyd George and the Generals*, pp. 221-52.
7. Robertson to Derby, November 15, 1917, Woodward, *Military Correspondence of Robertson*, p. 252.
8. House to Wilson, 14 November 1917, House Papers, Box 121, fol. 4281; and entry of 13 November 1917, Seymour, *Intimate Papers of Colonel House*, 3:218.
9. Wilson to House, 16 November 1917, *WWP*, 45:69.
10. United Kingdom, *Parliamentary Debates* (Commons), 5th ser., vol. 99 (19 November 1917).
11. The standard work on American participation in the SWC is Trask, *United States in the Supreme War Council*.
12. As late as November 23, encouraged by the initial British success of the Battle of Cambrai and the failure of the Austro-German forces to exploit their Italian success, Robertson had told the civilians that "Germany's military power was probably a good deal less and the condition of the Austrian armies a good deal worse than we had thought to be the case." WC (281), 23 November 1917, Cab 23/4.
13. WC (274), 15 November 1917, Cab 23/4. The speaker is not identified, but it is likely that it was either Lloyd George or Milner.
14. In October, Lloyd George had wanted to send as many as eight of Haig's divisions to Palestine, but the minister of shipping, Sir Joseph Maclay, had discouraged him by emphasizing the tonnage required to do so. See Maclay to Lloyd George, 11 October 1917, Lloyd George Papers, F/35/2/30.
15. WO 106/467.
16. WC (302), 19 December 1917, Cab 23/4.
17. WO 106/467.
18. Ibid.
19. Baker to Wilson, 11 November 1917, *WWP*, 45:4-6.
20. Ministry of Shipping, "The Shipping Situation and American Assistance," Cabinet Paper G.T. 2728 of 21 November 1917, Cab 24/33.
21. Curzon, "Restriction of Imports. Interim Report," 1 December 1917, App., WC (292), 5 December 1917, Cab. 23/4.
22. For a discussion of what Kennedy describes as "the modest, even stingy, American maritime contribution to the war," see his *Over Here*, pp. 324-31.
23. Lloyd George, *War Memoirs*, 2:1798. The prime minister's emotional speech was apparently not without justification. The Ministry of Shipping informed the government

during this period that Britain's "imports, excluding food and munitions, which amounted to over 36 million tons in peace times, have this year fallen to about 8 million tons; and 6 million tons must, as stated above, be taken partly off this figure and partly off the food and munitions requirements for next year even apart from the conveyance of the further 2 million tons of cereals for the Allies." Cabinet Paper G.T. 2728 of 21 November 1917, Cab 24/33.

24. WC (295), 10 December 1917, Cab 23/4; J.A. Salter, *Allied Shipping Control: An Experiment in International Administration* (Oxford, 1921), p. 152.

25. MPC (3), 11 December 1917, Cab 27/14.

26. War College Division, "Statement of the General Staff Plan for the Organization and Despatch of Troops to Europe," October 1917, RG 165/10050-119.

27. Cabinet Paper G.T. 2755 of 23 November 1917, Cab 24/33.

28. Major Fulton Q.C. Gardner, "Memorandum for Colonel Lochridge: Subject: General Bliss' Cablegram of December 4th," 21 December 1917, RG 165/6576-23.

29. Bliss to Baker, 23 December 1917, RG 165/6291-60.

30. General Staff, "American Army," 8 December 1917, MPC 6, Cab 27/14.

31. Account by Gilbert W. Hall, Hall Papers, 77/132/1.

32. Bliss to Mrs. Bliss, 8 November 1917, Bliss Papers, Box 244.

33. Bliss, "Report of the Representative of the War Department," 14 December 1917, Department of State, *Foreign Relations, 1917, Supplement 2,* 1:391.

34. Benson, "Report of the Representative of the Navy Department," 14 December 1917, ibid., pp. 385-386.

35. House, "Report of the Special Representative of the United States Government," 15 December 1917, ibid., pp. 356-357.

36. Bliss, "Report of the Representative of the War Department," 14 December 1917; and House, "Report of the Special Representative of the United States Government," 15 December 1917, ibid., pp. 356-357, 389.

37. Department of State, *Papers Relating to the Foreign Relations of the United States, The Lansing Papers, 1914-1920,* 2:201-15.

38. Bliss, "Report of the Representative of the War Department," 14 December 1917, Department of State, *Foreign Relations, 1917, Supplement 2,* 1:388.

39. *WWP*, 45:323.

40. Ibid.

41. Baker to Wilson, note to Pershing enclosed, 18 December 1917, ibid., p. 328. For Spring Rice's paraphrase of this telegram, see Spring Rice to Balfour, 20 December 1917, Balfour Papers, BM Add 49740.

42. James G. Harbord (chief of staff) to Fox Conner, 1 January 1918, G-3, GHQ, AEF, Secret General Correspondence, No. 681, Pt. 4, Box 3112, RG 120.

43. Fox Conner, "Strategical Study Directed by the Chief of Staff," 7 January 1918, ibid.

44. Ibid.

45. Résumé of Pershing/Pétain interview, 23 December 1917, Department of the Army, *United States Army in the World War,* 2:106-7.

46. Note by Pershing, n.d. but almost certainly early January 1918, G-3, GHQ, AEF, Secret General Correspondence, No. 681, Pt. 4, Box 3112, RG 120.

47. For a description of House's attempt to involve the British in a joint statement on war objectives, see Kernek, *Distractions of Peace during War,* pp. 65-69.

48. War College Division, "Estimate of the Current Strategic Situation," n.d. but internal evidence suggests that this 1,204-page document was produced during the last half of February 1918. Twenty-five copies were printed, but there is no evidence in the Baker Papers that Wilson was sent a copy by his secretary of war. RG 165/8690-666.

49. Robertson to Haig, 15 September 1917, Woodward, *Military Correspondence of Robertson,* p. 224.

50. This valuable record of Labour's support for the war can be found in the Public Record Office, Kew, Richmond.

51. See Bourne, *Britain and the Great War*, pp. 199-224; T. Wilson, *Myriad Faces of War*, pp. 519-30, 653-59; and John N. Horne, *Labour at War: France and Britain, 1914-1918* (Oxford, 1991), p. 55.

52. David R. Woodward, "The Origins and Intent of David Lloyd George's January 5 War Aims Speech," *The Historian*, November 1971, pp. 22-39; and Rothwell, *British War Aims and Peace Diplomacy*, pp. 143-58.

53. See Arno J. Mayer, *Political Origins of the New Diplomacy, 1917-1918* (New Haven, Conn., 1959), p. 323.

54. Lloyd George, in fact, wanted Smuts to replace Balfour as head of the Foreign Office. See entry of 2 January 1918 (misdated for 3 or 4 January), Hankey Diary, 1/3.

55. Note by Smuts, 26 December, given to Lloyd George on 27 December 1917, Cab 1/25.

56. WC (314), 4 January 1918, Cab 23/5.

57. This was the way Lloyd George characterized the intent of the War Cabinet. WC (312), 3 January 1918, Cab 23/5.

58. Entry of 9 December 1917, McEwen, *Riddell Diaries*, p. 210.

59. For British efforts to ensure that the acceptance of the principle of self-determination would provide for British domination of the former German colonies, see Louis, *Germany's Lost Colonies*, pp. 97-100.

60. For the text of this speech, see Lloyd George, *War Memoirs*, 2:1510-17. According to Cecil, Lloyd George's statement was "composed as to two-fifths by Smuts, one-fifth by the Prime Minister himself, and two-fifths by me." Cecil to Balfour, 8 January 1918, Balfour Papers, BM Add 49738.

61. It should be noted that Haig was at this time much discouraged by the failure of the government to replace his losses. Smuts to Lloyd George, 22 January 1918, minuted by Hankey: "Prime Minister I fully confirm the following," Lloyd George Papers, F/45/9/9.

62. Entry of 9 January 1918, House Diary, *WWP*, 45:556-57.

63. A point-by-point comparison of Wilson's and Lloyd George's war aims statements can be found in Kernek, *Distractions of Peace during War*, pp. 73-76.

64. Scott to Hobhouse, 20 December 1917, T. Wilson, *Political Diaries of C.P. Scott*, p. 323.

8. Before the Storm

1. Lloyd George's minute on "Extracts from Sir W. Robertson's Memo," 19 November 1917, Lloyd George Papers, F/162/3.

2. See WC (295), 10 December 1917, Cab 23/4.

3. WC (316 A), 7 January 1918, Cab 23/13. Haig later tried to alter this view, which was used by the civilians to deny him the reinforcements he requested, but the damage had been done.

4. Amery to Wilson, 12 January 1918, H. Wilson Papers, File 8.

5. Milner to Lloyd George, 3 November 1917, Lloyd George Papers, F/38/2/20.

6. WC (351 A), 21 February 1918, Cab 23/13.

7. Board of Trade, "The American Army as a Problem of Imports and Shipping," n.d. but almost certainly the last half of December 1917, WO 106/478; and Robertson's cable to Haig, 3 January 1918, concerning amalgamation and the Board of Trade's memorandum, WO 106/466.

8. Pershing's memorandum for House, 28 November 1917, House Papers, Box 89, fol. 3072. Several days later Pershing informed the War Department: "It is very doubtful

if they [the Allies] can hold on until 1919 unless we give them a lot of support this year." See Pershing's cable to Baker and chief of staff, 2 December 1917, Department of the Army, *United States Army in the World War*, 2:88.

9. Pershing, *My Experiences*, 1:257.

10. WC (292), 5 December 1917, Cab 23/4.

11. The complicated and divisive story of British attempts to employ American battalions in British divisions can be followed in John P. Fisher, "The Creation of the American First Army: Anglo-American Relations and the Amalgamation Controversy, 1917-1918" (M.A. thesis, Marshall University, 1988); Smythe, *Pershing*, pp. 74-80, 105-112; Beaver, *Baker and the American War Effort*, pp. 110-50; Fowler, *British-American Relations*, pp. 127-63; Trask, *United States in the Supreme War Council*, pp. 70-99; and Thomas Clement Lonergan, *It Might Have Been Lost! A Chronicle from Alien Sources of the Struggle to Preserve the National Identity of the A.E.F.* (New York, 1929). Lonergan's account includes many then classified British official documents.

12. Baker to Wilson, 3 January 1918, and Pershing to War Department, sent 8 January, received 9 January 1918, Baker Papers.

13. "Account of a meeting between General Pershing—Sir W. Robertson and Sir J. Maclay, Shipping Controller on 9th January 1918," WO 106/466.

14. Robertson, "American Battalions for British Divisions," 12 January 1918, Lloyd George Papers, F/163/4/1.

15. Pershing, *My Experiences*, 1:288.

16. "Account of a meeting held on 10th January between General Pershing—Sir W. Robertson, and Sir J. Maclay," WO 106/466.

17. Robertson, "American Battalions for British Divisions," 12 January 1918, Lloyd George Papers, F/163/4/1.

18. WC (321), 14 January 1918, Cab 23/5.

19. AEF headquarters to the adjutant general (Washington), 13 January 1918, *WWP*, 46:8-11.

20. Baker to Wilson, 19 January 1918, Baker Papers.

21. See *New York Times*, 20 January 1918; Seward W. Livermore, *Politics Is Adjourned: Woodrow Wilson and the War Congress, 1916-1918* (Middletown, Conn., 1966), pp. 79-104; and Frederic L. Paxson, *American Democracy and the World War*, vol. 2, *America at War, 1917-1918* (New York, 1939), pp. 202-26.

22. Wilson to Baker, 20 January 1918, Baker Papers.

23. McCain to Bliss, [19] 21 January 1918, *WWP*, 46:44-45.

24. W. Kirke (for CIGS) to Hankey (War Cabinet), 27 January 1918, with enclosure, "Note by the French General Staff on American Military Assistance in 1918," WO 107/467; and WC (331), 25 January 1918, Cab 23/5.

25. See the graph in Salter, *Allied Shipping Control*, p. 87.

26. Ibid., pp. 173-74.

27. Smythe, *Pershing*, p. 78, and Coffman, *War to End All Wars*, p. 171.

28. Pershing, *My Experiences*, 1:308.

29. Entry of 29 January 1918, Haig Diary, Acc 3155, No. 123.

30. Bliss to Baker, 30 January 1918, *WWP*, 46:211.

31. WC (338), 4 February 1918, Cab 23/5.

32. Maurice, however, had earlier cautioned the War Cabinet not to include the Americans in any consideration of extending the British front, "as there could not be enough Americans in line to modify the situation seriously before June." WC (331), 25 January 1918, Cab 23/5.

33. Wiseman to Drummond (for Balfour), 3 February 1918, Balfour Papers, BM Add 49741.

34. Ibid.

35. Wilson to Baker, 4 February 1918, Baker Papers.

36. Reading to Foreign Office, 15 February 1918, *WWP*, 46:354.

37. Calhoun argues in *Power and Principle*, pp. 166-84, that "both symbolically and practically" Wilson emphasized international cooperation, including collective military security.

38. For a discussion of the failure to create an Allied General Reserve prior to the 1918 German offensive, see Woodward, *Lloyd George and the Generals*, pp. 253-81. See also Trask, *United States in the Supreme War Council*, pp. 53-62; and entry of 24 February 1918, E. David Cronon, ed., *The Cabinet Diaries of Josephus Daniels, 1913-1921* (Lincoln, Neb., 1963), p. 283.

39. See Ambrosius, *Wilson and the American Diplomatic Tradition*.

40. Barter to War Office, sent 27 November, received 29 November 1917, Cabinet Paper G.T. 2817, Cab 24/34.

41. See Richard H. Ullman *Anglo-Soviet Relations, 1917-1921*, vol. 1, *Intervention and the War* (Princeton, 1961), pp. 40-57.

42. Memorandum by Macdonogh, 20 November 1917, FO 371/3018.

43. WC (289), 3 December 1917, Cab 23/4.

44. WC (294), 7 December 1917, Cab 23/4. Robertson clearly had doubts about reviving the eastern front, but because of the shipping crisis he saw no other theater in which the Japanese army might play an active role in the land campaign. See his note to Lord Cecil and Balfour, 20 December 1917, FO 371/3020.

45. Quoted in Rothwell, *British War Aims and Peace Diplomacy*, p. 193.

46. Lloyd George, *War Memoirs*, 2:1895-96.

47. Lloyd George Papers, F/2/1/9.

48. See Amery, "The Military and Strategical Position in the Turkish Theatre and South Russia as a Whole," 4 January 1918, and "Memo by General Sir Henry Wilson, K.C.B., D.S.O. 1918 Campaign," n.d., Cab 25/68. See also Amery to Lloyd George, 18 January 1918, Lloyd George Papers, F/2/1/13.

49. Entry of 16 January 1918, H. Wilson Diary.

50. Amery to Lloyd George, 12 January 1918, Lloyd George Papers, F/2/1/11.

51. See the articles by David R. Woodward: "British Intervention in Russia during the First World War," *Military Affairs*, December 1977, pp. 171-75; and "The British Government and Japanese Intervention in Russia during World War I," *Journal of Modern History*, December 1974, pp. 663-85.

52. See Beaver, *Baker and the American War Effort*, pp. 181-82.

53. "Foreign Office Minutes on S.E. Russia etc." Cabinet Paper G.T. 3243 of 4 January 1918, Cab 24/38.

54. "Note by the Russia Committee on the Question of the Trans-Siberian Railway," Cabinet Paper G.T. 3421 of 16 January 1918, Cab 24/40.

55. Cecil later changed his mind and became a strong advocate of Japanese intervention, believing it "the only real safeguard against the eventual Germanisation of the whole of Russia." See his "Russia and Japan," Cabinet Paper G.T. 3892 of 12 March 1918, Cab 24/44.

56. See also his "Military Co-operation of Japan in the War," Cabinet Paper G.T. 2206 of 3 October 1917, Cab 24/28.

57. WC (330 A), 24 January 1918, Cab 23/13.

58. See Cabinet Paper G.T. 3624 of 14 February 1918, Cab 24/42.

59. WC (350), 20 February 1918, Cab 23/5.

60. Entry of 21 February 1918, H. Wilson Diary.

61. WC (353), 25 February 1918, Cab 23/5.

62. Wiseman, "Notes for a Cable from the Ambassador to the Foreign Office," 9 March 1918, *WWP*, 46:591; and Wiseman to Drummond, Reading to Balfour enclosed, 10 March 1918, Balfour Papers, BM Add 49741.

63. Smuts to Lloyd George, 15 March 1918, Lloyd George Papers, F/45/9/11.

64. WC (358), 4 March 1918, Cab 23/5.

65. Milner to Wilson, 5 March 1918, H. Wilson Papers, File 11.

66. Memorandum by Balfour, 7 March 1918, Balfour Papers, BM Add 49699, and WC (362), 8 March 1918, Cab 23/5. With his eyes fixed on Persia, Amery now argued that the German threat was much greater to the Middle East than to Siberia. "In any case, Japanese intervention cannot conjure away the immediate danger which threatens our whole position in the East. That danger can only be disposed of by immediate vigorous measures on the spot." Amery, "Germany and the Middle East," 12 March 1918, H. Wilson Papers, File 11.

67. Reading to Foreign Office, sent 5 March, received 6 March 1918, FO 371/3289. For a discussion of Wilson's change of heart, see Betty Miller Unterberger, *America's Siberian Expedition, 1918-1920* (Durham, N.C., 1956), pp. 29-34.

68. WC (363), 11 March 1918, Cab 23/5. The speaker is not identified in the minutes, but it was probably Smuts.

69. See H. Wilson, Cabinet Paper G.T. 3891 of March 11, 1918, Cab 24/44.

70. See H. Wilson, "The Present Situation in Russia," Cabinet Paper G.T. 3927 of 13 March 1918, Cab 24/45. See also "The Delay in the East," Cabinet Paper G.T. 3970 of 18 March 1918, Cab 24/45.

71. See the memoranda by Knox, Cabinet Paper G.T. 3927 of 13 March and Cabinet Paper G.T. 3970 of 18 March 1918, Cab 24/45; memoranda by H. Wilson, Cabinet Paper G.T. 3842 of 7 March and Cabinet Paper G.T. 3891 of 11 March 1918, Cab 24/44, and Cabinet Paper G.T. 4156 of 5 April 1918, Cab 24/47; memorandum by Poole, Cabinet Paper G.T. 4033 of 15 March 1918, Cab 24/46; and memorandum by Proctor, "Japanese Intervention and Seizure of Archangel. Policy of Activity in Russia as Opposed to Inactivity and Alliance with Bolsheviks," 14 March 1918, Cab 25/48.

72. Wiseman to Balfour, 25 January 1918, Balfour Papers, B.M. Add 49741. President Wilson's mixed signals encouraged the British to believe that he might ultimately be won over to armed intervention. On March 14 Wiseman cabled Drummond that the president was "endeavouring to find a way both to reconcile American people to need for intervention and to allay Russian fears of it." See Wiseman to Drummond (No. CXP 561), 14 March 1918, Wiseman Papers. I am indebted to Professor Betty Miller Unterberger for sharing her microfilm of Wiseman materials with me.

73. Lloyd George Papers, F/38/3/20.

74. WC (369), 21 March 1918, Cab 23/5.

75. Ibid.

9. The Western Front Imperiled

1. Hankey, *Supreme Command*, 2:785.

2. Entry of 23 March 1918, McEwen, *Riddell Diaries*, p. 223.

3. WC (371), 23 March 1918, Cab 23/5.

4. Ibid.

5. WC (372), 25 March 1918, Cab 23/5.

6. WC (375-76), 27-28 March 1918, Cab 23/5.

7. WC (374), 27 March 1918, Cab 23/5.

8. WC (373), 26 March 1918, Cab 23/5.

9. Pershing, *My Experiences*, 1:365.

10. Ibid., p. 376.

11. Milner to Lloyd George, 28 March 1918, Lloyd George Papers, F/38/3/22.

12. Department of the Army, *United States Army in the World War*, 2:257-58; and Trask, *United States in the Supreme War Council*, p. 81.

13. Reading to Balfour, 27 March 1918, Wiseman Papers, Box 1, fol. 7.

14. See the prime minister's comments in WC (377), 29 March 1918, Cab 23/5.

15. Outwardly, Baker supported Joint Note No. 18, but he remained as determined as ever to create an independent American army in 1918. See Trask, *United States in the Supreme War Council*, p. 82.

16. Wilson to Lansing, 4 February 1918, House Papers, Box 121, fol. 4282.

17. WC (357 A), 1 March 1918, Cab 23/16.

18. Ibid.

19. Hankey to Lloyd George, 2 March 1918, ibid.

20. Balfour to Reading, 23 March 1918, *WWP*, 47:130.

21. Walworth, *World Prophet*, p. 166.

22. Unfortunately, the only record of these discussions is the skimpy published diary of Josephus Daniels. For the frivolous nature of the cabinet meetings, see Cronon, *Cabinet Diaries of Daniels*, 294.

23. Wilson to Baker, 19 June 1918, Baker Papers.

24. I am especially indebted to the revisionist essay by Arthur S. Link and John Whiteclay Chambers II (see "Woodrow Wilson as Commander in Chief," pp. 317-75) that portrays Wilson as a commander-in-chief who closely supervised the American military establishment and who was intimately involved in military decisions both large and small. My research, however, does not suggest that Wilson was closely involved in many military questions concerning the early development of the AEF. And indeed almost all of the evidence cited by Link and Chambers for Wilson's personal involvement in the role of U.S. land forces abroad is for the period from March 1918 onward.

25. Wilson to Auchincloss (for House), 27 March 1918, *WWP*, 47:158.

26. Quoted in Sir William Robertson, *Soldiers and Statesmen, 1914-1918* (New York, 1926), 1:331; and Fowler, *British-American Relations*, p. 139.

27. Reading to Lloyd George, 28 March 1918, *WWP*, 47:183.

28. Lloyd George to Reading, sent 29 March, received 30 March 1918, *WWP* 47:203-5.

29. WC (378), 30 March 1918, Cab 23/5.

30. Wiseman to Balfour, c. 28 March 1918, *WWP*, 47:184.

31. Entry of 29 March 1918, House Diary, *WWP*, 47:206; *The Times* (London), 2 April 1918.

32. Wiseman, "Notes on Interview with the President," 1 April 1918, Balfour Papers, BM Add 49741.

33. *WWP*, 47:269.

34. WC (390), 12 April 1918, Cab 23/6. On the day this message was sent to Washington, the War Cabinet noted that it was "questionable whether the passage referring to India was well adapted to appeal to American opinion." WC (391), 15 April 1918, Cab 23/6; paraphrase of cable from Balfour to Reading, 15 April 1918, *WWP*, 47:355-57.

35. Smythe, *Pershing*, p. 111; and WC (389), 11 April 1918, Cab 23/6. British casualties including the sick totaled 221,000 from March 21 to April 15. WC (393), 17 April 1918, Cab 23/6.

36. WC (388 A), 10 April 1918, Cab 23/14.

37. For British discussions of the possibility that the Channel ports might have to be abandoned, exposing Britain to a cross-Channel invasion, see WC (400-401 A), 26 and 30 April 1918, Cab 23/14.

38. Memorandum by Macdonogh, 10 April 1918, WO 106/982; see also Milner to Esher, 13 April 1918, Esher Papers, 5/55.

39. Lloyd George to Reading, 2 April 1918, *WWP*, 47:229.

40. WC (385), 6 April 1918, Cab 23/6.

41. In an attempt to clear up the confusion, Reading cabled London: "President has replied that he agreed in principle that there should be brigading but did not commit

himself to total and reserved details for Generals Bliss and Pershing. I do not find any substantial difference between this and my report to you [of March 30] which I quote:— 'In principle he approves of employment of troops in manner desired but leaves details to military chiefs.' " Reading to Lloyd George, 7 April 1918, WO 106/475.

42. Memorandum by Fox Conner, 6 April 1918, Department of the Army, *United States Army in the World War*, 2:284.

43. March to Bliss, 6 April 1918, *WWP*, 47:271.

44. Sackville-West to Sir Henry Wilson, 8 April 1918, H. Wilson Papers, File 12 B/14.

45. Lloyd George to Reading, 9 April 1918, *WWP*, 47:307.

46. Reading to Balfour, 10 April 1918, *WWP*, 47:314.

47. Lloyd George to Reading, 14 April 1918, *WWP*, 47:338.

48. Entry of 15 April 1918, Cronon, *Cabinet Diaries of Daniels*, p. 299.

49. Beaver, *Baker and the American War Effort*, p. 140.

50. Reading to Lloyd George, sent 20 April, received 21 April 1918, *WWP*, 47:386-88.

51. Baker to Pershing, 29 April 1918, quoted in Beaver, *Baker and the American War Effort*, p. 141.

52. WC (397), 23 April 1918, Cab 23/6.

53. See "Memorandum of General Pershing's Visit to the British War Office, and Interview with General Sir Henry Wilson, and Lord Milner," 22 April, and "London Agreement," 24 April 1918, Department of the Army, *United States Army in the World War*, 2:340-44.

54. SWC, 1 May 1918, Cab 28/3/IC-57; and Smythe, *Pershing*, pp. 113-15.

55. Lonergan, *It Might Have Been Lost*, pp. 165-66.

56. WC (393 and 404), 17 April and 3 May 1918, Cab 23/6; and Baker to Wilson, 29 April 1918, Baker Papers.

57. WC (405), 6 May 1918, Cab 23/6. Milner calculated that the strength of a U.S. division attached to the BEF would be 20,104. The remainder of the division, chiefly artillerymen, would go directly to Pershing.

58. Baker to Wilson, 4 May, and Wilson to Baker, 6 May 1918, *WWP*, 47:517, 535. For a discussion of Pershing's misleading account of the Abbeville negotiations, see Smythe, *Pershing*, pp. 117-18.

59. See Woodward, *Lloyd George and the Generals*, pp. 296-304.

60. Lloyd George's defense may have satisfied the politicians, but it in no way appeased the War Office. On May 14 the adjutant general produced a memorandum arguing that the War Office's manpower calculations, which had been rejected by the government, had been proved right by events. Significantly, Lloyd George defended the government's manpower approach with the questionable assertion that "the incorporation of the American infantry had for some time been the accepted policy of the British and American Governments. Indeed, it formed an essential part of the Government's man-power policy." See "Man-Power. Remarks by the Prime Minister on the Adjutant-General's Memorandum dated 14th May, 1918," Cabinet Paper G.T. 4679 of 28 May 1918, Cab 24/52.

61. Waldorf Astor to J.L. Garvin (conservative editor), 11 May 1918, quoted in Turner, *British Politics and the Great War*, pp. 299-300.

62. Derby (now British Ambassador in Paris) to Balfour, 18 May 1918, Lloyd George Papers, F/52/1/33.

63. WC (411), 14 May 1918, Cab 23/6.

64. H. Wilson to General Sir Edmund Allenby, 9 May 1918, Keith Jeffery, ed., *The Military Correspondence of Field Marshal Sir Henry Wilson, 1918-1922* (London, 1985), pp. 42-43.

65. "X" Committee (1), 15 May 1918, Cab 23/17.

66. Edward M. Coffman, *The Hilt of the Sword: The Career of Peyton C. March* (Madison, Wis., 1966), pp. 64-65, 150.

67. Bliss to Rawlinson, 30 April 1918, Bliss Papers, Box 246.

68. The exception was the black Ninety-second Division. To avoid, as Lord Milner expressed it to Pershing, "a good deal of administrative trouble," the British War Office had asked Pershing and the War Department not to send them black soldiers; hence, the Ninety-second was assigned to the French. See Pershing, *My Experiences*, 2:45-46.

69. "X" Committee (2-3), 16-17 May 1918, Cab 23/17.

70. See Lloyd Griscom to Pershing, 16 July 1918, Pershing Papers, Box 85.

71. Rawlinson to Clive Wigram (private secretary to the king), 27 May, and Rawlinson to Sir Henry Wilson, 25 May 1918, Rawlinson Papers, Letter Book, IV.

72. House sent this comment on to Wilson. Griscom to House, 7 June 1918, House Papers, Box 53, fol. 1678.

73. Rawlinson to Sir Henry Wilson, 19 May 1918, Rawlinson Papers, Letter Book, IV.

74. "Interview on Occupation of American Sector," 19 May 1918, Department of the Army, *United States Army in the World War*, 2:413-14.

75. On the question of logistics, see Charles R. Shrader, "'Maconochie's Stew': Logistical Support of American Forces with the BEF, 1917-18" in Adams, *The Great War*, pp. 101-31.

76. "X" Committee (1), 15 May 1918, Cab 23/17; see also Pershing to Lloyd George, 28 April 1918, House Papers, Box 89, fol. 3072.

77. "X" Committee (2), 16 May 1918, Cab 23/17.

78. Entry of 9 May 1918, H. Wilson Diary.

79. "X" Committee (2), 16 May 1918, Cab 23/17.

10. A New Strategic Landscape

1. Amery, "Future Military Policy," 22 May 1918, Milner Papers, dep. 372.

2. "X" Committee (4), 27 May 1918, Cab 23/17.

3. WC (418), 27 May 1918, Cab 23/6.

4. Entry of 1 June 1918, H. Wilson Diary.

5. Bliss to Mrs. Bliss, 8 June 1918, Bliss Papers, Box 244.

6. This was clearly a concern for Baker, who wrote Wilson: "I have felt that we ought not be put in the position of failing to do what was suggested to us as essential to hold the German line, chiefly because I did not want the possibility of failure being attributed to us even if the course recommended by our Allies would not have prevented the failure." Baker to Wilson, 5 June 1918, Baker Papers.

7. See Baker to Pershing, 11 May 1918, *WWP*, 47:615-16, and Wiseman to Drummond, 30 May 1918, *WWP*, 48:205.

8. Smythe, *Pershing*, p. 135.

9. Believing that victory was more and more dependent upon American arms, Pershing and March placed the "highest importance" on "the rapid formation of complete American divisions." See Baker to Wilson, June 5, 1918, Baker Papers.

10. Pershing to House, 19 June 1918, House Papers, Box 89, fol. 3073.

11. Entry of 2 June 1918, H. Wilson Diary.

12. Entry of June 3, 1918, Robert Blake, ed., *The Private Papers of Douglas Haig, 1914-1919* (London, 1952), p. 313.

13. One study estimated that there was enough shipping to evacuate from 300,000 to 400,000 daily if all ports were utilized. See "X" Committee (7 and 8), 5 June 1918, Cab 23/17; and Fourth Sea Lord, "Arrangements for Evacuation from France," 25 June 1918, Milner Papers, dep. 374. In an appreciation never completed, Amery, after conferring with the Admiralty and War Office, argued that Britain, if it abandoned Europe (with the possible exception of Greece), would have the men to build ships and produce munitions

and could consequently fight more effectively in the eastern theaters. See L. S. Amery, *My Political Life*, vol. 2, *War and Peace 1914-1929* (London, 1953), p. 158.

14. Smuts to Lloyd George, 8 June 1918, Lloyd George Papers, F/45/9/18.

15. It should be noted that Bliss thought the plan to move the five American divisions to Alsace a grave strategical error on Pershing's part. Bliss wrote Baker on June 8 that he did not like "a movement which looks to a re-concentration of a large part of the American forces down towards the Swiss frontier. I should very much prefer to see them on the left flank of the French line and where they could, if necessary, operate with the British." Instead of cabling his views to Baker, Bliss had written a letter, dated June 8, which apparently did not reach Washington for almost two weeks. See *WWP*, 48:383-90.

16. Within days of this pledge, however (June 17), Foch tried to persuade Pershing to amalgamate the remaining five American divisions in the British zone with twenty exhausted French divisions, one American regiment to each French division. See Smythe, *Pershing*, p. 145.

17. Entry of 7 June 1918, H. Wilson Diary; and Blake, *Private Papers of Haig*, pp. 314-15.

18. "X" Committee (10-13), 10 and 12-14 June 1918, Cab 23/17.

19. Griscom to Pershing, 14 June 1918, Pershing Papers, Box 85.

20. "X" Committee (14), 17 June 1918, Cab 23/17.

21. Pershing to Baker, and Wilson to Baker, 19 June 1918, Baker Papers; and Beaver, *Baker and the American War Effort*, p. 148.

22. "X" Committee (15), 19 June 1918, Cab 23/17.

23. Entry of 8 June 1918, H. Wilson Diary.

24. "X" Committee (12), 13 June 1918, Cab 23/17.

25. "X" Committee (19), 1 July 1918, Cab 23/17.

26. Milner to Lloyd George, 9 June 1918, Lloyd George Papers, F/38/3/37.

27. Amery to Lloyd George, 8 June 1918, Lloyd George Papers, F/2/1/24.

28. All of the above remarks were made by Lloyd George on 11 June 1918. See IWC (15), 11 June 1918, Cab 23/43.

29. IWC (30), 13 August 1918, Cab 23/43.

30. See Rothwell, *British War Aims and Peace Diplomacy*, p. 290.

31. IWC (30), 13 August 1918, Cab 23/43.

32. See Carl J. Richard, "'The Shadow of a Plan': The Rationale behind Wilson's 1918 Siberian Intervention," *The Historian*, November 1986, pp. 64-84. See also Betty Miller Unterberger, ed., *American Intervention in the Russian Civil War* (Lexington, Mass., 1969).

33. A study, utilizing both British and American sources, which would differ with this conclusion concerning the motivation of Anglo-American policy is Gardner, *Safe for Democracy*, pp. 151-202. My basic disagreement with Professor Gardner is that I think he relies too much on the motivation of men peripheral to the decision to intervene and underestimates, in particular, the desperation of imperial-minded statesmen in seeking means to contain the Turko-German threat to the now exposed British position in Asia.

34. See, e.g., the discussion in the Eastern Committee (14 and 16), 18 and 24 June 1918, Cab 27/24.

35. IWC (18), 18 June 1918, Cab 23/43.

36. Balfour to Reading, 20 June 1918, *WWP*, 48:379.

37. Sir Henry Wilson, "Situation in Murmansk," 18 May 1918, WO 106/314.

38. See Unterberger, *America's Siberian Expedition*, pp. 39-66; Ullman, *Intervention and the War*, pp. 195-96; and George F. Kennan, *Soviet-American Relations, 1917-1920*, vol. 2, *The Decision to Intervene* (New York, 1967), pp. 270-71.

39. Memorandum by Gregory, 17 June 1918, FO 371/3319.

40. See Beaver, *Baker and the American War Effort*, pp. 181-84.

41. Memorandum by March, 24 June 1918, *WWP*, 48:419.

42. See Woodward, "British Intervention in Russia," p. 174, and "British Government and Japanese Intervention," pp. 679-82.

43. IWC (20), 25 June 1918, Cab 23/43.

44. Lloyd George, Milner, Hankey, and Amery had discussed the "conditions under which the War would have to be carried on if by any chance our European Allies were unable to continue"; if the war were thus confined to the east, American participation on that front was essential. "X" Committee (18), 28 June 1918, Cab 23/17.

45. Sir Eric Drummond to Hankey, 27 June 1918, Drummond Papers, FO 800/329.

46. Peyton C. March, *The Nation at War* (Garden City, N.Y., 1932), p. 126.

47. Lansing, "Memorandum of a Conference at the White House in Reference to the Siberian Situation," 6 July 1918, *WWP*, 48:542-43.

48. See Robert J. Maddox, *The Unknown War with Russia: Wilson's Siberian Intervention* (San Rafael, Calif., 1977), pp. 49-50; and Richard, "Shadow of a Plan," pp. 78-84.

49. Wilson to Frank Lyon Polk, 17 July 1918, Enclosure, *WWP*, 48:640-43.

50. Entry of 10 July 1918, Hankey Diary, 1/3.

51. See the president's angry remarks to the French Ambassador about articles in the *New York Times*. Jean Jules Jusserand to Foreign Ministry, received 25 July 1918, *WWP*, 49:93.

52. Quoted in Beaver, *Baker and the American War Effort*, p. 183.

53. Pershing, *My Experiences*, 2:121; Coffman, *Hilt of the Sword*, pp. 84-94; and Army War College (Historical Section), *The Genesis of the American First Army* (Washington, D.C., 1929), pp. 40-45.

54. On July 13, 1918, Milner "expressed strong personal preference" for the establishment of the American army "between them and the French." Griscom to Pershing, 13 July 1918; see also Milner's discussion of the formation of an American Corps in the British zone, Griscom to Pershing, 22 June 1918, Pershing Papers, Box 85.

55. *The Times* (London), July 5-6, 1918; Pershing, *My Experiences*, 2:137-38; Arthur W. Page, *Our 110 Days' Fighting* (New York, 1920), pp. 204-5; John Terraine, *To Win a War: 1918, the Year of Victory* (New York, 1981), pp. 67-72; and Coffman, *War to End All Wars*, pp. 287-89.

56. Rawlinson to Clive Wigram, 7 July 1918, Rawlinson Papers, Letter Book, IV; Terraine, *To Win a War*, pp. 69-70.

57. "X" Committee (19), 1 July 1918, Cab 23/17.

58. Tardieu had attempted to accelerate the flow of Americans across the Atlantic without consulting London, which had to provide most of the additional shipping.

59. SWC, 3 July 1918, Cab 28/4/IC-70; and Woodward, *Lloyd George and the Generals*, p. 319.

60. Sir Henry Wilson, perhaps envious of Foch's status, had unsuccessfully lobbied his political leadership to support his being made the strategic tsar for "all theatres over the salt water except France and Italy." Entry of 3 July 1918, H. Wilson Diary.

61. Ibid.

62. Entry of 4 July 1918, ibid.

11. Disunity of Command

1. Bridges to Baker, 25 July 1918, Baker Papers.

2. See Barclay (Washington) to Balfour, 17 September 1918, Balfour Papers, FO 800/209.

3. Bliss to Baker and March, 14 August 1918, *WWP*, 49:259.

4. WC (442), 8 July 1918, Cab 23/7.

5. WC (444 A), 11 July 1918, Cab 23/14.

6. "X" Committee (20), 12 July 1918, Cab 23/17.

7. Lloyd George to Clemenceau, 13 July 1918, Lloyd George Papers, F/50/3/7.

8. Entry of 13 July 1918, Haig Dairy, Acc 3155, No. 129.

9. Lloyd George to Milner, 14 July 1918, Lloyd George Papers, F/38/4/1.

10. For Lloyd George's relationship to Borden, see George L. Cook, "Sir Robert Borden, Lloyd George, and British Military Policy, 1917-1918," *Historical Journal*, March 1971, pp. 371-95.

11. Entry of 13-14 July 1918, McEwen, *Riddell Diaries*, pp. 230-31.

12. When Smuts talked with Haig, the field marshal argued that the Beauvais Agreement meant that he must "obey his orders [from Foch] and to protest, if he considered necessary, afterwards." As a practical matter, Haig was correct. In an emergency he really had to obey Foch, or the existing unity of command would be meaningless. From a legal standpoint, however, Lloyd George correctly contended that Haig had the right to appeal to his government *before* obeying any order from Foch that placed the BEF in grave danger. Prime Minister Hughes of Australia put it best: the Beauvais Agreement was "not an easy matter to interpret; Field Marshal Haig would naturally look at it from the point of view of a soldier and not from that of a lawyer." See IWC (24 B), 16 July 1918, Cab 23/44.

13. Entry of 14 July 1918, H. Wilson Diary; IWC (24 A), 15 July 1918, Cab 23/44; and Wilson to Haig (by telephone, 12:25 A.M.), 15 July 1918, Haig Papers, Acc 3155, No. 129.

14. Balfour to Derby (Paris), 18 July 1918 (following from prime minister to M. Clemenceau), Lloyd George Papers, F/50/3/8.

15. Foch also argued that the raw American troops with the BEF offered far less security than the "trained" French divisions which would be sent north in an emergency. See Foch to Sir Henry Wilson, 16 July 1918, Lloyd George Papers, F/47/7/31.

16. "X" Committee (23), 18 July 1918, Cab 23/17.

17. IWC (24 B), 16 July 1918, Cab 23/44.

18. WC (449), 19 July 1918, Cab 23/7.

19. Foch, "Memorandum," 10 July 1918, Department of the Army, *United States Army in the World War*, 2:520.

20. Conner, memorandum for chief of staff on Foch-Pershing conversations 10 July at Bombon, 14 July 1918, G-3, GHQ, AEF, Secret General Correspondence, File No. 1003, Folder No. 681, Pt. 4, Box 3112, RG 120.

21. Pershing, *My Experiences*, 2:168-70. Sensing victory, the BEF's leadership now had abandoned all idea of amalgamation and wholeheartedly supported the early creation of an American army. Visiting the front at this time, Griscom reported to House: "The British higher command in France also told me personally that they had never approved of the attitude which the British politicians took toward our Army and they had expressed themselves vigorously in London." Griscom to House, 27 July 1918, House Papers, Box 53, fol. 1678.

22. Reading to Foreign Office, sent 7 July, received 8 July 1918, and Foreign Office to Reading, 11 July 1918, WO 106/522.

23. Reading to Balfour and Milner, sent 23 July, received 24 July 1915, and Reading to Foreign Office, 25 July 1918, WO 106/522.

24. Entry of 25 July 1918, Hankey Diary, 1/5.

25. General Sir John P. Du Cane (British liaison officer with Foch) to Sir Henry Wilson, 25 July 1918, WO 106/522.

26. Entry of 26 July 1918, H. Wilson Diary; and "X" Committee (25), 26 July 1918, Cab 23/17.

27. WC (452), 26 July 1918, Cab 23/7.

28. Cipher telegram to Lord Derby (Paris), 2 August 1918 (following for Clemenceau from Lloyd George), Lloyd George Papers, F/50/3/9. The prime minister's earlier draft of this communication had been much more direct, emphasizing France's monopoly of American forces in Europe. See rough draft for letter from prime minister to

Clemenceau, enclosed in Hankey to Lloyd George, 27 July 1918, Lloyd George Papers, F/23/3/7.

29. Geddes to Lloyd George, 8 August 1918, Lloyd George Papers, F/18/2/8; Lloyd George to Clemenceau, 6 August 1918, WO 106/522; and IWC (29 B), 12 August 1918, Cab 23/44.

30. It has been erroneously argued that the British at this time were motivated by a desire "to advance their own economic interests and to constrict Wilson's power to forge the armistice and peace terms." See Edward B. Parsons, "Why the British Reduced the Flow of American Troops to Europe in August-October 1918," *Canadian Journal of History*, December 1977, pp. 173-91; and Parsons, *Wilsonian Diplomacy*.

31. David French, *The British Way in Warfare, 1688-2000* (London, 1990), p. 172.

32. WC (449), 19 July 1918, Cab 23/7.

33. Lloyd George made this statement during the meeting of the Imperial War Cabinet when these figures were given. See IWC (27 B), 1 August 1918, Cab 23/44.

34. Memorandum by Sir Henry Wilson, 25 July 1918, Cab 25/85.

35. Entry of 30 July 1918, Hankey Diary, 1/5.

36. IWC (27 A), 31 July 1918, Cab 23/44.

37. Ibid.

38. Ibid.

39. Smuts was perhaps the British leader most alarmed by the potential German threat outside of Europe at this juncture. See his comments in IWC (27 A), 31 July 1918, Cab 23/44, and Eastern Committee (23), 8 August 1918, Cab 27/24.

40. Entry of 1 August 1918, Hankey Diary, 1/5. Significantly, this is also what Milner told the Empire statesmen on July 31.

41. IWC (27 B), 1 August 1918, Cab 23/44.

42. IWC (27 A and 27 B), 31 July and 1 August 1918, Cab 23/44.

43. IWC (27 C), 6 August 1918, Cab 23/44.

44. IWC (29 B), 12 August 1918, Cab 23/44.

45. Entry of 21 August 1918, Blake, *Private Papers of Haig*, p. 324.

46. Entry of 13 August 1918, Hankey Diary, 1/5.

47. It should be noted that the BEF, besides inflicting heavy casualties on the Germans, took over 60,000 prisoners during this same period. See Terraine, *To Win a War*, p. 110.

48. See Lloyd George's comments about British war aims in Africa and the Pacific. IWC (32B), 16 August 1918, Cab 23/44.

49. "Report of the Committee of Prime Ministers. Preliminary Draft as a Basis for Consideration," 14 August 1918, IWC (32 B), 16 August 1918, Cab 23/44.

50. IWC (32 B), 16 August 1918, Cab 23/44.

51. Ibid.

52. Ironically, on this same day, Griscom wrote House: "I am satisfied that all responsible officers in England are using all their power to prevent any relaxation of war effort on account of our entry into the war." Griscom to House, 16 August 1918, House Papers, Box 53, fol. 1678.

53. IWC (31), 14 August 1918, Cab 23/43.

54. IWC (32), 15 August 1918, Cab 23/7.

55. General Sackville-West, Sir Henry's successor at Versailles, had earlier made this proposal. IWC (27 C), 6 August 1918, Cab 23/44.

56. Radcliffe to Wilson, 9 August 1918, WO 106/522.

57. IWC (32 B), 16 August 1918, Cab 23/44; Griscom to House, 9 August 1918, House Papers, Box 53, fol. 1678; and Pershing, *My Experiences*, 2:219.

58. A recent revisionist work gives Foch rather than Haig the credit for originating the concentric offensive strategy, describing Haig as "the tea boy to Foch's managing director." See Denis Winter, *Haig's Command: A Reassessment* (London, 1991), p. 210.

59. John Charteris, *Field-Marshal Earl Haig* (New York, 1929), p. 360.

60. Terraine, *To Win a War*, p. 112.

61. Griscom to Pershing, sent 22 August, received 23 August 1918, Pershing Papers, Box 85.

62. Derby to Lloyd George (Clemenceau's note enclosed) sent 17 August, received 18 August 1918, Lloyd George Papers, F/50/3/15.

63. Note ("American Troops") to J.T. Davies (Lloyd George's private secretary), 21 August 1918, Lloyd George Papers, F/47/7/40.

64. Baker to Wilson (Pershing's telegram of 8 August, enclosed), 8 August, and Wilson to Baker, 9 August 1918, Baker Papers.

65. Kennedy, *Over Here*, p. 329; and Trask, *Captains & Cabinets*, p. 207.

66. Telegram ("Tonnage for Transport and Supply of American Troops") from British Section, SWC, n.d. but almost certainly in late July 1918, Lloyd George Papers, F/47/7/40.

67. Bliss to Baker and March, 14 August 1918, *WWP*, 49:258-61; entry of 21 August 1918, Cronon, *Cabinet Diaries of Daniels*, p. 332.

68. Baker to Wilson, 17 August 1918, *WWP*, 49:277.

69. Clemenceau told Derby and Reading that he and Foch had insisted that Pershing leave two divisions on the British front. Clemenceau, in fact, "begged" Lloyd George to believe that France was "seeking to be just and not to gain any special advantage for herself." See Derby to Lloyd George, 13 September 1918, Lloyd George Papers, F/52/2/31; and Reading to Lloyd George, 6 September 1918, Reading Papers, Eur F. 118/117.

70. See Sir Henry Wilson's report in "X" Committee (27), 31 August 1918, Cab 23/17.

71. Ibid. Although Lloyd George was especially concerned with American forces, General Wilson's instructions to Haig were that the War Cabinet "would not approve of attacks on the Hindenburg line involving heavy casualties whether by British or American troops."

72. WC (468), 3 September 1918, Cab 23/7.

73. Lloyd George to Reading, 26 August 1918, Lloyd George Papers, F/43/1/15.

74. Lloyd George to Clemenceau, 31 August 1918, Lloyd George Papers, F/50/3/17. Lloyd George later produced figures alleging to show that Britain and the Dominions had since January 1917 sent an additional 2,000,000 men to France, including 1,576,000 "fighting men." See War Cabinet (471), 10 September 1918, Cab 23/7.

75. Reading to Lloyd George, 3, 4, 6 September 1918, Reading Papers, Eur F. 118/117.

76. "X" Committee (27), 31 August 1918, Cab 23/17.

77. Foch had formally requested Pershing on August 23 to leave the American Twenty-seventh and Thirtieth Divisions with the British. Pershing had agreed, but he was determined that no more American divisions would either train or fight with the BEF. See Pershing, *My Experiences*, 2:229-30.

78. "X" Committee (27), 31 August 1918, Cab 23/17. For Allied strategy, see entries of August 27 and 29 1918, Blake, *Private Papers of Haig*, p. 325; De Groot, *Douglas Haig*, p. 388; Smythe, *Pershing*, pp. 174-76; and B.H. Liddell Hart, *The Real War, 1914-1918* (Boston, 1930), pp. 452-54.

79. Pershing, *My Experiences*, 2:243-48; Smythe, *Pershing*, p. 176.

80. "Notes on Conference between General Pershing, Marshal Foch and General Pétain at Bombon," 2 September 1918, Department of the Army, *United States Army in the World War*, 2:589-92.

81. Quoted in Coffman, *War To End All Wars*, p. 300.

82. Army War College, *Genesis of the American First Army*, p. 55.

83. Pershing, *My Experiences*, 2:270.

84. Hunter Liggett, *A.E.F.: Ten Years Ago in France* (New York, 1928), p. 159.

85. Eastern Committee (30), 11 September 1918, Cab 27/24. Smuts, however, continued to worry about Turkish aggrandizement in Asia. Fearing that the initiative was passing to Turkey, he believed that Britain would not be able to get favorable peace terms in the Middle East. See Eastern Committee (32), 18 September 1918, Cab 27/24.

86. WC (472), 13 September 1918, Cab 23/7. See also WC (468), 3 September 1918, Cab 23/7.

87. Entry of 10 September 1918, Blake, *Private Papers of Haig*, p. 326.

88. Milner to Lloyd George, 17 September 1918, Lloyd George Papers, F/38/4/17.

89. John Terraine, "Field Marshal Haig," *Stand To! The Journal of the Western Front Association*, Summer 1989, p. 10. It must be noted that a large number of these casualties were flu victims. The BEF's improved use of the new weaponry, especially artillery, limited its losses. On the first day of the Somme, 1 July 1916, the British had had almost 20,000 killed. The Fourth Army, however, sustained some 20,000 killed between August and November 1918, a period of sustained and dramatic advance. See Robin Prior and Trevor Wilson, *Command on the Western Front: The Military Career of Sir Henry Rawlinson, 1914-18* (Oxford, 1992), 391.

90. Entry of 23 September 1918, H. Wilson Diary.

91. The CIGS reported on September 27 that in addition to the rout of the enemy in Palestine, both the Germans and Turks were in disarray in the Caucasus-Caspian area. WC (479), 27 September 1918, Cab 23/7.

92. See Trask, *United States in the Supreme War Council*, pp. 144-46.

93. March to Wilson (Joint Note No. 37 enclosed), 3 October, and Wilson to March, 4 October 1918, *WWP*, 51:195-203, 211.

94. The BEF, in fact, incurred 853, 361 casualties in 1918, its most costly year of the war. See Terraine, "Field Marshal Haig," p. 10.

95. Edmonds, *Military Operations, France and Belgium, 1918*, 5:584.

96. Entries of 27 and 28 September 1918, McEwen, *Riddell Diaries*, p. 239.

97. See Baker to Wilson, 23 September 1918, Baker Papers; and Griscom to House (copy of Pershing), 21 September 1918, Pershing Papers, Box 85.

98. Lloyd George Papers, F/35/2/82.

99. Lloyd George to Milner, 29 September 1918, Lloyd George Papers, F/38/4/20.

100. Shrader, "Maconochie's Stew," p. 121, has the following estimates for Americans serving with the BEF at the beginning of the following months: April, 31,000; May 42,300; June, 174,400; July, 111,200; August, 109,200; September 59,900; October, 58,000; November, 46,900.

101. See Griscom, *Diplomatically Speaking*, pp. 434-35. The Americans were not above using their flow of troops across the Atlantic to pressure the British: e.g., House advised that Wilson "quietly diminish the transport of troops" to force the Allies to accept the American peace program. See House to Wilson, 30 October 1918, *WWP*, 51:514.

102. *WWP*, 51:435. This statement was furnished by Baker.

103. See Baker to Wilson, 23 September 1918, Baker Papers.

104. See Cabinet Paper G.T. 5932, n.d., Cab 24/66; and WC (487), 16 October 1918, Cab 23/8.

105. This understanding, however, did not resolve Anglo-American conflicts over shipping, which, as the German menace declined, tended to focus on commercial rivalry. E.g., the Geddes mission to Washington in October 1918 was unsuccessful in its efforts to reach agreement with the Americans on the postwar relationship between the British and American merchant marines. See Trask, *Captains & Cabinets*, pp. 281-312; and Beaver, *Baker and the American War Effort*, pp. 176-78.

106. See Lansing's memorandum, 27 September 1918, *WWP*, 5:140-41.

107. Joseph P. Tumulty, *Woodrow Wilson as I Know Him* (Garden City, N.Y., 1921), p. 309.

12. Pax Americana?

1. See WC (481), 2 October 1918, Cab 23/8; WC (482 A), 3 October 1918, Cab 23/14; and entry of 6 October 1918, Hankey Diary, 1/6.
2. "X" Committee (29), 19 October 1918, Cab 23/17; and entry of 23 October 1918, Blake *Private Papers of Haig*, p. 335.
3. Quoted in Coffman, *War to End All Wars*, p. 301.
4. Smythe, *Pershing*, p. 200.
5. Quoted in ibid., p. 208.
6. Barclay to Foreign Office, 7 October 1918, *WWP*, 51:263.
7. House to Wilson, 3 September 1918, House Papers, Box 121, fol. 4286.
8. "An Address in the Metropolitan Opera House [speaking copy]," 27 September 1918, *WWP*, 51:127-33.
9. For enlightening though in some important respects differing interpretations of the pre-Armistice negotiations, see Klaus Schwabe, *Woodrow Wilson, Revolutionary Germany, and Peacemaking, 1918-1919: Missionary Diplomacy and the Realities of Power* (Chapel Hill, N.C., 1985), pp. 30-117; Tillman, *Anglo-American Relations at the Paris Peace Conference*, pp. 39-54; Kernek, *Distractions of Peace during War*, pp. 96-108; Arthur Walworth, *America's Moment, 1918: American Diplomacy at the End of World War I* (New York, 1977), pp. 18-74; and Stevenson, *First World War and International Politics*, pp. 221-35.
10. Quoted in Ambrosius, *Wilson and the American Diplomatic Tradition*, p. 49.
11. See House to Wilson, 6 October 1918, *WWP*, 51:254.
12. Lansing's response, 8 October 1918, quoted in Ferdinand Czernin, *Versailles, 1919: The Forces, Events, and Personalities That Shaped the Treaty* (New York, 1965), pp. 6-7.
13. Entry of 12 October 1918, McEwen, *Riddell Diaries*, p. 241.
14. Entry of 15 October 1918, House Diary, *WWP*, 51:340.
15. On October 17 the War Cabinet decided to compile what would be in effect a lawyer's brief on British contributions to victory. Smuts, who had been a lawyer in his youth, was assigned the task of preparing Britain's negotiating position. See WC (488), 17 October 1918, Cab 23/8; and Erik Goldstein, *Winning the Peace: British Diplomatic Strategy Peace Planning, and the Paris Peace Conference, 1916-1920* (Oxford, 1991), pp. 94-98.
16. WC (489 B), 22 October 1918, Cab 23/14. The special correspondent's comments, datelined 19 October, appeared in the *Times* on 22 October 1918.
17. WC (485), 14 October 1918, Cab 23/8.
18. IWC (30), 13 August 1918, Cab 23/17.
19. IWC (32), 15 August 1918, Cab 23/43. See also Amery to Lloyd George, 16 August 1918 (with enclosure, "United States and British War Aims," 15 August 1918), Lloyd George Papers, F/2/1/29.
20. "Notes on an Interview with the President at the White House, Wednesday, October 16th, 1919," quoted in full in Fowler, *British-American Relations*, pp. 287-88.
21. See entry of 22 October 1918, Cronon, *Cabinet Diaries of Daniels*, p. 343; and "A Memorandum by Franklin Knight Lane," 23 October 1918, *WWP*, 51:413-15.
22. WC (491 B), 26 October 1918, Cab 23/14.
23. Sir Henry Wilson had told the War Cabinet three days earlier that there was "nothing to warrant the assumption that the present military situation justified the Germans in giving in." WC (487), 16 October 1918, Cab 23/8.

24. "X" Committee (29), 19 October 1918, Cab 23/17; and Haig's memorandum, 19 October 1918, App. II, WC (489 A), 21 October 1918, Cab 23/14.

25. See Cabinet Papers G.T. 6017 of 17 October, G.T. 6021 of 18 October, and G.T. 6035 of 19 October 1918, Cab 24/67.

26. See General Sir Herbert Lawrence's comments to Haig just before he left for London, entry of 17 October 1918, Blake, *Private Papers of Haig*, p. 332.

27. See, e.g., Haig's talk with Churchill, entry of 19 March 1918, ibid., p. 294.

28. Coffman, "American Military and Strategic Policy," p. 81.

29. Pershing to SWC, 30 October 1918, House Papers, Box 89, fol. 3073.

30. Wilson to House, 28 October 1918, *WWP*, 51:473.

31. See Bullitt Lowry, "Pershing and the Armistice," *Journal of American History*, September 1968, pp. 281-91.

32. Pershing to House, 30 October 1918, House Papers, Box 89, fol. 3073. Pershing had just reorganized his now unwieldy force of over 1,000,000 men (when the 135,000 French troops attached to his command are included) into two armies. The Second Army, activated on 12 October, was positioned east of the Meuse River to strike at Metz; as Pershing told Griscom, "Our second army is ready and waiting to march on Metz." See Griscom, *Diplomatically Speaking*, p. 440.

33. Pershing to House, 6 November 1918, House Papers, Box 89, fol. 3074.

34. Quoted in Griscom, *Diplomatically Speaking*, p. 446.

35. Quoted in Walworth, *America's Moment*, p. 44.

36. Entry of 19 October 1918, McEwen, *Riddell Diaries*, p. 243.

37. See entry of 22 October 1918, H. Wilson Diary.

38. WC (491 A), 26 October 1918, Cab 23/14.

39. WC (491 B), 26 October 1918, Cab 23/14; Smuts, "A Note on the Early Conclusion of Peace," Cabinet Paper G.T. 6091 of 24 October 1918, Cab 24/67.

40. Entry of 12 October 1918, McEwen, *Riddell Diaries*, p. 240.

41. "X" Committee (29), 19 October 1918, Cab 23/17.

42. "X" Committee (29 and 31), 19 and 23 October 1918, Cab 23/17.

43. WC (489 A), 21 October 1918, Cab 23/14.

44. Sir Henry Wilson told the War Cabinet that he had identified at least twenty-seven German divisions on the American front, but he also noted that one of these had infantry numbering only 785, "one of the most remarkable pieces of evidence we had regarding the decline in strength of the German armies." WC (490), 24 October 1918, Cab 23/17.

45. "X" Committee (31), 23 October 1918, Cab 23/17.

46. Quoted in Smythe, *Pershing*, p. 216.

47. As is often the case, there is disagreement about World War I statistics. The above numbers are taken from Pershing, *My Experiences*, 2:294, 388-90. Pershing, for example, claims the capture of 26,000 prisoners, while Millett lowers the number of POWs to 16,000. Recent examinations of the AEF's operational and tactical effectiveness have been quite critical. See especially the important studies by Millett, "The AEF and the American Strategy for Victory," Nenninger, "American Military Effectiveness in the First World War," Smythe, *Pershing*, and Paul F. Braim, *The Test of Battle: The American Expeditionary Forces in the Meuse-Argonne Campaign* (Newark, 1987).

48. Vera Brittain, *Testament of Youth: An Autobiographical Study of the Years 1900-1925* (New York, 1934), pp. 420-21.

49. Hunter Liggett, *Commanding an American Army: Recollections of the World War* (New York, 1925), pp. 124-25.

50. WC (491 B), 26 October 1918, Cab 23/14.

51. Minutes of SWC, 29 October 1918, quoted in Czernin, *Versailles*, p. 26.

52. See French, *British Way in Warfare*, pp. 173, 180.

53. House to Wilson, 30 October 1918, *WWP*, 51:514. Lloyd George did not exaggerate Dominion apprehension. Concerned that reports of the SWC discussions contained no mention of the German colonies, the War Cabinet telegraphed Lloyd George that the Dominions' claim to "certain of them cannot possibly be waived." WC (495 A) 1 November 1918, Cab 23/14.

54. The delicate question of "freedom of the seas" that divided London and Washington is well described in Walworth, *America's Moment*, pp. 56-65.

55. Error in original.

56. House to Wilson, 5 November 1918, *WWP*, 51:594.

57. IWC (36), 5 November 1918, Cab 23/8.

Bibliography

Papers of Individuals

Asquith, Herbert H. Department of Western Manuscripts, Bodleian Library, Oxford.

Baker, Newton D. Library of Congress Manuscript Division, Washington, D.C.

Balfour, Arthur J. Public Record Office, Kew, Richmond.
Manuscript Collections, British Library, London.

Bliss, Tasker H. Library of Congress Manuscript Division, Washington, D.C.

Bonar Law, Andrew. House of Lords Record Office, London.

Cecil, Lord Robert. Manuscript Collections, British Library, London.

Curzon, 1st Marquess. Oriental and India Office Collections, British Library, London.

Derby, 17th Earl of. Liverpool City Library.

Drummond, Sir Eric. Public Record Office, Kew, Richmond.

Esher, 2nd Viscount. Churchill College Archives Centre, Cambridge.

Grey, Sir Edward. Public Record Office, Kew, Richmond.

Haig, Sir Douglas. National Library of Scotland, Edinburgh.

Hall, Gilbert W. Department of Documents, Imperial War Museum, London.

Hankey, Maurice. Churchill College Archives Centre, Cambridge.

House, Edward M. Manuscripts and Archives Department, Sterling Memorial Library, Yale University, New Haven.

Lloyd George, David. House of Lords Record Office, London.

Milner, 1st Viscount. Department of Western Manuscripts, Bodleian Library, Oxford.

Northcliffe, 1st Viscount. Manuscript Collections, British Library, London.

Pershing, John J. Library of Congress Manuscript Division, Washington, D.C.

Rawlinson, Sir Henry. National Army Museum, London.

Reading, Rufus Isaacs, 1st Marquess of. Oriental and India Office Collections, British Library, London.

Robertson, Sir William. Liddell Hart Centre for Military Archives, King's College, London.

Scott, Hugh L. Library of Congress Manuscript Division, Washington, D.C.

Smuts, Jan Christiaan. University Library, Cambridge.

Wilson, Sir Henry. Department of Documents, Imperial War Museum, London.

Wiseman, Sir William. Manuscripts and Archives Department, Sterling Memorial Library, Yale University, New Haven.

Official Documents

Public Record Office, Kew, Richmond
    Files of the Cabinet Office, including:
        Cabinet Memoranda
        Committee of Prime Ministers
        Eastern Committee
        Imperial War Cabinet
        International Conferences
        Man-Power Committee
        Russia Committee
        Supreme War Council
        War Cabinet
        War Committee
        War Policy Committee
        "X" Committee
    Files of the War Office
    Files of the Foreign Office
National Archives, Washington, D.C.
    Record Group 120 (American Expeditiory Forces).
    Record Group 165 (Chief of Staff, War Plans, and
        Army War College files).

Published Primary Sources

Amery, L.S. *My Political Life*. Vol. 2, *War and Peace, 1914-1929*. 1953.

Army War College (Historical Section). *The Genesis of the American First Army*. 1929.

Baker, R.S., and William E. Dodd, eds. *The New Democracy: Presidential Messages, Addresses, and Other Papers (1913-1917)*. 2 vols. 1926.

Barnes, John, and Julian Amery, eds. *The Leo Amery Diaries*. Vol. 1, 1896-1929. 1980.

Blake, Robert, ed. *The Private Papers of Douglas Haig, 1914-1919*. 1952.

Bridges, Sir Tom, *Alarms & Excursions: Reminiscences of a Soldier*. 1938.

Brittain, Vera. *Testament of Youth: An Autobiographical Study of the Years 1900-1925*. 1934.

Cronon, E. David. ed. *The Cabinet Diaries of Josephus Daniels, 1913-1921*. 1963.

Department of the Army (Historical Division). *United States Army in the World War, 1917-1919*. 17 vols. 1948.

Department of State. *Papers Relating to the Foreign Relations of the United States, 1917:* Supplement 1, *The World War*. 1931.

———. *Papers Relating to the Foreign Relations of the United States, 1917:* Supplement 2, *The World War*. 2 vols. 1932.

———. *Papers Relating to the Foreign Relations of the United States, 1918: The World War*. 1930.

———. *Papers Relating to the Foreign Relations of the United States, 1918:* Supplement 1, *The World War*. 2 vols. 1933.

———. *Papers Relating to the Foreign Relations of the United States, 1918:* Supplement 2, *The World War.* 1933.

———. *Papers Relating to the Foreign Relations of the United States, 1918: Russia.* 3 vols. 1931-32.

———. *Papers Relating to the Foreign Relations of the United States: The Lansing Papers, 1914-1920.* 2 vols. 1939-40.

Edmonds, James E., ed. and comp. *Military Operations, France and Belgium.* 14 vols. 1922-49.

Griscom, Lloyd G. *Diplomatically Speaking.* 1940.

Hankey, Lord. *The Supreme Command, 1914-1918.* 2 vols. 1961.

Harbord, James G. *The American Army in France, 1917-1929.* 1936.

[House, Edward Mandell]. *Philip Dru, Administrator: A Century of Tomorrow, 1920-1935.* 1912.

Jeffery, Keith, ed. *The Military Correspondence of Field Marshal Sir Henry Wilson, 1918-1922.* 1985.

Liggett, Hunter. *A.E.F.: Ten Years Ago in France.* 1928.

———. *Commanding an American Army: Recollections of the World War.* 1925.

Link, Arthur S., ed. *The Papers of Woodrow Wilson.* Vols. 30-51. 1979-85.

Lloyd George, David. *War Memoirs of David Lloyd George.* 2 vols. 1938 ed.

Lonergan, Thomas Clement. *It Might Have Been Lost! A Chronicle from Alien Sources of the Struggle to Preserve the National Identity of the A.E.F.* 1929.

Ludendorff, Erich von. *Ludendorff's Own Story: August 1914-November 1918.* 2 vols. 1919.

McEwen, J.M., ed. *The Riddell Diaries, 1908-1923.* 1986.

March, Peyton, C. *The Nation at War.* 1926.

Palmer, Frederick. *Bliss, Peacemaker: The Life and Letters of General Tasker Howard Bliss.* 1934.

Pershing, John J. *My Experiences in the World War.* 2 vols. 1931.

Repington, C. à Court. *The First World War, 1914-1918.* 2 vols. 1920.

Riddell, Lord. *Lord Riddell's War Diary.* 1933.

Robertson, Sir William. *Soldiers and Statesmen, 1914-1918.* 2 vols. 1926.

Roskill, Steven. *Hankey: Man of Secrets.* Vol. 1, *1877-1918.* 1970.

Seymour, Charles, ed. *The Intimate Papers of Colonel House.* 4 vols. 1926-28.

Taylor, A.J.P., ed. *Lloyd George: A Diary by Frances Stevenson.* 1971.

Tumulty, Joseph P. *Woodrow Wilson as I Know Him.* 1921.

United Kingdom. *Parliamentary Debates* (Commons). 5th ser., vol. 99. 1918.

Willert, Arthur. *The Road to Safety: A Study in Anglo-American Relations.* 1953.

Wilson, Trevor, ed. *The Political Diaries of C.P. Scott, 1911-1928.* 1970.

Woodward, David R., ed. *The Military Correspondence of Field-Marshal Sir William Robertson, Chief Imperial General Staff, December 1915-February 1918.* 1989.

Secondary Sources

Abrahamson, James L. *American Arms for a New Century: The Making of a Great Military Power.* 1981.

Adams, R.J.Q., and Philip Poirier. *The Conscription Controversy in Britain, 1900-1918*. 1987.

Allard, Dean C. "Anglo-American Naval Differences during World War I." In *In Defense of the Republic*, ed. David Curtis Skaggs and Robert S. Browning III. 1991.

Ambrosius, Lloyd E. *Woodrow Wilson and the American Diplomatic Tradition: The Treaty Fight in Perspective*. 1987.

Asprey, Robert B. *The German High Command at War: Hindenburg and Ludendorff Conduct World War I*. 1991.

Auerbach, Jerold S. "Woodrow Wilson's 'Prediction' to Frank Cobb: Words Historians Should Doubt Ever Got Spoken." *Journal of American History*, December 1967.

Bartlett, C.J. *British Foreign Policy in the Twentieth Century*. 1989.

Beaver, Daniel R. *Newton D. Baker and the American War Effort, 1917-1918*. 1966.

Beloff, Max. *Imperial Sunset*. Vol. 1, *Britain's Liberal Empire, 1897-1921*. 1970.

———. "The Special Relationship: An Anglo-American Myth." In *A Century of Conflict, 1850-1950: Essays for A.J.P. Taylor*, ed. Martin Gilbert. 1967.

Blake, Robert. *The Decline of Power, 1915-1964*. 1985.

Bond, Brian. *The First World War and British Military History*. 1991.

Bourne, J.M. *Britain and the Great War, 1914-1918*. 1989.

Braim, Paul F. *The Test of Battle: The American Expeditionary Forces in the Meuse-Argonne Campaign*. 1987.

Burk, Kathleen. *Britain, America, and the Sinews of War, 1914-1918*. 1985.

———. "Great Britain in the United States, 1917-1918: The Turning Point." *International History Review*, April 1979.

Burton, David H. *Cecil Spring Rice: A Diplomat's Life*. 1990.

Calder, K.J. *Britain and the Origins of the New Empire*. 1976.

Calhoun, Frederick S. *Power and Principle: Armed Intervention in Wilsonian Foreign Policy*. 1986.

Calvert, P.A.R. "Great Britain and the New World, 1905-1914." In *British Foreign Policy under Sir Edward Grey*, ed. F.H. Hinsley. 1977.

Campbell, A.E. *Great Britain and the United States, 1895-1903*. 1974.

Chambers, John Whiteclay II. *To Raise an Army: The Draft Comes to Modern America*. 1987.

Charteris, John. *Field-Marshal Earl Haig*. 1929.

Clements, Kendrick A. *Woodrow Wilson: World Statesman*. 1987.

Coffman, Edward M. "The AEF Leaders' Education for War." In *The Great War: Essays on the Military, Political and Social History of the First World War*, ed. R.J.Q. Adams. 1990.

———. "The American Military Strategic Policy in World War I." In *War Aims and Strategic Policy in the Great War, 1914-1918*, ed. Barry Hunt and Adrian Preston. 1977.

———. "Conflicts in American Planning: An Aspect of World War I Strategy." *Military Review*, June 1963.

———. *The Hilt of the Sword: The Career of Peyton C. March*. 1966.

———. *The War to End All Wars: The American Military Experience in World War I*. 1968.

Coletta, Paolo E. "The American Naval Leaders' Preparations for War." In *The*

Great War, 1914-1918: Essays on the Military, Political and Social History of the First World War, ed. R.J.Q. Adams. 1990.

Collier, Basil. *The Lion and the Eagle: British and Anglo-American Strategy, 1900-1950*. 1972.

Coogan, John W. *The End of Neutrality: The United States, Britain, and Maritime Rights, 1899-1915*. 1981.

Cook, George L. "Sir Robert Borden, Lloyd George, and British Military Policy, 1917-1918." *Historical Journal*, March 1971.

Cooper, John Milton, Jr. "The British Response to the House-Grey Memorandum: New Evidence and New Questions." *Journal of American History*, March 1973.

———. *Causes and Consequences of World War I*. 1972.

———. *The Vanity of Power: American Isolationism and the First World War, 1914-1917*. 1969.

———. *Walter Hines Page: The Southerner as American, 1855-1918*. 1977.

———. *The Warrior and the Priest: Woodrow Wilson and Theodore Roosevelt*. 1983.

Cruttwell, C.R.M.F. *The Role of British Strategy in the Great War*. 1936.

Czernin, Ferdinand. *Versailles, 1919: The Forces, Events, and Personalities That Shaped the Treaty*. 1965.

De Groot, Gerard J. *Douglas Haig, 1861-1928*. 1988.

Devlin, Patrick. *Too Proud to Fight: Woodrow Wilson's Neutrality*. 1975.

DeWeerd, Harvey A. *President Wilson Fights His War: World War I and the American Intervention*. 1968.

Dimbleby, David, and David Reynolds. *An Ocean Apart: The Relationship between Britain and America in the Twentieth Century*. 1988.

Dulles, Foster Rhea. *America's Rise to World Power, 1898-1954*. 1963 ed.

Egerton, George W. *Great Britain and the Creation of the League of Nations: Strategy, Politics, and International Organization, 1914-1919*. 1979.

Esposito, David M. "Force without Stint or Limit: Woodrow Wilson and the Origins of the American Expeditionary Force." Ph.D. diss., Pennsylvania State University, 1988.

Falls, Cyril. *The Great War*. 1959 ed.

Farrar, L.L. "Opening to the West: German Efforts to Conclude a Separate Peace with England, July 1917-March 1918." *Journal of Canadian History*, April 1975.

Ferrell, Robert H. *Woodrow Wilson and World War I, 1917-1921*. 1985.

Finnegan, John Patrick. *Against the Specter of a Dragon: The Campaign for Military Preparedness, 1914-1917*. 1974.

Fischer, Fritz. *Germany's Aims in the First World War*. 1967 ed.

Fisher, John P. "The Creation of the American First Army: Anglo-American Relations and the Amalgamation Controversy, 1917-1918." M.A. thesis, Marshall University, 1988.

Floto, Inga. *Colonial House in Paris: A Study of American Policy at the Paris Peace Conference, 1919*. 1980.

Fowler, W.B. *British-American Relations, 1917-1918: The Role of Sir William Wiseman*. 1969.

French, David. *British Strategy and War Aims, 1914-1916*. 1986.

———. *The British Way in Warfare, 1688-2000*. 1990.

Fromkin, David. *A Peace to End All Peace: The Fall of the Ottoman Empire and the Creation of the Modern Middle East.* 1989.

Fry, M.G. "The Imperial War Cabinet, the United States, and the Freedom of the Seas." *Journal of the Royal United Services Institute,* November 1965.

————. *Lloyd George and Foreign Policy.* Vol. 1, *The Education of a Statesman, 1890-1916.* 1977.

Galbraith, John S. "British War Aims in World War I: A Commentary on 'Statesmanship.'" *Journal of Imperial and Commonwealth History,* October 1984.

Gardner, Lloyd C. *Safe for Democracy: The Anglo-American Response to Revolution, 1913-1923.* 1984.

George, Alexander L., and Juliette L. George. *Woodrow Wilson and Colonel House: A Personality Study.* 1956.

Gilmore, Russell. "'The New Courage': Rifles and Soldier Individualism, 1876-1918." *Military Affairs,* October 1976.

Goldstein, Erik. *Winning the Peace: British Diplomatic Strategy, Peace Planning, and the Paris Peace Conference, 1916-1920.* 1991.

Gollin, A.M. *Proconsul in Politics: A Study of Lord Milner in Opposition and in Power.* 1964.

Gough, Sir Hubert. *The Fifth Army.* 1931.

Graebner, Norman A. *Foundations of American Foreign Policy: A Realistic Appraisal from Franklin to McKinley.* 1985.

Grenville, John A.S., and George Berkeley Young. *Politics, Strategy, and American Diplomacy, 1873-1917.* 1966.

Grieves, Keith. "'Total War'?: The Quest for a British Manpower Policy, 1917-1918." *Journal of Strategic Studies,* March 1986.

Grigg, John. *Lloyd George: From Peace to War, 1912-1916.* 1985.

Guinn, Paul. *British Strategy and Politics, 1914 to 1918.* 1965.

Hassler, Warren W., Jr. *The President as Commander in Chief.* 1971.

Heckscher, August. *Woodrow Wilson.* 1991.

Herwig, Holger H., and David F. Trask. "The Failure of Germany's Undersea Offensive against World Shipping, February 1917-October 1918." *Historian,* August 1971.

Horne, John N. *Labour at War: France and Britain, 1914-1918.* 1991.

Howard, Michael. "British Grand Strategy in World War I." In *Grand Strategies in War and Peace,* ed. Paul M. Kennedy. 1991.

Hughes, Clive. "The New Armies." In *Nation in Arms: A Social Study of the British Army in the First World War,* ed. Ian F.W. Beckett and Keith Simpson. 1985.

Huttenback, Robert A. *The British Imperial Experience.* 1966.

Jordan, Gerald, ed. *British Military History: A Supplement to Robin Higham's Guide to the Sources.* 1988.

Kaspi, André. *Le temps des américains: Le concours américain à la France en 1917-1918.* 1976.

Kennan, George F. *Soviet-American Relations, 1917-1920.* Vol. 2, *The Decision to Intervene.* 1967 ed.

Kennedy, David M. *Over Here: The First World War and American Society.* 1980.

Kennedy, Paul M. "Britain in the First World War." In *Military Effectiveness,* vol. 1, *The First World War,* ed. Allan R. Millett and Williamson Murray. 1988.

―――. "The First World War and the International Powers System." In *Military Strategy and the Origins of the First World War: An International Security Reader,* ed. Steven E. Miller. 1985.

Kernek, Sterling. "The British Government's Reactions to President Wilson's 'Peace' Note of December 1916." *Historical Journal,* December 1970.

―――. *Distractions of Peace during War: The Lloyd George Government's Reactions to Woodrow Wilson, December 1916-November, 1918.* 1975.

Kettle, Michael. *Russia and the Allies, 1917-1920.* Vol. 1, *The Allies and the Russian Collapse.* Vol. 2, *The Road to Intervention March-November 1918.* 1981-88.

Kihl, Mary R. "A Failure of Ambassadorial Diplomacy." *Journal of American History,* December 1970.

Kreidberg, Marvin A., and Merton G. Henry. *History of Military Mobilization in the United States Army, 1775-1945.* 1955.

LaFeber, Walter. *The American Age: United States Foreign Policy at Home and Abroad since 1750.* 1989.

Liddell Hart, B.H. *The Real War, 1914-1918.* 1930.

Link, Arthur S. "The Higher Realism of Woodrow Wilson." *Journal of Presbyterian History,* March 1963.

―――. *Wilson.* Vol. 5, *Campaigns for Progressivism and Peace, 1916-1917.* 1965.

―――. *Wilson the Diplomatist: A Look at His Major Foreign Policies.* 1974.

―――, ed. *Woodrow Wilson: A Profile.* 1968.

―――, and John Whiteclay Chambers II. "Woodrow Wilson as Commander in Chief." In *The United States Military under the Constitution of the United States,* ed. Richard H. Kohn. 1991.

Livermore, Seward W. *Politics Is Adjourned: Woodrow Wilson and the War Congress, 1916-1918.* 1966.

Louis, Wm. Roger. *Great Britain and Germany's Lost Colonies, 1914-1919.* 1967.

Lowry, Bullitt. "Pershing and the Armistice." *Journal of American History,* September 1968.

McCarthy, Michael. "'Lafayette, We Are Here': The War College Division and American Military Planning for the AEF in World War I." M.A. thesis, Marshall University, 1992.

McKercher, B.J.C., ed. *Anglo-American Relations in the 1920s: The Struggle for Supremacy.* 1990.

Maddox, Robert J. *The Unknown War with Russia: Wilson's Siberian Intervention.* 1977.

Marshall, S.L.A. *World War I.* 1985.

Martin, Laurence W. *Peace without Victory: Woodrow Wilson and the British Liberals.* 1958.

May, Ernest R. *The World War and American Isolation, 1914-1917.* 1966.

―――, ed. *The Ultimate Decision: The President as Commander in Chief.* 1960.

Mayer, Arno J. *Political Origins of the New Diplomacy, 1917-1918.* 1959.

Millett, Allan R., "Cantigny, 28-31 May 1918." In *America's First Battles, 1776-1965,* ed. Charles E. Heller and William A. Stofft. 1986.

―――. "Over Where? The AEF and the American Strategy for Victory, 1917-

1918." In *Against All Enemies: Interpretations of American Military History from Colonial Times to the Present*, ed. Kenneth J. Hagan and William R. Roberts. 1986.

Morgan, Kenneth O. "Lloyd George's Premiership: A Study in 'Prime Ministerial Government.'" *Historical Journal*, March 1970.

Morgenthau, Hans J. *In Defense of the National Interest: A Critical Examination of American Foreign Policy.* 1951.

Neilson, Keith. "'Greatly Exaggerated': The Myth of the Decline of Great Britain before 1914." *International History Review*, November 1991.

———. *Strategy and Supply: The Anglo-Russian Alliance, 1914-17.* 1984.

Nelson, Harold I. *Land and Power: British and Allied Policy on Germany's Frontiers.* 1963.

Nelson, Keith L. "What Colonel House Overlooked in the Armistice. *Mid-America*, April 1968.

Nenninger, Timothy K. "American Military Effectiveness in the First World War." In *Military Effectiveness*, vol. 1, *The First World War*, ed. Allan R. Millett and Williamson Murray. 1989.

———. *The Leavenworth Schools and the Old Army: Education, Professionalism, and the Officers Corps of the United States Army, 1881-1918.* 1978.

Offer, Avner. *The First World War: An Agrarian Interpretation.* 1989.

Osgood, Robert Endicott. *Ideals and Self-Interest in America's Foreign Relations.* 1953.

Page, Arthur W. *Our 110 Days' Fighting.* 1920.

Palmer, Frederick. *Newton D. Baker: America at War.* 2 vols. 1931.

Parsons, Edward B. "Why the British Reduced the Flow of American Troops to Europe in August-October 1918." *Canadian Journal of History*, December 1977.

———. *Wilsonian Diplomacy: Allied-American Rivalries in War and Peace.* 1978.

Paterson, Thomas G., Garry J. Clifford, and Kenneth J. Hagan. *American Foreign Policy: A History, 1900 to the Present.* 1991.

Paxon, Frederic L. *American Democracy and the World War.* Vol. 2, *America at War, 1917-1918.* 1939.

Perkins, Bradford. *The Great Rapprochement: England and the United States, 1895-1914.* 1968.

Prior, Robin, and Trevor Wilson. *Command on the Western Front: The Military Career of Sir Henry Rawlinson, 1914-1918.* 1992.

Rainey, James W. "Ambivalent Warfare: The Tactical Doctrine of the AEF in World War I." *Parameters*, September 1983.

Rhodes, Benjamin D. *The Anglo-American Winter War with Russia, 1918-1919: A Diplomatic and Military Tragicomedy*, 1988.

Richard, Carl J. "'The Shadow of a Plan': The Rationale behind Wilson's 1918 Siberian Intervention." *Historian*, November 1986.

Robbins, Keith. *The Abolition of War: The Peace Movement in Britain, 1914-1919.* 1976.

Rothwell, V.H. *British War Aims and Peace Diplomacy, 1914-1918.* 1971.

Safford, Jeffrey J. "Anglo-American Maritime Relations during the Two World Wars: A Comparative Analysis." *American Neptune*, October 1981.

———. *Wilsonian Maritime Diplomacy, 1913-1921.* 1978.

Salter, J.A. *Allied Shipping Control: An Experiment in International Administration.* 1921.

Sargent, Herbert Howland. *The Strategy on the Western Front, 1914-1918.* 1920.

Schulzinger, Robert D. *American Diplomacy in the Twentieth Century.* 1984.

Schwabe, Klaus. *Woodrow Wilson, Revolutionary Germany, and Peacemaking, 1918-1919: Missionary Diplomacy and the Realities of Power.* 1985.

Shrader, Charles R. "'Maconochie's Stew': Logistical Support of American Forces with the BEF, 1917-18." In *The Great War, 1914-1918: Essays on the Military, Political, and Social History of the First World War,* ed. R.J.Q. Adams. 1990.

Simpson, Michael, ed. *Anglo-American Naval Relations, 1917-1919.* 1991.

Smith, Daniel M. "Robert Lansing, 1915-1920." In *An Uncertain Tradition: American Secretaries of State in the Twentieth Century,* ed. Norman A. Graebner. 1961.

———. *Robert M. Lansing and American Neutrality, 1914-1917.* 1958.

———, ed. *American Intervention, 1917: Sentiment, Self-Interest, or Ideals.* 1966.

Smythe, Donald. "AEF Strategy in France, 1917-1918." *Army Quarterly and Defence Journal,* April 1985.

———. *Pershing: General of the Armies.* 1986.

———. "St. Mihiel: The Birth of an American Army." *Parameters,* June 1983.

Spector, Ronald. "'You're Not Going to Send Soldiers Over There Are You!': The American Search for an Alternative to the Western Front, 1916-1917." *Military Affairs,* February 1972.

Steiner, Zara S. *Britain and the Origins of the First World War.* 1977.

Stevenson, David. "The Failure of Peace by Negotiation in 1917." *Historical Journal,* March 1991.

———. *The First World War and International Politics.* 1988.

Stokesbury, James L. *A Short History of World War I.* 1981.

Swartz, Marvin. *The Union of Democratic Control in British Politics during the First World War.* 1971.

Terraine, John. "Field Marshal Haig." *Stand To! The Journal of the Western Front Association,* Summer 1989.

———. *To Win a War: 1918, The Year of Victory.* 1981.

Thompson, J.A. "Woodrow Wilson and World War I: A Reappraisal." *Journal of American Studies,* December 1985.

Tillman, Seth P. *Anglo-American Relations at the Paris Peace Conference of 1919.* 1961.

Toland, John. *No Man's Land: 1918—The Last Year of the Great War.* 1980.

Trask, David F. "The American Navy in a World at War, 1914-1918." In *In Peace and War: Interpretations of American Naval History, 1775-1978,* ed. Kenneth J. Hagan. 1978.

———. *Captains & Cabinets: Anglo-American Naval Relations, 1917-1918.* 1972.

———. *The United States in the Supreme War Council: American War Aims and Inter-Allied Strategy, 1917-1918.* 1961.

———. "Woodrow Wilson and World War I." In *American Diplomacy in the Twentieth Century,* ed. Warren F. Kimball. 1980.

Travers, Tim. *How the War Was Won: Command and Technology in the British Army on the Western Front, 1917-1918.* 1992.

———. *The Killing Ground: The British Army, the Western Front, and the Emergence of Modern Warfare, 1900-1918.* 1987.

Tuchman, Barbara W. *The Zimmerman Telegram.* 1958.

Turner, John. *British Politics and the Great War: Coalition and Conflict, 1915-1918.* 1992.

Ullman, Richard H. *Anglo-Soviet Relations, 1917-1921.* Vol. 1, *Intervention and the War.* 1961.

Unterberger, Betty Miller. *America's Siberian Expedition, 1918-1920.* 1956.

———, ed. *American Intervention in the Russian Civil War.* 1969.

Vandiver, Frank E. *Black Jack: The Life and Times of John J. Pershing.* 2 vols. 1977.

———. "Commander-in-Chief–Commander Relations: Wilson and Pershing." *Rice University Studies,* Winter 1971.

Walworth, Arthur. *America's Moment: 1918: American Diplomacy at the End of World War I.* 1977.

———. *Woodrow Wilson.* Vol. 2, *World Prophet.* 1958.

Watt, D. Cameron. *Succeeding John Bull: America in Britain's Place: A Study of the Anglo-American Relationship and World Politics in the Context of British and American Foreign-Policy-Making in the Twentieth Century.* 1984.

Weigley, Russell F. *The American Way of War: A History of United States Military Strategy and Policy.* 1973.

———. *History of the United States Army.* 1967.

———. "To the Crossing of the Rhine." In *In Defense of the Republic: Readings in American Military History,* ed. David Curtis Skaggs and Robert S. Browning III. 1991.

Weinstein, Edwin A. *Woodrow Wilson: A Medical and Psychological Biography.* 1981.

Wilson, Trevor. *The Myriad Faces of War: Britain and the Great War, 1914-1918.* 1986.

Winter, Denis. *Haig's Command: A Reassessment.* 1991.

Winter, J.M. *The Great War and the British People.* 1985.

Woodward, David R. "Britain in a Continental War: The Civil-Military Debate over the Strategical Direction of the Great War of 1914-1918." *Albion,* Spring 1980.

———. "Britain's 'Brass Hats' and the Question of a Compromise Peace, 1916-1918." *Military Affairs,* April 1971.

———. "The British Government and Japanese Intervention in Russia during World War I." *Journal of Modern History,* December 1974.

———. "British Intervention in Russia during the First World War." *Military Affairs,* December 1977.

———. "David Lloyd George, A Negotiated Peace with Germany, and the Kuhlmann Peace Kite of September, 1917." *Canadian Journal of History,* March 1971.

———. "Did Lloyd George Starve the British Army of Men prior to the German Offensive of 21 March 1918?" *Historical Journal,* March 1984.

———. "Great Britain and President Wilson's Efforts to End World War I in 1916." *Maryland Historian,* Spring 1970.

———. "The Imperial Strategist: Jan Christiaan Smuts and British Military Policy, 1917-1918." *Military History Journal,* December 1981.

————. *Lloyd George and the Generals.* 1983.

————. "The Origins and Intent of David Lloyd George's January 5 War Aims Speech." *Historian,* November 1971.

————. "United States in World War I." In *Encyclopedia of the American Military,* ed. John E. Jessup. Forthcoming.

Woodward, David R., and Robert Franklin Maddox, eds. *America and World War I: A Selected Annotated Bibliography of English-Language Sources.* 1985.

Index

Doullens: Anglo-French agreement on unity of command at, 152-53, 166

Drum, Col. Hugh A., 201, 207

Drummond, Sir Eric, 62, 67, 101, 179, 241 n 72

Du Cane, Gen. Sir John P., 203

Duke, H.E., 151

Dulles, Foster Rhea, 2

Eastern Committee: established, 147

Emergency Peace Federation, 37

Ferrell, Robert H.: quoted, 45

Foch, Gen. Ferdinand, 97, 183-84, 199, 215, 245 n 16, 246 n 60; given "coordinating" authority over Anglo-French forces at Doullens, 152; authority over Pershing after Doullens, 152; extension of his power at Beauvais, 159; conflict with Pershing over amalgamation, 160-61; powers conferred on, as Allied commander, 165-66, 183, 187-89, 194-95, 206, 247 n 12; British suspicious of his leadership, 165-66, 170-72, 183-85, 191; asks for 100 U.S. divisions, 168; confronts Pershing over limited U.S. assistance, 169; incurs British anger by removal of U.S. troops from British sector, 171-72; and armed intervention in Russia, 179-80; and independent AEF, 181, 189-90; alarms British with reaction to fifth German offensive in 1918, 186-89, 247 n 15; offensive plans in 1918, 197, 200-201, 248 n 58; and British threats to reduce shipping, 199, 249 n 69; conflict with Pershing over deployment of U.S. forces, 200-201; praises Haig's generalship, 203; agrees to leave two U.S. divisions with BEF, 249 n 77

Fourteen Points, 129, 176, 205, 210-11, 218-19

France: sends mission to Washington, 50, 53-55; Lloyd George urges continuation of offensive (1917), 73; determination to keep AEF on French front, 82, 114, 124. *See also* army, French; Clemenceau, Georges; Foch, Gen. Ferdinand

freedom of the seas, 210-11, 216-18, 253 n 54

French, Field-Marshal Sir John, 56, 107, 152

Funston, Camp (Kansas), 119

Galt, Edith Bolling, 10

Gardner, Lloyd C., 245 n 33

Garrison, Lindley M., 20

Geddes, Rt. Hon. Sir Eric, 192; mission to Washington, D.C., 208, 250 n 105

General Board (U.S. Navy), 19, 65

General Staff (U.S. War Department), 118; establishment and role of, 18-19; initial plans for war with Germany, 33-36, 40-41; takes back seat to Pershing, 81; defends deployment of AEF in France, 94-97; and instability of leadership, 155

General Staff College (Ft. Leavenworth), 81

George V, King, 182, 214

German colonies, 60, 128, 211, 218, 229 n 54, 232 n 28, 238 n 59, 248 n 48

Germany: and peace negotiations, 14-15, 21-25, 30, 99-104, 126; decision for unrestricted U-boat warfare, 30-31; sues for peace, 205-12. *See also* German colonies; Ludendorff, Gen. Erich; U-boat warfare

Glynn, Martin, 20

Gough, Gen. Sir Hubert, 90, 149

Graebner, Norman: quoted, 7

Gregory, John D., 178

Grey, Rt. Hon. Sir Edward, 28, 67, 92; and American mediation, 12-15, 21, 23

Griscom, Col. Lloyd C., 214, 252 n 32; appointed Pershing's personal representative in British War Office, 164; meets with Haig, 172; and British War Office's lobbying for location of U.S. force in British sector, 197; and British fury over Pershing's removal of three U.S. divisions from British sector, 198; account of Baker-Lloyd George showdown over shipping, 204; discovers a disappointed Pershing on 11 Nov. 1918, 214; reports that British high command has dropped amalgamation, 247 n 21; reports no relaxation of British war effort, 248 n 52

Haig, Field-Marshal Sir Douglas, 21, 131-32, 164, 182; placed under Nivelle's strategic control, 71; given permission for Flanders offensive (1917), 74-76; "wearing-out" phase of offensive, 88, 233 n 13; lobbies for U.S. participation

military mission to Washington, D.C. (1917), 53-55, 229 n 37

Johnston, Col. W.H., 54

Joint Army and Navy Board, 19

Kaledin, A.M., 140-41, 144

Kennan, Col. Francis E., 57

Kerr, Philip, 91, 210

Kirke, Col. Walter, 149

Kitchener, Field-Marshal 1st Earl, 14, 44; and suggestion of Anglo-American military cooperation (1916), 15-16; and opposition to negotiated peace, 16

Knox, Brig. Gen. A.W.F., 143, 146

Kühlmann, Richard von: German peace kite in 1917, 99-103

Kuhn, Brig. Gen. Joseph E., 34-35; on necessity of military coordination with Allies, 41; opposed to sending small U.S. force to Europe, 41, 54

Lancken, Baron Oskar von der, 100-101

Lansdowne, Rt. Hon. 5th Marquess of: supports negotiated peace, 27, 125

Lansing, Robert, 10, 30, 49, 52, 78, 180; account of 21 March 1917 Cabinet meeting, 39-40

Lawrence, Gen. Sir Herbert, 189, 252 n 26

Lawrence, Col. T.E., 106

League of Nations, 12, 27, 211

Le Hamel, Battle of, 181-82

Liggett, Gen. Hunter, 202, 216

Ligny-en-Barrois: Foch-Pershing confrontation at, 200-201

Link, Arthur, 9, 227 n 44, 242 n 24; quoted, 7

Lloyd George, Rt. Hon. David, 2, 165, 174, 206, 231 nn 6, 7, 236 n 13, 246 n 44; and U.S. ability to support its diplomacy with force, 16-17, 21-23; and opposition to U.S. mediation, 22-25, 27, 29, 92, 223 n 36; W. Wilson suspicious of, 25, 92, 112, 136; composition of inner circle, 28-29; urges W. Wilson to join Allies, 45; predicts victory, 45-47; and importance of American manpower to final victory, 47-48; and German colonies, 60, 218, 229 n 54, 232 n 28, 248 n 48, 253 n 53; critical of U.S. war mobilization, 67, 174-75; sends Lord Northcliffe on special mission to

Washington, D.C., 67, 230 n 80; uses Hankey as alternative to General Staff's advice, 69-71; and political objectives of "eastern" strategy, 70-71, 139-40; desires summit meeting with W. Wilson, 77-78; personality compared with W. Wilson's, 79; growing opposition to Haig's Flanders offensive, 90; attempts to use W. Wilson to reverse Allied military policy, 91-92; considers compromise peace with Germany at Russia's expense, 99-103, 125, 127-28; war plans for 1918, 104, 110-11, 115, 125, 129, 236 n 14; refuses to keep BEF up to strength, 105-6, 151; uses H. Wilson and Lord French to undermine General Staff, 107-9; role and motives in establishing SWC, 109-10, 113-14; AEF's role in his stategic views for 1918-19, 117, 167-68, 182-83, 193-94, 196-97, 199; stresses British economic sacrifices in war, 117-18, 236 n 23; disappointed by U.S. response for manpower assistance in late 1917, 122, 125, 174-75; 5 Jan. war aims statement, 126-29, 176, 238 nn 57, 60; rejects warning of all-out offensive in 1918, 130-31; and armed intervention in Russia, 141-47; response to destruction of Fifth Army, 149-51; pressures W. Wilson to send reinforcements to BEF, 152-56, 158-60, 161-62; critical of W. Wilson's liberal diplomacy, 154; and Maurice debate, 162, 243 n 60; creates "X" Committee, 163; wants U.S. troops on British front as soon as possible, 164; supports Foch's expanded powers, 166; confronts Pershing at SWC, 169; and Smuts's desire to replace Pershing, 171; furious with Foch over transfer of U.S. troops from BEF, 171-72; determined to continue war if U.S. remains ally, 173; comments on his ignorance of Pershing's intentions, 173; rejects peace negotiations with a triumphant Germany, 175; and W. Wilson's comment to foreign journalists about Allied war aims, 176; suggests that W. Wilson might accept conquered territory, 176; angered by W. Wilson's limited intervention in Russia, 181; speaks to U.S. troops, 182; confronts

Moore, George G., 56
Morning Post, 103
Murray, Gen. Sir A.J., 44

Nation, 30
National Defense Act of 1916, 19-20
Naval Act of 1916, 19
New York Times, 31, 134, 170, 246 n 51
New York World, 39
Nivelle, Gen. Robert, 47, 71; failure of
  spring offensive (1917), 55, 69, 71, 88
Northcliffe, 1st Viscount, 78; chosen to
  head British war mission to U.S., 67

Offer, Avner: quoted, 6

Page, Walter Hines, 10, 49, 100; notes
  war is becoming one between English-
  speaking people and Germany, 232 n
  26
Painlevé, Paul: and possibility of
  negotiated peace with Germany, 101, 103
Parsons, Edward B.: quoted, 248 n 30
Passchendaele Offensive (Third Ypres),
  82; origins of, 71-74, 88; course of, 90,
  99, 104, 110, 199, 203
Patiala, Maharaja of, 173
Percy, Lord Eustace, 48, 228 n 17
Perkins, Bradford: quoted, 6
Pershing, Gen. John J., 1, 197;
  biographical sketch, 55-56; relationship
  with W. Wilson, 56-58; instructions
  from civilian superiors, 57-58, 82;
  escalates demands for men, 58, 97,
  135, 181; views on U.S. response to
  Allied missions (1917), 67; desires
  British shipping assistance for AEF, 71;
  departs for France, 81; deployment of
  AEF, 81-82, 124, 165-66, 181, 200-201,
  245 n 15, 252 n 32; offensive objectives
  (1918-19), 82-87, 94, 122-24, 209, 213;
  tactical doctrine, 88-90, 164; sends W.
  Wilson combat pictures, 97; and
  response to Baker telegram on
  amalgamation, 122-24; understanding
  with Pétain on location of U.S. troops,
  124; and German threat in 1918, 132,
  238 n 8; negotiations with British over
  use of U.S. troops, 132-37, 160-61;
  relationship with Foch after Doullens
  and Beauvais agreements, 152, 159;
  offer to put four U.S. divisions in line
  rejected, 152; efforts to avoid

integration of his forces with BEF
  (1918), 153, 160-61, 168-69, 171-73, 244 n
  9; and London Agreement, 160-61;
  appoints Col. Griscom to represent
  him in British War Office, 164; and
  pooling of Allied supplies, 165; and
  reluctance to commit U.S. troops to
  combat, 165, 182, 234 n 2; believes AEF
  superior to Allied forces, 170; Smuts
  wants to replace, 171; and British
  pressure to establish an American
  front next to BEF, 172; request to Foch
  for independent AEF with own sector,
  181; furious with British use of U.S.
  troops at Le Hamel, 182; gains Allied
  acceptance of independent AEF,
  189-90; wants to remove U.S. divisions
  from Haig's command, 191; angers
  British by recalling three divisions
  from BEF, 197-98; learns of British
  threat to reduce shipping of U.S.
  troops, 198; conflict with Foch over use
  of U.S. troops, 200-201; confers with
  Baker during St. Mihiel offensive,
  201-2; believes great opportunity lost
  when St. Mihiel Offensive terminated,
  202; reluctant to replace losses of
  American corps with BEF, 207;
  emotional reaction to American losses
  at Meuse-Argonne Offensive, 207-8;
  wants to command Allied forces, 213;
  conflict with W. Wilson over
  unconditional surrender, 213-14; nature
  of his "memoirs," 226 n 24;
  deployment of his forces questioned
  by Bliss, 245 n 15; instructed by Foch
  to leave two U.S. divisions with BEF,
  249 nn 69, 77; creates Second Army,
  252 n 32. *See also* Meuse-Argonne
  Offensive; St. Mihiel Offensive
Pétain, Marshal Philippe, 132, 190, 201;
  cautious approach to battle with
  German Army, 88, 104, 107; wants to
  keep U.S. troops in French sector, 124;
  rejects Pershing's offer to put four
  divisions in line, 152; makes
  arrangement with Pershing to move
  U.S. troops with BEF to Lorraine, 165,
  170, 190
Poole, Maj. Gen. F.C., 146
preparedness campaign, 20-21, 33
Proctor, Capt. Alex, 146
Punitive Expedition, 17, 20